"Not many books should be recommended for both beginning Bible readers and mature Bible readers, but this is one of them. Utilizing brief and pointed expositions of often overlooked Bible verses, John Piper helpfully explains why we should be reading the Bible, the work of the Spirit in our Bible reading, and the fundamental skills and habits of faithful Bible reading. I cannot imagine a serious Christian who would not benefit from a thoughtful reading of this book."

D. A. Carson, Research Professor of New Testament, Trinity Evangelical Divinity School; Cofounder, The Gospel Coalition

"I have been reading the Bible daily for thirty-five years. *Reading the Bible Supernaturally* challenged my motives, effort, and enjoyment. I doubt I will read the Scriptures the same way again. I look forward to deeper and more wonderful times alone in the Word in the days ahead. This book is a must-read for anyone wanting to take Bible study seriously."

Francis Chan, *New York Times* best-selling author, *Crazy Love* and *Forgotten God*

"Stunning. Profound. Powerful. *Reading the Bible Supernaturally* will move you to captivated and awestruck worship at the Divine's plan for his Word as an instrument to magnify his unrivaled glory. Seeing and savoring the God of the Scriptures is an extraordinarily high calling every believer must pursue, and no man can move us to that place quite like John Piper. This book, accessibly written and weighty in content, is so much more than a manual or study guide to the Scriptures. Rather, it's an invitation to the experience God intended we have with his Word—an experience that is Spirit dependent, faith building, and worship inciting."

Louie Giglio, Pastor, Passion City Church, Atlanta; Founder, Passion Conferences; author, *The Comeback*

"The seemingly mundane topic of reading the Bible ushers us into a world of supernatural grace for sinners. With constant reference to the Holy Scriptures, John Piper shows us how to beware the leaven of the Pharisees and to read by the light of Christ. Yet Piper commends no passive mysticism, but studious labor over the best of books; he is thorough, practical, and engaging throughout. Take up and read!"

Joel R. Beeke, President, Puritan Reformed Theological Seminary

"*Reading the Bible Supernaturally* reminds us why we cannot rest until every person on earth has access to the Bible in their own tongue. Tribes, languages, peoples, and nations are perishing without access to, or opportunity to know, this glorious God through this glorious book. John Piper stokes the urgency of our calling as the church of Jesus Christ to deepen our appreciation for the Word that God uses toward a missional end—his global and eternal glory."

Michael Oh, Global Executive Director, the Lausanne Movement

"*Reading the Bible Supernaturally* is a thorough and compelling wake-up call to lethargic, passive, resistant, mechanical Bible readers (which is all of us at one point or another) to become hungry, eager, inquisitive, aggressively observant miners for the treasure in the text—fully expectant that God will bring us from death to life, from foolishness to wisdom, from damning despair to glorious hope through his Word."

Nancy Guthrie, Bible teacher; author, *Seeing Jesus in the Old Testament* Bible study series

"If you disconnect the Bible from God's glory, you lose your grip on both. What terrible things we hear people say about each of them, taken in isolation. John Piper puts them together, and finds himself preaching an astonishingly high doctrine of Scripture, right alongside an intimately experiential doctrine of God's glory. *Reading the Bible Supernaturally* is not just one of the helpful activities that make up the Christian life. Kept in proper context, seen in full perspective, and received in wide-awake recognition of the living voice of the triune God, reading the Bible is the central act of Christian existence. This book, a kind of extended Christian hedonist gloss on Psalm 119, is an invitation to the miracle of Bible reading."

Fred Sanders, Professor of Theology, Torrey Honors Institute, Biola University; author, *The Deep Things of God: How the Trinity Changes Everything*

"No book has inspired me to approach Scripture with as much anticipation as *Reading the Bible Supernaturally*. Read this book at your own risk, for it will ignite your devotional life. You will find yourself actively hunting for treasure in the Bible, looking carefully at each passage, praying and trusting that God himself will open your eyes to see and savor his glory. Don't let the length of this book fool you; it is clear, accessible, and inspiring. In fact, it is the most practical, passionate, and motivating book on reading the Bible I have ever read. Read it. Apply it. Test it. It will transform your approach to God's Word."

Vaneetha Rendall Risner, author, *The Scars That Have Shaped Me*

"Having read *Reading the Bible Supernaturally*, readers will not return to Scripture carelessly or indifferently but with renewed and stimulated appetite to meet with the God of glory who inspired it and can be found and freshly encountered through its pages. John Piper's own insatiable appetite for fellowship with God communicates inspiringly."

Terry Virgo, Founder, Newfrontiers

Reading the Bible Supernaturally

Reading the Bible Supernaturally

Seeing and Savoring the Glory of God in Scripture

John Piper

WHEATON, ILLINOIS

Reading the Bible Supernaturally: Seeing and Savoring the Glory of God in Scripture

Copyright © 2017 by Desiring God Foundation

Published by Crossway
       1300 Crescent Street
       Wheaton, Illinois 60187

Cover design: Josh Dennis

First printing 2017

Printed in the United States of America

Hardcover ISBN: 978-1-4335-5349-3
ePub ISBN: 978-1-4335-5352-3
PDF ISBN: 978-1-4335-5350-9
Mobipocket ISBN: 978-1-4335-5351-6

Library of Congress Cataloging-in-Publication Data

Names: Piper, John, 1946– author.
Title: Reading the Bible supernaturally : seeing and savoring the glory of God in Scripture / John Piper.
Description: Wheaton, Illinois : Crossway, 2017. | Includes bibliographical references and indexes.
Identifiers: LCCN 2016029650 (print) | LCCN 2016031894 (ebook) | ISBN 9781433553493 (hc) | ISBN 9781433553509 (pdf) | ISBN 9781433553516 (mobi) | ISBN 9781433553523 (epub)
Subjects: LCSH: Bible—Reading. | Bible—Devotional use. | Glory of God—Biblical teaching.
Classification: LCC BS617 .P56 2017 (print) | LCC BS617 (ebook) | DDC 220.6—dc23
LC record available at https://lccn.loc.gov/2016029650

RRDC		27	26	25	24	23	22	21	20	19	18	17
15	14	13	12	11	10	9	8	7	6	5	4	3	2	1

To
all who have helped me see
the light of the glory of God in Scripture,
a legacy of shared illumination

Contents

PART 2

The Supernatural Act of Reading the Bible

PART 3

The Natural Act of Reading the Bible Supernaturally

Spiritually to understand the Scripture, is to have the eyes of the mind opened, to behold the wonderful spiritual excellency of the glorious things contained in the true meaning of it, and that always were contained in it, ever since it was written; to behold the amiable and bright manifestations of the divine perfections, and of the excellency and sufficiency of Christ, and the excellency and suitableness of the way of salvation by Christ, and the spiritual glory of the precepts and promises of the Scripture, etc. Which things are, and always were in the Bible, and would have been seen before, if it had not been for blindness, without having any new sense added by the words being sent by God to a particular person, and spoken anew to him, with a new meaning.[1]

JONATHAN EDWARDS

1. Jonathan Edwards, *Religious Affections*, ed. John E. Smith and Harry S. Stout, rev. ed., vol. 2, *The Works of Jonathan Edwards* (New Haven, CT: Yale University Press, 2009), 281.

Preface

To write a book that you hope will help others see more of God in the Christian Scriptures is to acknowledge that God intends that a reader of his word understand it and enjoy it with the help of others. Writing books, teaching lessons, preaching sermons, raising children "in the instruction of the Lord"—all of these imply that God has planned for us to understand the Bible with the help of human teachers. Another way to say it is that God reveals more of himself through his word when it is read in community than he does when it is read in isolation.

The New Testament shows repeatedly that Jesus Christ gives teachers to his church "to equip the saints for the work of ministry, for building up the body of Christ" (Eph. 4:11–12). Those teachers do not replace the Bible as God's inspired word. They help us understand it. In fact, the aim of human teachers is to help all believers grow to the point of being teachers themselves—not necessarily in an official capacity, but at least having the ability to use the word of God for both oneself and others.

> Though by this time you ought to be teachers, you need someone to teach you again the basic principles of the oracles of God. You need milk, not solid food, for everyone who lives on milk is unskilled in the word of righteousness, since he is a child. (Heb. 5:12–13)

Therefore, I see myself, and this book, as one small part of God's unfathomably complex matrix of influences that make up the Christian community of discovery and illumination. Therefore, nothing in this book should be construed to imply that its aim is to produce isolated Bible readers. It is a stone tossed into a pool of people. Its ripple effect, if any, will flow through relationships. Its aim is to be part of God's global purpose to create a beautiful bride for his Son—"the church . . . in splendor, without spot or wrinkle . . . holy and without blemish" (Eph. 5:27). The beauty of that bride consists largely in the humble, holy, happy, loving way Christians treat each other. If the *end* is corporate glory, we should not be surprised that the *means* is corporate growth. We read the word together; we reach the end together.

God has used hundreds of people to help me understand and love the Bible. I would like to help you—so you can help others. This is as it should be: a legacy of shared illumination until God's purposes for the church and the world are complete. May God turn your own ripple into a wave of blessing for the few that you know, and the thousands you don't. I am praying to this end.

The gospel of the blessed God does not go abroad a-begging for its evidence, so much as some think: it has its highest and most proper evidence in itself. . . . The mind ascends to the truth of the gospel but by one step, and that is its divine glory.

JONATHAN EDWARDS

Those who are under the power of their natural darkness and blindness . . . cannot see or discern that divine excellency in the Scripture, without an apprehension whereof no man can believe it aright to be the word of God.

JOHN OWEN

Introduction

This is a book about what it means to read the Bible supernaturally. I know that sounds strange. If there is anything obvious about you and me, it is that we are natural, ordinary, finite, mortal. We are not angels or demons; and we are certainly not God. But if the Bible is what it claims to be—namely, inspired by God—then it has a supernatural origin. And what I will try to show is that such a book calls for more than your natural kind of reading. Not less. But more. In fact, it calls for the very best of natural reading. But also for more—something beyond what is merely human.

As with all strange-sounding claims, there is a backstory. I tried to write this book a year ago, but within a matter of days, another book pushed its way into my mind and demanded to be written first. So I postponed this one and wrote *A Peculiar Glory: How the Christian Scriptures Reveal Their Complete Truthfulness*.[1] The question "Is the Bible true?" begged to be answered first.

In a sense, this is backward. Surely you must read a book before you can decide whether it's true. So shouldn't a book about how to read the Bible *precede* a book about its truthfulness? Maybe. But in my case, the discoveries I made writing *A Peculiar Glory* proved essential for the way this book is written. The way the Bible shows itself to be true and completely trustworthy carries indispensable implications for how to read it. This has become much clearer to me through writing *A Peculiar Glory* first.

You don't have to read *A Peculiar Glory* in order to understand this book. But it will clarify what I am doing in this book if you know

---

1. *A Peculiar Glory: How the Christian Scriptures Reveal Their Complete Truthfulness* (Wheaton, IL: Crossway, 2016).

how that book argues for the truth of the Bible. So I'll give a summary. The point of that first book, which shapes this one throughout, is that the Bible reveals its complete truthfulness by the shining forth of a self-authenticating, peculiar, divine glory. That too may sound strange. But it may not seem as strange if you compare that kind of argument with several others in the Bible of the same kind.

The Glory of God Authenticates the Creator

For example, how does the Bible expect all humans to know that God exists, and that he is all-powerful and generous, and should be thanked and glorified? Not many questions, if any, are more important than this. The answer is that the Bible expects all humans to see the self-authenticating glory of God in the universe he created. "The heavens declare the glory of God, and the sky above proclaims his handiwork" (Ps. 19:1).

Just this morning, I was walking home from a prayer meeting at church. As I crossed the bridge over the interstate, I saw, to my left, on the horizon, that the sun was just rising. It was white with brightness. I could only let my eyes glance briefly to the side of the sun. The ball itself was too brilliant to allow a direct sight. Everything from horizon to horizon was luminous with its own color and shape in the crystal-clear air. It is wonderful how natural light—the brightest and most beautiful of all lights—can cheer the soul. But none of that beauty and none of this natural cheerfulness is the glory of God. It is "declaring the glory of God." We are not pantheists. To see the glory of *God*, we must experience something supernatural. But it is there to see.

So there is a *divine* glory shining through the natural world—not just a natural glory. It's not just the glory of beautiful sunrises, and the stunning complexity of the human eye, and the solar system. It is something ineffable, but real and discernible. We are expected to see not just natural glory, but the glory *of God*.

The apostle Paul realizes that people do not see this divine glory by themselves. He explains why this is true and yet why none of us has an excuse for this spiritual blindness. It's because

> what can be known about God is plain to them, because God has shown it to them. For his invisible attributes, namely, his eternal power and divine nature, have been clearly perceived, ever since the

creation of the world, in the things that have been made. So they are without excuse. For although they knew God, they did not honor him as God or give thanks to him. (Rom. 1:19–21)

This means that God has shown everyone the glory of his power and deity and generosity. If we do not see God's glory, we are still responsible to see it, and to treasure it as supremely glorious, and to give God thanks. If we don't, we are, Paul says, "without excuse."

The Glory of God Authenticates Jesus

There is another, similar argument for how people should have recognized the divinity of Jesus. How did Jesus expect his first followers to know that he was the divine Son of God? The answer is that his whole way of life, the kind of person he was, and the works that he did revealed a self-authenticating, divine glory. His closest disciple wrote, "The Word became flesh and dwelt among us, and *we have seen his glory, glory as of the only Son from the Father*, full of grace and truth" (John 1:14).

But many people did not see this glory. Judas certainly didn't, in spite of three years of nearness. The Pharisees didn't. Even his disciples were slow to see. To such people Jesus said, "Have I been with you so long, and you still do not know me . . . ?" (John 14:9). He had shown them enough. They were responsible to see the glory—and to know that he was the divine Son of God. To be sure, Jesus was really human. He was natural, ordinary, finite, mortal. But he was also the virgin-born, supernatural Son of God (Luke 1:35). There was a glory shining through. Those who heard his teaching and saw his ministry were responsible to see it. This is how they were to know the truth.

The Glory of God Authenticates the Gospel

Consider one more example of how glory authenticates truth. This one relates to the gospel itself—the heart of the good news about Jesus's death and resurrection for sinners. How are people who hear the good news of the Christian gospel supposed to know that it's from God? The apostle Paul answered: they can know that it's from God because they see in it "the light of the gospel of the glory of Christ, who is the image of God" (2 Cor. 4:4). Or, putting it slightly differently, they can know because they see in it "the light of the knowledge of the glory of God in the face of Jesus Christ" (2 Cor. 4:6).

But many people hear the gospel and do not see divine glory. Why? It is not because the glory of God is unreal. It is not because the glory of God is not there in the gospel. It is because human beings, by nature, "are darkened in their understanding . . . due to their hardness of heart" (Eph. 4:18). It is not owing mainly to ignorance, but to hardness. This hardness is a deep antipathy to the truth. They are "perishing, because *they refused to love the truth* and so be saved" (2 Thess. 2:10). Satan, the "god of this world," exploits this hardness. Paul says he "has blinded the minds of the unbelievers, to keep them from seeing the light of the gospel of the glory of Christ" (2 Cor. 4:4). But the glory is really there in the gospel. To hear the gospel faithfully and fully presented is to be responsible to see divine glory.

The Glory of God Authenticates Scripture

The point of *A Peculiar Glory* is that the glory of God authenticates Scripture in a way similar to these three examples. In and through the Scriptures we see the glory of God. What the apostles saw face-to-face in Jesus Christ they impart to us through the words of Scripture. "That which we have seen and heard we proclaim also to you, so that you too may have fellowship with us; and indeed our fellowship is with the Father and with his Son Jesus Christ" (1 John 1:3). The glory that they saw in Christ, we can see through their words. The human words of Scripture are seen to be divine the way the human man Jesus was seen to be divine. Not all saw it. But the glory was there. And it is here, in the Scriptures.

All People Know God

One more illustration might help clarify how this actually works in the human soul. How is the glory of God seen? To be sure, the natural eyes and ears and brains are part of the process. Without them we cannot even see or hear or construe the natural things that reveal God's glory—creation, incarnation, gospel, Scripture. But this natural seeing is not decisive in seeing the glory of God. "Seeing they do not see," Jesus said (Matt. 13:13). Something more than the use of the natural eyes and ears and brains must happen.

The way the apostle Paul puts it is that you must "have the eyes of your hearts enlightened, that you may know" (Eph. 1:18). This too is strange—the heart has eyes! But perhaps not beyond comprehension. Most people are at home speaking of "the heart" as something more than the blood-pumping organ in our chest. Such language is not foreign to us. This "heart" is the real us. Intuitively we know that there is more to us than flesh and bones. We know we are not mere chemicals in a sack of skin. We would not talk the way we do about things like justice and love if we didn't believe that.

Is it so strange, then, to add to this immaterial personhood the idea of immaterial eyes—"the eyes of the heart"? This inner person, who is the real us, sees and knows things that are not identical with what the eyes of the body can see. Pascal said, "The heart has its reasons, which reason does not know. We feel it in a thousand things."[2] There is a spiritual seeing through and beyond natural seeing. There is a spiritual hearing through and beyond natural hearing. There is spiritual discerning through and beyond natural reasoning.

How may we conceive of what happens when the heart sees the glory of God? I found a clue in the way Paul speaks of our knowledge of the glory of God in nature. On the one hand, Paul says that we all "know God." "Although *they knew* God, they did not honor him as God or give thanks to him" (Rom. 1:21). That is astonishing. Everyone knows God! But in other places, Paul emphatically says that by nature people do *not* know God. For example, "In the wisdom of God, *the world did not know God* through wisdom" (1 Cor. 1:21). The "Gentiles . . . *do not know God*" (1 Thess. 4:5). Formerly "*you did not know God*" (Gal. 4:8; see 2 Thess. 1:8; 1 John 4:8).

So, what does Paul mean in Romans 1:21 when he says that all human beings "know God"? To answer this, we might simply quote Romans 1:19–20, "What can be known about God is plain to them, because God has shown it to them. For his invisible attributes, namely, his eternal power and divine nature, have been clearly perceived, ever since the creation of the world, in the things that have been made." In other words, we might say that "knowing God" in Romans 1:21 simply means having the witness of creation available and clearly seeing it by the natural eye.

---

2. Blaise Pascal, *Pascal's Pensées.*, no. 227, Kindle ed., loc. 1,531.

But is that all Paul means when he says, "They knew God"? I think there is more. In Romans 2:14–15, Paul says that people who have never heard of the law of God sometimes do what the law requires. Their consciences witness to God's will. He puts it like this: "They show that the work of the law is written on their hearts."

The Template of Divine Glory

So here is my suggestion. "Knowing God" in Romans 1:21 includes this deeper heart experience of Romans 2:15. The analogy that I find helpful is to conceive of the innate knowledge of God and his will as a kind of template or mold in the human heart. This template is designed by God in every human heart with a shape, or a form, that corresponds to the glory of God. In other words, if the glory of God were seen with the eyes of the heart, it would fit the template so perfectly that we would know the glory is real. We would know we were made for this.

So when Paul says that all humans "know God," or that all humans have the work of the law "written on their hearts," he means that there is a glory-shaped template in every heart waiting to receive the glory of God. We all "know God" in the sense that we have this witness in our hearts that we were made for this glory. There is a latent expectancy and longing, and the shape of it is buried deep in our souls.

Hearts Packed Hard with Alien Loves

The reason we do not see the glory of God is not that the template is faulty or that God's glory is not shining. The reason is "hardness of heart" (Eph. 4:18). This hardness is a deep aversion to God, and a corresponding love for self-exaltation. Paul said that the mind-set of the flesh is hostile to God (Rom. 8:7). And Jesus said that "light has come into the world, and people loved the darkness rather than the light" (John 3:19). Our problem is not that we lack the light, but that we love the dark. This is the hardness of our hearts.

So, in my analogy of the template, this means that the hollowed-out shapes of the mold, which are perfectly shaped for the all-satisfying glory of God, are instead packed hard with the love of other things. So when the glory of God shines into the heart—from creation or incarnation or Jesus or the gospel—it finds no place. It is not felt or perceived as fitting. To the natural mind—the mind whose glory-shaped mold is packed hard with idols—the glory of God is "foolishness" (1 Cor. 2:14 KJV). It doesn't fit. As Jesus said to those whose hardness pushed them to the point of murder, "You seek to kill me because *my word finds no place in you*" (John 8:37). Of course, they could construe his words, and remember his words. But they could not see them as glorious or compellingly beautiful. They heard the words, but they did not love them. They loved the darkness that filled the template that was designed for the brightness of the glory of God.

The Supernatural Excavation of the Template

Perhaps you can see now why I said that the present book is about what it means to read the Bible supernaturally. If we are on the right track, the only hope for seeing the glory of God in Scripture is that God might cut away the diamond-hard, idolatrous substitutes for the glory of God that are packed into the template of our heart. The Bible speaks of this supernatural act in many ways. For example, it describes this supernatural in-breaking as a shining into our hearts of divine glory (2 Cor. 4:6), and as a granting of truth and repentance (2 Tim. 2:25), and as the giving of faith (Phil. 1:29), and as raising us from the dead (Eph. 2:5), and as new birth by the word (1 Pet. 1:23; James 1:18), and as the special revelation of the Father (Matt. 16:17) and the Son (Matt. 11:27), and as the enlightening of the eyes of the heart (Eph. 1:18), and as being given the secret of the kingdom of God (Luke 8:10).

When this miracle happens to us, the glory of God cuts and burns and melts and removes from the template the suicidal cement of alien loves and takes its rightful place. We were made for this. And the witness of this glory to the authenticity of the Scriptures is overwhelming. Where we saw only foolishness before, we now see the all-satisfying beauty of God. God has done this—supernaturally.

No one merely decides to experience the Christian Scriptures as the all-compelling, all-satisfying truth of one's life. Seeing is a gift. And so the free embrace of God's word is a gift. God's Spirit opens the eyes of our heart, and what was once boring, or absurd, or foolish, or mythical, is now self-evidently real.

So my argument in *A Peculiar Glory* was that the glory of God, in and through the Scriptures, is a real, objective, self-authenticating reality. It is a solid foundation for a well-grounded faith in the truth of the

Bible. This faith is not a leap in the dark. It is not a guess, or a wager. If it were, our faith would be no honor to God. God is not honored if he is picked by the flip of a coin. A leap into the unknown is no tribute to one who has made himself unmistakably known by a peculiar glory.

It Is a Peculiar Glory

Up to this point in my recap of *A Peculiar Glory*, I have not emphasized the word *peculiar*. What does that word imply? It implies that the way the Scripture reveals its complete truthfulness is by means of a *peculiar* glory. In other words, the power of Scripture to warrant well-grounded trust is not by *generic* glory. Not by mere dazzling. Not by simply boggling the mind with supernatural otherness. Rather, what we see as inescapably divine is a *peculiar* glory. And at the center of this peculiar glory is the utterly unique glory of Jesus Christ.

There is an essence, or a center, or a dominant peculiarity in the way God glorifies himself in Scripture. That dominant peculiarity is the revelation of God's majesty in meekness, his strength in suffering, and the wealth of his glory in the depth of his giving. This *peculiar* glory is at the heart of the gospel of Jesus Christ. Along with countless manifestations in Scripture, this is the central brightness of "the light of the gospel of the glory of Christ, who is the image of God" (2 Cor. 4:4). This is what bursts upon the heart and mind of the person in whom God shines with the "light of the knowledge of the glory of God in the face of Jesus Christ" (2 Cor. 4:6).

Encountering the Glory in Jesus

This peculiar brightness shines through the whole Bible but finds its most beautiful radiance in the person and work of Jesus Christ. My guess is that the vast majority of people who come to believe in the divine inspiration and complete truthfulness of the Bible come to this conviction through an irresistible encounter with Jesus Christ. The peculiar glory that authenticates the Bible shines first and most clearly in Jesus.

How does that happen? Sometimes it is one particular word or deed of Jesus that penetrates the heart and begins to shatter the hardness that hinders the light of Christ's beauty. But sooner or later, it is the whole biblical portrait—climaxing in the crucifixion and resurrection—that conquers us and overcomes all resistance.

When the churches of Galatia were starting to drift away from the gospel of Jesus, Paul wrote to them and said, "O foolish Galatians! Who has bewitched you? It was before your eyes that Jesus Christ was publicly portrayed as crucified" (Gal. 3:1). This "portrayal" came with *words*, not pictures. But it was so real, and so vivid, that Paul said it was an appeal to their *eyes*—"before *your eyes* Jesus Christ was publicly portrayed." They *saw* the peculiar glory of Christ in the preaching of the gospel.

Paul was so taken back by their apparent departure that he called it a kind of witchcraft. "Who has *bewitched* you?" They had been converted by seeing the peculiar glory of Jesus, most vividly in his crucifixion. His hope was that his letter would blow the demonic vapors away and restore the vivid sight of Christ's glory. This is how most people come to a well-grounded faith in Christ and his word.

A Sketch of the Biblical Portrait of Jesus

It may be that you do not have a clear sense of what I mean by the "whole biblical portrait" of Christ. Perhaps you do not resonate with the idea that your mind and heart can be brought to a well-grounded confidence in Christ through the peculiar glory of his biblical portrayal. If so, let me try to sketch a small version of that portrayal. The aim here is to illustrate the luminous constellation of Jesus's words and deeds, in the hope that you will see how his divine glory shines through their cumulative, multifaceted uniqueness.

No One Loved God and Man More

Jesus was a person of unwavering and incomparable love for God and man. He became angry when God was dishonored by irreligion (Mark 11:15–17), and when man was destroyed by religion (Mark 3:4–5). He taught us—and showed us how—to be poor in spirit, meek, hungry for righteousness, pure in heart, merciful, and peaceable (Matt. 5:3–9). He urged us to honor God from the heart (Matt. 15:8) and to put away all hypocrisy (Luke 12:1). And he practiced what he preached. He was meek and lowly in heart (Matt. 11:29). His life was summed up as "doing good and healing" (Acts 10:38).

He took time for little children and blessed them (Mark 10:13–16). He crossed social barriers to help women (John 4), foreigners (Mark

7:24–30), lepers (Luke 17:11–19), harlots (Luke 7:36–50), tax collectors (Matt. 9:9–13), and beggars (Mark 10:46–52). He washed his disciples' feet, like a slave, and taught them to serve rather than be served (John 13:1–20).

Even when he was exhausted, his heart went out in compassion to the pressing crowds (Mark 6:31–34). Even when his own disciples were fickle and ready to deny him and forsake him, he wanted to be with them (Luke 22:15), and he prayed for them (Luke 22:32). He said his life was a ransom for many (Mark 10:45), and as he was being executed, he prayed for the forgiveness of his murderers (Luke 23:34).

No One Was More Truthful and Authentic

Not only is Jesus portrayed as full of love for God and man; he is also presented as utterly truthful and authentic. He did not act on his own authority to gain worldly praise. He directed men to his Father in heaven. "The one who speaks on his own authority seeks his own glory; but the one who seeks the glory of him who sent him is true, and in him there is no falsehood" (John 7:18). He does not have the spirit of an egomaniac or a charlatan. He seems utterly at peace with himself and God. He is authentic.

This is evident in the way he saw through sham (Matt. 22:18). He was so pure, and so perceptive, that he could not be tripped up or cornered in debate (Matt. 22:15–22). He was amazingly unsentimental in his demands, even toward those for whom he had a special affection (Mark 10:21). He never softened the message of righteousness to increase his following or curry favor. Even his opponents were stunned by his indifference to human praise: "Teacher, we know that you are true, and care for no man; for you do not regard the position of men, but truly teach the way of God" (Mark 12:14 author's translation). He never had to back down from a claim, and could be convicted of no wrong (John 8:46).

No One Spoke with Such Unassuming Authority

But what made all this peculiarly amazing was the unobtrusive yet unmistakable *authority* that rang through all he did and said. The officers of the Pharisees speak for all of us when they say, "No one ever spoke like this man!" (John 7:46). There was something unquestionably different about him. "He was teaching them as one who had authority, and not as their scribes" (Matt. 7:29). Yet he felt no need to flaunt it. It was natural to him.

His claims were not the open declaration of worldly power that the Jews expected from the Messiah. But they were unmistakable nonetheless. Though no one understood it at the time, there was no doubt that he had said, "Destroy this temple, and in three days I will raise it up" (John 2:19; cf. Matt. 26:61). They thought it was an absurd claim that he would single-handedly rebuild an edifice that took forty-six years to build. But he was claiming, in his typically veiled way, that he would rise from the dead. And he would rise by his own power. "I will build it."

In his last debate with the Pharisees, Jesus silenced them with this question: "What do you think of the Messiah? Whose son is he?" They answered, "David's son." In response, Jesus quoted King David from Psalm 110:1, "The Lord said to my Lord: Sit at my right hand, until I make your enemies your footstool." Then, with only slightly veiled authority, Jesus asked, "David thus calls him Lord, so how is he his son?" (Luke 20:44). In other words, for those who have eyes to see, the son of David—and *far more than the son*—is here.

That's the way he put it more than once. "I tell you, *something greater* than the temple is here" (Matt. 12:6). "*Something greater* than Jonah is here. . . . *Something greater* than Solomon is here" (Matt. 12:41–42). This kind of veiled claim runs through all that Jesus said and did. For those who have eyes to see, and ears to hear, something unimaginably great—and glorious—is here.

The Veil Is Lifted

Then there were words that were not at all veiled, and indeed were blasphemously self-exalting—unless they were true. He commanded evil spirits (Mark 1:27) and all the forces of nature (Mark 4:40), and they obeyed him. He issued forgiveness for sins (Mark 2:5), which only God can do (Mark 2:7). He summoned people to leave all and follow him in order to have eternal life (Mark 10:17–22; Luke 14:26–33). He said he would stand at the judgment day and declare who will enter heaven and who will not (Matt. 7:23). And he made the astonishing claim that "everyone who acknowledges me before men, I also will acknowledge before my Father who is in heaven, but whoever denies me before men,

I also will deny before my Father who is in heaven" (Matt. 10:32–33). He said he was the final arbiter of the universe.

Love and Sacrifice to the Uttermost

Then, with all this power—all this potential to make a life of exquisite pleasure and fame on earth—he sacrifices it all for the eternal happiness of sinners. He says uncompromisingly, "The Son of Man came not to be served but to serve, and to give his life as a ransom for many" (Mark 10:45). Over and over he told his disciples what was going to happen—it was the plan: "The Son of Man must suffer many things and be rejected by the elders and the chief priests and the scribes and be killed, and after three days rise again" (Mark 8:31).

In all of his self-giving, he was intentionally fulfilling Scripture. "The Son of Man goes as it is written of him" (Mark 14:21). So he not only submitted himself to death; he also entirely submitted himself to his Father in heaven (John 5:19)—and to God's word in Scripture. He was not caught in a web of tragic circumstances. He was willingly laying down his life. "I lay down my life that I may take it up again. No one takes it from me, but I lay it down of my own accord. I have authority to lay it down, and I have authority to take it up again" (John 10:17–18).

The aim of his sacrifice, he said, was the forgiveness of sins. "This is my blood of the covenant, which is poured out for many for the forgiveness of sins" (Matt. 26:28). This was the greatest love that had ever been shown in all of history, because the greatest person made the greatest sacrifice for the greatest gift to the least deserving. "Having loved his own who were in the world, he loved them to the end" (John 13:1).

Risen, Reigning, Coming

When he rose from the dead on the third day, as he said he would (Luke 24:6–7), he appeared to his disciples for forty days, giving them many proofs that he was not a ghost but the very person—body and spirit—whom they had known for three years (Luke 24:39–42; Acts 1:3). He gave them a global command to make disciples from every nation (Matt. 28:19) and promised to send his Spirit and be with them to the end of the age (John 14:26; Matt. 28:20). He ascended into heaven where he reigns over the world (Rev. 17:14; 1 Pet. 3:22) at the right hand of God the Father (Matt. 22:44; 26:64). And he promised he would come again to the earth in power and great glory (Matt. 16:27; 24:30) and bring all his people into everlasting joy (Matt. 25:21).

This is one sketch of the biblical portrait of Jesus. My argument in *A Peculiar Glory* is that the peculiar glory of God in Scripture comes to its clearest expression in this Jesus. His glory shines through the biblical account of his life and work. This glory is a real, objective, self-authenticating reality. It is a solid foundation for a well-grounded faith in the truth of the Bible.

Answering the Charge of Circularity

Someone may raise the objection that I am arguing in a circle. They may say that I am assuming the reliability of the biblical portrait of Jesus (by citing all these texts), even as I argue for it. There are two kinds of answer to this objection. One is the scholarly answer that says, no, even if you assume the most critical stance toward the New Testament records, there is no Gospel writer, and (to use the language of critical scholars) no layer of the tradition, where this kind of portrait is not present. This is the Jesus we know from history. There is no comfortable, natural Jesus that fits into preconceptions. There is no reconstruction of another Jesus more historically reliable than this one.[3]

The other answer to the objection of circularity is that the portrait of Jesus in the New Testament is self-authenticating. Most people have no access to the scholarly historical arguments for the reliability of the Gospels. My argument is that this need not be a hindrance to well-grounded faith. The reality of Jesus himself, as the New Testament portrays him, carries in it sufficient marks of authenticity that we can have full confidence that this portrait is true. I am calling the self-authenticating beauty, which shines through the New Testament portrait of Jesus, the peculiar glory of God.

Well-Grounded Faith for Nonhistorians

In fact, one of the key impulses behind the argument of *A Peculiar Glory* is the concern that there must be a way for the simplest person to have well-grounded confidence that the gospel is true. For example, what about a preliterate tribesman in the mountains of Papua New Guinea

---

3. I have argued for this more fully in John Piper, *What Jesus Demands from the World* (Wheaton, IL: Crossway, 2006), 29–39.

who has just heard the gospel story unfolded for the first time by a missionary? Or what about a child who is nine or ten years old and has heard the gospel from his parents for years? These people have no access to historical arguments about the authenticity of the New Testament documents. Can they come to a well-grounded confidence (not a leap in the dark) that the gospel is true and that the Scriptures are reliable?

Jonathan Edwards shared this concern more than 250 years ago. He had taken a position as missionary to the Native Americans of New England. He knew that if they were to have a well-grounded confidence in the truth of the gospel, it would not be by scholarly, historical reasoning. My approach to this problem builds on Edwards's answer. He said, "The gospel of the blessed God does not go abroad a-begging for its evidence, so much as some think: it has its highest and most proper evidence in itself. . . . The mind ascends to the truth of the gospel but by one step, and that is its divine glory."[4] Extending that argument to all of Scripture—that is what I tried to explain and defend in *A Peculiar Glory*.

The Scope of the Whole Is to Give Glory to God

Another way to put it is to say that *A Peculiar Glory* was an extended investigation and explanation of the words of the Westminster Larger Catechism. Question 4 reads, "How doth it appear that the Scriptures are of the Word of God?" Answer: "The Scriptures manifest themselves to be the Word of God, *by . . . the scope of the whole, which is to give all glory to God.*" In other words, the whole Bible, properly understood, has this divine purpose to communicate and display the glory of God. This pervasive aim of the Scriptures is carried through in such a way that God himself stands forth unmistakably as the unerring author guiding the human authors of the Bible.

The Bible, God's Book

Therefore, my conclusion (with about three hundred pages of argumentation and explanation) is that "the Bible, consisting of the sixty-six books of the Old and New Testaments, is the infallible Word of God, verbally inspired by God, and without error in the original manuscripts."[5] This

---

4. Jonathan Edwards, *A Treatise Concerning Religious Affections*, ed. Paul Ramsey, vol. 2., *The Works of Jonathan Edwards* (New Haven, CT: Yale University Press, 1957), 299, 307.

5. Paragraph 1.1 of the *Bethlehem Baptist Church Elder Affirmation of Faith*.

also implies that the Scriptures are the supreme and final authority in testing all claims about what is true and right and beautiful. It implies, in matters not explicitly addressed by the Bible, that what is true and right and beautiful is to be assessed by criteria consistent with the teachings of Scripture. All of this implies that the Bible has final authority over every area of our lives, and that we should, therefore, try to bring all our thinking and feeling and acting into line with what the Bible teaches.

I do not write those words lightly. They make a staggering claim. Breathtaking. If they are not true, they are outrageous. The Bible is not the private charter of a faith community among other faith communities. It is a total claim on the whole world. God, the creator, owner, and governor of the world, has spoken. His words are valid and binding on all people everywhere. That is what it means to be God.

To our astonishment, God's way of speaking with infallible authority in the twenty-first century is through *a book*! One book. Not many. Not this one! But the Bible. That is the breathtaking declaration of the Christian Scriptures. The implications of this are huge—including implications about how to read the Bible.

Two Facts Full of Implications

But now we've seen that there is another spectacular fact that is full of implications about how we should read the Bible. First, there was the fact that the Creator of the universe has spoken through *a book*. And, second, there is the fact that he has shown this book to be completely true by the divine glory revealed through it. Both of these facts are laden with implications for how to read the book. On the one hand, it is a book composed with ordinary human language that needs to be understood—it is, after all, a real human book. And on the other hand, it is luminous with the supernatural light of divine glory. Which means, as we said at the beginning, the Bible calls for more than your natural kind of reading. Not less. But more. Natural *and* supernatural. If either is missing, we will misread God's word.

The Structure of the Book

This book has three parts. Part 1 poses the all-important question, *What does the Bible tell us is the ultimate goal of reading the Bible?* I propose an answer with six implications and then devote ten chapters to unfolding and testing those implications. Part 2 works out the inference from part 1 that reading the Bible really must be a supernatural act, if God's goals for our reading the Bible are to be reached. Finally, part 3 treats the practical outworking of such a claim in the seemingly ordinary human act of reading—the natural act of reading the Bible supernaturally.

PART 1

The Ultimate Goal of
Reading the Bible

. . . that God's infinite worth and beauty *would be exalted in the everlasting, white-hot worship of the blood-bought bride of Christ from every people, language, tribe, and nation.*

Introduction to Part 1

The Proposal

Some authors leave marks of their authorship that have nothing to do with the point of their book. That seems to be the case, for example, with the letters of the apostle Paul. He wrote, "I, Paul, write this greeting with my own hand. This is the sign of genuineness in every letter of mine; it is the way I write" (2 Thess. 3:17). Again in Galatians 6:11, he wrote, "See with what large letters I am writing to you with my own hand." In other words, these marks of his authorship are not the great burden of his letters. They are not the vision of God and Christ and the Christian life that moved him to write in the first place. These are signatures. And even though signatures are important for authentication, they are not essential to the message.

Other authors develop a style of writing that is so unique that it functions as a mark of their own authorship. One thinks of G. K. Chesterton's use of paradox, or Ernest Hemingway's staccato sentences. Or Charles Dickens's florid descriptions. Or Emily Dickinson's deceptively simple brevity of verse. Of course, these styles are not artificially disconnected from the message or the purpose of the writings. But neither are they the main point. Probably each author would say they are essential to what they are trying to do overall. But I doubt that any of them would say, "The main thing I want people to take away from my work is my style."

The Meaning of Glory Is the Marker of Divinity

But things are different when we think of God's relationship to the Bible. He did not sign it with a distinctive signature. And when he inspired it (2 Tim. 3:16), he did not overrule the individual styles of the human authors so as to create a style of his own—such as a divine diction, or heavenly vocabulary, or Godlike cadence. When the officers of the Pharisees said of Jesus, "No one ever spoke like this man!" they were not referring to his accent or his vocabulary or his oratorical skill. They were referring to the overall nature and impact of the man as he spoke. The Pharisees saw where this was going and said, "Have you also been deceived? Have any of the authorities or the Pharisees believed in him?" (John 7:47–48). In other words, they saw that the officers were starting to see something that awakens faith. But it was not a signature or a style.

What is different about the way God authenticates the Bible is that the ground he gives for the Bible's truth is the same as the center and aim of the Bible's message. The peculiar glory of God is both the substance and the seal of the story that the Bible tells. It is not as though God speaks in his word, revealing his nature and his purposes, and then must add a separate marker for his divinity—like a signature or a style. His glory, through his word, is the message *and* his marker.

To be sure, God often "bore witness to the word of his grace, granting signs and wonders" (Acts 14:3). But the signs and wonders were not decisive. They could be denied, distorted, and rejected as completely as his word was—which we know from the life of Judas, and from certain people who saw Jesus raise Lazarus from the dead and then helped his murderers (John 11:45–53). Rather, those miracles were woven together with God's word into a tapestry of the revelation of the peculiar glory of God. That glory is the ultimate meaning of the tapestry and the decisive mark of its divine reality.

Implications for the Big Picture

If that is true, then we would not be surprised that the Bible calls for a supernatural reading, since seeing divine glory in human words is not your ordinary way of reading a book. But we are getting ahead of ourselves. Is it, in fact, true that the peculiar glory of God is the ultimate meaning of the tapestry of Scripture? Is this what we should aim to see when we read the Bible? That is our first key question in this book. That is what part 1 is about.

The way I would like to put the question is this: What does the Bible itself say is the ultimate goal of reading the Bible? If the Bible makes clear that the goal of reading the Bible is to see what can only be supernaturally seen, then the implications for how we read the Bible will be profound. So we ask in part 1 what the Bible tells us is the ultimate goal of reading the Bible. Then, in part 2, we examine the implication that this calls for a supernatural reading of the Bible. And finally, in part 3, we present the implications of this for the ordinary human act of reading.

The Proposal

So, first, what does the Bible tell us is the ultimate goal of reading the Bible? What follows is my proposed answer to this question, with six implications. The aim of part 1 of this book is to see whether this proposal and its implications are true.

The Bible itself shows that our ultimate goal in reading the Bible is that God's infinite worth and beauty would be exalted in the everlasting, white-hot worship of the blood-bought bride of Christ from every people, language, tribe, and nation. In other words, each time we pick up the Bible to read, we should intend that reading would lead to this end. The way that we as individuals are caught up into this ultimate aim as we read the Bible becomes clear as we spell out six implications that flow from this proposed answer to our question. When we say that the ultimate goal of reading the Bible is that God's infinite worth and beauty would be exalted in the everlasting, white-hot worship of the blood-bought bride of Christ from every people, language, tribe, and nation, we imply that:

1. the infinite worth and beauty of God are *the ultimate value and excellence* of the universe;
2. that the supremely *authentic and intense worship* of God's worth and beauty is the ultimate aim of all his work and word;
3. that we should always read his word in order to *see* this supreme worth and beauty;
4. that we should aim in all our seeing to *savor* his excellence above all things;
5. that we should aim to be *transformed* by this seeing and savoring into the likeness of his beauty,
6. so that more and more people would be drawn into the worshiping family of God until the bride of Christ—across all centuries and cultures—is complete in number and beauty.

The following chapters in part 1 focus on the parts of this proposal and put them all to the test: What does the Bible itself say about this proposed goal of reading and its implications?

The great end of God's works, *which is so variously expressed in Scripture, is indeed but one; and this one end is most properly and comprehensively called the glory of God.*

JONATHAN EDWARDS

[He] works all things according to the counsel of his will . . . to the praise of his glory.

EPHESIANS 1:11–12

1

Reading the Bible toward
God's Ultimate Goal

"Whatever you do, do all to the glory of God."

The Proposal

Our ultimate goal in reading the Bible is that God's infinite worth and beauty would be exalted in the everlasting, white-hot worship of the blood-bought bride of Christ from every people, language, tribe, and nation. This implies:

1. that the infinite worth and beauty of God are *the ultimate value and excellence* of the universe;
2. that the supremely *authentic and intense worship* of God's worth and beauty is the ultimate aim of all his work and word;
3. that we should always read his word in order to *see* this supreme worth and beauty;
4. that we should aim in all our seeing to *savor* his excellence above all things;
5. that we should aim to be *transformed* by this seeing and savoring into the likeness of his beauty,
6. so that more and more people would be drawn into the worshiping family of God until the bride of Christ—across all centuries and cultures—is complete in number and beauty.

Our proposal elevates the worth and beauty of God to the highest place possible. The ultimate aim of all Bible reading, I argue, is that *God's infinite worth and beauty would be exalted in everlasting, white-hot worship.* There is nothing higher than the worth and beauty of God. That is what the first implication expresses: *the infinite worth and beauty of God are the ultimate value and excellence of the universe.*

So the first thing we need to do is clarify from Scripture the meaning and then the supremacy of the *glory* of God. That may seem strange since I didn't even use the word *glory* in my proposal or its implications. Nevertheless, the reality is there, and it is the most important one. I used other words for it, namely, the pairs "worth and beauty" and "value and excellence."

Finding Words for the Glory of God

I recall one day when I was in college, Clyde Kilby, my favorite English teacher, said something to this effect: "One of the greatest tragedies of the fall is that we get tired of familiar glories." That simple statement sank deep into my consciousness. It made me very sad, because I saw how superficial and unresponsive I was to so many wonders around me. It filled me with a longing not to be like that. I did not want to arrive in the Alps, be filled with wonder for a couple days, but by the end of the week be watching television in the chalet. I lamented my ability to actually yawn during Handel's "Hallelujah Chorus."

Which means I loathe the thought of speaking of the glory of God in a way that is so familiar or stale or clichéd that it wakens no sense of wonder. Of course, I realize that only God can waken true wonder at the glory of God. Kilby was right. The fall has left us deeply dysfunctional emotionally. We are excited by trivia and bored by grandeur. We strain out a gnat to admire and swallow a camel of glory unnoticed. Nevertheless, I want to try to use language that helps us see what the glory of God is, if I can. Hence the effort to find other words besides *glory*—like *worth* and *beauty* and *value* and *excellence.*

What Is the Glory of God?

My understanding of the glory of God has been deeply shaped by its relationship to the holiness of God. I have in mind the way this relationship comes to expression in Isaiah 6:1–3:

In the year that King Uzziah died I saw the Lord sitting upon a throne, high and lifted up; and the train of his robe filled the temple. Above him stood the seraphim. Each had six wings: with two he covered his face, and with two he covered his feet, and with two he flew. And one called to another and said: "Holy, holy, holy is the LORD of hosts; the whole earth is full of his glory!"

Why did the prophet not say, "Holy, holy, holy is the LORD of hosts; the whole earth is full of his *holiness!*"? My suggestion is that the glory of God is the holiness of God put on display. When God's holiness shines into creation, it is called "God's glory."

The Holiness of God

This pushes the question about the meaning of *glory* back into the holiness of God. What is that?[1] The root meaning of the Old Testament word for *holy* (Hebrew *chadōsh*) is the idea of being separate—different from and separated from something. When applied to God, that means God's holiness is his separateness from all that is not God. This, then, means he is in a class by himself. And like all good things that are rare, the more rare it is, the more valuable it is. Therefore, God is supremely valuable.

We can see this meaning of God's holiness in the following two illustrations. First, when Moses struck the rock instead of speaking to it the way God had instructed him, God said, "Because you did not believe in me, to uphold me as *holy* in the eyes of the people of Israel, therefore you shall not bring this assembly into the land that I have given them" (Num. 20:12; see 27:14). In other words, when Moses distrusted God, he did not treat him as being in a magnificent class of power and trustworthiness by himself. He treated him as just another common person to be distrusted as unwilling or unable to do what he said. But God is not common. He is not like others. He is holy.

Second, in Isaiah 8:12–13, God says to Isaiah, "Do not call conspiracy all that this people calls conspiracy, and do not fear what they fear, nor be in dread. But the LORD of hosts, him you shall honor as *holy*. Let him be your fear, and let him be your dread." In other words,

---

1. In what follows I am adapting some things I wrote about holiness in *Acting the Miracle: God's Work and Ours in the Mystery of Sanctification*, ed. John Piper and David Mathis (Wheaton, IL: Crossway, 2013), 29–41, 127–38.

don't lump God into the same group as all your other fears and dreads. Treat him as an utterly unique fear and dread. Set him apart from all the ordinary fears and dreads.

So here is how I conceive of the holiness of God. God is so separate, so above, so distinct from all else—all that is not God—that he is self-existent and self-sustaining and self-sufficient. Thus he is infinitely complete and full and perfect in himself. He is separate from, and transcendent above, all that is not God. So he was not brought into existence by anything outside himself. He is, therefore, self-existent. He depends on nothing for his ongoing existence and so is self-sustaining. And, therefore, he is utterly self-sufficient. Complete, full, perfect.

The Bible makes plain that this self-existing, self-sustaining, self-sufficient God exists as three divine persons in one divine essence. Thus the Father knows and loves the Son perfectly, completely, infinitely; and the Son knows and loves the Father perfectly, completely, infinitely. And the Holy Spirit is the perfect, complete, infinite expression of the Father's and the Son's love of each other. This perfect Trinitarian fellowship is essential to the fullness and perfection of God. There is no lack, no deficiency, no need—only perfect fullness and completeness and self-sufficiency.

The Moral Dimension of God's Holiness

This is the holiness of God: his transcendent completeness and self-sufficiency. But there is a missing dimension in that description of holiness. This is the dimension I mentioned above that flows from his absolute rareness—being one of a kind in his perfection. This implies that he is of infinite value. One of the reasons it is crucial to focus on this aspect of God's holiness is that it helps us understand why the Bible treats God's holiness not just as transcendent *being*, but also as transcendent *purity or goodness*.

In other words, introducing God's infinite worth helps us conceive of God's holiness in moral categories. We take this so for granted that we don't ponder how this can be. How can God be thought of as infinitely good or right or pure, when there are no standards outside of God by which to measure him? Before creation, all there was was God. So, when there is only God, how do we define good? How can holiness mean more than transcendence? How can there be holiness with a *moral* dimension?

My answer is this: the moral dimension of God's holiness is that every affection, every thought, and every act of God is consistent with the infinite worth of his transcendent fullness. In other words, holiness is not only the infinite worth of God's transcendent fullness but also the harmony that exists between the worth of that transcendent fullness and all God's affections, thoughts, and acts. This harmony of God's acts with his infinite worth we may call "the beauty of God's holiness." Stephen Charnock (1628–1680) uses a quaint phrase to express what I am trying to say. God's holiness, he says, is that he "works with a becomingness to his own excellency."[2] The old word *becomingness* means "suitableness, agreeableness, fittingness, harmony." That's how an act of God is good or pure or perfect. It is agreeable to—perfectly expressive of, in harmony with—the worth of God.

The Glory of God as the Beauty of God's Holiness

This brings us back to the relationship between God's holiness and his glory. We experience the beauty of God's holiness as the glory of God. As God's holiness becomes expressive—creating and penetrating the world—we call it the "glory of God."[3] His glory is the streaming out of his holiness for the world to see and admire. Gerhard Kittel's lengthy article on glory in *The Theological Dictionary of the New Testament* concludes that God's glory "denotes divine and heavenly radiance . . . that which makes God impressive to man, the force of His self-manifestation."[4]

We must constantly remind ourselves that we are speaking of a glory that is ultimately beyond created comparison. "The glory of God" is the way you designate the infinite beauty and the infinite greatness of the person who was there before anything else was there. In other words, it is the worth and beauty and greatness that exists without origin, without comparison, without analogy, without being judged or assessed by any external criterion. It is the all-defining, absolute original of worth

---

2. Stephen Charnock, *The Existence and Attributes of God*, vol. 2 (Grand Rapids, MI: Baker, 1979), 115.

3. I don't mean to imply an ironclad limitation of the word *glory* for the manifestation of the radiance of God's holiness *in the world*. For example, Jesus prays, "Father, I desire that they also, whom you have given me, may be with me where I am, to see *my glory that you have given me because you loved me before the foundation of the world*" (John 17:24). But, in general, it holds that the glory of God is the radiance of God—that which shines out from his essence.

4. *Theological Dictionary of the New Testament*, ed. Gerhard Kittel, Geoffrey W. Bromiley, and Gerhard Friedrich (Grand Rapids, MI: Eerdmans, 1964–), 237–38.

and greatness and beauty. All created worth and greatness and beauty come from it, and point to it, but do not comprehensively or adequately reproduce it.

"The glory of God" is a way of saying that there is objective, absolute reality to which all human admiration, wonder, awe, veneration, praise, honor, acclaim, and worship are pointing. We were made to find our deepest pleasure in admiring what is infinitely admirable, that is, the glory of God. The glory of God is not the psychological projection of human longing onto reality. On the contrary, inconsolable human longing is the evidence that we were made for God's glory.

The Supreme Importance of God's Glory

So when the Bible puts the glory of God on display as the goal of all that God does, this is another way of saying that God's infinite worth and beauty—or his ultimate value and excellence—is the supreme reality in the universe. And that is, in fact, what we find in the Bible. From beginning to end, God tells us and shows us that his ultimate goal in all he does is to communicate his glory for the world to see and for his people to admire and enjoy and praise.

We can show this by pointing to six stages of redemption, beginning in eternity past and moving through creation and history to eternity future. At each of these stages, God says explicitly that his purpose is that his glory be known and praised—that is, gladly admired, expressively enjoyed, heartily treasured.

Predestination

> Blessed be the God and Father of our Lord Jesus Christ, who has blessed us in Christ with every spiritual blessing in the heavenly places, even as he chose us in him before the foundation of the world, that we should be holy and blameless before him. In love he predestined us for adoption through Jesus Christ, according to the purpose of his will, *to the praise of the glory of his grace.* (Eph. 1:3–6 author's translation)

Redemption begins in eternity past in the heart of God. He predestines a people "for adoption . . . through Jesus Christ." Paul tells us the deepest root and the highest goal of this predestination. He says it is rooted in "the purpose of his will" (Eph. 1:5). And he says its ultimate goal is "the praise of his glorious grace" (Eph. 1:6).

How quickly do we pass over that last statement! Whose purpose is being expressed in the words "he predestined us for adoption . . . to the praise of his glorious grace"? It is *God's* purpose. And what is that purpose? That we praise. That we praise what? His glory. The peculiar glory of his grace. So from all eternity, God's plan was to have a family adopted "through Jesus Christ" who would praise his glory to all eternity. There are few things more important to know than that. Few things will shape more of your life than that—if it penetrates to the center of your soul.

The plan from eternity past was praise for eternity future. The one who planned and the one to be praised are the same: God. And the focus of the praise is his own peculiar glory—which shines most brightly as the glory of grace in the person and work of Jesus.

Creation

> I will say to the north, Give up,
>> and to the south, Do not withhold;
> bring my sons from afar
>> and my daughters from the end of the earth,
> everyone who is called by my name,
>> whom I created *for my glory*,
>> whom I formed and made. (Isa. 43:6–7)

What does "for my glory" mean? It doesn't mean that the creation will bring God's glory into being. He has glory already. Creation is overflow. It means that creation will show, or display, or communicate God's glory. That is why Israel was created. And that is why all of us were created. This is the point of Genesis 1:27–28:

> God created man in his own image, in the image of God he created him; male and female he created them. And God blessed them. And God said to them, "Be fruitful and multiply and fill the earth."

If you are very great and you fill the earth with seven billion images of yourself, what is your aim? Your aim is to be known and admired for your greatness. But, of course, since sin entered the world, human beings prefer to live for their own glory, not God's. That is why God planned a history of redemption—so that those who put their hope in Christ "might be to the praise of his glory" (Eph. 1:12). We were created for God's glory in our first birth. And through Christ we are born again—made new as new creations—for his glory. *Human existence is for the glory of God.* That is why he created the world (Ps. 19:1) and the human race (Gen. 1:27–28), and the new race in Christ (Eph. 1:12).

Incarnation

> The Word became flesh and dwelt among us, and *we have seen his glory, glory as of the only Son from the Father*, full of grace and truth. (John 1:14)

The incarnation of the eternal Son of God—the Word who "was with God, and . . . was God" (John 1:1)—put God's glory on display as never before. "We have seen his glory, glory as of the only Son from the Father." This was why God sent him, and why he came.

Paul makes this point in Philippians 2:6–11. He describes the incarnation like this:

> Though he was in the form of God . . . he was born in the likeness of men. And being found in human form, he . . . was obedient to the point of death. . . . Therefore God has highly exalted him . . . so that at the name of Jesus . . . every tongue would confess that Jesus Christ is Lord, *to the glory of God the Father.* (author's translation)

If you follow the line of thought carefully, what you see is that God exalted Christ because he took on human form and was obedient to death. He was an obedient human; therefore God exalted him. And the aim of that incarnation and consequent exaltation was *God's glorification.* "Therefore God has highly exalted him . . . to *the glory of God the Father.*" Thus God's aim in the incarnation of the Son was the display of the peculiar glory of the Father in the incarnation and work of Christ.

Propitiation

> "Now is my soul troubled. And what shall I say? 'Father, save me from this hour'? But for this purpose I have come to this hour. *Father, glorify your name.*" Then a voice came from heaven: "*I have glorified it, and I will glorify it again.*" (John 12:27–28)

Father, the hour has come; glorify your Son that the Son may glorify you. (John 17:1)

The hour Jesus is speaking of is the hour of his death. He had come to die. "I lay down my life for the sheep" (John 10:15). And the reason that needs to be done is that all humans are under the wrath of God. There is no hope for any of us without a propitiation—that is, a sacrifice that removes the wrath of God. Jesus gives himself as that sacrifice. The result is that "whoever believes in the Son has eternal life; whoever does not obey the Son shall not see life, but the wrath of God remains on him" (John 3:36). There are only two options. Believe and escape God's wrath. Or disobey the command to believe and remain under the wrath. Jesus said that he came to provide this escape for the glory of the Father. "For this purpose I have come to this hour. Father, *glorify your name*" (John 12:27–28).

The apostle Paul explained more fully how this aspect of Christ's death actually works. He wrote in Romans 3:25–26:

God put [Christ] forward as a propitiation by his blood, to be received by faith. *This was to show God's righteousness*, because in his divine forbearance he had passed over former sins. It was *to show his righteousness* at the present time, so that he might be righteous and the one who declares the one righteous who has faith in Jesus. (author's translation)

Twice Paul says that God sent Christ as a propitiation "to *show* God's righteousness." Also he says that the purpose is "that he might *be* righteous." So three times Paul describes the death of Jesus as the vindication of the righteousness of God.

Did Christ die for us or for God? I once preached a sermon at the student gathering called Passion under the title "Did Christ Die for Us or for God?" This passage, Romans 3:25–26, was my text. The answer to the question was that *Christ died for God's glory* so that his death might count for our salvation. Why did Christ need to die to show that God is righteous? Indeed, why did he need to die so that God, in declaring sinners righteous, might himself *be* righteous? The answer is given plainly: "because in his divine forbearance he had passed over former sins." God had not punished the sins of the Old Testament saints. He had passed over them. Just like he is still passing over the sins of all who trust Jesus.

But he had just said in Romans 3:23 that these sins belittle the glory of God. "All have sinned and *fall short of the glory of God.*" When a person sins, he is expressing a preference for something other than God. He is saying that God and his way are less satisfying than the way of sin. This is an outrageous insult to God. We are exchanging the glory of God for another glory (Rom. 1:23).

Therefore *sinning is a discounting of the value of the glory of God.* If God passes over this attitude and this behavior, as though his glory were not of infinite value, he is acting unrighteously. He is agreeing that other things are more to be desired than he is. That is unrighteous. It is a lie.

Nevertheless, that is what God has done. He has passed over former sins. He looks unrighteous. And this, Paul says, is why God put Christ forward as a propitiation by his blood. In Christ's death for the glory of God (John 12:27), Jesus showed the world that God does not ignore the belittling of his glory. He does not sweep God-demeaning sins under the rug of the universe. He shows, in the death of Christ, that his glory is of infinite value. He is not unrighteous; he did not treat his glory as worthless. When he passes over sin for Christ's sake, all creation can see that this is not because the glory of God is negligible, but because in Christ there has been an infinite display of the worth of the glory of God. "For this purpose I have come to this hour. Father, *glorify your name*" (John 12:27–28).

Therefore, we know that *Christ died for the glory of God.* Christ gave himself as a propitiation of the wrath of God to vindicate the righteousness of God in passing over God-belittling sins. And in doing this, Christ himself, in his death and resurrection, became part of the magnificent divine display of the peculiar glory of God.

Sanctification

> It is my prayer that your love may abound more and more, with knowledge and all discernment, so that you may approve what is excellent, and so be pure and blameless for the day of Christ, filled with the fruit of righteousness that comes through Jesus Christ, *to the glory and praise of God.* (Phil. 1:9–11)

> We always pray for you, that our God may make you worthy of his calling and may fulfill every resolve for good and every work of faith by his power, *so that the name of our Lord Jesus may be glorified in you.* (2 Thess. 1:11–12)

God makes his people holy—sanctifies them—in order to put his own glory on display. He works in us to "fill us with the fruit of righteousness." Why? "To the glory and praise of God." We can easily overlook in Philippians 1:9–11 that Paul is praying *to* God. That is, he is asking *God* to glorify God in the righteousness of his people. This is God's purpose and God's doing, not just Paul's.

Similarly, in 2 Thessalonians 1:11–12, Paul prays that the believers be able to carry through every good work "so that the name of our Lord Jesus may be glorified in you." *Good deeds are for the glory of Christ.* And through him for the glory of God. This is what we should expect if God *predestined* us for his glory, and *created* us for his glory, and *died to save* us for his glory. Step by step in the history of redemption, God is working all things for the communication of his glory for the enjoyment of his people.

Consummation

> They will suffer the punishment of eternal destruction, away from the presence of the Lord and from the glory of his might, when he comes on that day *to be glorified* in his saints, and *to be marveled at* among all who have believed, because our testimony to you was believed. (2 Thess. 1:9–10)

At the last day—the end of history as we know it—Jesus is coming back to this earth. Why? The reason given here is so that he might "be glorified in his saints, and to be marveled at among all who have believed." The word *glorify* does not mean "make glorious." It means to *show* as glorious—or to acclaim or praise or exalt or magnify as glorious.

Magnify. Yes, that is a good word for *glorify.* But it is ambiguous. We do not magnify him the way a microscope magnifies. We magnify him the way a telescope magnifies. A microscope makes tiny things look bigger than they are. Telescopes make huge things, which already look tiny, appear more like what they really are. That is why he is coming back: finally to be shown and seen and enjoyed for who he really is.

For Our White-Hot Worship

So from eternity to eternity—in predestination, creation, incarnation, propitiation, sanctification, and consummation—the Bible makes explicit that God's ultimate aim in all things is the revelation and exaltation of his glory. It is evident from this that the glory of God is the supreme treasure over all else that exists. That is (as the first implication of the proposal states) *the infinite worth and beauty of God are the ultimate value and excellence of the universe.*

The proposal I am making about the ultimate goal of reading the Bible, however, is not only that the glory of God—the worth and beauty of God—be revealed and shown to be an exalted glory. The proposal is *that God's infinite worth and beauty would be exalted in everlasting, white-hot worship.* And this implies that the ultimate aim of all God's work and word is the supremely authentic and intense worship of his worth and beauty. In other words, as I will try to show in the next chapter, the ultimate goal of reading the Bible is not only the world-wide exaltation of God's worth, but also the white-hot exultation of his people in worship. That joyful exultation in worship is the way God planned the highest exaltation of his glory.

Though you do not now see him, you believe in him and rejoice with joy that is inexpressible and filled with glory.

1 PETER 1:8

O God, you are my God; earnestly I seek you;
    my soul thirsts for you;
my flesh faints for you,
    as in a dry and weary land where there is no water.

PSALM 63:1

2

Reading the Bible toward
White-Hot Worship

"Because you are lukewarm,
. . . I will spit you out of my mouth."

The Proposal

Our ultimate goal in reading the Bible is that God's infinite worth and
beauty would be exalted in the everlasting, white-hot worship of the
blood-bought bride of Christ from every people, language, tribe, and
nation. This implies:

1. that the infinite worth and beauty of God are *the ultimate
   value and excellence* of the universe;
2. **that the supremely *authentic and intense worship* of God's
   worth and beauty is the ultimate aim of all his work and word;**
3. that we should always read his word in order to *see* this
   supreme worth and beauty;
4. that we should aim in all our seeing to *savor* his excellence
   above all things;
5. that we should aim to be *transformed* by this seeing and
   savoring into the likeness of his beauty,
6. so that more and more people would be drawn into the worshiping family of God until the bride of Christ—across all
   centuries and cultures—is complete in number and beauty.

We are asking in part 1, "What is our ultimate goal in reading the Bible?" Our proposed answer is *that God's infinite worth and beauty would be exalted in the everlasting, white-hot worship of the blood-bought bride of Christ from every people, language, tribe, and nation.*

Our first step in establishing this was to show from Scripture, in the previous chapter, that *the infinite worth and beauty of God are the ultimate value and excellence of the universe.* What we saw was that from beginning to end, God lifts up his glory as the supreme aim of all things. If there is something of greater value or excellence, then God would seem to be an idolater. He would be leading us to glorify most what is not most glorious. But he is not an idolater. He is righteous. Therefore (affirming our first implication), the worth and beauty of God are indeed the ultimate value and excellence in the universe. Nothing is more valuable or beautiful.

The Worship of God Is the Aim of Exalting His Worth

The second implication of our proposal follows from the first one. *The supremely authentic and intense worship of God's worth and beauty is the ultimate aim of all his work and word.* This is implicit in the first implication. It is also explicit in the Bible. If God reveals himself to be the supreme value and excellence in the universe, then it follows that we should worship him for his supreme worth and beauty—and not just in a casual way but with white-hot devotion. Our worship follows our values. For that is what worship is. It is the experience of valuing, and cherishing, and treasuring what we perceive to be our greatest treasure.

This second implication is also explicit in the Bible. Jesus says plainly that God is seeking *worshipers.* "The hour is coming, and is now here, when the true worshipers will worship the Father in spirit and truth, for *the Father is seeking such people to worship him*" (John 4:23). Not surprisingly, then, the Bible commands us to worship him in accord with his supreme worth.

> Ascribe to the LORD, O heavenly beings,
>   ascribe to the LORD glory and strength.
> Ascribe to the LORD the glory due his name;
>   worship the LORD in the splendor of holiness. (Ps. 29:1–2)

There is a glory that belongs to his name. It is "due his name." This is what we have seen in God's zeal to exalt his glory as the goal of all things. Now here it is made explicit that there is a *response* from us—worship—that accords with this glory. This is why God was exalting his glory—that we might worship. God's exaltation *of* God aims at our exultation *in* God.

Worship Is the Aim of Every Stage of Redemption

The Bible makes this explicit in relation to all six of the stages of redemptive history that we saw in the previous chapter. The goal is worship.

- In regard to *predestination*, "he predestined us . . . to the praise of his glory" (Eph. 1:5, 14). Not just to know it but to praise it. The aim is worship.

- In regard to *creation*, the heavenly beings cry out, "Worthy are you, our Lord and God, to receive glory and honor and power, for you created all things" (Rev. 4:11). Everlasting worship in heaven happens precisely in response to God's creating all things.

- In regard to Christ's *incarnation* and saving death, the angels of heaven cry, "Worthy is the Lamb who was slain, to receive power and wealth and wisdom and might and honor and glory and blessing!" (Rev. 5:12). The glory of Christ's saving work will be worshiped forever.

- In regard to propitiation, and the great work of Christ's decisive wrath-removing ransom, heaven worships with a new song, saying, "Worthy are you to take the scroll and to open its seals, for you were slain, and by your blood you ransomed people for God from every tribe and language and people and nation" (Rev. 5:9).

- In regard to the *sanctification* of God's people, Paul tells us that the ultimate aim of being "filled with the fruit of righteousness" is that this transformation might be "to the glory and praise of God" (Phil. 1:11). Not just glory but also *praise*. Which makes explicit that the aim of holiness in the Christian life is that God be worshiped.

- And in regard to the *consummation* of all things at the second coming of Christ, the aim is not just that his glory might be seen, but that it might "be *marveled* at among all who have believed" (2 Thess. 1:10).

So the Bible is explicit in affirming that the aim of all God's acts is that we might praise and worship him for his supreme worth and beauty.

Two Pressing Questions

Two questions are pressing on us for answers at this point.

> First, what is the worship that the Bible says is the ultimate aim of all God's work and word?

> Second, why is God not a megalomaniac in demanding this kind of worship for himself?

I pose these two questions together because the answer to the first is key in answering the second.

C. S. Lewis on the Consummation of Praise

I first saw the relationship between these two questions with the help of C. S. Lewis. Before he was a Christian, God's demand for worship was a great obstacle to Lewis's faith. He said it seemed to him like "a vain woman who wants compliments." But then as he discovered the nature of worship, the question about God's seeming vanity (or megalomania) was also answered. He wrote:

> But the most obvious fact about praise—whether of God or anything—strangely escaped me. I thought of it in terms of compliment, approval, or the giving of honor. I had never noticed that all enjoyment spontaneously overflows into praise. . . . The world rings with praise—lovers praising their mistresses, readers their favorite poet, walkers praising the countryside, players praising their favorite game—praise of weather, wines, dishes, actors, horses, colleges, countries, historical personages, children, flowers, mountains, rare stamps, rare beetles, even sometimes politicians and scholars.
>
> My whole, more general difficulty about the praise of God depended on my absurdly denying to us, as regards the supremely Valuable, what we delight to do, what indeed we can't help doing, about everything else we value.
>
> I think we delight to praise what we enjoy because the praise not merely expresses but completes the enjoyment; it is its appointed consummation. It is not out of complement that lovers keep on telling one another how beautiful they are, the delight is incomplete till it is expressed.[1]

---

1. C. S. Lewis, *Reflections on the Psalms* (New York: Harcourt, Brace & World, 1958), 93–95.

In other words, genuine, heartfelt praise is not artificially added to joy. It is the consummation of joy itself. The joy we have in something beautiful or precious is not complete until it is expressed in some kind of praise.

The Answer to God's Seeming Megalomania

Lewis saw the implication of this for God's seemingly vain command that we worship him. Now he saw that this was not vanity or megalomania. This was love. This was God seeking the consummation of our joy in what is supremely enjoyable—himself.

If God demeaned his supreme worth in the name of humility, *we* would be the losers, not God. God is the one being in the universe for whom self-exaltation is the highest virtue. For there is only one supremely beautiful being in the universe. There is only one all-satisfying person in the universe. And because of his supreme beauty and greatness, what the psalmist says in Psalm 16:11 is true: "In your presence there is fullness of joy; at your right hand are pleasures forevermore." If God hides that, or denies that, he might seem humble, but he would be hiding from us the very thing that would make us completely happy forever.

But if God loves us the way the Bible says he does, then he will give us what is best for us. And what is best for us is himself. So if God loves us fully, God will give us God, for our enjoyment and nothing less. But if our enjoyment is not complete until it comes to completion in praise, then God would not be loving if he was indifferent to our praise. If he didn't pursue our praise in all that he does (as we have seen!), he would not be pursuing the fullness of our satisfaction. He would not be loving.

So what emerges is that God's pervasive self-exaltation in the Bible— his doing everything to display his glory and to win our worship—is not unloving; it is the way an infinitely all-glorious God loves. His greatest gift of love is to give us a share in the very satisfaction that he has in his own excellence, and then to call that satisfaction to its fullest consummation in praise. This is why I maintain that the supremely authentic and intense worship of God's worth and beauty is the ultimate aim of all his work and word.

Supremely Authentic and Intense

But what about those words "supremely authentic and intense"? And what about that phrase "white-hot worship"? Our ultimate aim in reading the Bible, I am arguing, is that God's infinite worth and beauty would be exalted in everlasting, *white-hot* worship. When I use the phrase "white-hot worship," I am calling out the visceral implications of the words "supremely authentic and intense." The reason words like these are important is that there is a correlation between the measure of our intensity in worship and the degree to which we exhibit the value of the glory of God. Lukewarm affection for God gives the impression that he is moderately pleasing. He is not moderately pleasing. He is infinitely pleasing. If we are not intensely pleased, we need forgiveness and healing. Which, of course, we do.

We know this because Jesus said to the church at Laodicea, "Because you are lukewarm . . . I will spit you out of my mouth" (Rev. 3:16). The opposite of being lukewarm in our affections for Jesus is what Paul commands in Romans 12:11, "Do not be slothful in zeal, be *fervent in spirit* . . ." The word *fervent* in the original (Greek ζέοντες, *zeontes*), means "boiling." The intensity of our worship matters. Jesus indicted the hypocrites of his day by saying, "This people honors me with their lips, but their heart is far from me" (Matt. 15:8). Authentic worship comes from the heart, not just the lips.

Undivided and Fervent

A key measure of a heart's worship is whether it is authentic and intense or divided and tepid. Authentic means undivided, genuine, real, sincere, unaffected. Intensity implies energy, vigor, ardor, fervor, passion, zeal.

The Bible does not leave us wondering what kind of worship God is aiming at in all his work and word. Over and over God calls for our hearts to be authentic and undivided in our worship. "You shall love the Lord your God with *all* your heart and with *all* your soul and with *all* your strength and with *all* your mind" (Luke 10:27). You shall "search after him with *all* your heart and with *all* your soul" (Deut. 4:29); and "serve the LORD your God with *all* your heart" (Deut. 10:12); and turn to him with *all* your heart (1 Sam. 7:3); and "trust in the LORD with *all* your heart" (Prov. 3:5); and "rejoice and exult with *all* your heart" (Zeph. 3:14); and give thanks to the Lord with your *whole* heart (Ps. 9:1). No competitors. No halfhearted affections.

And the Bible makes clear what level of worship intensity God is pursuing. When Peter wrote to the churches of Asia Minor, he did not consider *inexpressible* joy to be exceptional, but typical: "Though you do not now see him, you believe in him and rejoice with joy that is *inexpressible* and filled with glory" (1 Pet. 1:8). The psalmist had tasted this kind of joy and made it his lifelong quest. "As a deer pants for flowing streams, so pants my soul for you, O God. My soul thirsts for God, for the living God" (Ps. 42:1–2). "O God, you are my God; earnestly I seek you; my soul thirsts for you; my flesh faints for you, as in a dry and weary land where there is no water" (Ps. 63:1).

Similarly, the early Christians had tasted the joy set before them, and when they were called on to suffer with their imprisoned friends, they showed how intensely they cherished their heavenly treasure by the way they responded to losing their earthly one: "You had compassion on those in prison, and you *joyfully* accepted the plundering of your property, since you knew that you yourselves had a better possession and an abiding one" (Heb. 10:34; cf. 11:24–26; 12:2).

God is not pursuing lukewarm worship, but worship that is supremely authentic and intense—*everlasting, white-hot worship*. It will never end. "To him who sits on the throne and to the Lamb be blessing and honor and glory and might forever and ever!" (Rev. 5:13). White-hot and without end. That's the goal of creation and redemption.

The Sorrow of Our Shortfall

Of course, one of the great sorrows of this fallen age is that we fall short of that measure of authenticity and intensity every day. God knows our frame, that we are dust (Ps. 103:14). He knows his own children. He can discern worship that is true, even if flawed. And he will not leave us in this frustrated brokenness forever. When Jesus prayed that we would see his glory beyond the dimness and dysfunction of this world (John 17:24), he also prayed that our love for him would be purified and made unimaginably intense. "[Father, I pray] that the love with which you have loved me may be in them, and I in them" (John 17:26).

Someday we will love Jesus with the very love that God the Father has for God the Son. This is literally unimaginable. For the Father loves the Son with infinite love—a love whose authenticity and intensity cannot be measured. So don't lose heart in all your struggles to love him as you ought. The day is coming when we will see him as he is. We will be changed. We will love him with a love beyond imagination. It will be supremely authentic and supremely intense.

Worship in Spirit and Truth

God created and governs the world in order to put his all-satisfying glory on display for the enjoyment of his creatures. And the aim of that display is the white-hot worship of his people. I have stressed the authenticity and intensity of worship. But, of course, truth and feeling are both essential. Doctrine and delight are indispensable. "True worshipers will worship the Father in spirit *and* truth" (John 4:23). Truth matters. There is no real worship without it. Intense affections for God, when we do not know God, are not truly affection for God. They are affections for a distortion of God in our imagination.

According to Paul, this could not be more serious. He said it is possible to have zeal (intensity!) for God and not be saved: "Brothers, my heart's desire and prayer to God for them is that they may be saved. For I bear them witness that they have *a zeal for God*, but *not according to knowledge*" (Rom. 10:1–2). Passion for God that is not based on a true vision of God is not a saving passion. So we are playing with fire either way: tepid affections and false doctrine are both deadly. God does not want us to die. Therefore, he exalts his glory for our all-satisfying enjoyment in everything he does.

No Song without Sight

That is the point of this chapter: *the supremely authentic and intense worship of God's worth and beauty is the ultimate aim of all his work and word.* And if it is the ultimate aim of all his work and word, then it is the ultimate aim of the Bible—and of reading the Bible. In all our reading, we are aiming and hoping and praying that God would use his word to make us a vital part of the everlasting, white-hot worship of his infinite worth and beauty. How does that happen in reading the Bible? That is where we turn next. It happens by *seeing* in Scripture God's supreme worth and beauty. There is no song in worship without a *sight* of God's wonders.

That . . . which we have seen with our eyes, which we looked upon and . . . was made manifest to us . . . we proclaim also to you.

1 JOHN 1:1–3

When you read this, you can perceive my insight into the mystery of Christ . . . the unsearchable riches of Christ.

EPHESIANS 3:4, 8

3

Reading to See Supreme
Worth and Beauty, Part 1

"When you read this, you can perceive
my insight into the mystery of Christ."

The Proposal

Our ultimate goal in reading the Bible is that God's infinite worth and beauty would be exalted in the everlasting, white-hot worship of the blood-bought bride of Christ from every people, language, tribe, and nation. This implies:

1. that the infinite worth and beauty of God are *the ultimate value and excellence* of the universe;
2. that the supremely *authentic and intense worship* of God's worth and beauty is the ultimate aim of all his work and word;
3. **that we should always read his word in order to *see* this supreme worth and beauty;**
4. that we should aim in all our seeing to *savor* his excellence above all things;
5. that we should aim to be *transformed* by this seeing and savoring into the likeness of his beauty,
6. so that more and more people would be drawn into the worshiping family of God until the bride of Christ—across all centuries and cultures—is complete in number and beauty.

If the ultimate aim of God in creation and redemption is to have a family who worships him with white-hot affection because of his all-satisfying beauty, then being part of that family must mean having eyes to see that beauty. Not the eyes located in our skull, but what Paul called the eyes of the heart (Eph. 1:18). A person born blind in the physical sense may see a thousand times more glory in the gospel of Jesus than a person with eyes. That was certainly true of Fanny Crosby, the Christian songwriter who was blind from childhood and wrote more than five thousand songs to celebrate the glory she saw in Jesus. Without physical eyes, she saw the "great things" of God.

> To God be the *glory*, great things He has done;
> So loved He the world that He gave us His Son,
> Who yielded His life an atonement for sin,
> And opened the life gate that all may go in.
>
> Praise the Lord, praise the Lord,
> Let the earth hear His voice!
> Praise the Lord, praise the Lord,
> Let the people rejoice!
> O come to the Father, through Jesus the Son,
> And give Him the *glory*, great things He has done.[1]

The Aim of Reading—Always

In the next three chapters, we focus on this all-important aim of life—seeing the glory of God. And the point we are trying to understand and establish is expressed above in the third implication of our proposal: we should always read God's word in order to see his supreme worth and beauty—*his glory*. In other words, I am not only saying that seeing the glory of God does happen in reading God's word; I am also saying that this should always be our aim in reading the Bible. There may be a hundred practical reasons—good ones—that we turn to God's word. This aim should be in and under and over all of them—always.

To see this, we turn first to the witness of the apostles John and Paul. John is explicit in his concern about later generations seeing the glory of Christ. And Paul is explicit that by reading what he writes, we can see the glory he saw.

---

1. Fanny J. Crosby, "To God Be the Glory, Great Things He Has Done" (1875); emphases added.

Putting the Glory of Christ Front and Center

The apostle John made clear that he saw his role as helping later generations. He knew that later Christians would wonder if they could have the same spiritual sight of the glory of Christ as the first eyewitnesses. He believed that they could, and that it would happen through what he wrote. He put the glory of the Son of God front and center as he wrote his Gospel. It begins, "The Word became flesh and dwelt among us, and we have seen his glory, glory as of the only Son from the Father, full of grace and truth" (John 1:14). He showed how the signs Jesus did were aimed to reveal his glory and that this glory was the ground of faith.

For example, when Jesus turned water into wine, John wrote, "This, the first of his *signs*, Jesus did at Cana in Galilee, and manifested his *glory*. And his disciples believed in him" (John 2:11). And again, the raising of Lazarus from the dead was described as a manifestation of the glory of God. "Jesus said to her, 'Did I not tell you that if you believed you would see the *glory* of God?'" (John 11:40).

See the Glory of Jesus without Seeing His Body

But what about the generations that follow that did not see the Lord firsthand? How would they "see the glory of God" and believe? John's answer is that the Holy Spirit would come and enable him and the other eyewitnesses to put what they saw into words (John 14:26; 16:13), so that people could see the glory of Christ *by reading* and so believe and have eternal life. We can see how John thought about this by the way he connects believing without seeing together with his own writing. Later generations do not "see" the physical form of Jesus the way the eyewitnesses did. But they can still believe and have eternal life. Why? Because of what happens when they read the apostolic testimony. They see the glory of Christ.

> "Blessed are those who have not seen and yet have believed." Now Jesus did many other [glory-revealing] signs in the presence of the disciples, which are not written in this book; but *these* [glory-revealing signs] are written so that you may believe that Jesus is the Christ, the Son of God, and that by believing you may have life in his name. (John 20:29–31)

So eternal life comes by believing on Jesus. And believing comes by reading what is written, because reading what is written is a window onto the glory of Christ.

The Holy Spirit guided the writing of the apostles with a specific goal of making the glory of Jesus evident. Jesus implied this in John 16:13–14: "When the Spirit of truth comes . . . *he will glorify me,* for he will take what is mine and declare it to you." The work of the Spirit in the writings of the New Testament is to *reveal the glory of Christ.* This glory is seen by reading.

What We Have Seen, We Proclaim

In his first epistle, John made this connection even clearer—the connection between what he saw as an eyewitness of the glory of Christ and what he wrote for those who had not been eyewitnesses. His epistle begins like this:

> That which was from the beginning, which we have heard, which we have *seen with our eyes,* which we *looked upon* and have touched with our hands, concerning the word of life—the life was *made manifest,* and we have *seen* it, and testify to it and proclaim to you the eternal life, which was with the Father and was *made manifest* to us—that which we have *seen* and heard we proclaim also to you, so that you too may have fellowship with us; and indeed our fellowship is with the Father and with his Son Jesus Christ. And we are writing these things so that our joy may be complete. (1 John 1:1–4)

Six times he refers to what was "seen" or "manifest." And four times he says that what he had seen is now being turned into what he testifies and proclaims and writes. The intention is that the faith and life he received by seeing the glory of Christ, his readers would also be able to receive by seeing what he saw—the glory of Christ shining through the inspired writing.

By Reading You Can See What I See

Turning from John's testimony to Paul's, we see the same conviction. But we get to hear an apostle talk explicitly about the reading of his own writing. In Ephesians 3:4, the apostle Paul makes a rare and crucial reference to the aim of reading his own epistle:

The mystery was made known to me by revelation, as I have written briefly. *When you read this, you can perceive my insight into the mystery of Christ,* which was not made known to the sons of men in other generations as it has now been revealed to his holy apostles and prophets by the Spirit. This mystery is that the Gentiles are fellow heirs, members of the same body, and partakers of the promise in Christ Jesus through the gospel. Of this gospel I was made a minister according to the gift of God's grace, which was given me by the working of his power. To me, though I am the very least of all the saints, this grace was given, to preach to the Gentiles the unsearchable riches of Christ. (Eph. 3:3–8)

When Paul ponders how the Ephesians will read his letter to them, he focuses their attention on his "insight into the mystery of Christ." He says, "The mystery was made known to me by revelation, as I have written briefly. *When you read this, you can perceive my insight into the mystery of Christ.*" This is the great pattern of Scripture.

The Pattern of Revelation

First, there is a mystery—not something unintelligible, but something unknown, kept in the mind of God. Then there is revelation of that mystery to a divinely chosen spokesman. Then the spokesman puts the revelation of the mystery into writing—in this case the epistle to the Ephesians. Then there is the reading of the inspired writing. And by means of this reading, the readers may "perceive my insight" (Greek νοῆσαι τὴν σύνεσίν μου) into the revealed mystery. That is, by reading they may "see," or get a glimpse, into what Paul was shown by God. And from there flows everything else in the Christian life—faith, hope, love, transformed relationships, new community, impact on the world.

So, if seeing comes by reading, the question is, "What was Paul telling the Ephesian readers to see?" He said that by reading they could perceive his insight into "the mystery of Christ" (Eph. 3:4). What riches did that phrase carry for Paul?

The Unsearchable Riches of Christ

He defines the phrase "mystery of Christ" in verse 6: "This mystery is that the Gentiles are fellow heirs, members of the same body, and partakers of the promise in Christ Jesus through the gospel." His readers are those Gentiles (Eph. 2:11, "You Gentiles . . ."). So this is spectacular news for them. The wall between Jew and Gentile has been torn down by Christ's death for sinners. He "has broken down in his flesh the dividing wall of hostility" (Eph. 2:14). So the Gentiles "are no longer strangers and aliens, but fellow citizens with the saints and members of the household of God" (Eph. 2:19). The mystery that Paul reveals is that the promises made to Israel and her Messiah now count for the Gentiles who are "in Christ" (Eph. 2:13). They are full "fellow citizens," full "members of the household of God." They will inherit what the household inherits.

That's the first answer to the question, what Paul wanted them to see by reading: the mystery that Gentiles are now full fellow heirs with Israel in Christ. Now the question becomes, "How did Paul summarize the spectacular benefits this brought to the Gentiles?" Two verses later, he puts it like this: "To me . . . this grace was given, to preach to the Gentiles the unsearchable riches of Christ" (Eph. 3:8). When he says that the readers can perceive his insight into the mystery of Christ, he has in mind these unsearchable riches of Christ.

The Riches of God's Glory

What's the connection between the mystery and the riches of Christ? Paul had said that the mystery is that they are "fellow heirs." Note the word *heirs*. He had already prayed in Ephesians 1:18 that God would enlighten "the eyes of your hearts" so that they could see (with heart-eyes) "the riches of his glorious *inheritance*." So we may surely infer that "the unsearchable riches of Christ" (referred to in Ephesians 3:8) are primarily what Paul had in mind when he said that the Gentiles would be fellow heirs of Christ. And we notice that these riches of Christ are called (in Ephesians 1:18) "the riches of glory"—God's glory.

The Riches of the Glory of This Mystery

In other words, the mystery that the readers could "perceive by reading" was the revelation of the riches of God's glory, that is, "the unsearchable riches of Christ." This connection between the riches of God's glory and the mystery of the unsearchable riches of Christ is confirmed by the parallel passage in Colossians 1:27. There Paul says,

"God chose to make known how great among the Gentiles are the riches of the glory of this mystery." The mystery, which in Ephesians is the Gentile enjoyment of "the riches of Christ," is in Colossians the Gentile enjoyment of "the riches of glory." The "riches of glory" and the "unsearchable riches of Christ" are the same riches. They are comprehensive terms for all that God is in Christ for the sake of Gentiles who are now fellow heirs.

A Surge of Joy Goes through Me

To me, it is simply wonderful that God would lead Paul, in Ephesians 3:4, to make unmistakably explicit this breathtaking fact about reading, namely, that *the riches of the glory of God are perceived through reading*. It is wonderful because reading is so ordinary, but the unsearchable riches of Christ are so extraordinary. It's as if he said that you can fly by sitting. Or that you can be on the top of Mount Everest by breathing. By reading we can see divine glory! By the most ordinary act, we can see the most wonderful reality. A surge of joy goes through me when I think about this. In that book, by the act of reading, I may see the glory of God. O Lord, incline my heart to that book and not to vanity! That is my prayer—for myself and you.

But I must not lose sight of the point I am trying to make: that we should read God's word in order to see his supreme worth and beauty. The least we can say at this point, from Ephesians 3:4–8, is that Paul has given us a great push in that direction. Do you want access to the riches of the glory of God in Christ? Do you want to "perceive" them (Eph. 3:4)? Do you want to know them (Eph. 1:18)? Do you want to be empowered by them "to comprehend . . . the breadth and length and height and depth, and to know the love of Christ that surpasses knowledge" (Eph. 3:16–19)? Then, Paul says, read! Read what I have written. Or we may say, read the Bible.

Never See Anything Apart from the Glory of Christ

Of course, someone may, rightly, say, "But the book of Ephesians contains so many other things to see! Are you saying that we neglect those things and focus only on the riches of God's glory?" It is certainly true that Ephesians touches on dozens of things that matter for our daily lives: humility, gentleness, patience, forbearance (4:2), baptism (4:5), church offices (4:11), love (4:16), hardness of heart (4:18), deceit (4:22), righteousness and holiness (4:24), anger (4:26, 31), honest work (4:28), covetousness (5:5), the Holy Spirit (5:18), marriage (5:22–33), spiritual warfare (6:10–20), and more.

When I say that we should read—*always* read—to see God's glory, I don't mean that reading to see God's glory means *not* seeing the life issues that are there in front of us. On the contrary, I mean, by all means, see them! See them all. See them with meticulous clarity in all their relations as Paul intended. But never see them apart from the glory of God. Never see them apart from the unsearchable riches of Christ.

The glory of the triune God is not an item to see alongside, and distinct from, other items. It is an all-encompassing and all-pervading reality. It is over all and in all and under all. If there is a list of life issues, the glory of God is not one of them. Rather, God's glory is the paper and the ink and the light on the sheet and the meaning of the words. It is the ground of all and the goal of all. Therefore, the point is never to see the glory of God *instead of* other things. The point is always to see the glory of God *in and through* all things.

When Paul said, "Whether you eat or drink, or whatever you do, do all to the glory of God" (1 Cor. 10:31), he meant, see *all things* in relationship to the glory of God—starting with the most ordinary things, like food and drink. Then treat all things in such a way as to show how those things find their true significance in relation to the glory of God. Treat them, deal with them, in a way that shows the supreme value of the glory of God in and above them all.

So I conclude from Ephesians 3:4–8 that reading is a God-appointed means of seeing the riches of God's glory, the unsearchable riches of Christ. This is why God inspired Paul to write Scripture. This is why he wrote. And this is what we should see when we read.

See God through Reading

Both John and Paul put the glory of Christ (who is the *image* of God!) in the foreground of their inspired writing. And both show us the great importance they put on reading the very words they wrote. Both believe and teach that by such reading, the followers of Jesus who were not eyewitnesses may indeed see the glory of Christ and have eternal life. This is the wonder of Scripture. The sight of divine glory that the apostles saw in the presence of Jesus we too may see through what they wrote. This was, in fact, the main thing they wanted us to see. This was the most important thing to see. "The light of the gospel of the glory of Christ" (2 Cor. 4:4). This is what we should *aim* to see in all our reading of God's word.

To this day, when they read the old covenant, that same veil remains unlifted, because only through Christ is it taken away. Yes, to this day whenever Moses is read a veil lies over their hearts. But when one turns to the Lord, the veil is removed.

2 CORINTHIANS 3:14–16

4

Reading to See Supreme
Worth and Beauty, Part 2

"When one turns to the Lord, the veil is removed."

The Proposal

Our ultimate goal in reading the Bible is that God's infinite worth and beauty would be exalted in the everlasting, white-hot worship of the blood-bought bride of Christ from every people, language, tribe, and nation. This implies:

1. that the infinite worth and beauty of God are *the ultimate value and excellence* of the universe;
2. that the supremely *authentic and intense worship* of God's worth and beauty is the ultimate aim of all his work and word;
3. **that we should always read his word in order to *see* this supreme worth and beauty;**
4. that we should aim in all our seeing to *savor* his excellence above all things;
5. that we should aim to be *transformed* by this seeing and savoring into the likeness of his beauty,
6. so that more and more people would be drawn into the worshiping family of God until the bride of Christ—across all centuries and cultures—is complete in number and beauty.

Bring the Books, and Above All the Parchments

The apostle Paul breathed the air of books. While imprisoned in Rome, he wrote to Timothy and requested his books: "When you come, bring the cloak that I left with Carpus at Troas, *also the books, and above all the parchments*" (2 Tim. 4:13). Of course, when he says "books," he does not have in mind the three-hundred-page, finely bound, thin-paper books we think of. He lived in the first century. The earliest books, as we think of them, were called "codices"—stacked sheets of parchment or papyrus or leather or wood, sewn or bound together to make a "book." Before that, longer documents were rolled up in scrolls. No one knows when the first codex was introduced in history. They were not uncommon in the second century AD among Christians.[1] So it is possible that Paul possessed books sewn together like this. Whatever their form, he wanted them with him in prison in Rome.

Paul was a Pharisee before his conversion (Phil. 3:5). That means he was an expert in the written law of Moses. He used the word *book* to refer to the Mosaic law: "Cursed be everyone who does not abide by all things written in the *Book* of the Law, and do them" (Gal. 3:10). He once identified himself as a rigorous student of this law, with the best training available: "I am a Jew, born in Tarsus in Cilicia, but brought up in this city, educated at the feet of Gamaliel according to the strict manner of the law of our fathers, being zealous for God" (Acts 22:3).

Paul's evangelistic strategy was to go to an urban center and start with the Jewish synagogue. This was strategic not only because the Jews had a special place in God's redemptive plan (Acts 3:26; Rom. 1:16), but also because the synagogue had the holy books that Paul loved and trusted. This was common ground. Every Sabbath these Scriptures were read publicly. Peter had said to the Jerusalem Council in Acts 15:21, "From ancient generations Moses has had in every city those who proclaim him, for *he is read every Sabbath in the synagogues.*" This is what

---

1. "The first recorded Roman use of the codex for literary works dates from the late first century C.E., when Martial experimented with the format. At that time the scroll was the dominant medium for literary works and would remain dominant for secular works until the fourth century. Julius Caesar, traveling in Gaul, found it useful to fold his scrolls concertina-style for quicker reference, as the Chinese also later did. As far back as the early second century, there is evidence that the codex—usually of papyrus—was the preferred format among Christians: In the library of the Villa of the Papyri, Herculaneum (buried in 79 C.E.), all the texts (Greek literature) are scrolls; in the Nag Hammadi 'library,' secreted about 390 C.E., all the texts (Gnostic Christian) are codices." Accessed March 12, 2016, http://www.newworldencyclopedia.org/entry/Codex.

Paul could count on as he entered the synagogue. They would read from the books that he had mastered. He had been a former Pharisee.

This experience of dealing with Jewish people who read the books of Scripture every week caused Paul to think deeply about reading. They read the same books that he now read, but they did not see what he saw. They did not see the glory of God the way he saw it. And when he showed them the connections between the old covenant and the new, they could not see the wonder of it the way he did. At this point, it would be illuminating to ask, "What did Paul's understanding of this tragedy tell us about the aims of reading?"

A Sweeping and Pointed Text

One of the most sweeping, yet pointed, passages about seeing the glory of God through reading is 2 Corinthians 3:7–4:6. It is *sweeping* in reaching back across the entire old-covenant era to the giving of the law at Mount Sinai, then moving forward through the centuries-long reading of Moses, and then finally relating all of that to the new covenant and gospel of Christ. Few passages take in so much history of God's work. But it is not only sweeping. It is *pointed*. It deals specifically with the glory of God in both covenants, new and old.

I know that the passage is long. But I'll quote it all so that when I refer to specific verses you will be able more easily to check out my thinking.

> Now if the ministry of death, carved in letters on stone, came with such *glory* that the Israelites could not gaze at Moses' face because of its *glory*, which was being brought to an end, will not the ministry of the Spirit have even more *glory*? For if there was *glory* in the ministry of condemnation, the ministry of righteousness must far exceed it in *glory*. Indeed, in this case, what once had *glory* has come to have no *glory* at all, because of the glory that surpasses it. For if what was being brought to an end came with *glory*, much more will what is permanent have *glory*.
>
> Since we have such a hope, we are very bold, not like Moses, who would put a veil over his face so that the Israelites might not gaze at the outcome of what was being brought to an end. But their minds were hardened. For to this day, when they read the old covenant, that same veil remains unlifted, because only through

Christ is it taken away. Yes, to this day whenever Moses is read a veil lies over their hearts. But when one turns to the Lord, the veil is removed. Now the Lord is the Spirit, and where the Spirit of the Lord is, there is freedom. And we all, with unveiled face, beholding the *glory* of the Lord, are being transformed into the same image from one degree of *glory* to another. For this comes from the Lord who is the Spirit.

Therefore, having this ministry by the mercy of God, we do not lose heart. But we have renounced disgraceful, underhanded ways. We refuse to practice cunning or to tamper with God's word, but by the open statement of the truth we would commend ourselves to everyone's conscience in the sight of God. And even if our gospel is veiled, it is veiled to those who are perishing. In their case the god of this world has blinded the minds of the unbelievers, to keep them from seeing the light of the gospel of the *glory* of Christ, who is the image of God. For what we proclaim is not ourselves, but Jesus Christ as Lord, with ourselves as your servants for Jesus' sake. For God, who said, "Let light shine out of darkness," has shone in our hearts to give the light of the knowledge of the *glory* of God in the face of Jesus Christ. (2 Cor. 3:7–4:6)

The Vanishing of Old-Covenant Glory

Paul uses the word *glory* fourteen times in 2 Corinthians 3:7–4:6. It will become plain that the glory of God—in relation, first, to the law of Moses and, then, to the gospel of Christ—is his primary concern. In regard to Moses, the main point is that the glory of that old covenant has virtually vanished when compared to the glory of the new covenant. Candlelight vanishes when sunlight streams through the windows. This vanishing is expressed most boldly in 2 Corinthians 3:10: "Indeed, in this case, what once had glory has come to have no glory at all, because of the glory that surpasses it."

That is an astonishing statement, because Paul had just said, "The ministry of death, carved in letters on stone, came with such glory that the Israelites could not gaze at Moses' face because of its glory" (3:7; cf. Ex. 34:30). There *was* glory in the old covenant. It was *God's* glory. It was not nothing. It was not to be despised—then or now. Not to see it and value it for what it was is to miss the meaning of the old covenant—and the surpassing value of the new. But by God's own design, the old-covenant glory was temporary, not permanent. "If what was being brought to an end came with glory, much more will what is permanent [the gospel, the new covenant] have glory" (3:11).

God reveals more or less of his glory in different times and settings. But it is always *his* glory! It is never minor. Never insignificant. Never negligible. It is always some measure of the infinite excellence. It is always worthy of seeing and knowing and loving.

Supernovas Vanish in the Light of the Gospel

But by comparison with the glory of the gospel, the glory of the Mosaic covenant has virtually vanished. By comparison with the 20-watt bulbs of television and bank accounts and vocational success, the glory of the Mosaic covenant—yes, the *Mosaic* covenant—shines like a supernova. Be careful that you don't diminish the glory of the gospel by diminishing the glory of Sinai, which vanishes in relation to the glory of the gospel. The point is not that candles go out when Jesus comes. The point is that supernovas vanish before the gospel, as if they were candles. But they are not nothing. When we read the Old Testament, we should probably put on safety glasses—unless we are blind.

Now the Link between Glory and Reading

Tragically, most Jewish readers in Paul's day were just that—spiritually blind. Here is where Paul makes the connection between the glory of God and reading. Paul compares the Jewish readers of his day to the generation at Mount Sinai. He adapts the Sinai situation to his own situation in two different ways. Paul was reading Exodus 34:34–35:

> Whenever Moses went in before the LORD to speak with him, he would remove the veil, until he came out. And when he came out and told the people of Israel what he was commanded, the people of Israel would see the face of Moses, that the skin of Moses' face was shining. And Moses would put the veil over his face again, until he went in to speak with him.

On the one hand, Paul compares the bulk of Jewish readers in his day to the people at Sinai who were kept from seeing the glory: "To this day, when they read the old covenant, that same veil remains unlifted" (2 Cor. 3:14). But on the other hand, these same readers are also compared to

Moses, who lifted the veil when he turned to the Lord in the tent of meeting: "When one turns to the Lord, the veil is removed" (3:15–16).

The point I want to stress is that the occasion for seeing the glory of God—or not seeing it—is the act of *reading* the Scriptures. Verse 14: "When they *read* the old covenant . . ." Verse 15: "Whenever Moses is *read* . . ." At this precise point in life—the *reading* of Moses—the glory of God was to be seen. The reason it was not seen was that "their minds were hardened" (3:14). It was as though a veil came over them. To be sure, that veil let a lot of facts about God and his law shine through. That is why the Pharisees were so full of knowledge of the Old Testament and yet could not see the true glory of God. "Seeing they do not see" (Matt. 13:13). The veil, the hardening, kept out the peculiar glory of God.

Hardening and the Great Need for Right Reading

Already in Moses's own day he was aware of this hardening in spite of great manifestations of the glory of God. For example, we read in Deuteronomy 29:2–4:

> Moses summoned all Israel and said to them: "You have seen all that the LORD did before your eyes in the land of Egypt, to Pharaoh and to all his servants and to all his land, the great trials that your eyes saw, the signs, and those great wonders. *But to this day the LORD has not given you a heart to understand or eyes to see or ears to hear.*"

All through the history of Israel (Isa. 6:9–10; 63:17; John 8:43; Acts 28:26; Rom. 11:8–10), there was a seeing, believing remnant. But there was also a predominant bent toward spiritual blindness, a fact that God ordained, in order to open a door of salvation to the Gentile nations, a mystery that Paul unfolds in Romans 11:11–32: "Through their [Israel's] trespass salvation has come to the Gentiles" (v. 11). "A partial hardening has come upon Israel, until the fullness of the Gentiles has come in" (v. 25).

Oh, how we should earnestly and faithfully join Paul in prayer for his kinsmen, the Jewish people! "Brothers, my heart's desire and prayer to God for them is that they may be saved" (Rom. 10:1). His hope was that his prayers and ministry would "make my fellow Jews jealous, and thus save some of them" (Rom. 11:14). And he promised that when the fullness of the Gentiles comes in, "all Israel will be saved" (Rom. 11:26).

In other words, the veil over Israel's eyes and the hardening that kept them from seeing the true nature of God's peculiar glory (2 Cor. 3:14–15) was not unique to Paul's day. It was true already in Deuteronomy 4:29. It was true in Paul's time (2 Cor. 3:15). And it is true today (Rom. 11:25). And this throws into sharp relief what the great need is—for Jew and Gentile. We need to read the Scriptures in such a way that we see the glory of God.

The Supernatural Unveiling as Christians Read

Paul proceeds to contrast his own ministry with the experience of Moses. "We are very bold, *not* like Moses, who would put a veil over his face" (2 Cor. 3:12–13). The Greek word for boldness (παρρησίᾳ) connotes openness, frankness, and plainness, not just boldness. The contrast is that in Moses's ministry the glory of God was being veiled, and in Paul's ministry the glory of God is being unveiled.

Then Paul draws out a comparison between Moses and all Christians. A Christian is a person who has turned to the Lord Jesus and has thus seen the glory of the Lord unveiled. "When one turns to the Lord, the veil is removed. . . . And we all, with unveiled face, beholding the glory of the Lord . . ." (2 Cor. 3:16–18). In other words, all believers have "turned to the Lord"—like Moses when he entered the tent.

This experience of every Christian is supernatural. It does not come from merely human powers. In turning to Jesus, believers experience the work of the Holy Spirit. That is implied in Paul's words, "Now the Lord is the Spirit, and where the Spirit of the Lord is, there is freedom" (2 Cor. 3:17). That is, the Spirit sets us free from the bondage of blindness and hardening.

Turning to the Lord and seeing the Lord are one thing. Opening the eye and seeing light are not sequential. They are simultaneous. Turning to the light and seeing light are one. And this one great miracle of liberation from spiritual blindness is a gift. "For this comes from the Lord who is the Spirit" (2 Cor. 3:18).

"Beholding the Glory of the Lord"—by Reading

So Paul has shifted our focus from the old covenant to the new—from the law of Moses to the gospel of Christ. From the veiled, temporary glory, to the unveiled, permanent glory. And his central point is that when the veil is lifted—when the hardening and blindness are removed—we see the glory of the Lord. "We all, with unveiled face, *beholding the glory of the Lord*, are being transformed" (2 Cor. 3:18). Beholding glory was the partial and fading experience of the old covenant, and now, with the veil lifted, is the greater, brighter experience of the new covenant. Seeing the glory of God was, and is, preeminent.

Recall that the point of contact with the glory of God was, at one time, supposed to be the *reading* of Moses (2 Cor. 3:14–15). Reading! This was supposed to be the way the glory of God was seen. Has that changed? No. There has been no criticism or abandonment of this window we call "reading." So we may assume that the value of this window remains.

The difference is that once there was reading with a veil. Now there is reading with no veil. Once there was a window with a curtain, and now the curtain has been pulled aside. But the window of reading remains, as we saw in Ephesians 3:4. It remains God's plan for the revelation of his glory. Once the glory of the Lord was veiled in reading. Now the glory of the Lord is unveiled in reading. "Beholding the glory of the Lord with unveiled face" (2 Cor. 3:18) happens through reading. This is true both for a new Spirit-illumined reading of the old covenant as well as a reading (or hearing) of the gospel of Christ.

"The Light of the Gospel of the Glory of Christ"

Paul focuses here in 2 Corinthians not on the old covenant, but on seeing the glory of God in *the gospel*. But he concedes that not everyone sees the glory of the Lord in the gospel. "We are the aroma of Christ to God among those who are being saved and among those who are perishing, to one a fragrance from death to death, to the other a fragrance from life to life" (2 Cor. 2:15–16). Or, as he puts it here in 2 Corinthians 4:3–4, "Even if our gospel is veiled, it is veiled to those who are perishing. In their case the god of this world has blinded the minds of the unbelievers."

They were blinded to what? To the glory of God—the glory of Christ—*in the gospel*. He "has blinded the minds of the unbelievers, to keep them from seeing *the light of the gospel of the glory of Christ, who is the image of God*" (2 Cor. 4:4). In other words, the same blindness that kept Israel from the seeing the peculiar glory of God in the Mosaic covenant is still at work blinding people to the glory of Christ in the gospel.

God's Sovereign Shining

The remedy for this blindness is given in verse 6: "God, who said, 'Let light shine out of darkness,' has shone in our hearts to give the light of the knowledge of the glory of God in the face of Jesus Christ." God himself, speaking an omnipotent word, as on the day of creation, gives to the blind "the light of the knowledge of the glory of God in the face of Jesus Christ." God creates the seeing of divine glory in the gospel. He removes the hardening. He takes away the blindness. He lifts the veil.

To see what? Notice the similar phrases in verses 4 and 6:

Verse 4: "the light of the gospel of the *glory of Christ*, who is the image of God."

Verse 6: "the light of the knowledge of the *glory of God* in the face of Jesus Christ."

Verse 4 refers to the glory of Christ. Verse 6 refers to the glory of God. But when the glory of Christ is mentioned, Christ is called "the image of God." And when the glory of God is mentioned, his glory is seen "in the face of Christ." Therefore, these are *not* two glories, but one. It is Christ's glory and it is God's glory, but these are one glory. For Christ is the image of God. And God is known in the face of Christ.

Seeing Glory by Reading and Hearing

This glory is seen (2 Cor. 4:4) as a kind of spiritual light that shines in the gospel. That is why it is called here "the light of the gospel of the glory of Christ." And this gospel—this news of Christ's death and resurrection for sin (1 Cor. 15:3–5)—is both *proclaimed* aloud (1 Cor. 9:14; Gal. 2:2) and *written* down. It is heard and read.

We know that Paul thought of it as *written for reading*—not just proclaimed for hearing—because he used the term *gospel*, as we saw, in Ephesians 3:6 to describe what the Ephesians could *read*. He said, "When you *read* this, you can perceive my insight into the mystery of Christ" (Eph. 3:4). And then he said, "This mystery is that the Gentiles are fellow heirs . . . *through the gospel."* Thus in Ephesians 6:19, Paul calls it "the mystery of *the gospel."*

So when Paul says in 2 Corinthians 4:4–6 that God enables believers to see "the light of the gospel of the glory of Christ," we know that this seeing happens by *reading* the gospel as well as hearing. And so we know the same is true for 2 Corinthians 3:18. When Paul says, "We all, with unveiled face, beholding the glory of the Lord," we know this beholding glory happens not only through hearing but also through reading the gospel.

The Whole Apostolic Witness Reveals the Glory

Does this not imply that our window onto the glory of God is not only the reading of a portion of Paul's writing called "the gospel," but also the reading of all of his inspired writing? Would it not be artificial to say that the apostle Paul only intended for *part* of his letters to reveal "the light of the knowledge of the glory of God" (2 Cor. 4:6)? He did not limit the supernatural origin and impact of his letters in that way. Rather, he spoke of all his apostolic teaching as having this supernatural design.

> Among the mature we do impart wisdom, although it is not a wisdom of this age. . . . But we impart a secret and hidden wisdom of God. . . . We have received . . . the Spirit who is from God. . . . And we impart this in words not taught by human wisdom but taught by the Spirit. (1 Cor. 2:6–13)

This is the way he viewed all of his writings as an apostle. This was the ground of his authority. It caused him to say, even about nonessential matters, "If anyone thinks that he is a prophet, or spiritual, he should acknowledge that the things I am writing to you are a command of the Lord. If anyone does not recognize this, he is not recognized" (1 Cor. 14:37–38). All Paul's letters—indeed all of the apostolic witness of the New Testament—bear the marks of this divine authority. These writings as a whole—not just a slice of them called "gospel"—are our window onto the glory of God. And through this window we *see* the peculiar glory of God *by reading.*

In the creature's knowing, esteeming, loving, rejoicing in, and praising God, the glory of God is both exhibited and acknowledged; his fullness is received and returned. Here is both an *emanation* and *remanation*. The refulgence shines upon and into the creature, and is reflected back to the luminary. The beams of glory come from God, and are something of God, and are refunded back again to their original. So that the whole is *of* God, and *in* God, and *to* God; and God is the beginning, middle and end in this affair.

JONATHAN EDWARDS

5

Reading to See Supreme
Worth and Beauty, Part 3

"My eyes have seen the King, the LORD of hosts!"

The Proposal

Our ultimate goal in reading the Bible is that God's infinite worth and beauty would be exalted in the everlasting, white-hot worship of the blood-bought bride of Christ from every people, language, tribe, and nation. This implies:

1. that the infinite worth and beauty of God are *the ultimate value and excellence* of the universe;
2. that the supremely *authentic and intense worship* of God's worth and beauty is the ultimate aim of all his work and word;
3. **that we should always read his word in order to *see* this supreme worth and beauty;**
4. that we should aim in all our seeing to *savor* his excellence above all things;
5. that we should aim to be *transformed* by this seeing and savoring into the likeness of his beauty,
6. so that more and more people would be drawn into the worshiping family of God until the bride of Christ—across all centuries and cultures—is complete in number and beauty.

Always Read to See the Glory of God

We focus in this chapter on the word *always* in the third implication of our proposal: "We should *always* read God's word in order to see his supreme worth and beauty." In the preceding two chapters, we looked closely at Ephesians 3:4–8; 2 Corinthians 3:7–4:6; and John's writing. These passages have shown that we should read the inspired Scriptures with the aim of seeing the glory of God. But none of those passages made explicit that this should *always* be the aim of our reading. I think that was implicit. But there is an argument that confirms this truth by rooting it in the very nature of God's design for all things.

Nothing Rightly Understood except in Relationship to God

The argument that settles the matter for me is the relationship between God and all things. The argument is this: *the relationship between God and all things is such that nothing can be rightly understood apart from its connection with God.* And since God intends for Scripture to be rightly understood, therefore, we should *always* aim to see everything in it in relation to God.

Moreover, we saw in chapters 1 and 2 that God's ultimate aim is to be known and enjoyed as having the greatest worth and beauty in the universe. It follows from this that a right understanding of all that is in the Bible will include its relationship to the worth and beauty of God—the glory of God. No biblical author would say, "If you see the content of my book in relation to God's worth and beauty, you will distort what I am trying to communicate." Seeing that relationship is never a distortion of a text's meaning, but a completion.

Why, then, do I think that nothing in Scripture can be rightly understood apart from its relationship to the glory of God? Here's my answer:

God is the origin and ground of all things.

- From him and through him and to him are all things. To him be glory forever. Amen. (Rom. 11:36)
- By [him] all things exist. (Heb. 2:10)
- All things come from you. (1 Chron. 29:14)
- You created all things, and by your will they existed and were created. (Rev. 4:11)

God owns all things.

- The heavens are yours; the earth also is yours; the world and all that is in it. (Ps. 89:11)
- The earth is the LORD's and the fullness thereof, the world and those who dwell therein. (Ps. 24:1)

God holds all things in being.

- He upholds the universe by the word of his power. (Heb. 1:3)
- In him [Christ] all things hold together. (Col. 1:17)
- In him we live and move and have our being. (Acts 17:28)

God designs the purpose of all things.

- The LORD has made everything for its purpose. (Prov. 16:4)

God governs all things according to his will.

- [He] works all things according to the counsel of his will. (Eph. 1:11)
- All things are your servants. (Ps. 119:91)

God's purpose in creation is to make all things new.

- Behold, I am making all things new. (Rev. 21:5)

God appointed his Son heir of all things.

- He has spoken to us by his Son, whom he appointed the heir of all things. (Heb. 1:2)

God is the end and goal of all things.

- For [him] all things exist. (Heb. 2:10)
- From him and through him and *to him* are all things. (Rom. 11:36)

A Pathetically Parochial Point of View

In view of these facts, I would say that any so-called understanding of anything—in the Bible or anywhere else—*apart* from its relation to God is a *failed* understanding. We live in such a pervasively secular culture that the air we breathe is godless. God is not part of the social consciousness. Christians, sad to say, absorb this. It combines with our own self-exalting bent, and we find ourselves slow to see the obvious— that God is a million times more important than man, and his glory is the ultimate meaning of all things.

The world thinks that because we can put a man on the moon and cure diseases and build skyscrapers and establish universities, therefore we can understand things without reference to God. But this is a pathetically parochial point of view. It is parochial because it assumes that the material universe is large and God is small. It is parochial because it thinks that being able to do things with matter, while being blind to God, is brilliant. But in fact, a moment's reflection, in the bracing air of biblical God-centeredness, reminds us that when God is taken into account, the material universe is "an infinitely small part of universal existence."[1]

Those are the staggering words of Jonathan Edwards. To be impressed with the material universe and not be impressed with God is like being amazed at Buck Hill in Minnesota and bored at the Rockies of Colorado. If God wore a coat with pockets, he would carry the universe in one of them like a peanut. To ponder the meaning of that peanut, without reference to God's majesty, is the work of a fool.

So, yes, the portrait of God in the Bible demands that we always read the Bible with the aim of seeing the glory of God. When Paul said that "from him and through him and to him are all things" (Rom. 11:36), he did not mean "all things except the things in the Bible." He meant all things. And then he added, "To him be glory forever." Which means: it is God's glory to be the beginning, middle, and end of all things. It is God's glory to be the origin, foundation, and goal of all things. It is his glory to be the alpha and the omega of all things—and every letter in between. And therefore his glory belongs to the meaning of all things. And would we not blaspheme to say that this glorious God is anything less than the ultimate meaning of all things?

We Should Aim to See Trinitarian Glory

When God summons us in the Bible to read his word in order to see his supreme worth and beauty, he means the worth and beauty of God

---

1. Jonathan Edwards, *Ethical Writings*, ed. Paul Ramsey and John E. Smith, vol. 8, *The Works of Jonathan Edwards* (New Haven, CT: Yale University Press, 1989), 601.

the Father and God the Son and God the Holy Spirit. And since the supreme work of the Holy Spirit is to glorify the Son (John 16:14), and since the Father and the Son are committed to glorify each other (John 17:1, 4–5), therefore, our aim in reading the Bible should be to see, by the power of the Holy Spirit, the glory of the Father and the glory of the Son, which are one glory.

We have seen the oneness of this glory in the relationship between 2 Corinthians 4:4 and 4:6.[2] The peculiar glory of God shines most brightly in the gospel—the great work of the Father and the Son in accomplishing our salvation through death and resurrection. In 2 Corinthians 4:4, this glory is called "the light of the gospel of *the glory of Christ*, who is the image of God." In 2 Corinthians 4:6, it is called "the light of the knowledge of *the glory of God* in the face of Jesus Christ." *The glory of God* shining in Christ's face and *the glory of Christ* shining as the image of God are one glory. That is the glory we aim to see in reading the Bible. And this seeing, Paul says, "comes from the Lord who is the Spirit" (2 Cor. 3:18).

What this means is that the divine glory, manifest in Scripture from beginning to end, is the glory of the triune God—the glory of the Father and the Son, personified in, and revealed by, the divine Spirit. Therefore, everywhere that the glory of God shines forth in the biblical history of creation and redemption, it is the glory of the Son as well as the glory of the Father.

Isaiah Saw the Glory of Jesus

This is why the apostle John says that the glory of God, for example, revealed in Isaiah 6, was, in fact, also the glory of Jesus. First, John points out the unbelief of the crowd who had gathered to hear Jesus (John 12:29). Even though they had seen his signs, they did not believe. "Though he had done so many signs before them, they still did not believe in him" (John 12:37). Then he said that this unbelief was the fulfillment of Isaiah's prophecy. "For again Isaiah said, 'He has blinded their eyes and hardened their heart, lest they see with their eyes, and understand with their heart, and turn, and I would heal them'" (John 12:39–40). Then John says the astonishing words: "Isaiah said these things because he saw his glory and spoke of him" (John 12:41). In

---

2. See chap. 4, pp. 82–84.

other words, John applies Isaiah's words about the blindness of the people in Isaiah's day (Isa. 6:9–10) to the people who could not recognize Jesus, the eternal Son of God.

Isaiah said that he "saw the Lord sitting upon a throne" and heard the seraphim say, "The whole earth is full of his glory!" Then Isaiah cried out, "My eyes have seen the King, the LORD of hosts!" (Isa. 6:1–5). What he had seen was the glory of the Son of God. Henry Alford comments, "Indeed, strictly considered, the glory which Isaiah saw *could only* be that of the Son, Who is the ἀπαύγασμα τῆς δόξης ["radiance of the glory," Heb. 12:3] of the Father, Whom no eye hath seen."[3] What this passage in John 12:36–43 implies, therefore, is that wherever the glory of God shines forth in the Bible, it is not just the glory of the Father, but also the glory of the Son, for they are one glory.

The Glory of Yahweh Is the Glory of Christ

Another example of how the Bible presents the unity of the glory of the Father and the glory of the Son is found in Philippians 2:5–11. Paul describes the love-driven condescension of the Son from heaven and the fullness of divine glory that he enjoyed there. "He was in the form of God, did not count equality with God a thing to be grasped, but emptied himself" (Phil. 2:6–7). In this self-emptying, the Son descended willingly to the depths of dishonor in his crucifixion as a criminal.

This is why Jesus prayed, in the days of his self-emptying, "Father, glorify me in your own presence with the glory that I had with you before the world existed" (John 17:5). He had laid aside great glory. But when Jesus had accomplished the great work of our salvation by his "death on a cross" (Phil. 2:8), Paul says something astonishing about the glory of Christ. He says, in effect, that the glory of Christ and the glory of God the Father are one glory:

> Therefore God has highly exalted him and bestowed on him the name that is above every name, so that at the name of Jesus every knee should bow, in heaven and on earth and under the earth, and every tongue confess that Jesus Christ is Lord, *to the glory of God the Father.* (Phil. 2:9–11)

3. Henry Alford, *Alford's Greek Testament: An Exegetical and Critical Commentary*, vol. 1 (Grand Rapids, MI: Guardian Press, 1976), 838; emphasis original.

At first, it may look like the relationship between the exaltation of Jesus "above every name" is simply a means by which the Father receives glory—verse 11: "to the glory of God the Father." But it's not that simple. The words that Paul uses to describe Jesus's being honored by the bowing of every knee and the allegiance of every tongue are words from Isaiah 45:23, which refer to Yahweh himself, the God of Israel: "By myself I have sworn; from my mouth has gone out in righteousness a word that shall not return: 'To me every knee shall bow, every tongue shall swear allegiance.'"

N. T. Wright shows that Isaiah 45:23, which Paul quotes in reference to Jesus, occurs in a context in which the whole point "is that the one true God does not, cannot, and will not share his glory with anyone else. It is his alone. Paul, however, declares that this one God has shared his glory with—Jesus. How can this be?" Wright's answer is: "Of course, it will strain all our categories to [the] breaking point and beyond. But if we are going to let Paul speak in his own terms we cannot help it. For him, the meaning of the word 'God' includes not only Jesus, but, specifically, the crucified Jesus."[4]

Read to See the Glory of God, the Glory of Christ

For our purposes, there is a massive implication in the fact that Isaiah 45:23 is not an explicit prophecy about Jesus and yet applies to Jesus. There is no explicit reference to the Messiah in this verse. It is one of those many great Old Testament assertions about the God-centeredness of God. "By myself I have sworn . . . : 'To me every knee shall bow, every tongue shall swear allegiance.'" The fact that Paul can apply it to Jesus shows that the glory of God and the glory of Jesus are one glory. This is true not just where the Bible makes it explicit, but also, as here, where there is no explicit reference to Jesus at all. Therefore, if we are to read the Bible in order to see the glory of God, this includes—*always* and *everywhere*—seeing the glory of Christ.

Wherever the Glory of God Is Seen, the Glory of Christ Is Seen

It cannot be otherwise in view of what the New Testament says about the divinity of Christ:

---

4. N. T. Wright, *What Saint Paul Really Said: Was Paul of Tarsus the Real Founder of Christianity?* (Grand Rapids, MI: Eerdmans, 1997), 68–69.

- In the beginning was the Word, and the Word was with God, and the Word was God. . . . And the Word became flesh and dwelt among us, and we have seen his glory. (John 1:1, 14)
- Jesus said to them, "Truly, truly, I say to you, before Abraham was, I am." (John 8:58)
- Of the Son he [God] says, "Your throne, O God, is forever and ever." (Heb. 1:8)
- We wait "for our blessed hope, the appearing of the glory of our great God and Savior Jesus Christ." (Titus 2:13)
- Though he was in the form of God, [he] did not count equality with God a thing to be grasped, but emptied himself. (Phil. 2:6–7)
- To Israel belong "the patriarchs, and from their race, according to the flesh, is the Christ, who is God over all, blessed forever. Amen." (Rom. 9:5)

When Jesus said, "I and the Father are one" (John 10:30), the implications were vast for how to read the Bible. It implies that the presence and the glory of the Son of God are as pervasive as God himself in all his relations. It implies that wherever the glory of God is seen, Christ's glory is seen. It implies that the identity of the God who exalts his glory in the all-encompassing providence of creation is always the triune God of Father, Son, and Holy Spirit.

This is not a call for abandoning distinctions in the persons of the Trinity, or in their distinct roles in history and redemption. The Father is not the Son. Nor is the Son the Father. And the Spirit is not the Father or the Son. They are three persons with a single divine nature, and thus one God. Nevertheless, their oneness—their sharing a single divine nature—means that whenever we truly see and love any of these divine persons, we also see and love the others. When the Spirit grants us to see the glory of the Father or the Son, we also see the glory of the other. Therefore, when we read the Bible, in order to see the worth and beauty of God, we are always aware that to see such glory is to see the glory of the Father and the Son perfectly united in the Holy Spirit.

All Creation Is for the Father—and the Son

On the one hand, the apostle Paul could distinguish the roles of the Father and the Son, for example, in creation: "There is one God, the Father, from whom are all things and *for whom we exist*, and one Lord,

Jesus Christ, through whom are all things and through whom we exist" (1 Cor. 8:6). Yet, on the other hand, he could turn around and, from a different angle, see in the Son the same role as the Father:

> [Christ] is the image of the invisible God, the firstborn of all creation. For by him all things were created. . . . All things were created through him and *for him*. And he is before all things, and in him all things hold together. (Col. 1:15–17)

So the Father creates all things through the Son *for* the Father and the Son. In the words, "for him" (εἰς αὐτὸν, Christ) in Colossians 1:17 and "for whom" (εἰς αὐτον, the Father) in 1 Corinthians 8:6, we have an explicit affirmation of what I am trying to show. The *purpose* of all things is to make much of the Father *and* the Son—to glorify them. And in order to exalt and magnify their glory, we must *see* it. Therefore, the aim of reading the Bible *always* includes the aim to see the glory of the triune God.

What the Point of This Chapter Is Not

The point of this chapter is not to draw you into the distinct and specific ways that the New Testament finds Christ in the Old Testament. This is not a chapter about how to see Jesus in explicit prophecies (Mic. 5:2 = Matt. 2:6; Isa. 53:7–8 = Acts 8:32–33), and foreshadowings (Heb. 8:5; 10:1), and types (Rom. 5:14; 1 Cor. 10:6), and covenant transitions (Jer. 31:31; Luke 22:20; 2 Cor. 3:6; Heb. 8:8), and tacit prophecies by contextual implications (Psalm 16:8–11 = Acts 2:25–31), and more. That is a crucial aspect of biblical study. Reading the Bible well will always make us alert to seeing Christ that way.

Jesus said, "You search the Scriptures because you think that in them you have eternal life; and it is they that bear witness about me" (John 5:39). After his resurrection, he said to the disciples on the Emmaus road, "'O foolish ones, and slow of heart to believe all that the prophets have spoken!' . . . And beginning with *Moses and all the Prophets*, he interpreted to them *in all the Scriptures* the things concerning himself" (Luke 24:24–27). And the apostle Paul makes one of the most wonderful and sweeping statements: "All the promises of God find their Yes in him" (2 Cor. 1:20). In other words, if you are in Christ—whatever your ethnicity—you are an heir of all the benefits promised in the Old

Testament. So Christ is the sum of those benefits, and the price paid, so that we could enjoy them. Or more precisely, Christ paid the price so that in and above all his benefits we might enjoy Christ himself!

Glory in the Details

But this is not a chapter about the specific ways Christ was prophesied or foreshadowed in the Old Testament. Rather, the point of this chapter is the more sweeping claim that, in all the details and particulars of what we find in the Bible—Old Testament and New—the aim of reading is always to see the worth and beauty of God. Notice that I say "*in* all the details and particulars." There is no other way to see the glory.

God's greatness does not float over the Bible like a gas. It does not lurk in hidden places separate from the meaning of words and sentences. *It is seen in and through the meaning of texts.* We will have much more to say about this in part 3. But the point here is that in all our reading—in all our necessary attention to words and grammar and logic and context—we will not see what is supremely important to see if we do not see the glory of God, and all other things in relation to that. Therefore, we should aim in *all* our reading to see this.

No True Savoring without True Seeing

There is a special reason for lingering so long (chapters 3–5) over the necessity of reading the Bible in order to *see* the glory of God. The reason is that any emotional response to the Bible that is not the fruit of a true sight of the worth and beauty of God is, in the end, worthless. "Whatever does not proceed from faith is sin" (Rom. 14:23). Emotions for God that do not spring from seeing God cannot honor God. Paul warned that there is "a zeal for God, but not according to knowledge" (Rom. 10:2). That is, there are emotions and affections that seem to be godly. But they are not, because at the root is not a true sight of the glory of God in Christ.

Therefore, these three chapters have laid the foundation for the emotional response to God that I am going to call *savoring* God. If there is no true *seeing* of the glory of God, there can be no true *savoring* of the glory of God. And without savoring—delighting, cherishing, enjoying, treasuring—there will be no true transformation into the image of God. And if the people of God fail to be transformed into the image of Christ—from glory to glory—the ultimate purpose of God will fail. That cannot happen. God cannot fail in his ultimate purpose. Therefore, if we would be part of his Christ-reflecting, Christ-exalting family, we must read the Bible in order to *see* his glory—and then savor him above all things. That is what we turn to next.

The design of the whole of Scripture, and all the parts of it, hath an impress on it of divine wisdom and authority: and hereof there are two parts: first, To reveal God unto men; and, secondly, To direct men to come unto the enjoyment of God.

JOHN OWEN

Delight yourself in the LORD,
    and he will give you the desires of your heart.

PSALM 37:4

Rejoice in the Lord always; again I will say, rejoice.

PHILIPPIANS 4:4

6

Reading to Savor His Excellence, Part 1

"You have tasted that the Lord is good."

The Proposal

Our ultimate goal in reading the Bible is that God's infinite worth and beauty would be exalted in the everlasting, white-hot worship of the blood-bought bride of Christ from every people, language, tribe, and nation. This implies:

1. that the infinite worth and beauty of God are *the ultimate value and excellence* of the universe;
2. that the supremely *authentic and intense worship* of God's worth and beauty is the ultimate aim of all his work and word;
3. that we should always read his word in order to *see* this supreme worth and beauty;
4. **that we should aim in all our seeing to *savor* his excellence above all things;**
5. that we should aim to be *transformed* by this seeing and savoring into the likeness of his beauty,
6. so that more and more people would be drawn into the worshiping family of God until the bride of Christ—across all centuries and cultures—is complete in number and beauty.

A Life Calling

I have spent virtually all of my adult life encouraging people to pursue their supreme satisfaction in God.[1] I have argued that saving faith in Jesus Christ does not just bear the *fruit* of joy, but in fact, even more profoundly, is *itself* a species of joy. Saving faith at its root means being satisfied with all that God is for us in Jesus.[2] I have celebrated the way George Müller[3]—that great prayer warrior and lover of orphans—approached the Bible, when he said, "I saw more clearly than ever, that the first great and primary business to which I ought to attend every day was, to have my soul happy in the Lord."[4] Though he was a thoroughly doctrinal man with a strong commitment to Reformed theology,[5] he was never content to find doctrine in the Bible. Unless some unusual obstacle hindered him, he would not rise from his knees until sight had become savoring.

True Illumination before Proper Affections

To be sure, Müller agreed with his contemporary and friend Charles Spurgeon that seeing precedes savoring. And we must read the Bible with a diligent pursuit of right understanding before there are to be right emotions.

> Certainly, the benefit of reading must come to the soul by the way of the understanding. . . . The mind must have illumination before the affections can properly rise towards their divine object. . . . There must be knowledge of God before there can be love to God: there must be a knowledge of divine things, as they are revealed, before there can be an enjoyment of them.[6]

Yes. Illumination precedes and warrants and shapes the affections. But Müller agreed just as much with John Owen that the "ravishing

---

1. See esp. John Piper, *Desiring God: Meditations of a Christian Hedonist*, rev. ed. (Colorado Springs: Multnomah, 2011).
2. John Piper, *Future Grace: The Purifying Power of the Promises of God* (Colorado Springs: Multnomah, 2012). For a short argument on this point, see http://www.desiringgod.org/articles/love -is-the-main-thing-in-saving-faith (accessed March 1, 2016).
3. For my examination and celebration of Müller's life and ministry see John Piper, *A Camaraderie of Confidence: The Fruit of Unfailing Faith in the Lives of Charles Spurgeon, George Müller, and Hudson Taylor* (Wheaton, IL: Crossway, 2016), 63–83.
4. George Müller, *Autobiography of George Müller: A Million and a Half in Answer to Prayer* (London: J. Nisbet, 1914), 152.
5. George Müller, *A Narrative of Some of the Lord's Dealings with George Müller*, vol. 1 (London: J. Nisbet, 1860), 45–48.
6. C. H. Spurgeon, *The Metropolitan Tabernacle Pulpit Sermons*, vol. 25 (London: Passmore & Alabaster, 1879), 627.

joys and exultations of spirit that multitudes of faithful martyrs of old" have tasted came "by a view of the glory of Christ."[7] Therefore, neither Owen, nor Spurgeon nor Müller was satisfied with "mere notions" about the glory of Christ. They read their Bibles not only to see but to savor. Owen put it like this:

> If we satisfy ourselves in mere notions and speculations about the glory of Christ as doctrinally revealed unto us, we shall find no transforming power or efficacy communicated unto us thereby. . . . Where light leaves the affections behind, it ends in formality or atheism; and where affections outrun light, they sink in the bog of superstition, doting on images and pictures, or the like.[8]

The Double Dangers of Intellectualism and Emotionalism

These men understood—and we should understand—the double dangers of intellectualism and emotionalism. Intellectualism stresses the use of the intellect and its discoveries without the corresponding awakening of all the emotions that those discoveries are meant to kindle. Emotionalism stresses the energetic stirring of the emotions that are untethered to truth as their warrant and guide. Owen gives sound counsel about how the emotions of the heart should be rooted in and shaped by the truth that the mind sees in Scripture.

> When the heart is cast indeed into the mold of the doctrine that the mind embraceth,—when the evidence and necessity of the truth abides in us,—when not the sense of the words only is in our heads, but the sense of the things abides in our hearts,—when we have communion with God in the doctrine we contend for,—then shall we be garrisoned by the grace of God against all the assaults of men.[9]

I love this vision of how we seek and contend for truth. Is it not a beautiful prospect to "have communion with God in the doctrine we contend for"? How different our Bible reading and our Bible discussions would be if we refused to speak of our insights until they were sweetened by the real communion of our souls with God in them.

---

7. John Owen, *The Works of John Owen*, ed. William H. Goold, vol. 1 (Edinburgh: T&T Clark, n.d.), 399.
8. Ibid., 400–401.
9. Ibid., *lxiii–lxiv*.

The Aim of This Chapter: The Quest to Savor

The point of this chapter is that in all our effort to see more and more of the glory of God, *we are aiming, by that seeing, to savor the God we see.* That is, we are always aiming to experience spiritual affections in our heart wakened by the spiritual sight of truth in our minds. We are taking upon ourselves the same goal for our Bible reading that Jonathan Edwards had for his preaching when he said:

> I should think myself in the way of my duty to raise the affections of my hearers as high as possibly I can, provided that they are affected with nothing but truth, and with affections that are not disagreeable to the nature of what they are affected with.[10]

We read our Bibles to "raise the affections." Yes. But we aim to be affected by truth. And we aim that our affections accord with the nature of the truth we see.

I have proposed that our ultimate goal in reading the Bible—according to the Bible itself—is that God's infinite worth and beauty would be exalted in the everlasting, white-hot worship of the blood-bought bride of Christ from every people, language, tribe, and nation. To explain and test this proposal by the Scripture, we are focusing on six of its implications (see the box at the beginning of the chapter). The focus of this chapter and the next is the fourth implication: We should aim in all our seeing to savor his excellence above all things. The point of this fourth implication is that seeing the glory of God as we read the Bible should never be an end in itself. We read in order to see in order to savor. We seek insight in order to enjoy. We seek knowledge in order to love. We seek doctrine for the sake of delight. The eyes of the heart serve the affections of the heart.

Savoring the Bitter with the Sweet

One corrective is needed immediately to clarify the meaning of *savor*. I have treated *savoring* as though it were all positive—enjoying and loving and delighting. The reason is that this is how the peculiar glory of God does its deepest transforming work. We see it. Then we are profoundly satisfied by it. And then, by this satisfaction, we are changed at the root of our being.

---

10. Jonathan Edwards, *The Great Awakening*, rev. ed., ed. Harry S. Stout and C. C. Goen, vol. 4, *The Works of Jonathan Edwards* (New Haven, CT: Yale University Press, 2009), 387.

But it is also clear from Scripture that God uses not only *pleasant* emotions in response to seeing his glory, but also *painful* emotions. These too come from seeing the glory of God in Scripture. And these too are meant to be transforming, in their own way. They are meant to bring about change in a more indirect way, driving us away from destructive sins, in the hope that we will be drawn positively by the superior satisfaction of God's holiness.

God does not cease to be glorious when he disciplines his children. Yet this glory leads us first to sorrow. And then, through sorrow and repentance, to joy.

> "The Lord disciplines the one he loves, and chastises every son whom he receives." . . . For the moment all discipline seems painful rather than pleasant, but later it yields the peaceful fruit of righteousness to those who have been trained by it. (Heb. 12:6, 11).

God aims at "peaceful fruit," not pain. But he may cause pain for the sake of the pleasant experience of peace.

God does not cease to be glorious when he says to those who are entangled in sin, "Be wretched and mourn and weep. Let your laughter be turned to mourning and your joy to gloom. Humble yourselves before the Lord, and he will exalt you" (James 4:9–10). His aim is that we enjoy the experience of "he will exalt you." But on the way there, God's strategy may be rebuke. It is fitting. Together with all God's ways and purposes, it too is part of his peculiar glory. It may stretch the ordinary meaning of language, but this too we should "savor." "Count it all joy, my brothers, when you meet trials of various kinds, for you know that the testing of your faith produces steadfastness" (James 1:2–3). There are foods that blend the sour and the sweet in such a way as to make the sweet all the richer.

What this means for our reading the Scriptures is that seeing the glory of God may not always awaken, first, the sweetness of his worth and beauty. It may awaken the sorrows of remembered sin and remaining corruption in our hearts. "Savoring" this painful truth would mean welcoming it rather than denying it or twisting it. It would mean being thankful and letting the rebuke and the correction have their full effect in contrition and humility. And it would mean letting it lead us to the mercies of God and the sweet relief that comes from his saving grace in Christ.

We Always Read in Pursuit of Passion

So the principle remains: we never read the Bible merely to *see* the glory of God. Never merely to *learn* or merely to *know* or merely to *amass doctrinal truth*. We always see and learn and know in the pursuit of affections, and feelings, and emotions, and passions that are suitable to the truth we have seen. The range of emotions in response to reading the Bible is as broad as the kinds of truth revealed. The truth may be horrible, like the infants being slaughtered in Bethlehem (Matt. 2:16), and our emotions should include revulsion and anger and grief. The truth may be precious beyond words, like the words to a lifelong thief who hears, just before he dies, "Today you will be with me in Paradise" (Luke 23:43). So our emotions should include wonder and thankfulness and hope. The divine fingers of Scripture are meant to pluck every string in the harp of your soul. We never read just to know.

How Does the Bible Teach This?

How does the Bible itself make plain that in all our Bible reading we should move through the act of seeing the glory of God to savoring the glory of God? The answer can be given in two steps: (1) Scriptures that encourage us to pursue joy in God generally and (2) Scriptures that connect that pursuit explicitly with the Scriptures themselves. In this chapter, we will deal with the first, and in the next chapter we will deal with the second.

Even though I just tried to show that God pursues painful emotions in his people when we need them, nevertheless I will focus now on the positive ones. The reason is that this is, in fact, the ultimate aim for our emotions. God created human emotion for the ultimate purpose of white-hot worship of his worth and beauty. In this ultimate experience, we will be supremely satisfied, and he will be supremely glorified. So I focus on the savoring of God that we ordinarily call "joy." This may include numerous positive emotions—like thankfulness and admiration and hope and pleasure. So when I speak of joy in what follows, think of the large, overarching positive savoring of all that God is for us in Jesus.

1. We Are Commanded to Be Joyful in God

The most obvious foundation in Scripture for pursuing joy in God is that we are commanded to do so. I was once exhorted by a friend that we should pursue *obedience* to God, not *joy* in God. My response was that this is like saying, "We should pursue fruit, not apples." Apples *are* fruit. And the pursuit of joy in God *is* the pursuit of obedience to God, because we are commanded to pursue joy in God. And doing what you are commanded is obedience.

For example, in the Psalms we are told, "*Delight yourself in the* LORD, and he will give you the desires of your heart" (Ps. 37:4). "*Be glad in the* LORD, *and rejoice, O righteous, and shout for joy, all you upright in heart!*" (Ps. 32:11). "*Make a joyful noise to the* LORD, all the earth! Serve the LORD with gladness! Come into his presence with singing!*" (Ps. 100:1–2). Similarly, in the New Testament, the command to rejoice is not infrequent: "*Rejoice in the Lord always*; again I will say, rejoice" (Phil. 4:4; cf. Matt. 5:12; Rom. 12:12; Phil. 3:1; 1 Thess. 5:16). None of these passages tells us explicitly to read the Bible for the sake of joy in the Lord. But that we should will become clear shortly.

But for now, the amazing point is that God leaves us no option. He aims for us to be happy. It is amazing to me how many good, Christian people have a knee-jerk reaction against saying this. Just last week I was rebuked by a good man for saying that God pursues our happiness. He said, "That's not biblical. God pursues our holiness." I said to him. "Don't push me away. I'm on your side. Of course God pursues our holiness. But spiritual people find holiness to be their joy." In fact, what is holiness if it is not first *treasuring the worth and beauty of God so highly that all worldliness loses its attraction*? I would say there is no such thing as holiness where the heart does not find God to be its greatest happiness.

I suppose some of the people who have this knee-jerk reaction against saying that God pursues our happiness, feel this way because in their mind the word *happiness* is superficial and circumstantial—like preferring chocolate over vanilla, and if we don't get it, we are not "happy." If that's what they mean, then I agree with them. God does not work to see to it that we always get chocolate. Amen.

But the Bible does not use the word *happy* that way—as if *happy* were superficial and worldly, but *joy* were deep and Godward. Randy Alcorn's book *Happiness* is the most thorough treatment of happiness and joy in the Bible that I am aware of. He devotes an entire section (chapters 20–29) to the topic "The Bible's Actual Words for

Happiness." He shows that the Bible's words for happiness are stunningly diverse and touch on every dimension of the heart's positive experience of life and God:

> I looked up all references to these words in the English Standard Version: happiness, joy, enjoy, rejoice, gladness, merry, pleasure, delight, celebration, cheerful, please, pleasant, laugh, laughter, smile, jubilant, jubilee, relax, rest, feast, festival, and exult. These and their related words appear more than 1,700 times. When we add the times the word blessed is used to translate words that mean "happy," the total comes to about two thousand.[11]

I think, therefore, it would be good for my friends who have this knee-jerk reaction to God's pursuit of our full and everlasting happiness to soak themselves in the vast language of the Bible concerning the happiness of God's people. And if they are going to object to God commanding us to pursue happiness, let them make it clear that they mean idolatrous happiness in things, not happiness in God.

What I am focusing on, when I say God commands us to pursue happiness, is the happiness in God himself, not his creation. There is a proper happiness in God's gifts (1 Tim. 4:4; 6:17). But my focus is on happiness in *God himself*, which we experience *in and above* the enjoyment of things, and which keeps the enjoyment of things from being idolatry. "I will go to the altar of God, to *God my exceeding joy*" (Ps. 43:4). "I will *rejoice in the* LORD; I will take joy in the God of my salvation" (Hab. 3:18). "We *rejoice in hope of the glory of God*" (Rom. 5:2). This is why Christian joy flourishes even in suffering—because God himself is our joy, not mainly his gifts or our circumstances. "We rejoice in our sufferings, knowing that suffering produces endurance, and endurance produces character, and character produces hope"—namely, hope in the everlasting, pain-free presence of the glory of God (Rom. 5:2). "I consider that the sufferings of this present time are not worth comparing with the *glory* that is to be revealed to us" (Rom. 8:18).

2. God Threatens Terrible Things If We Will Not Be Happy

God threatens us with trouble if we don't pursue satisfaction in God: "Because you did not serve the LORD your God with joyfulness and

---

11. Randy Alcorn, *Happiness* (Carol Stream, IL: Tyndale, 2015), 179.

gladness of heart, because of the abundance of all things, therefore you shall serve your enemies" (Deut. 28:47–48). God does not want begrudging service. He wants joyful service. Which is why the apostle Paul said, "God loves a cheerful giver" (2 Cor. 9:7), and why Peter tells the elders to do their work willingly and eagerly, that is, joyfully. "Shepherd the flock of God that is among you, exercising oversight, not under compulsion, but *willingly*, as God would have you; not for shameful gain, but *eagerly*" (1 Pet. 5:2). Psalm 100:2 had already said, "Serve the LORD with gladness," and the command has not been rescinded.

3. Saving Faith Contains Joy in God

The nature and necessity of saving faith shows that we must pursue our joy in God. The apostle John makes clear that saving faith is essentially *receiving*. He says in John 1:11–12, "[Jesus] came to his own, and his own people did not *receive* him. But to all who did *receive* him, who *believed* in his name, he gave the right to become children of God." John puts "believing in his name" in apposition to "receiving him." They are essentially the same.

So the question becomes: Receive as what? The common evangelical answer—and it is gloriously true—is: Receive him as your personal *Savior* and *Lord*! But did the Scripture ever mean that saving faith receives Christ as anything less than *supreme treasure*? Did the Bible ever mean: Receive him as Lord, but not as *treasured Lord*? Did the Bible ever mean: Receive him as Savior, but not as *treasured Savior*?

No. Receiving Christ *as he is* means receiving him as the supreme treasure that he is. Isn't Jesus's parable about the treasure meant to describe the true nature of coming into contact with the King? "The kingdom of heaven is like treasure hidden in a field, which a man found and covered up. Then in his joy he goes and sells all that he has and buys that field" (Matt. 13:44). The point of that one-verse parable is not that the kingdom can be bought, but that there is no greater treasure than being in the kingdom—where the King is.

So saving faith receives Jesus as what he truly is. He is the supreme treasure of all who receive him. Jesus shows us how essential this kind of receiving is when he says, "Whoever loves father or mother more than me is not worthy of me, and whoever loves son or daughter more than me is not worthy of me" (Matt. 10:37). You can't be saved if Jesus has second place in your heart. This is because saving faith includes receiving Jesus for who he really is, namely, the supreme treasure of the universe.

We see this view of faith again in the words of Jesus in John 6:35: "I am the bread of life; whoever comes to me shall not hunger, and whoever believes in me shall never thirst." Notice that coming to Jesus for the stilling of soul-hunger is parallel to *believing* in Jesus for the stilling of soul-thirst. I think these are two ways of saying the same thing, since the hunger and thirst of the soul are indistinguishable. So *believing* is described, then, as coming to Jesus for the satisfaction of the soul's deepest longings. Saving faith, therefore, may be more, but it is not less, than seeking and finding fullest satisfaction in Jesus.

The writer to the Hebrews points us in the same direction. Saving faith believes in God as an all-satisfying rewarder: "Without faith it is impossible to please him, for whoever would draw near to God must believe that he exists and that he rewards those who seek him" (Heb. 11:6). Faith does not come to God out of some disinterested benevolence, thinking to do God a favor with our presence. Faith comes to God full of hunger for God and finds him to be faith's great reward.

Therefore, I conclude that saving faith, by its nature and necessity, teaches us to pursue our satisfaction in God. Saving faith is *necessary* for eternal life (John 3:15), and the *nature* of saving faith includes resting in Jesus as the soul's final and supreme satisfaction. Therefore, saving faith summons everyone to pursue joy in God.

4. Evil Is Forsaking Happiness in God

The nature of evil teaches us to pursue our satisfaction in God. Jeremiah describes two features of evil that make this clear:

> Be appalled, O heavens, at this;
> > be shocked, be utterly desolate, declares the LORD,
> for my people have committed two evils:
> they have forsaken me,
> > the fountain of living waters,
> and hewed out cisterns for themselves,
> > broken cisterns that can hold no water. (Jer. 2:12–13)

What are the two evils? One is that they have forsaken God as the fountain of all-satisfying, life-giving water. The other is that they are desperately trying to replace God by digging in the dirt. These are two sides of the one coin of evil. The essence of evil is turning away from God as our all-satisfying treasure in the hope of finding something better elsewhere. As Paul put it in Romans 1:22–23, "Claiming to be wise, they became fools, and exchanged the glory of the immortal God for images." This exchange is the heart of all evil. Every other kind of sin comes from this root: preferring anything over God. Therefore, if we are to avoid evil, the central task of our lives is to pursue our greatest satisfaction in God, not other things.

5. Deny the Self Every Comfort That Would Diminish Joy in Christ

Jesus's call for self-denial teaches us to pursue our satisfaction in God. This may seem counterintuitive. In fact, over the years, one of the most common objections to the point I am making—that the Bible teaches us to pursue our joy in God—is that Jesus, on the contrary, teaches us to deny ourselves. But when you look at how Jesus actually argues for self-denial, you see that he is, in fact, calling for us to find our soul's supreme delight in God, not this world. Here is what he says:

> If anyone would come after me, let him deny himself and take up his cross and follow me. For whoever would save his life will lose it, but whoever loses his life for my sake and the gospel's will save it. For what does it profit a man to gain the whole world and forfeit his soul? (Mark 8:34–36)

Far from repudiating what I call Christian Hedonism,[12] Jesus makes it the basis of his argument. His assumption is that no one wants to lose his soul. Nor should anyone want to lose his soul. It would be a dishonor to Jesus if we did not want to be in the joy of his presence forever. So Jesus tells us how not to lose our lives. "Whoever would save his life will lose it." And he tells us how to save our lives: "Whoever loses his life for my sake and the gospel's will save it."

The foundation of Jesus's argument is his approval of our desire not to lose our lives. To be sure, there is real self-denial. Saving our eternal life may cost us our earthly life. As Jesus says in John 12:25, "Whoever loves his life loses it, and whoever hates his life *in this world* will keep

---

12. This term is explained and defended in the book mentioned earlier: Piper, *Desiring God*. The key point of Christian Hedonism is that God is most glorified in us when we are most satisfied in him.

it for eternal life." Notice the words "in this world." Here is where self-denial may bring many losses in this world, as in the case of Moses:

> [He chose] rather to be mistreated with the people of God than to enjoy the fleeting pleasures of sin. He considered the reproach of Christ greater wealth than the treasures of Egypt, for he was looking to the reward. (Heb. 11:25–26)

Jesus himself was sustained by the same way of thinking: "Looking to Jesus, the founder and perfecter of our faith, who *for the joy that was set before him* endured the cross, despising the shame, and is seated at the right hand of the throne of God" (Heb. 12:2). It is precisely the greatness of the future joy that gives us the ability to deny ourselves lesser joys here in this life. But never in the Bible are we told to sacrifice supreme pleasure in God—not for anything.

The measure of our longing for true life with Christ is the amount of worldly comfort we are willing to give up to get it. The gift of eternal life in God's presence is glorified if we are willing to "hate our lives in this world" in order to have it (John 12:25). Therein lies the God-centered value of self-denial.

C. S. Lewis saw things accurately. He said:

> The New Testament has lots to say about self-denial, but not about self-denial as an end in itself. We are told to deny ourselves and to take up our crosses in order that we may follow Christ; and nearly every description of what we shall ultimately find if we do so contains an appeal to desire.[13]

The reason some people think Jesus's teaching on self-denial contradicts the pursuit of our joy is that they fail to think deeply into the paradox of his words. Saint Augustine captured the paradox like this:

> If you love your soul, there is danger of its being destroyed. Therefore you may not love it, since you do not want it to be destroyed. But in not wanting it to be destroyed you love it.

So everything hangs on how we love our souls. If you love your soul in wanting it to have as many comforts in this world as possible, then

---

13. C. S. Lewis, *The Weight of Glory and Other Addresses* (Grand Rapids, MI: Eerdmans, 1965), 1.

self-denial will be an insuperable obstacle. But if you love your soul in wanting it to be supremely and eternally happy in God, then self-denial is not an impediment but a path. Therefore, Jesus's teaching about self-denial presses us onward in the pursuit of maximum joy in God.

6. *Love for People Presses Us On to Pursue Our Joy in God*

The demand to love people teaches us to pursue satisfaction in God. This claim is the foundation of chapters 8 and 9, that savoring the glory of Christ transforms us into his likeness. But a few comments here may be helpful. In the same way that self-denial seems to some people like an obstacle to the pursuit of our joy, similarly, the command to love others with self-sacrificing love seems like a similar obstacle to the pursuit of our own joy. They point to 1 Corinthians 13:5 with its literal (and accurate) King James Version translation, "[Love] seeketh not her own." And they ask, "How can you truly love another person if, in loving them, you are 'seeking your own' joy? Isn't that just using them?"

The solution to this apparent problem is that Paul is clearly not telling us that "seeking our own" is wrong in *every* sense. We know this because of the way he argues for love in 1 Corinthians 13:3. He says, "If I give away all I have, and if I deliver up my body to be burned, but have not love, *I gain nothing.*" If genuine love dare not set its sights on its own *gain*, isn't it strange that Paul would warn us that not having love will rob us of gain? But this is, in fact, what he says in verse 3: "If you don't have real love, you won't have real gain."

So what Paul means by "love seeks not its own" is that love seeks not its own private benefit at the expense of others. If seeking your own good in God leads you to lay down your life for others, as it did for Jesus in Hebrews 12:2, then the pursuit of your own joy is not contrary to love but the power of love.

We can see love pressing us toward the pursuit of our joy in a passage like Acts 20:35. Paul is speaking to the elders of Ephesus and tells them:

> In all things I have shown you that by working hard in this way we must help the weak and remember the words of the Lord Jesus, how he himself said, "*It is more blessed to give than to receive.*"

What is especially powerful about this verse is the word *remember*. Jesus is not saying, "When it comes to motivating the love of generosity and self-giving, be sure to *forget* the words of Jesus about how rewarding it is. Be sure to get out of your mind any thought of seeking blessing in your act of giving." On the contrary, Paul actually says, "Remember!" As you struggle with whether to be generous and loving today, remember the reward. Remember the blessing. Remember, "It is more blessed to give than to receive."

So Jesus does not think that the pursuit of your joy, your reward, your blessedness contaminates love. He thinks it is essential to love. Why is that? Two reasons. One is that people do not feel loved when we do good for them *begrudgingly*. They feel loved when our acts of love are *cheerful*. This is one reason Paul says, "God loves a cheerful giver" (2 Cor. 9:7). So real love depends in part on our finding joy in and through loving.

The other reason pursuing joy is essential to love is that our aim in loving is that those we love would *join us in the all-satisfying reward we seek*. If someone were to accuse me of exploiting the person I claim to love by doing good to them for my own greater enjoyment of God, I would respond by saying, "No, I am not exploiting them; my aim and prayer is that, because of my good deed, they would *join me* in the everlasting enjoyment of God's presence." In fact, I would say that if I do not pursue the "blessedness" that Jesus promises to those who love, I am not truly loving, because I am not pursuing the joy of drawing the other person into the greatest joy imaginable.

So the biblical command that we love our neighbor is not an obstacle to the point we are making, but a support. Genuine love is the *glad* effort to make others glad in God forever. Genuine love is being willing to suffer and die to draw as many people as we can into the pursuit and enjoyment of God.

7. God Is Glorified in Us When We Are Satisfied in Him

The biblical demand to glorify God in all things teaches us to pursue our satisfaction in God. This is the most important argument of all. It brings us back to the connection with chapters 3–5. There we argued that all Bible reading should be aimed at *seeing* the glory of God. Now I am arguing that we should never settle for seeing, but always experience seeing as *savoring*. We should always want to see in order to savor. That is what I am trying to show. The pursuit of joy in God in all our Bible reading is what the Bible calls for.

At this point, the argument is that *God is most glorified in us when we are most satisfied in him.* This is one of the most foundational insights the Scriptures have to give. You can see it in Philippians 1:20–21, where Paul says:

> It is my eager expectation and hope that I will not be at all ashamed, but that with full courage now as always Christ will be magnified in my body, whether by life or by death. For to me to live is Christ, and to die is gain. (author's translation)

What I want us to see here is how Paul believes Christ will be magnified, or glorified, in his body. Notice that Paul says he is confident that Christ will be magnified in his body by life or death. Then comes the explanation of the ground he gives: "For to me to live is Christ and to die is gain." Now put together the two corresponding phrases: "Christ magnified by life or death" and "to live is Christ and to die is gain." What we see is that living to Christ corresponds to magnifying Christ by life. And experiencing death as gain corresponds to magnifying Christ by death.

Think with me about that last pair: magnifying Christ by death and experiencing death as gain. How does that work? Why is Christ *magnified* when Paul experiences death as *gain*? The answer is partially given in verse 23, where Paul says, "My desire is to depart and be with Christ, for that is *far better.*" Dying is gain because dying means departing and being *with Christ*, which, Paul says, is "far better" than living here.

So here is what we see: Christ is magnified in Paul's death because in Paul's dying he experiences the presence of Christ as great gain. And what else is this than Paul's being supremely satisfied in Christ? Christ is even better than life. This, Paul says, is what magnifies Christ. Therefore, I conclude: Christ is most magnified in Paul because Paul is most satisfied in Christ. It is precisely Paul's manifest treasuring of Christ above life that makes Christ look magnificent.

So I say again, the main reason we should read the Bible in pursuit of supreme satisfaction in God is that God is most glorified in us when we are most satisfied in him. Moving from seeing the glory of God to savoring the glory of God is one of the great ways that God is glorified in us.

Jonathan Edwards wrote more deeply and compellingly about this than anyone I know. He argues that this way of glorifying God is profoundly rooted in the very nature of God. His conclusion goes like this:

> God glorifies Himself toward the creatures also in two ways: 1. By appearing to . . . their understanding. 2. In communicating Himself to their hearts, and in their rejoicing and delighting in, and enjoying, the manifestations which He makes of Himself. . . . *God is glorified not only by His glory's being seen, but by its being rejoiced in.* When those that see it delight in it, God is more glorified than if they only see it. . . . He that testifies his idea of God's glory [doesn't] glorify God so much as he that testifies also his approbation of it and his delight in it.[14]

Read that key sentence once more: *"God is glorified not only by His glory's being seen, but by its being rejoiced in."* I believe that is what Paul implied in Philippians 1:20–21. And that is why reading the Bible both to *see* the glory of God and to *savor* it is essential. God's glory shines most brightly not just in the soul that *sees* him, but in the soul that sees him truly and *savors* him duly.

Pursue Joy in All You Do

So I conclude that the Bible itself encourages us to pursue joy in God generally—to savor his glory wherever we see it. In all we think and do, we should be hoping and aiming and praying that God would not only reveal to us his glory, but so waken our hearts to his worth and beauty that we savor his glory over all other treasures in the world. The Scriptures that we have looked at so far teach us to pursue our happiness in God in all we do. But they did not make an explicit connection between our pursuit of joy and our reading of Scripture. That is what we turn to next.

---

14. Jonathan Edwards, *The "Miscellanies": (Entry Nos. A–z, Aa–zz, 1–500)*, corrected ed., ed. Thomas A. Schafer and Harry S. Stout, vol. 13, *The Works of Jonathan Edwards* (New Haven, CT: Yale University Press, 2002), 495; emphasis added.

The law of the LORD is perfect,
    reviving the soul;
the testimony of the LORD is sure,
    making wise the simple;
The precepts of the LORD are right,
    rejoicing the heart;
the commandment of the LORD is pure,
    enlightening the eyes;
the fear of the LORD is clean,
    enduring forever;
the rules of the LORD are true,
    and righteous altogether.
More to be desired are they than gold,
    even much fine gold;
sweeter also than honey
    and drippings of the honeycomb.
Moreover, by them is your servant warned;
    in keeping them there is great reward.

PSALM 19:7–11

These things I have spoken to you, that my joy may be in you, and
that your joy may be full.

JOHN 15:11

Like newborn infants, long for the pure spiritual milk, that by it
you may grow up into salvation—if indeed you have tasted that the
Lord is good.

1 PETER 2:2–3

7

Reading to Savor His Excellence, Part 2

"These things I speak . . .
that they may have my joy."

The Proposal

Our ultimate goal in reading the Bible is that God's infinite worth and beauty would be exalted in the everlasting, white-hot worship of the blood-bought bride of Christ from every people, language, tribe, and nation. This implies:

1. that the infinite worth and beauty of God are *the ultimate value and excellence* of the universe;
2. that the supremely *authentic and intense worship* of God's worth and beauty is the ultimate aim of all his work and word;
3. that we should always read his word in order to *see* this supreme worth and beauty;
4. **that we should aim in all our seeing to *savor* his excellence above all things;**
5. that we should aim to be *transformed* by this seeing and savoring into the likeness of his beauty,
6. so that more and more people would be drawn into the worshiping family of God until the bride of Christ—across all centuries and cultures—is complete in number and beauty.

The Sorrow of Reading without Savoring

In this chapter, we continue to test biblically the claim that in all our reading of Scripture we should seek "to *savor* God's excellence above all things" (see the fourth implication above). That is, we should pray and hope and labor to be awakened emotionally by the Scriptures. Specifically, we should aim to experience affections of the heart that correspond to the reality we are seeing in the Bible. The conviction behind this aim is that seeing without savoring "ends in formality or atheism," and "has no transforming power or efficacy."[1] Therefore, seeing without savoring does not lead to the ultimate purpose of God for his people—*the everlasting, white-hot worship of God's infinite worth and beauty.*

Spiritual Affections Are Not Physical

In the previous chapter, I clarified that there are a whole range of emotions implied in the word *savoring*. The emotion of *savoring God's holy wrath* is not identical to the emotion of *savoring God's merciful tenderness*. Now there are two more clarifications that may be helpful to make at this point.

First, when I speak of "emotions" or "affections" or "feelings"—all of which are implied in "savoring" what we see in the Scripture—I am not referring to physical experiences such as sweaty palms, knocking knees, racing heart, trembling lips, or tearful eyes. Those are bodily reactions. They may be reactions to true affections of the heart—and therefore truly precious. Or they may be mere reactions to music, or communal fervor, or desperate circumstances, or a dozen other things that are not born of the Holy Spirit. I am not talking about those physical experiences.

By "affections" I mean emotions such as gratitude, hope, joy, contentment, peacefulness, desire, compassion, fear, hate, anger, and grief. None of these is merely physical. Angels, demons, and departed saints without bodies can have these "feelings." God himself experiences what the Bible calls anger (Jer. 15:14) and grief (Eph. 4:30) and hate (Ps. 5:5) and compassion (Hos. 11:8) and desire (James 4:5) and joy (Zeph. 3:17). These are not physical events. When they are awakened and

---

1. John Owen, *The Works of John Owen*, ed. William H. Goold, vol. 1 (Edinburgh: T&T Clark, n.d.), 401.

formed by the Holy Spirit, the Bible calls them "spiritual" (1 Cor. 2:13). You do not need a physical body to experience them.

Jonathan Edwards has written what may be, apart from the Bible, the most important book on such *affections* in the Christian life. It's called *The Religious Affections*. His definition of these affections is "the more vigorous and sensible[2] exercises of the inclination and will of the soul."[3] In other words, the feelings that really matter are not mere physical sensations. They are the stirring up of the soul with some perceived treasure or threat. When the will embraces or rejects something vigorously, that is what Edwards means by an *affection*.

Of course there is a connection between the feelings of the soul and the sensations of the body. This is owing, Edwards says, to "the laws of union which the Creator has fixed between the soul and the body." In other words, heartfelt gratitude can make you cry. Fear of God can make you tremble. The crying and the trembling, as mere physical movements of the body, are insignificant. But the gratitude and the fear are essential in the Christian life. And if those are spiritual, the crying and trembling share in the true value that they have. Which is why God can say, "This is the one to whom I will look: he who is humble and contrite in spirit and *trembles at my word*" (Isa. 66:2).

Affections Are Essential

I use the word *essential* carefully when I say that gratitude and fear are essential in the Christian life. The Bible puts a far greater weight on our affections than many people realize. Negatively, the apostle Paul says that those who go on in the same old way of "strife," "jealousy," "fits of anger," and "envy" "will not inherit the kingdom of God" (Gal. 5:20–21). These are all affections. It is essential that they change. Positively, Christians are commanded to have God-honoring affections, like joy (Phil. 4:4), hope (Psalm 42:5), fear (Luke 12:5), peace (Col. 3:15), zeal (Rom. 12:11), grief (Rom. 12:15), desire (1 Peter 2:2), tenderheartedness (Eph. 4:32), brokenness, and contrition (James 4:9). These are not icing on the cake of Christian living. They are essential.

The great lesson of the Pharisees is that cleaning up the visible,

---

2. *Sensible* here has the old-fashioned meaning of "the capacity to be sensed," not the newer meaning of "reasonable."

3. Jonathan Edwards, *Religious Affections*, rev. ed., ed. John E. Smith and Harry S. Stout, vol. 2, *The Works of Jonathan Edwards* (New Haven, CT: Yale University Press, 2009), 96.

physical outside of our lives, while the inward affections remain unchanged, is deadly.

> Woe to you, scribes and Pharisees, hypocrites! For you clean the outside of the cup and the plate, but inside they are full *of greed and self-indulgence.* You blind Pharisee! First clean the inside of the cup and the plate, that the outside also may be clean. (Matt. 23:25–26)

"Greed and self-indulgence" must be replaced with contentment (Heb. 13:5–6) and the treasuring of Christ over the comforts of this world (Phil. 3:8). This is essential. And the Pharisees could not see it.

So when we speak of moving from *seeing* the glory of God in the Bible to *savoring* that glory, we are not talking about a peripheral issue. It is essential. That is why I am arguing for the fourth implication above: *We should aim in all our seeing to savor God's excellence above all things.*

The Reality behind the Words of Scripture

There is a second clarification we need to make before we continue our defense of this fourth implication. When I speak of moving from *seeing* to *savoring*, or from seeing truth in Scripture to savoring what we see, I mean savoring the *reality behind the words*, not just the words themselves. Perhaps this is obvious. But I know from my own experience the danger of being excited merely with the structure of a text that I just discovered. I've tasted the danger of being excited merely with the logic of a passage that I finally caught onto, or, even worse, being excited that I might now be able to win an argument with this new insight. In other words, there are superficial, and even evil, ways to experience happy emotions when reading the Bible.

This is not what I am calling for. When I say, in the fourth implication above, that *we should aim in all our seeing to savor God's excellence above all things,* I mean the very excellence of God himself, not merely the excellence of words about God's excellence. Of course, there is nothing wrong with loving literary beauty and logical clarity. The subtle danger is when that kind of savoring deludes us into thinking we are really savoring divine reality behind those words. Unbelievers can savor the Bible as literature. There is nothing necessarily spiritual about it.

God warned us about this kind of savoring in Isaiah 29:13:

Because this people draw near with their mouth
    and honor me with their lips,
      while their hearts are far from me,
and their fear of me is a commandment taught by men . . .

This kind of thing can happen when we are "worshiping," and it can happen when we are reading the Bible. A real emotion can arise—even a kind of "fear of God," as Isaiah calls it—and it is no more than a response to a biblical commandment. It is not a response to the living God. You can, perhaps, feel the weight of this—and the difficulty. There are glories of God that we can see only by reading the Scriptures, so words and linguistic structures and logical arrangements of propositions are crucial. But we can get lost on the very bridge designed by God to take us to the reality. Or, to change the image, we can become like the dog who, when we point to his food, only wags his tail with delight at our finger. Or, to change the image one more time, we can admire the shape and position and cleanness of the window and miss the mountains beyond.

Where Are We in the Argument?

So much for the two clarifications. Now we take up the main argument. We asked in the previous chapter how the Bible teaches us that *we should aim in all our seeing to savor God's excellence above all things.* How does it make plain that in all our Bible reading we should move through the act of seeing the glory of God to savoring the glory of God? I suggested that there are two ways. The first we dealt with in chapter 6—the Scriptures encourage us to pursue joy in God generally and thus, by implication, in reading the Scriptures. In this chapter, we take up the second way: Scripture connects savoring the glory of God explicitly with reading the Scriptures themselves.

The Gift of Jesus's Joy through Words

Two times Jesus says that he has given us his words so that we might share in his own joy—once in his teaching and once in his praying: "These things I have spoken to you, *that my joy may be in you*, and that your joy may be full" (John 15:11). "But now I am coming to you

[Father], and these things I speak in the world, *that they may have my joy fulfilled in themselves*" (John 17:13).

Response 1

How are we to respond to Jesus's statement and prayer that the reason he has given us his words is that we might share his joy? The first response is to say yes to Jesus's intention for his words—his intention for our reading! "Yes, Lord, yes! I will rejoice in your word. I will not ignore what you have said as I read your words. I will not simply try to *learn* your truth without trying to *feel* your joy. You gave your words for my joy. So I will not analyze without seeking to be affected with joy by your word."

Response 2

The second response is to realize that the joy he says we should seek in reading his words is the very joy he has: "These things I have spoken to you, that *my* joy may be in you." This is vastly more than if he had only said, "These things I have spoken to you that you may have joy." That would be great enough. But he said that his aim in speaking is that we experience a joy *through reading* that is the very joy of the Son of God. Christ dwells in us by the Spirit. This was his promise and prayer: "I in them and you [Father] in me, that they may become perfectly one, so that the world may know that you sent me and loved them even as you loved me" (John 17:23). Christ himself is in us by his Spirit: The Father "will give you another Helper . . . even the Spirit of truth. . . . You know him, for he dwells with you and will be in you" (John 14:16–17). This Spirit bears the fruit of joy (Gal. 5:22), and that joy is the joy of the Spirit of Christ.

Response 3

The third response we should have to Jesus's words in John 15:11 and 7:13 is amazement that the joy of the Son of God is ultimately and finally joy in God the Father. When Jesus said, "I love the Father" (John 14:31) and that his food was to do the will of the Father (John 4:34), he did not mean he loved him with a disinterested love, as if the Father were difficult to love. He meant that his supreme delight was in the Father—as it had been in the fellowship of the Trinity from all eternity. The thought that this love and this delight between the Son and the Father should be in us by the Spirit, and that our love and our joy should be even now, in some measure, a participation in the Son's love for the Father—this thought should astonish us. It should make us passionate to have as much of this joy as we can.

Response 4

And it should lead into the fourth response to Jesus's words, namely, the wonder that this divine joy is mediated to us *through the words of Jesus*, that is, *through reading the Scriptures*. Supernatural joy is created in us through the natural act of reading. No, it is not automatic. We will see later what a miracle it is, and how we are to pursue it. But for now, let the wonder sink in. One of the greatest experiences in the world—rejoicing in God with the very joy of the Son of God—is offered to us through the words of Jesus: "These things I have spoken to you, that my joy may be in you." It is offered to us *through reading*.

Response 5

A fifth response to Jesus's words should be that we are even more astonished at the word "full." "These things I have spoken to you, that my joy may be in you, and *that your joy may be full*" (John 15:11). The divine aim of Scripture is not that by reading we be *moderately* joyful. The aim is that our joy—the joy of Christ in us—be *full*. Full would mean, at least, so strong that it pushes any idolatrous competing pleasures out of our heart. It would mean that selfishness has come to an end. We are no longer to be a sinkhole of craven neediness, but a fountain of life—givers, not takers. That is what Jesus meant when he said, "The water that I will give him will become in him a spring of water welling up to eternal life." (John 4:14). That water is drunk through his word. And the overflowing joy he promises, therefore, comes *through reading*. I am sure there is a fullness of divine joy that we will not attain until we see his unmediated glory (John 17:24–26; 1 John 3:1–2); but who can tell what measures of joy in God are possible, even in this fallen world, if we give ourselves utterly to the word of God?

The final response to Jesus's words I will mention follows from these five; namely, we should read the Scriptures with great expectation, and, in all our reading, *aim to savor God's worth and beauty above all things*.

Faith, Including Savoring, Comes by Hearing the Word

I argued in chapter 6 that saving faith is more, but not less, than being satisfied with all God is for us in Jesus. In other words, authentic faith is never a mere human decision that can be made by willpower without a transformed heart. It is the opening of the eyes of the heart (Eph. 1:18) to see Jesus as more precious than anything. Therefore, faith overlaps with what we are talking about in this chapter—the aim to savor God's worth and beauty above all things. That savoring is part of what saving faith is.

Therefore, whatever brings saving faith into being and sustains it and strengthens it is to be pursued with all our heart. The apostle Paul tells us what this is. It is the word of Christ:

> "Everyone who calls on the name of the Lord will be saved." How then will they call on him in whom they have not believed? And how are they to believe in him of whom they have never heard? And how are they to hear without someone preaching? And how are they to preach unless they are sent? . . . *So faith comes from hearing, and hearing through the word of Christ.* (Rom. 10:13–17)

This "hearing" may be through audible preaching, or it may be through reading. Whichever way "the word of Christ" comes, the point is the same: faith is brought into being and sustained "through the word." And since faith includes being satisfied in all that God is for us in Jesus, we know that this satisfaction—this savoring of the glory of God in the gospel and in the person of Christ—comes "through the word." Therefore, we should give ourselves to this word, not halfheartedly, but with a passion to see and savor the very beauty of Christ that the word is designed to impart.

Written That You Might (Read, See, Savor, and) Believe

John makes the same point Paul does, only he explicitly refers to books and writing, whereas Paul referred to preaching:

> Now Jesus did many other signs in the presence of the disciples, which are not *written in this book*; but *these are written* so that you *may believe* that Jesus is the Christ, the Son of God, and that by believing you may have life in his name. (John 20:30–31)

Now it is clear: the Scriptures are written to help us believe. And believing means receiving Jesus as the living water and the bread of life so that our soul's longing for joy is satisfied (John 6:35). And, therefore, *the Scriptures are written to create in us a savoring of the glories of Christ.* How then can we ever come to the Scriptures as if the only aim were practical guidance or doctrinal clarification? No. We will go "as a deer pants for flowing streams" (Ps. 42:1). We will go to drink and eat. We will go to see and savor the glories of all that God is for us in Jesus. That is, we will go for the strengthening of our *faith.*

Desire to Taste the Milk of God's Goodness—in the Word

The apostle Peter commands every Christian to feel strong desire for the word of God because in it we taste the goodness of the Lord. That is, in the word, we find delight in the glories of God's kindness. In other words, he makes it a matter of Christian obedience to see and savor, in the word, the glory of God's goodness. The key passage is 1 Peter 1:23–2:2:

> You have been born again, not of perishable seed but of imperishable, through the living and abiding word of God; for "All flesh is like grass and all its glory like the flower of grass. The grass withers, and the flower falls, but the word of the Lord remains forever." And this word is the good news that was preached to you. . . . Like newborn infants, long for the pure spiritual milk, that by it you may grow up into salvation—if indeed you have tasted that the Lord is good.

Notice the flow of thought. He begins by reminding them that they were born again "through the living and abiding word of God." Then he says that "this word is the good news that was preached to you"—the gospel. Then he tells them—*commands* them—to "long for the pure spiritual milk." In the flow of thought, we move from a *newborn* in 1:23 to a hungry *infant* in 2:2. The newborn came into being by the "word of God." And the infant is told to "long for the pure spiritual milk." There is no serious doubt, therefore, that the "milk" is the word.

Only not simply the word. Because as soon as he tells us to desire this milk that we may grow up into salvation, he adds, "if indeed you have *tasted* that the *Lord* is good." He doesn't say, "If you have tasted the milk." Surely the word *taste* connects with the milk, but what we taste is not just the milk of the word, but the goodness of the Lord in and behind the word.

So Peter is saying to every Christian: God in his great mercy and goodness (1:3, 23) brought us into existence by the new birth. He extended this miracle-working goodness to us "through the living and abiding word of God." So by this word we have already "tasted" the goodness of the Lord. Now the way to maintain our new life and "grow up into [our final] salvation" is never to lose our desire for this goodness that comes to us through the milk of the word.

A key phrase is "long for." "*Long for* the pure spiritual milk." He is not simply telling us to develop the *discipline* of reading the Bible. He is telling us to develop a *yearning* for the word. Hunger for it. Crave it. Desire it. This is the language of savoring. And the object of our savoring is the worth and beauty of God's goodness offered to us *in the word of God*. Therefore, Peter is telling us—commanding us—to read the Scriptures not just for doctrine and guidance, but in order to "taste and see that the LORD is good" (Ps. 34:8). He wants our experience of the word to be such that we go beyond testing to *tasting*. Beyond knowing to *loving*. Beyond doctrine to *delight*. Beyond seeing to *savoring*.

Joy Inexpressible and Glorified

We can feel the passion Peter has in mind with this *tasting* if we go back to 1 Peter 1:8. There he refers to Christ like this: "Though you have not seen him, you love him. Though you do not now see him, you believe in him and rejoice with *inexpressible and glorified joy*" (author's translation). He admits that, in one sense, we do not now see Jesus Christ. He is raised from the dead and has ascended to the right hand of God (1 Pet. 3:22). "Though you have *not* seen him. . . . Though you do *not* now see him. . . ." Nevertheless, they have "tasted" (2:2) the worth and beauty of Jesus.

How did they taste this? Peter says in verse 1:6, "In *this* you rejoice." He is referring back to what he just wrote in verses 3–5—that according to God's great mercy they had been born again through the resurrection of Jesus, and that they had an indestructible inheritance waiting for them at the coming of Christ. "In *this*" they rejoice. In this they *tasted* the worth and beauty of Christ. In fact, the word *taste* falls far short of what they experienced. Peter uses words that are unparalleled in the New Testament. He says that even though they can't see Jesus with their physical eyes, nevertheless "you love him" and you rejoice over him "with inexpressible and glorified joy" (1:8).

Why is this joy called "glorified" (my literal translation—ESV "filled with glory")? My own suggestion goes back to what we saw about our joy in John 15:11. Jesus spoke to us so *his* joy might be in us. Jesus is glorious. He has now entered into the glory that he had with the Father before the world was created (John 17:24). Our joy is his joy. Therefore, in some measure, our joy is the very joy of the glorified Jesus.

Or to come at it another way, Paul says in 2 Corinthians 3:18, "We all, with unveiled face, beholding the glory of the Lord, are being transformed into the same image from one degree of glory to another." This would suggest that as the Christians in 1 Peter *beheld the glory of Jesus* in the inspired words of Peter, they themselves were in some measure glorified—"transformed into the same image from one degree of *glory* to another." So their joy was, to some degree, a glorified joy. That is, it reflected the glory of Christ.

Peter describes the experience of those Christians in 1 Peter 1:8 without any hint that this was unique to them. This is what *Christians* experience. This is who we are. We are those who come to the word—in this case it is 1 Peter 1:3–7—and in the word taste the goodness of the Lord. We see, with the eyes of the heart, the glory of Christ, and we experience a response of "inexpressible and glorified joy."

This is what I mean by savoring the worth and beauty of God in Scripture. And it is clear that Peter intends for this to happen through what he writes. "In *this* you rejoice" (1 Pet. 1:6). Therefore, as we come to Scripture, *we should aim in all our seeing to savor God's excellence above all things.*

The Psalms Model Savoring

It is hard to escape the impression that the psalms are written to show us that when we come to the Bible, we should come with the unabashed aim of enjoying God and his word. Of course, the word may have to devastate us before we can enjoy it fully. But can we really avoid seeing that the psalms are modeling for us how to savor and celebrate the glory of God—what the psalmists themselves saw in the word of God?

His Delight Is in the Law of the Lord

One of the strongest evidences to this effect is that the first psalm and the longest psalm (119) are both devoted explicitly to this savoring of God's word. It is as though those who put the Psalter together said, "Let's make the first psalm and the longest psalm a resounding summons to treasure and enjoy and ponder the written word of God. Psalm 1 begins:

> Blessed is the man
> > who walks not in the counsel of the wicked,
> nor stands in the way of sinners,
> > nor sits in the seat of scoffers;
> but his delight is in the law of the LORD,
> > and on his law he meditates day and night.
>
> He is like a tree
> > planted by streams of water
> that yields its fruit in its season,
> > and its leaf does not wither.
> In all that he does, he prospers. (vv. 1–3)

The word *law* comes from the Hebrew word for "teach" (*torah*; see Ps. 119:33). It is very broad. It refers not just to legislation the way the English word *law* usually does. It *can* refer to that. But it also can refer to all of God's revelation—all his "teaching" to mankind. For example, in the New Testament, the corresponding word for *law* (Greek νόμος, *nomos*) can refer to the Psalms themselves (John 15:25) or to the Prophets (1 Cor. 14:21). Therefore, when Psalm 1:2 says, "His delight is in the *law* of the LORD, and on his *law* he meditates day and night," it should not be limited to "legislation." This delight is in all of God's revelation—all of his instruction.

So the very first thing this collection of 150 psalms aims to communicate to us is that there is a profound difference between the righteous and the wicked. "The LORD knows the way of the *righteous*, but the way of the *wicked* will perish" (Ps. 1:6). And the main thing about this difference between the righteous and the wicked is that the righteous *person delights in the word of God and meditates on it day and night.*

That is the main summons of the whole Psalter—the banner over all the psalms. This is very important. It waves like a banner over the whole collection. As we walk through the gate of Psalm 1 into the whole Psalter, the summons to all of us is: Come, see (by your meditation[4]) and savor (by your delight) the wonders of God revealed in this great, divine instruction. This is to be our aim, our prayer, as we come to God's word: "Open my eyes, that I may behold wondrous things out of your law" (Ps. 119:18).

The Redwood among the Mighty Psalms

And then standing like a giant redwood tree among the other 149 psalms is the longest psalm of all, Psalm 119. It is more than twice as tall as its nearest competitor (Psalm 78 has seventy-two verses; Psalm 119 has 176 verses). The remarkable height is owing to its structure. Psalm 119 is an acrostic. Each group of eight verses begins with a different letter of the Hebrew alphabet. There are twenty-two letters of the alphabet, hence 22 x 8 = 176.

There is no doubt what this psalmist is doing. He is celebrating God by celebrating the word of God. He is savoring with his spiritual eyes every facet of the diamond of God's revelation. He refers to this revelation as God's "law," "testimonies," "precepts," "statutes," "commandments," "ordinances" (or "rules"), "word," and "promise." But the unmistakable evidence of what he is doing comes not mainly from these words for God's revelation, but mainly from the words he uses for his own *joyful experience* of this revelation. That is what he wants to draw us into. Let your eyes run down over this sampling of love language for the law of God:

In the way of your testimonies I *delight*
   as much as in all riches. (v. 14)

I will *delight* in your statutes;
   I will *not forget* your word. (v. 16)

My soul is consumed with *longing*
   for your rules at all times. (v. 20)

---

4. It will become clear in the remainder of this book what I mean by "meditation." That is, in fact, what this book is about—how to meditate faithfully on Scripture. It is not an attempt to empty the mind of thought with a view to divine filling. Rather it is an intentional directing of the mind to think God's thoughts after him, with earnest prayer that he would grant all the spiritual effects that such a sacred communion can offer.

Your testimonies are my *delight*;
  they are my counselors. (v. 24)

Lead me in the path of your commandments,
  for I *delight* in it. (v. 35)

Behold, I *long for* your precepts;
  in your righteousness give me life! (v. 40)

I find my *delight* in your commandments,
  which I *love*. (v. 47)

I will lift up my hands toward your commandments, which I *love*,
  and I will meditate on your statutes. (v. 48)

Their heart is unfeeling like fat,
  but I *delight* in your law. (v. 70)

Those who fear you shall see me and rejoice,
  because I have *hoped* in your word. (v. 74)

Let your mercy come to me, that I may live;
  for your law is my *delight*. (v. 77)

If your law had not been my *delight*,
  I would have perished in my affliction. (v. 92)

Oh how I love your law!
  It is my meditation all the day. (v. 97)

How sweet are your words to my taste,
  sweeter than honey to my mouth! (v. 103)

Your testimonies are my heritage forever,
  for they are the *joy* of my heart. (v. 111)

I hate the double-minded,
  but I love your law. (v. 113)

All the wicked of the earth you discard like dross,
  therefore I *love* your testimonies. (v. 119)

Therefore I *love* your commandments
  above gold, above fine gold. (v. 127)

I open my mouth and pant,
    because I long for your commandments. (v. 131)

Your promise is well tried,
    and your servant *loves* it. (v. 140)

Trouble and anguish have found me out,
    but your commandments are my *delight*. (v. 143)

Consider how I *love* your precepts!
    Give me life according to your steadfast love. (v. 159)

Princes persecute me without cause,
    but my heart *stands in awe* of your words. (v. 161)

I *rejoice* at your word
    like one who finds great spoil. (v. 162)

I hate and abhor falsehood,
    but I *love* your law. (v. 163)

Great peace have those who *love* your law;
    nothing can make them stumble. (v. 165)

My soul keeps your testimonies;
    I *love* them exceedingly. (v. 167)

I long for your salvation, O LORD,
    and your law is my *delight*. (v. 174)

I suppose I could rest my case on the basis of Psalm 119 alone. Yes, *we should aim in all our seeing (all our meditating on God's word) to savor his excellence above all things.* Yes, savoring is indispensable. This is what seeing is for.

Delighting in the Word or in God through the Word?

If anyone is inclined to object that Psalm 119 is only about delighting in the word rather than the glories of God revealed in the word, Derek Kidner gives the right answer:

This untiring emphasis [of the psalmist on loving the word] has led some to accuse the psalmist of worshipping the word rather than the Lord; but it has been well remarked that every reference here to Scripture, without exception, relates it explicitly to its Author; indeed every verse from 4 to the end is a prayer or affirmation addressed to him. This is true piety: a love of God not desiccated by study but refreshed, informed and nourished by it. . . .

Verse 132 goes to the heart of the matter in the expression, "who love thy name." It is on God's account that we love the writings that reveal him. The psalmist's longing (20, 40), which he pictures now as pleasurable appetite ("thy words . . . sweeter than honey," 103), now as gasping urgency ("with open mouth I pant," 131), is for God himself, as the context shows. Note the emphatic *thou* immediately before 103, and the prayer, "Turn to me . . ." which follows 131 (Today's English Version: the Psalms, 1970). Cf. the seeking of "him" in verse 2, the emphatic "Thou" in verse 4; above all, verse 151: "You are all I want, Lord" (as TEV paraphrases it).[5]

There is no hint in all the Bible that the word of God is pursued or enjoyed primarily because of some aesthetic effect that makes it enjoyable. Such effects are real. And the Bible is filled with admirable literary traits. But that is not what the biblical authors celebrate with greatest pleasure. Literary brilliance is a means to an end: the revelation of the brilliant glories of God and his ways. When the word of God came, what thrilled the recipients was that God himself "appeared" through the word. "*The* LORD *appeared* again at Shiloh, for *the* LORD *revealed himself* to Samuel at Shiloh *by the word of the* LORD" (1 Sam. 3:21). This was the great wonder and the great joy. In all our "seeing," we aim to "savor," because this is what we see.

Psalm 119 deserves a thousand pages of meditation. It inspires long, deep, and happy meditation on God's word. Charles Bridges wrote five hundred pages on this psalm.[6] Thomas Manton preached 190 sermons on this psalm, published in three volumes totaling 1,677 pages.[7] That is what this psalm is worthy of. But for my limited aim here, the point is simple: the longest chapter in God's written word is devoted to modeling for us how to savor God's written word. We fall short in our reading when we do not follow this model.

---

5. Derek Kidner, *Psalms 73–150: An Introduction and Commentary*, vol. 16, Tyndale Old Testament Commentaries (Downers Grove, IL: InterVarsity Press, 1975), 453–55.

6. Charles Bridges, *Psalm 119: An Exposition* (1827; repr. Edinburgh: Banner of Truth, 1974).

7. Thomas Manton, *Psalm 119* (1680; repr. Edinburgh: Banner of Truth, 1990).

Savor the Excellence of God

If, as Psalm 19 says, the commandments of the Lord give light and the precepts of the Lord give joy (v. 8), then would it not be contrary to God's design for his word if we do not seek, in all our Bible reading, to *see* that light and *savor* that joy? If his word is more to be desired than gold, and if it is sweeter to the soul than honey to the tongue (v. 10), then it is clearly the calling of every Christian to dig through every line of the Scriptures for the gold of God's glory and to savor every sight with a pleasure in the soul greater than honey on the lips. I conclude, therefore, that the fourth implication of our proposal (see the box at the beginning) is true: *We should aim in all our Bible reading not only to see, but also to savor the excellence of God above all things.*

No man can have the least ground of assurance that he hath seen Christ and his glory by faith, without some effects of it in changing him into his likeness.

JOHN OWEN

We all, with unveiled face, beholding the glory of the Lord, are being transformed into the same image from one degree of glory to another. For this comes from the Lord who is the Spirit.

2 CORINTHIANS 3:18

8

Reading to Be Transformed, Part 1

"We all . . . , beholding the glory of the Lord,
are being transformed from one
degree of glory to another."

The Proposal

Our ultimate goal in reading the Bible is that God's infinite worth and beauty would be exalted in the everlasting, white-hot worship of the blood-bought bride of Christ from every people, language, tribe, and nation. This implies:

1. that the infinite worth and beauty of God are *the ultimate value and excellence* of the universe;
2. that the supremely *authentic and intense worship* of God's worth and beauty is the ultimate aim of all his work and word;
3. that we should always read his word in order to *see* this supreme worth and beauty;
4. that we should aim in all our seeing to *savor* his excellence above all things;
5. **that we should aim to be *transformed* by this seeing and savoring into the likeness of his beauty,**
6. so that more and more people would be drawn into the worshiping family of God until the bride of Christ—across all centuries and cultures—is complete in number and beauty.

God Is Most Glorified in Us When We Are Most Satisfied in Him?

God's purpose in Scripture does not end with our seeing and savoring his glory. I say this, knowing that it may sound like a contradiction of my favorite slogan, "God is most glorified in us, when we are most satisfied in him." One might think, well, if God is *most* glorified when we are most *satisfied* in him—that is, when we are fully *savoring* his glory—then why would this not be the end point of God's purposes?

Here's the catch. Saying, "God is most glorified in us, *when* we are most satisfied in him," is not the same as saying, "God is most glorified in us, *only because* we are most satisfied in him." There may be *other facts* about us that also need to be true for God to be "most glorified" in us.

The point of saying, "God is most glorified in us, *when* we are most satisfied in him," is to stress how indispensable it is that we pursue satisfaction in God. That pursuit is *never* negligible. It is always essential. We will always fall short in our aim to glorify God "most" if we do not pursue our heart's satisfaction in God. Whatever else we attain, if our hearts are *more* satisfied in some other person or some other thing, rather than God, we will not attain our aim to glorify him most. We will always be saying, in effect, "God falls short of satisfying me." This robs him of the glory he should receive from us—no matter how outwardly decent our behavior is.

God Did Not Create Visible Reality So That His Value Would Stay Invisible

So I will say it again: God's purpose in Scripture does not end with our seeing and savoring his glory. The reason it doesn't is that the savoring of God that goes on in the heart (which is the only place that spiritual savoring happens) is *invisible* to other human beings. Only God looks on the heart (1 Sam. 16:7). So God is delighted with the heart that is satisfied in him. But no one else can see this. Yet God's purpose in creating a material universe, and not just a world of invisible spirits, is so that his glory would be displayed visibly in millions of ways. Not only does he say, "The heavens declare the glory of God" (Ps. 19:1), but he also says, "Let your light shine before others, so that they may *see your good works* and give glory to your Father who is in heaven" (Matt. 5:16).

God did not create the world to keep his glory invisible, and he did not re-create Christians to keep our passion for his glory invisible. All things—including human beings—were created the first time for the glory of God (Isa. 43:6–7). And all Christians were created the second time for a kind of outward life that calls attention to the glory of God: "We are his workmanship, created in Christ Jesus *for good works*, which God prepared beforehand, that we should walk in them" (Eph. 2:10). These are the "good works" that people "see" and that cause them to "*give glory to your Father who is in heaven*" (Matt. 5:16).

The Fifth Implication: Transformation

This chapter and the next are an explanation and justification of how the Scriptures function to bring us from *seeing* the glory of God to *savoring* the glory of God to *being transformed*—inside and outside—into the likeness of Christ. The fifth implication of our proposal (in the box at the beginning of the chapter) says, "We *should aim to be transformed by this seeing and savoring into the likeness of his beauty.*" What we are now seeing is that God's purpose for creation and redemption is the *outward, visible, manifest* display of his glory—not only the glorifying that happens when we are most satisfied with him in our hearts.

Outward Sanctity Is Only Good as the Fruit of Inward Savoring

Therefore, God's purpose for us in reading the Scripture is not only that we *see* his glory, and that we *savor* his glory, but also that we be *transformed* by this seeing and savoring, so that our visible, audible, touchable lives display the worth and beauty of God. This, of course, is vastly different from merely trying to do morally better things. Jesus knew and taught that the tree is known by its fruit. That is, the inner life is known by its outer life:

> Either make the tree good and its fruit good, or make the tree bad and its fruit bad, for the tree is known by its fruit. You brood of vipers! How can you speak good, when you are evil? For out of the abundance of the heart the mouth speaks. The good person out of his good treasure brings forth good, and the evil person out of his evil treasure brings forth evil. (Matt. 12:33–35)

But many people miss half the point. They hear only the half that the aim of the inner life is a *better outer life*. So they think getting the outer life morally renewed is what really matters. They neglect the heart and work on the appearance. Jesus was unsparing in his criticism of those who tried to keep up a good moral exterior while their hearts did not savor God:

> Woe to you, scribes and Pharisees, hypocrites! For you clean the outside of the cup and the plate, but inside they are full of greed and self-indulgence. You blind Pharisee! First clean the inside of the cup and the plate, that the outside also may be clean. (Matt. 23:25–26)

That is the way God has designed the Scriptures to work. They reveal the glory of God so that, first, it may be seen. This seeing is the first act of the new heart, which then *savors* the glory of God above everything else. This is a real heart experience that precedes all God-exalting outward behavior. The Bible is not aiming to create hypocrites—"whitewashed tombs, which outwardly appear beautiful, but within are full of dead people's bones and all uncleanness" (Matt. 23:27). The Bible aims to create authentic people who are so satisfied in God that their outward behavior shows that God is their greatest treasure—not money, or power, or fame, or sexual pleasure, or family, or church, or even sickness-free heaven. God's value is supreme in the heart, and this has changed everything.

Ordinary Outward Morality Does Not Impress the World

Outward morality that only avoids notorious sins is not impressive to the world. Seldom do unbelievers—or believers for that matter—respond with praises to God that I as Christian have not killed anyone or embezzled or committed adultery. So, then, what did Jesus (in Matthew 5:16) and Peter (in 1 Peter 2:12) have in mind when they said we should do good deeds *so that others would glorify God when they see them?* The answer to this question shows how essential it is that savoring the glory of God be the ground of our outward transformation. The answer will show that, first, God must become the supreme treasure and satisfaction of our hearts. Then, like fruit from the tree of this deep and unshakable joy in God, the kinds of behaviors grow that cause people to see the worth and beauty of God.

For Jesus, the answer lies in the flow of thought from Matthew 5:11–16; for Peter the answer lies in the flow of thought in 1 Peter

3:13–17. Let's take these one at a time. Remember, what we are looking for is the secret to the kind of "good deeds" that draw people to
glorify God.

What Kind of Good Deeds Get Glory for God?

Let's begin with Matthew 5:11–16:

> Blessed are you when others revile you and persecute you and utter
> all kinds of evil against you falsely on my account. Rejoice and be
> glad, for your reward is great in heaven, for so they persecuted the
> prophets who were before you. You are the salt of the earth, but
> if salt has lost its taste, how shall its saltiness be restored? It is no
> longer good for anything except to be thrown out and trampled
> under people's feet. You are the light of the world. A city set on a
> hill cannot be hidden. Nor do people light a lamp and put it under
> a basket, but on a stand, and it gives light to all in the house. In the
> same way, let your light shine before others, so that they may see
> your good works and give glory to your Father who is in heaven.

Immediately before saying that his disciples are the salt of the earth
(v. 13) and the light of the world (v. 16), Jesus tells them to rejoice and
be glad when they are reviled and persecuted and slandered (vv. 11–
12). The basis of this rejoicing in the face of suffering is "for your
reward is great in heaven" (v. 12). In other words, disciples should be
so happy with who God will be for them in the age to come that no sorrow in this world can take away their happiness in God. Jesus prayed
for them that in heaven they might see his glory (John 17:24). He told
them that he will welcome them into his own joy in heaven—"into
the joy of your master" (Matt. 25:21). They know that to die will be
gain because they will be "with Christ" (Phil. 1:23). And they know
that in God's presence there will be "fullness of joy" and "pleasures
forevermore" (Ps. 16:11).

On the basis of this indestructible joy in God, Jesus commands them
to do what is utterly against all ordinary human experience. If they
could do this, it would be inexplicable to ordinary people. It would
be stunning and amazing and wonderful. It would be like changing a
tasteless, boring, ordinary life into an astonishing, attractive, spicy life.
Like putting salt on a piece of tasteless meat. It would be like lighting a

lamp in a dreary room so that everything looks beautiful. This utterly counterintuitive thing is "rejoice and be glad" when people "persecute you and utter all kinds of evil against you falsely on my account." Be happy when people do their worst to you.

That is what I think Jesus means by "salt" and "light." Immediately after telling us to do the humanly impossible and utterly counterintuitive thing—rejoicing in our persecution—he says, "You are the salt of the earth. . . . You are the light of the world." What he means is that the good deeds you do, *in this utterly inexplicable spirit of indestructible joy in God*, will have a flavor about them that causes people to look for the explanation for your joy. And the explanation will be that your joy comes not from the things their joy comes from, but from God. And, if God gives grace, they will "see your good works and give glory to your Father who is in heaven" (Matt. 5:16). Your savoring of God over all things will prove to be the secret of how your good deeds give God glory.

If You Suffer, You Are Blessed

That's my answer to the question, "What is the secret to the kind of 'good deeds' that draw people to glorify God?" It is the savoring of the glory we see over all that this world can offer. The same answer is found in the flow of thought in 1 Peter 3:13–17:

> Now who is there to harm you if you are zealous for what is good? But even if you should suffer for righteousness' sake, you will be blessed. Have no fear of them, nor be troubled, but in your hearts honor Christ the Lord as holy, always being prepared to make a defense to anyone who asks you for a reason for the hope that is in you; yet do it with gentleness and respect, having a good conscience, so that, when you are slandered, those who revile your good behavior in Christ may be put to shame. For it is better to suffer for doing good, if that should be God's will, than for doing evil.

In verse 15, Peter says that you should always be "prepared to make a defense to anyone who asks you for a reason for the hope that is in you." Notice that the question they ask has to do explicitly with our *hope*. Why is that? It must be because our behavior in some way gives the impression that we are not hoping in the same things they are. When you act just like everyone else, they don't say, "What hope prompted that?"

Evidently we are to be acting in a way that shows our treasure is not on earth but in heaven. Our hope for security and lasting satisfaction is not in money, or security alarm systems, or a good neighborhood, or a great job, or a substantial health insurance policy, or an ample nest egg, or a solid marriage, or a good reputation, or anything else in this world. The key is in verse 14: "Even if you should suffer for righteousness' sake, you will be blessed." This is exactly the same promise Jesus made in Matthew 5:12. Peter was more explicit in 1 Peter 4:13: "Rejoice insofar as you share Christ's sufferings, that *you may also rejoice and be glad when his glory is revealed.*"

For both Jesus and Peter, there is a great reward "when his glory is revealed." This glory-laden reward is so satisfying—inexpressibly satisfying according to 1 Peter 1:8—that our hope and our joy are unshakable. This revolution of our heart's affections is so deep and so pervasive that it leads to the kinds of choices and sacrificial risks that may cause people to wonder, "What are you really hoping in? What reward are you living for?" In that way, we pray that "they may see your good deeds and glorify God" (1 Pet. 2:12). So the secret to the kind of good deeds that get glory for God is a deep underlying satisfaction in God's promise of blessing that frees us to take risks in the cause of love that the world finds inexplicable. In other words, savoring God over all leads to radical transformation.

How the Scriptures Serve Transformation

This is how God has designed the Scriptures to work for human transformation and for the glory of God: the Scriptures *reveal* God's glory. This glory, God willing, is *seen* by those who read the Bible. This seeing gives rise, by God's grace, to *savoring* God above all things—treasuring him, hoping in him, feeling him as our greatest reward, tasting him as our all-satisfying good. And this savoring *transforms* our lives—freeing us from the slavery of selfishness and overflowing in love to others. This joy-sustained, God-exalting transformation of love is then *seen by others*, who, by God's grace, glorify God because of it. This movement rises and falls through history according to the faithfulness of Christ's people and the renewal of God's mercies.

The Most Illuminating Text on Transformation

The passage of Scripture that most explicitly connects seeing the glory of God with being transformed into his likeness is 2 Corinthians 3:18–4:6. In my own experience, it has proved to be one of the most important passages in all of the Bible.

> We all, with unveiled face, beholding the glory of the Lord, are being transformed into the same image from one degree of glory to another. For this comes from the Lord who is the Spirit. Therefore, having this ministry by the mercy of God, we do not lose heart. But we have renounced disgraceful, underhanded ways. We refuse to practice cunning or to tamper with God's word, but by the open statement of the truth we would commend ourselves to everyone's conscience in the sight of God. And even if our gospel is veiled, it is veiled to those who are perishing. In their case the god of this world has blinded the minds of the unbelievers, to keep them from seeing the light of the gospel of the glory of Christ, who is the image of God. For what we proclaim is not ourselves, but Jesus Christ as Lord, with ourselves as your servants for Jesus' sake. For God, who said, "Let light shine out of darkness," has shone in our hearts to give the light of the knowledge of the glory of God in the face of Jesus Christ.

We have already seen how important 2 Corinthians 4:4–6 is in showing us that the glory of Christ is revealed in the gospel. Paul says that when God does his new-creation work of opening our eyes and saving us, we see "the light of the knowledge of the *glory of God* in the face of Jesus Christ" (v. 6), or, as he calls it in verse 4, "the light of the gospel of *the glory of Christ*, who is the image of God." The unsurpassed importance of "the glory of Christ" stands out in this passage because the gospel is called "the gospel of the glory of Christ." In other words, Christ's death and resurrection were a brutal and beautiful display of the glory of Christ. But not only that: by the very act of displaying that glory, Christ purchased our everlasting enjoyment in it.

This was his aim in dying for us: "Christ suffered once for sins, the righteous for the unrighteous, *that he might bring us to God*" (1 Pet. 3:18). All the countless benefits of the cross lead to this as their essence and aim: to bring us to God. For in his presence is fullness of joy and pleasures forevermore (Ps. 16:11). So Paul calls the good news a "gospel of glory" both because Christ is supremely glorious in his work of redemption, *and* because the aim of that redemption is that we might come to God and enjoy that glory forever. It is a "gospel of glory" because the means is glorious and the end is glory.

The Saving Sight (4:6) and the Transforming Sight (3:18)

The chapter division between 2 Corinthians 3 and 4 can obscure something that is all-important—the connection between 2 Corinthians 3:18 and 4:6.

> We all, with unveiled face, *beholding the glory of the Lord*, are being transformed into the same image from one degree of glory to another. (3:18)

> For God, who said, "Let light shine out of darkness," has shone in our hearts to give the light of the knowledge of the glory of God in the face of Jesus Christ. (4:6)

This "beholding the glory of the Lord" in 3:18 happens because of the miracle that God brings about in 4:6. In verse 4, Satan is blinding unbelievers. What he keeps them from seeing is "the light of the gospel of *the glory of Christ*." Then, in verse 6, that blinding work of Satan is overcome by God's power as the Creator. The one who said, "Let there be light!" has shone in our hearts.

The result of God's act in our hearts is that he gives "the light of the knowledge of the glory of God in the face of Jesus Christ." This "light" is not physical or natural. It is, to use the words of Jonathan Edwards, "a divine and supernatural light."[1] As he says in one of his most famous sermons, "there is such a thing, as a spiritual and divine light, immediately imparted to the soul by God, of a different nature from any that is obtained by natural means."[2]

God Irradiates the Mind with Spiritual Light

This is what Paul prayed for in Ephesians 1—that *the eyes of our hearts* would be enlightened. Not the eyes of our heads. So the seeing is not a natural seeing, but a "divine and supernatural" seeing. He prayed:

---

1. Jonathan Edwards, "A Divine and Supernatural Light," in *Sermons and Discourses, 1730–1733*, ed. Mark Valeri and Harry S. Stout, vol. 17, *The Works of Jonathan Edwards* (New Haven, CT: Yale University Press, 1999), 405–26.
2. Ibid., 410.

> . . . having the eyes of your hearts enlightened, that you may know what is the hope to which he has called you, what are the riches of his glorious inheritance in the saints, and what is the immeasurable greatness of his power toward us who believe. (Eph. 1:18–19)

This "enlightened" seeing with "the eyes of your hearts" is what Satan was preventing in 2 Corinthians 4:4 and what God granted in 2 Corinthians 4:6. This miracle of seeing divine glory with the eyes of the heart is the same as regeneration, or the new birth. Oh, how crucial it is to realize what God does in this moment of divine illumination. "He irradiates the mind," as John Owen puts it, "with a spiritual light, whereby it is enabled to discern the glory of spiritual things."[3] This miracle is absolutely decisive in everything else that happens in the Christian's life.

It is the creation of a new spiritual sense or awareness or discernment—a new spiritual ability to know and be enthralled by a divine beauty that is not visible to the physical human eye. Edwards described the creation of 2 Corinthians 4:6 like this: "The first effect of the power of God in the heart in regeneration, is to give the heart a Divine taste or sense; to cause it to have a relish [for] the loveliness and sweetness of the supreme excellency of the Divine nature."[4]

The Connection

Now we are ready to appreciate the connection between 2 Corinthians 4:6 and 3:18. The glory that we are now supernaturally able to see (4:6) is the glory of the Lord in 2 Corinthians 3:18, which transforms us from one degree of glory to another. "We all, with unveiled face, *beholding the glory of the Lord*, are being transformed into the same image from one degree of glory to another." What is now clear is that this "beholding the glory of the Lord" is not a mere neutral sight, as if we looked accidentally or casually on some great person. In fact, that is precisely the way unbelievers look on Christ and his gospel *before* the miracle of 2 Corinthians 4:6. But *after* that miracle, the light of the glory of Christ shines through the gospel as through a window. Once the gospel was an uninteresting painting on the wall. Then suddenly we see, for the

---

3. John Owen, *The Works of John Owen*, ed. William H. Goold, vol. 4 (Edinburgh: T&T Clark, n.d.), 57.

4. Jonathan Edwards, *Treatise on Grace*, ed. Paul Helm (Cambridge, UK: James Clarke, 1971), 48–49.

first time with wonder, that it is not a painting after all, but a window onto the Himalayas of the glories of Christ. Through the window of the gospel shines "the light of the gospel of the glory of Christ, who is the image of God" (2 Cor. 4:4).

It Is Seeing with Savoring That Transforms

When the miracle of 2 Corinthians 4:6 happens, no one looks through that gospel window on the glory of Christ neutrally. This new seeing is not like the old seeing. It is a seeing with savoring. As Edwards said, the heart now has a new taste (remember 1 Peter 2:3), a new sense, a new "relish for the loveliness and sweetness of the supreme excellency" of Christ. This is how we "behold the glory of the Lord" in 2 Corinthians 3:18. And *this is why beholding glory leads to becoming glorious.* Disinterested, casual glimpses of glory do not transform. But *this* beholding transforms. "Beholding the glory of the Lord, *[we] are being transformed into the same image from one degree of glory to another.*" We are transformed because this mere seeing has become seeing with savoring. Discerning with delighting. Looking with loving. Sensing with satisfaction. The beauty of Christ—and all that God is for us in him—no longer stands in our minds as an irrelevant religious notion, or even as a mere doctrinal truth, but as our supreme treasure. We see glory as glory. Beauty as beauty. Supreme value as supreme value. And this seeing is now simultaneous with savoring. This is why beholding transforms us.

Beholding Glory and Becoming Glorious

And this is why Paul speaks of *our own* glory. "Beholding the glory of the Lord, [we] are being transformed into the same image *from one degree of glory to another.*" By seeing Christ in this new way—treasuring him above all things—we are *now* becoming glorious. This is not yet the glory we will have fully when we are "glorified" at the coming of the Lord (Rom. 8:17; 2 Thess. 1:12), with new resurrection bodies (1 Cor. 15:43), in a new and glorious creation (Rom. 8:18–25), completely free from sin and totally conformed to the risen Christ (1 John 3:2). Nevertheless, it is real. Something is changing now. The glory of Christ is in some way being imparted to us through beholding the glory of the Lord. How is that happening?

We can see the answer if we ask, "What is our shortfall in glory?"

If we leave aside for a moment the fallenness of our bodies and mental faculties, what is our fallenness? What is the ugliness that ought to be glorious? Paul gives the answer in Romans 1–3. He says in Romans 3:23, "All have sinned and fall short of the glory of God." The word for "fall short" (Greek ὑστεροῦνται, *husterountai*) means "to lack" or "to be in need of." The idea is not so much that we had a target and missed it, but that we had a treasure and lost it—squandered it.

That is exactly the way Paul talks about our loss of the glory of God in Romans 1:23 because we treasured something else more—we savored the glory of the creation more than the glory of God: "Claiming to be wise, they became fools, and exchanged the glory of the immortal God for images" (Rom. 1:22–23). Therefore, the essence of our fallenness is our outrageous preference for the glory of the world—including our own—over the glory of God. This is the essence of all sin. At the root of all evil is the devaluing of God, in our preference for other things. This is the loss of the divine radiance we were meant to reflect. Our inner glory, our moral or spiritual beauty, is a heart that sees God so clearly and feels his worth so fully that he is our supreme treasure. Wherever that is true, the exchange of Romans 1:23 has been reversed.

God-Savoring Is Our Glory

That is what 2 Corinthians 3:18 says is happening when we "behold the glory of the Lord." That is what it means to "be transformed from one degree of glory to another." It means that gradually our savoring the supreme worth and beauty of Christ is pushing out of our hearts all competing desires. *The glory of a Christian is that Jesus Christ is our glory.* Our glory lies not intrinsically in ourselves but in our actualized capacity to see and savor the glory of our Creator and Redeemer. Therefore, to be changed "from one degree of glory to another" is to be increasingly controlled by surpassing joy in the all-satisfying glory of Christ.

The Spirit of the Mind

Paul says in Ephesians 4:22 that our old self was "corrupt through deceitful desires." In other words, we were deceived into feeling that other things were more desirable than God. The remedy, he says, is to "be renewed in the spirit of your minds" (Eph. 4:23)—not just renewed in your mind, but in the *spirit* of your mind. The newness of a Christian is not just a new way of thinking. A new spirit, a new taste, a new love, a new treasure penetrates our thinking.

I mention this in relation to 2 Corinthians 3:18 because I am concerned that some Christians may use Romans 12:2 as a description of how we are transformed, without any reference to the emotional transformation that comes from beholding the glory of Christ. Paul says:

> Do not be conformed to this world, but *be transformed by the renewal of your mind*, that by testing you may discern what is the will of God, what is good and acceptable and perfect. (Rom. 12:2)

Without an awareness of how Paul describes the process of transformation in 2 Corinthians 3:18, one might infer from Romans 12:2 that transformation is merely an intellectual affair. Get a new way of thinking and test behaviors and choose the best one. What a travesty of the Christian life that would be! The "renewal of your mind" that Paul refers to in Romans 12:2 includes what he calls in Ephesians 4:23 the "renewal of the *spirit* of the mind." And this new "spirit of the mind" is the remedy for "deceitful *desires*" (Eph. 4:22). The old, unrenewed mind was the mind whose "spirit" exchanged the glory of God for images: "They became *futile in their thinking, and their foolish hearts were darkened*. Claiming to be wise, they became fools, and exchanged the glory of the immortal God for images" (Rom. 1:21–23).

Therefore, when Paul calls for the renewal of the mind in Romans 12:2, he means much more than a mere intellectual change. He means a renovation of the soul's capacity to feel as well as think—a renovation of the *spirit of the mind*. He means that the "futility" and the "darkness" and the "foolishness" that made images feel more desirable than God must be done away with. The mind must be continually renewed in its capacity to "discern what is the will of God" by the miraculous seeing and savoring of the heart.

See, Savor, Be Changed

Therefore, the most fundamental thing that changes us is our beholding the glory of the Lord as our supreme and all-satisfying treasure. Renewing the mind means bringing all our thinking—again and again—into accord with this supernatural sight of the worth and beauty of Jesus.

This is how we move from one degree of glory to another. This is how we image forth the beauty of Christ. And this is how good deeds are done in a way that the world finds inexplicable, because they spring up from a profound contentment in God that the world does not know and cannot feel—until the miracle of 2 Corinthians 4:6 happens to them. This is the prayer and aim of all who are being transformed into the image of Christ.

This is the first part of our explanation and justification of the fifth implication highlighted in the box at the beginning of this chapter: *We should aim to be transformed into the likeness of Christ's beauty, by seeing and savoring the glory of the Lord.* That glory shines forth from his word. Therefore, the goal of all our Bible reading is to see and savor and be changed by this revealed glory.

In a severe test of affliction, their abundance of joy and their extreme poverty have overflowed in a wealth of generosity on their part.

2 CORINTHIANS 8:2

The only way to dispossess the heart of an old affection, is by the expulsive power of a new one.

THOMAS CHALMERS

No one who keeps on sinning has seen God.

1 JOHN 3:6 (AUTHOR'S TRANSLATION)

9

Reading to Be Transformed, Part 2

"Their abundance of joy . . .
overflowed in . . . generosity."

The Proposal

Our ultimate goal in reading the Bible is that God's infinite worth and beauty would be exalted in the everlasting, white-hot worship of the blood-bought bride of Christ from every people, language, tribe, and nation. This implies:

1. that the infinite worth and beauty of God are *the ultimate value and excellence* of the universe;
2. that the supremely *authentic and intense worship* of God's worth and beauty is the ultimate aim of all his work and word;
3. that we should always read his word in order to *see* this supreme worth and beauty;
4. that we should aim in all our seeing to *savor* his excellence above all things;
5. **that we should aim to be *transformed* by this seeing and savoring into the likeness of his beauty,**
6. so that more and more people would be drawn into the worshiping family of God until the bride of Christ—across all centuries and cultures—is complete in number and beauty.

Jesus, Peter, and Paul United in How Christians Change

In the previous chapter, we saw the strikingly similar way that Jesus, Peter, and Paul explain the way Christians are transformed "from one degree of glory to another." Jesus traced this transformation back to unshakable joy in our "great reward" that frees from revenge and releases the risks of love in God-glorifying good deeds (Matt. 5:11–16). Peter traced it back to unshakable joy in God's promised blessing that overcomes our bent to return evil for evil and empowers us to do good, even while suffering, so that others ask "a reason for the hope" that is in us (1 Pet. 3:9, 13–17; 4:13). And Paul traced this transformation back to "beholding the glory of the Lord" with such a new savoring of his worth and beauty that we are changed "from one degree of glory to another" (2 Cor. 3:18).

It all starts with God's gift of seeing. This seeing gives rise to savoring. And this savoring pushes out the "deceitful desires" that tricked us into thinking anything is more satisfying than God. And that all-important seeing happens as we read the word of God. In effect, then, Jesus, Peter, and Paul trace authentic change back to seeing and savoring the glory of Christ as the supreme treasure of our lives—as we read the inspired Scriptures.

A Stunning Example of Transformation through Joy

That unity is striking. It is part of the faith-stirring glory of Scripture. But even more stirring, for me, is to actually watch this process at work in the lives of the Corinthians as Paul describes it in 2 Corinthians 8:1–2. The snapshot of Christian transformation that we are about to see is stunning. It gives us a glimpse of how being supremely satisfied in God bears the fruit of radical love. And so it shows us the kind of "good works" (Matt. 5:16; 1 Pet. 2:12) that could indeed lead someone to be converted and glorify God.

The situation is that Paul is trying to motivate the Corinthians to be generous participants in the collection he is taking up for the poor saints in Jerusalem (Rom. 15:25–33; 1 Cor. 16:3; 2 Cor. 8:18–19). As Paul goes from church to church among the Gentiles, he is making the case that "if the Gentiles have come to share in their [Jewish] spiritual blessings, they [the Gentiles] ought also to be of service to them in material blessings" (Rom. 15:27).

So now, in 2 Corinthians 8, he is writing to the Corinthians and using the example of the Macedonians (from the northern part of Greece where Philippi and Thessalonica were) to stir up the Corinthians to be equally generous. It is the example of these Macedonians that provides our stunning illustration of how joy in God's glorious grace severs the root of selfishness and sets us free for the radical risks and sacrifices of love:

> We want you to know, brothers, about the grace of God that has been given among the churches of Macedonia, for in a severe test of affliction, their abundance of joy and their extreme poverty have overflowed in a wealth of generosity on their part. (vv. 1–2)

A Living Illustration of Being Changed from Glory to Glory

There we have a living illustration of the transformation we read about just a few chapters earlier in 2 Corinthians 3:18. Paul had come to Macedonia and preached the gospel. God, he says in verse 1, gave his grace— "the grace of God . . . has been given among the churches of Macedonia." I take this to mean, at least, that God performed for them the miracle of 2 Corinthians 4:6, and they were converted to Christ. He "shone in our hearts to give the light of the knowledge of the glory of God in the face of Jesus Christ." They saw and they experienced the glory of God's grace.

The effect was simply amazing—beyond all human explanation. It's described in 2 Corinthians 8:2: "In a severe test of affliction, their abundance of joy and their extreme poverty have overflowed in a wealth of generosity on their part." The practical, visible effect of this experience of grace was "a wealth of generosity on their part." They responded to Paul's appeal for the poor in Jerusalem with extraordinary liberality. I say it was extraordinary, first because of its sacrificial amount and its eagerness. You can see that in verses 3–4: "For they gave according to their means, as I can testify, and *beyond their means*, of their own accord, *begging us earnestly for the favor of taking part* in the relief of the saints." They begged to be allowed to give more, and they gave beyond what they were materially able to give. As verse 2 says, it was a *"wealth* of generosity."

Liberating Joy in Affliction and Poverty

But those are not the main reasons the giving was extraordinary. The main reasons are in verse 2. The giving was "in a severe test of affliction," and it was out of "their extreme poverty." They had good human reasons not to give anything. And certainly not to give lavishly. They were extremely poor, and they were presently enduring fresh afflictions because of their new Christian faith. While many people, as you can imagine, might be complaining that God is not caring for them—allowing them to be persecuted and poor—these Christians were stunningly different. There is no hint of self-pity. There is rather "a wealth of generosity." The name for this generosity, as Paul makes clear in verses 7–8, is *love*. He says, "See that you excel in this act of grace also. I say this not as a command, but to prove by the earnestness of others that *your love* also is genuine."

The Origin of Inexplicable Sacrifice

Now the decisive question is: What was it about these Macedonians that gave rise to this humanly inexplicable sacrifice of generosity in the midst of affliction and poverty? The answer is explicit and crystal clear: "*Their abundance of joy . . .* overflowed in a wealth of generosity." Paul could not have been clearer about what it was that transformed these Macedonians into radically generous, loving people. It was their joy. Notice carefully. It is not just that they had joy *at the same time* that they had generosity. Joy did not just *accompany* their generosity. No. Joy was the *cause*. The joy itself "overflowed in . . . generosity." Joy was the spring; generosity was the stream. Joy was the root; generosity was the fruit.

Notice also that this joy was not moderate. It was an "abundance of joy" (Greek ἡ περισσεία τῆς χαρᾶς). It was huge. Nor was it in any way based on their outward circumstances. They were in "a severe test of affliction" (Greek ἐν πολλῇ δοκιμῇ θλίψεως) and they were in "extreme poverty" (Greek ἡ κατὰ βάθους πτωχεία). Paul is using language to make it crystal clear that their joy was not aroused or sustained by any part of their outward circumstances. What, then, were these Macedonians so happy about in these terrible circumstances?

The Source of Their Indomitable Joy

The answer is in verse 1: "The grace of God . . . has been given among the churches of Macedonia." If our response to grace is not this kind of joy, we do not yet know sin and wrath and hell and the cross and the resurrection and forgiveness and Christ and the hope of glory the way we should. But for the Macedonians, the glory of God's grace (Eph. 1:6) was more beautiful, more valuable, more satisfying than any riches or comfort could ever be. God had overcome the blinding effects of Satan and opened the eyes of their hearts to see the brilliant "light of the gospel of the glory of Christ." He had "shone in our hearts to give the light of the knowledge of the glory of God in the face of Jesus Christ." Nothing! Nothing could surpass the value of what they had seen and received in Jesus Christ. No affliction, no poverty could take away their joy.

They had "seen the glory of the Lord" and were being transformed from one degree of glory to another as they were set free from selfishness and sought to extend their joy into the lives of others. That is the nature of joy in the glory of an infinitely beautiful and infinitely resourceful Christ. It has an outward impulse. Its nature is to expand. It seeks to enlarge itself with the joy that others have in God. In other words, the pursuit of joy in the glory of God, far from making us self-absorbed, in fact, puts us on the quest of making others eternally glad in God. *Their* joy in God is the expansion and completion of *ours*.

The Expulsive Power of a New Affection

What is wonderfully clear and refreshing in the Macedonians is this truth: finding supreme joy in Jesus severs the root of sin with the power of a superior satisfaction. Or as Thomas Chalmers says, our selfishness is driven out with "the expulsive power of a new affection."

> There are two ways in which a practical moralist may attempt to displace from the human heart its love of the world—either by a demonstration of the world's vanity, so that the heart shall be prevailed upon simply to withdraw its regards from an object that is not worthy of it; or, by setting forth another object, even God, as more worthy of its attachment, so that the heart shall be prevailed upon not to resign an old affection, which shall have nothing to succeed it, but to exchange an old affection for a new one. My purpose is to show that from the constitution of our nature, the former method is altogether incompetent and ineffectual, and that the latter method will alone suffice for the rescue and recovery of the heart from the wrong affection that domineers over it.[1]

---

1. "The Expulsive Power of a New Affection," in *The Protestant Pulpit: An Anthology of Master Sermons from the Reformation to Our Own Day*, comp. Andrew Blackwood (Grand Rapids, MI: Baker, 1947), 50.

The Place of Warning and Fear

To be sure, part of God's way in working for our transformation is to use abundant warnings of dire things that will come if we press on in paths of disobedience. "I warn you, as I warned you before, that those who do such things will not inherit the kingdom of God" (Gal. 5:21). But the role of fear is always secondary. We are children of God, not slaves:

> You did not receive the spirit of slavery to fall back into fear, but you have received the Spirit of adoption as sons, by whom we cry, "Abba! Father!" The Spirit himself bears witness with our spirit that we are children of God. (Rom. 8:15–16)

The function of fear is to wake us up to the insanity of turning away from the fountain of life to dig useless cisterns in the dust (Jer. 2:12–13). The decisive means of transformation is not dread but delight. Even the Bible-wide prevalence of the call to "fear the Lord" is not in contradiction with this, because when we fear the Lord aright, it is our joy! "O Lord, let your ear be attentive . . . to the prayer of your servants who *delight to fear your name*" (Neh. 1:11; cf. Isa. 11:3).

We Read for Transformation

In these last two chapters, we have focused on the fifth implication of our proposal (see the box at the beginning of the chapter). In chapter 8, we saw Jesus, Peter, and Paul trace Christian transformation back to the seeing and savoring of all that God is for us in Jesus. By this seeing and savoring, we are being changed from one degree of glory to another.

In this chapter, we have now seen an actual example of how that worked in the lives of the Macedonian Christians. Their "abundance of joy" in the grace of God—that is, their savoring the glory of God's grace—had an expansive impulse. It transforms us from self-preoccupied, self-protecting, self-exalting people into Christlike servants who long for the temporal and eternal good of others.

Which means, therefore, that our Bible reading is never just for seeing, never just for learning and doctrine. It is not even just for savoring, if that savoring is thought of in a private way that leaves us unchanged in our relationship with others. No. We read the Bible—we *always* read the Bible—for the kind of seeing and savoring Christ that transforms us into his likeness.

Everything we have seen about being transformed, we have seen *in Scripture.* I say the obvious lest we miss the point of this book. I am not writing in general about the ultimate purpose of God. I am writing about how God pursues his ultimate purposes *through a book, the Bible.* It is the Bible that shows us how God is pursuing his ultimate purpose. And what the Bible shows us is that the Bible itself is indispensable in God's design.

A Clarification

There is perhaps a needed clarification before we end this chapter. What about the hundreds of Bible passages that help us in our pursuit of transformation but don't mention the glory of God? In saying that treasuring that glory above all things is the decisive means of Christ-exalting transformation, I do not intend to nullify, minimize, or twist any of those passages. I have written whole books to show how to take those motivations seriously, as they stand, with no dilution or alteration.[2]

None of those motivational statements should be isolated, as though it expressed everything important in a motivated act. Every part of Scripture has something to contribute to the whole. And there are kinds of revelations in the Scripture that are so central and so comprehensive as to shed light on all the rest. I think 2 Corinthians 3:18–4:6 is that kind of revelation. The necessity of the miracle of 2 Corinthians 4:6 is universally relevant for every person everywhere in the world.

This universally necessary and indispensable miracle enables the ongoing miracle of 2 Corinthians 3:18—"beholding the glory of the Lord, [we] are being transformed from one degree of glory to another." This is not a truth for one part of the church only. It is not a truth for one period of the church only. This is a truth for all Christians in all places at all times. It is relevant for every aspect of Christian transformation. And it is related to every aspect of biblical motivation.

Every Motivation Has to Do with the Enjoyment of God Himself

Therefore, whenever the Bible holds out a promise or a warning to us as a motivation for some act of love, we should never think that the thing

---

2. John Piper, *Future Grace: The Purifying Power of the Promises of God* (Colorado Springs: Multnomah, 2012); John Piper, *Battling Unbelief: Defeating Sin with Superior Pleasure* (Colorado Springs: Multnomah, 2007).

promised or the harm threatened is to be effective in our hearts without reference to the glory of God. If we are attracted by the desirability of something God promises, and hope to enjoy it *without enjoying God in it and by it*, then we are turning God's promise into a summons to idolatry.

A Promise of Provision Is a Promise to Know More of God

For example, when Paul promises the Philippians, "My God will supply every need of yours according to his riches in glory in Christ Jesus" (Phil. 4:19), it would be contrary to Paul's intention if the Philippians found their contentment in the sheer fact that there will be enough money to pay the bills. Paul did not mean for this promise of sufficient resources to be separated from everything else he has said about the all-satisfying greatness of God. He had said, "I count everything as loss because of the surpassing worth of knowing Christ Jesus my Lord" (Phil. 3:8). And he had said, "I know how to be brought low, and I know how to abound. In any and every circumstance, I have learned the secret of facing plenty and hunger, abundance and need" (Phil. 4:12).

In other words, when Paul promised them sufficient resources, he intended that in and by that provision they would see something of their God, their treasure. He intended that they would value the promise for God's sake. As Augustine prays, "He loves Thee too little who loves anything together with Thee, which he loves not for Thee."[3]

The Radiance in All Creation and All Motivation

God promises us many good things, not just himself—good things he has created for our use and enjoyment (1 Tim. 4:1–4; 6:17). He did not create the material world merely to test us with possible idols. The world is to be used and enjoyed with thankfulness and with an awareness that every good thing God has made communicates something of God. We may be rightly motivated by it when we see him in it and through it.

Therefore, when I say that we should always read the Bible to see and savor the glory of God, I am not referring to the glory of God as

---

3. Augustine, "The Confessions of St. Augustin," in *The Confessions and Letters of St. Augustin with a Sketch of His Life and Work*, ed. Philip Schaff, trans. J. G. Pilkington, vol. 1, A Select Library of the Nicene and Post-Nicene Fathers of the Christian Church, First Series (Buffalo, NY: Christian Literature Co., 1886), 153.

a "thing" separated from all the created things in the Bible and all the hundreds of motives in the Bible. Rather, the glory of God is the radiance of God, the beauty of God, the greatness of God in and through all created realities and all biblical motivations. In fact, what we have seen is that God's glory is the main thing in all those realities. When the Bible says that the heavens are telling the glory *of God*, that is the main thing about the heavens. There are ten thousand things to study about the heavens. But that is the main thing. And so it is with every created reality. And every biblical motive for holiness and for love.

Augustine's Transformation

Since I have quoted Augustine, it may be fitting to close this chapter with the story of his own transformation through savoring the glory of God in his word. Augustine is one of the greatest theologians in history (AD 354–430). But he was in bondage, as he himself admitted, to sexual sin until he was thirty-one years old. He had kept a concubine for fifteen years. Then, in a garden at Milan, Italy, everything changed. Here is Augustine's narration of his struggles and his transformation:

> I was asking myself these questions, weeping all the while with the most bitter sorrow in my heart, when all at once I heard the sing-song voice of a child in a nearby house. Whether it was the voice of a boy or girl I cannot say, but again and again it repeated the refrain "Take it and read." "Take it and read." At this I looked up, thinking hard whether there was any kind of game in which children used to chant words like these, but I cannot remember ever hearing them before. I stemmed my flood of tears and stood up, telling myself that this could only be a divine command to open my book of Scripture and read the first page on which my eyes should fall. . . .
>
> So I hurried back to the place where Alypius was sitting, for when I stood up to move away I had put down the book containing Paul's Epistles. I seized it and opened it, and in silence I read the first passage on which my eyes fell: *Not in reveling and drunkenness, not in lust and wantonness, not in quarrels and rivalries. Rather, arm yourselves with the Lord Jesus Christ; spend no more thought on nature and nature's appetites.*
>
> I had no wish to read more and no need to do so. For in an instant, as I came to the end of the sentence, it was as though the light

of confidence flooded into my heart and all the darkness of doubt was dispelled.[4]

Augustine's darkness-banishing experience of God's word was not superficially based on the mere *coincidence* of reading something so surprisingly relevant to his sexual sin. We know it was deeper than that because of its lasting effect, and because of his own insight into what really happened. He tells us later what began at that moment and continued through the rest of his life:

> How sweet all at once it was for me to be rid of those fruitless joys which I had once feared to lose! . . . *You drove them from me, you who are the true, the sovereign joy.* You drove them from me and took their place. . . . O Lord my God, my Light, my Wealth, and my Salvation.[5]

That is the way God has designed the Scriptures to transform his people. The glory of Christ is revealed. The eyes are opened. And Christ is seen and savored as "my Light, my Wealth, and my Salvation." And in that sight, "sovereign joy" drives out "fruitless joys" and takes their place. Beholding the glory of the Lord, by reading the word of the Lord, Augustine was changed from one degree of glory to another.

---

4. Aurelius Augustine, *Confessions,* trans. R. S. Pine-Coffin (New York: Penguin, 1961), bk. 8, chap. 12; emphasis added.
5. Ibid., bk. 9, chap. 1; emphasis added.

The creation waits with eager longing for the revealing of the sons of God. . . . The creation itself will be set free from its bondage to corruption and obtain the freedom of the glory of the children of God.

ROMANS 8:19–21

Worthy are you to take the scroll and to open its seals, for you were slain, and by your blood you ransomed people for God from every tribe and language and people and nation.

REVELATION 5:9

10

Reading toward the Consummation

"Ransomed . . . for God from every tribe."

The Proposal

Our ultimate goal in reading the Bible is that God's infinite worth and beauty would be exalted in the everlasting, white-hot worship of the blood-bought bride of Christ from every people, language, tribe, and nation. This implies:

1. that the infinite worth and beauty of God are *the ultimate value and excellence* of the universe;
2. that the supremely *authentic and intense worship* of God's worth and beauty is the ultimate aim of all his work and word;
3. that we should always read his word in order to *see* this supreme worth and beauty;
4. that we should aim in all our seeing to *savor* his excellence above all things;
5. that we should aim to be *transformed* by this seeing and savoring into the likeness of his beauty,
6. so that more and more people would be drawn into the worshiping family of God until the bride of Christ—across all centuries and cultures—is complete in number and beauty.

From Scripture's Words to Worshiping Family

Emanating from the Christian Scriptures is the glory of God for those who have eyes to see. There is a divine and supernatural light that infuses the whole inspired testimony of Scripture. Wherever we read in the Bible, if we see what is really there, we see the glory of what God is for us in Jesus. This kind of seeing wakens a savoring. There is not true seeing without savoring, for Jesus called such seeing a "not-seeing." "Seeing they do not see" (Matt. 13:13). True seeing sees the glory of God *as beautiful*—as precious, as satisfying, as a supreme treasure. It is a miracle. "This comes from the Lord who is the Spirit" (2 Cor. 3:18).

What we saw in chapters 8 and 9 is that this seeing and savoring is profoundly transforming. "Beholding the glory of the Lord, [we] are being transformed" (2 Cor. 3:18). Establishing God himself in the human soul as its supreme treasure disestablishes the "deceitful desires" of sin that betray us into believing that anything is more desirable than God. In this way, the seen and savored glory of God severs the root of selfishness and sets us on the path of love.

So God pursues his ultimate purpose by means of the inspired Scriptures. Through them he reveals his plan for the universe, his saving work in Christ, and the glory of all his ways. Through this revelation he creates, gathers, transforms, and finally perfects a family of worshipers to fill the coming new earth with the glory of the Lord.

The Sixth Implication

The proposal I am trying to clarify and justify is that our ultimate goal in reading the Bible is that God's infinite worth and beauty would be exalted in the everlasting, white-hot worship of the blood-bought bride of Christ from every people, language, tribe, and nation. We have come now to the sixth implication of this proposal: Through the transformation of a people by the seen and savored glory of Christ, more and more people will be drawn into the worshiping family of God until the bride of Christ—across all centuries and cultures—is complete in number and beauty.

A Beautiful Bride for the Son of God

It is astounding that God's ultimate purpose would include the creation of a new people transformed to be a beautiful bride for the Son of God. Surely, in revealing this to us in the Scriptures, God means for us to revel in the thrilling implications of this kind of family closeness to the Father and the Son. What this will mean for our glory and our joy is beyond imagination. But this is why we linger over and meditate on God's word, and why we write poems and songs, and why we worship and gather together to stir each other up with shared glimpses of glory.

We know the preparation of a bride for the Son of God was God's plan from the beginning. Paul makes this plain by connecting Christ's relation to the church with the marriage of Adam and Eve. First, he tells husbands to love their wives "as Christ loved the church and gave himself up for her" (Eph. 5:25). Then he describes how Christ's saving work on the cross was designed to create a beautiful bride:

> . . . that he might sanctify her, having cleansed her by the washing of water with the word, *so that he might present the church to himself in splendor*, without spot or wrinkle or any such thing, that she might be holy and without blemish. (Eph. 5:26–27)

This is the transforming work we focused on in chapters 8 and 9. Christ carries it out by his Spirit through the word.

Then Paul connects this marriage between Christ and the church with the marriage of Adam and Eve. He quotes Genesis 2:24, "Therefore a man shall leave his father and mother and hold fast to his wife, and the two shall become one flesh." Finally, Paul makes the application of Genesis 2:24 explicit: "This mystery is profound, and I am saying that it refers to Christ and the church" (Eph. 5:25–32). In other words, when God designed marriage for Adam and Eve as a covenant with each other in a new family unit, he was modeling human marriage on the divine marriage he already had in mind for Christ.

God's Roundabout Way of Preparing a Bride

Then God put in motion a plan to have a bride for his Son made up of redeemed and transformed people from every ethnic group on the earth. He went about this in a way that is so roundabout and baffling to ordinary human expectations that Paul finished telling the story by saying, "Oh, the depth of the riches and wisdom and knowledge of

God! How unsearchable are his judgments and how inscrutable his ways!" (Rom. 11:33).

Instead of launching the Great Commission in Genesis and gathering all the nations, he chose a single ethnic group to make the focus of his saving work—the Jews. "You are a people holy to the LORD your God. The LORD your God has chosen you to be a people for his treasured possession, out of all the peoples who are on the face of the earth" (Deut. 7:6). And in choosing Israel for his "treasured possession," he spoke of himself as her husband. "Your Maker is your husband, the LORD of hosts is his name; and the Holy One of Israel is your Redeemer, the God of the whole earth he is called" (Isa. 54:5). In some of the most vivid words in the Old Testament, God described his election of Israel as his betrothal to a bloody foundling:

> When I passed by you and saw you wallowing in your blood, I said to you in your blood, "Live!" I said to you in your blood, "Live!" I made you flourish like a plant of the field. And you grew up and became tall and arrived at full adornment. Your breasts were formed, and your hair had grown; yet you were naked and bare. When I passed by you again and saw you, behold, you were at the age for love, and I spread the corner of my garment over you and covered your nakedness; I made my vow to you and entered into a covenant with you, declares the Lord GOD, and you became mine. (Ezek. 16:6–8)

With some exceptions (like the stories of Ruth and Esther and Jonah and some psalms that summoned the nations), God focused his special revelation on one ethnic group, Israel. Nevertheless, from the beginning, in some strange way (which Paul calls a mystery in Eph. 3:6), God's purpose was that this focus on Israel was designed to eventually include all the nations of the world. The focus on Israel began with Abram (later called Abraham). And the promise to him included these words: "In you all the families of the earth shall be blessed" (Gen. 12:3).

God's (Temporary) Turn from Israel to the Nations

As it turned out, Israel was not obedient to God in a way that fitted them for the consummation of God's purposes. To be sure, there was always a remnant in Israel who were faithful to God (Isa. 10:22–23;

Rom. 9:27). But by and large, the people were rebellious. When the Messiah Jesus came and proclaimed the kingdom of God, only a small number from Israel embraced their King. For most, a crucified Messiah was a stumbling block (1 Cor. 1:23).

So Jesus told a parable about his rejection and interpreted it with these terrible words for Israel: "The kingdom of God will be taken away from you and given to a people producing its fruits" (Matt. 21:43). He pronounced the same judgment in Matthew 8:11–12: "Many will come from east and west and recline at table with Abraham, Isaac, and Jacob in the kingdom of heaven, while the sons of the kingdom will be thrown into the outer darkness."

So God turned his direct and special focus of special revelation and transformation away from Israel and focused his saving work on the creation of a family from all the nations. Paul pointed out that by faith in Jesus, a Gentile could be united with "the seed of Abraham" (Gal. 3:16 KJV), and so be a full beneficiary of all the promises made to faithful Israel. Here is Paul's great explanation of how there is only one people of God—from Jew and Gentile:

> In Christ Jesus you are all sons of God, through faith. For as many of you as were baptized into Christ have put on Christ. There is neither Jew nor Greek, there is neither slave nor free, there is no male and female, for you are all one in Christ Jesus. And if you are Christ's, then you are Abraham's offspring, heirs according to promise. (Gal. 3:26–29)

The Future of Israel in the People of the Messiah

So, when I say that God turned his direct and special focus of special revelation and transformation away from Israel, I don't mean that his new focus on gathering a people from all nations excluded Jews. In fact, Paul modeled in his own ministry that the gospel should be delivered "to the Jew first and also to the Greek" (Rom. 1:16). He prayed earnestly for his Jewish kinsmen to be saved (Rom. 10:1). And he said, "I magnify my ministry in order somehow to make my fellow Jews jealous, and thus save some of them" (Rom. 11:13–14). But the response to his evangelism among Israel was not great (similar to the response to Jesus) and, just as Jesus wept over Jerusalem (Luke 19:41–44), Paul had "great sorrow and unceasing anguish" that most of his Jewish kinsmen were "accursed and cut off from Christ" (Rom. 9:2–3).

Paul saw this failure of Israel to accept her Messiah as a mysterious part of God's plan to bring salvation to all the nations of the world. And he saw that the ingathering of the Gentiles, during what Jesus called "the times of the Gentiles" (Luke 21:24), would eventually lead to the removal of Israel's hardening so that a great turning to Christ would eventually come to Israel.

Thus Paul said, "If their [the Jews'] rejection means the reconciliation of the world, what will their acceptance mean but life from the dead?" (Rom. 11:15). A few verses later, he said, "I do not want you to be unaware of this mystery, brothers: a partial hardening has come upon Israel, until the fullness of the Gentiles has come in" (Rom. 11:25). Then, when that full number of the nations comes in, "all Israel will be saved" (Rom. 11:26).[1] Then just before crying out, "How unsearchable are his judgments and how inscrutable his ways!" (Rom. 11:33), Paul sums up God's mysterious, roundabout way of gathering a people:

> Just as you [Gentiles] were at one time disobedient to God but now have received mercy because of their [Jewish] disobedience, so they [Israel] too have now been disobedient in order that by the mercy shown to you [Gentiles] they [the Jews] also may now receive mercy. For God has consigned all [Jew and Gentile] to disobedience, that he may have mercy on all. (Rom. 11:30–32)

The Times of the Gentiles

We live in the period of history that God designed for the ingathering of his ransomed people from all the peoples of the world. During his lifetime, Jesus was still focusing on Israel. He said, "I was sent only to the lost sheep of the house of Israel" (Matt. 15:24). But after his rejection was decisive, he ended his earthly stay with these momentous words:

> All authority in heaven and on earth has been given to me. Go therefore and make disciples of *all nations*, baptizing them in the name

---

1. Not everyone construes the phrase "all Israel" here the way I do. Some refer it only to the elect from Jew and Gentile—the true Israel without reference to ethnicity. For a fuller explication of my view, see http://www.desiringgod.org/scripture/romans/11/messages.

of the Father and of the Son and of the Holy Spirit, teaching them to observe all that I have commanded you. And behold, I am with you always, to the end of the age. (Matt. 28:18–20)

This Great Commission—which we know only from Scripture—defines our time. All authority. All nations. All things he commanded. This is our task. With his authority, we preach to all nations. By the Scriptures and the Spirit, we seek the ingathering and the transformation of a people who *observe all he commanded.*

Jesus Is Preparing His Bride

When we say we do this "by his authority," we don't just mean Jesus authorized the mission. We mean he is presently the decisive force in the mission. He bought his bride by his own blood, and he is gathering her from all peoples. He said, "I will build my church, and the gates of hell shall not prevail against it" (Matt. 16:18). *He* is building—today! He also said, "I have other sheep that are not of this fold. I *must bring* them also, and *they will* listen to my voice. So *there will be* one flock, one shepherd" (John 10:16). Note the authority of his own involvement in the mission today. "I *must* bring them." "They *will* listen to my voice." "There *will* be one flock."

Jesus had died "not for the nation [of Israel] only, but also to gather into one the children of God who are scattered abroad" (John 11:52). "Scattered abroad" meant scattered among all the peoples of the world. We know this because the same author (John) celebrated the extent and diversity of Christ's purchase with these words: "Worthy are you to take the scroll and to open its seals, for you were slain, and by your blood you ransomed people for God *from every tribe and language and people and nation*" (Rev. 5:9).

There is no doubt that this ransom will be totally effective in its purpose. John says that these ransomed ones will, in fact, inhabit the future world with God. He has seen it in a vision. "I looked, and behold, [there was] a great multitude that no one could number, from every nation, from all tribes and peoples and languages, standing before the throne and before the Lamb, clothed in white robes" (Rev. 7:9).

This redeemed people from all the nations of the world is the bride of the Lamb, Jesus Christ:

"Let us rejoice and exult and give him the glory, for the marriage
of the Lamb has come, and his Bride has made herself ready; it was
granted her to clothe herself with fine linen, bright and pure"—for
the fine linen is the righteous deeds of the saints. (Rev. 19:7–8)

The time will come when her number will be complete. There is a "fullness" as Paul says. The second coming of Christ is being delayed until
the full number comes to repentance (2 Pet. 3:9). The bride will be
perfect, by God's reckoning, both in number and in beauty.

God's Plan for History Comes by Means of the Scriptures

The number and the beauty of the bride are brought about by the Scriptures. Without the Bible, there would be no ingathering of God's people,
and without the Bible, there would be no beautification of the bride.
"Faith comes from hearing, and hearing through the word of Christ"
(Rom. 10:17). So everyone who enters the people of God by faith comes
by the word. So it is, as we saw in chapters 8 and 9, with the beautification (that is, transformation) of God's people. The bride is beautified by
beholding the glory of the Lord (2 Cor. 3:18) in the word of the Lord
(2 Cor. 4:4). And that transformation itself becomes a means of more
and more people seeing the glory of God and wakening to his saving
reality.

The word-sustained process of transformation (or beautification),
which we focused on in chapters 8 and 9, continues until its completion
at the coming of Christ. At that moment, in the coming of the Lord, the
bride will be perfect in number and beauty. This completion is as sure
as the ultimate purpose of God—the purpose *that his infinite worth
and beauty would be exalted in the everlasting, white-hot worship of
the blood-bought bride of Christ from every people, language, tribe,
and nation.*

God's Work Is Decisive, and Ours Is Necessary

But this certainty stands side by side with contingency. That is, it is *sure*
that God will complete the number and beauty of his bride for the sake
of his worship, and this completion is also *dependent* on human means,
including the use of Scripture. The purpose of God will not succeed
without the word of God. That is the way he designed it.

So, on the one hand, Paul proclaims the certainty of the completion of the beautification of God's people—the certainty of their final holiness and blamelessness and love:

> May the God of peace himself sanctify you completely, and may your whole spirit and soul and body be kept blameless at the coming of our Lord Jesus Christ. He who calls you is faithful; *he will surely do it.* (1 Thess. 5:23–24)

> You wait for the revealing of our Lord Jesus Christ, *who will sustain you to the end, guiltless in the day of our Lord Jesus Christ. God is faithful,* by whom you were called into the fellowship of his Son, Jesus Christ our Lord. (1 Cor. 1:7–9).

> *I am sure of this,* that he who began a good work in you *will bring it to completion* at the day of Jesus Christ. (Phil. 1:6)

However, on the other hand, Paul also makes clear that this completion of our holiness is contingent on human acts. It is *certain* because *God* will see to it. It is *contingent* because *man* must also see to it. God's agency is *decisive.* But ours is *real.* This is possible because God works in and through our action. "It is *God who works in you,* both to will and to work for his good pleasure" (Phil. 2:13). He equips "you with everything good that you may do his will, *working in us that which is pleasing in his sight*" (Heb. 13:21).

Our Part in the Transformation Is Real

Our part in pursuing God's ultimate purpose to have a beautiful people is real: Christ "has now reconciled [you] in his body of flesh by his death, in order to present you holy and blameless and above reproach before him, *if indeed you continue in the faith*" (Col. 1:21–23). The completion of our holiness and blamelessness is *contingent.* We will be presented complete *if we continue in the faith.* But it is also *certain* because *God is faithful and he will do it* (1 Thess. 5:24).

The "if" is real. Will you "continue in the faith"? Will you endure to the end? "The one who endures to the end will be saved" (Matt. 24:13). "In due season we will reap, *if we do not give up*" (Gal. 6:9). "We are his house, *if indeed we hold fast our confidence*" (Heb. 3:6).

Will We Use the Scriptures to Pursue God's Great Goal?

This raises a related question: Will we "strive for the holiness without which no one will see the Lord" (Heb. 12:14)? That is, will we use the means God has appointed in the process of beautifying his Son's bride? Specifically, will we read and hear the word of God? Will we return again and again to behold the glory of the Lord in order to be changed by seeing and savoring him (2 Cor. 3:18)? And since that *seeing* happens by the word, will we store up the word in our heart (Ps. 119:11)? Will we cry out to God that he incline our hearts to his testimonies (Ps. 119:36)? Will we meditate on the instruction of the Lord day and night (Ps. 1:2)?

The ultimate purpose of God—to be worshiped with white-hot affection by a redeemed people, complete in number and beauty—*will* be accomplished by the one who "works all things according to the counsel of his will" (Eph. 1:11). There is no doubt about it. He cannot fail. And he will do it by his Spirit *through his word*. Through the reading of the Scriptures.

The New Heavens and the New Earth

Suppose someone asks this good question: Why do you express the ultimate purpose of God without reference to the new heavens and the new earth? I certainly asked it, as I formulated my proposal: . . . *that our ultimate goal in reading the Bible is that God's infinite worth and beauty would be exalted in the everlasting, white-hot worship of the blood-bought bride of Christ from every people, language, tribe, and nation.* And I thought about it in relation to the final implication: the transformation of God's people is *so that more and more people would be drawn into the worshiping family of God until the bride of Christ—across all centuries and cultures—is complete in number and beauty.*

My answer is that we are not told in Scripture that the written word of God would be the instrument by which God creates the new heavens and the new earth. But we are told that this written word would be the instrument by which a people would be re-created, gathered, transformed, and fitted to fill the new earth with the glory of the Lord. This is a book about how to use the Scripture in the pursuit of what the Scriptures were designed to accomplish. The Scriptures were not designed to create the new heavens and the new earth. But they were designed to create, gather, transform, and fit a people to fill the new earth. That is why I stated God's goal the way I did.

The Worshiping People over the Glorious Place

Lest I give the impression that this white-hot worship from a redeemed people is an immaterial, ethereal choir without body or place, let me close this chapter with a corrective. But even in the corrective, I will maintain the priority of the worshiping people over the spectacular universe of the new creation. The key passage is Romans 8:18–23. Note the italicized words:

> For I consider that the sufferings of this present time are not worth comparing with the glory that is to be revealed to us. For *the creation waits with eager longing for the revealing of the sons of God.* For the creation was subjected to futility, not willingly, but because of him who subjected it, in hope that the creation itself will be set free from its bondage to corruption and *obtain the freedom of the glory of the children of God.* For we know that the whole creation has been groaning together in the pains of childbirth until now. And not only the creation, but we ourselves, who have the firstfruits of the Spirit, groan inwardly as we wait eagerly for adoption as sons, the redemption of our bodies.

Since the fall of Adam and Eve into sin, the material creation has been subjected to "futility" (v. 20) and "bondage to corruption" (v. 21). That includes our bodies (v. 23), as well as the groaning of the "whole creation" (v. 22). But this groaning is intended by God not as the death gasps of a dying patient, but as the birth pangs of a new creation (v. 22). The creation was subjected to destruction *in hope* that it would be set free from corruption (v. 21). So the new heavens and the new earth are coming (Isa. 65:17; 66:22; 2 Pet. 3:13).

But the astonishing thing is that the great transformation of the natural order "waits with eager longing for *the revealing of the sons of God*" (Rom. 8:19). When the time for that transformation comes, Paul says, the creation will "*obtain the freedom of the glory of the children of God*" (v. 21). Both of these statements imply that the new heavens and the new earth are *the inheritance of the children*. The universe—new and old—is not important in itself. It is important as the playground of the children of God—and as the temple and the farm and the craft shop. God doesn't design his children for the universe. He designs the universe for his children. This was true from the beginning, and it is true in the end.

Therefore, I heartily and joyfully and expectantly affirm the cosmic scope of Christ's redeeming work. The ultimate goal of God in creation and redemption embraces the fullness and beauty of the bride, and the fullness and beauty of her place—the new heavens and the new earth. But the renewed cosmos exists for the sake of the bride, not the other way around. And the cosmos will reach its final purpose when the saints enjoy God *in* it and *through* it and *over* it with white-hot admiration for the Creator and the Redeemer.

Conclusion to Part 1

This will not happen without the Scriptures. God has made the *written* word as indispensable as the *incarnate* Word. For the achievement of God's ultimate purpose, he has made Christ essential and the Bible essential. The Bible is not as glorious, not as ultimate, not as foundational, as Christ. But both are indispensable.

They are both essential, but not in the same way. There is no forgiveness of sins, no righteousness before God, no new birth, no seeing, no savoring, no transformation without Christ and his death and resurrection. He purchased these things and became the foundation of our salvation in a way that the Scriptures never could and never will. We are not making Christ and the Scriptures interchangeable. Christ is the foundation of the Scriptures, not the other way around.

Nevertheless, God has made the Scriptures indispensable to the consummation of all things. He has ordained that without the written word—explaining and preserving who God is and what he has done—there would be no saving knowledge of God, no new birth, no faith, no seeing and savoring, no experience of forgiveness, no transformation, and, in the end, no completed and beautified bride for the Son and no white-hot worshiping family for the Father.

But we thank God with all our hearts that Christ has come and died and risen. And the Scriptures have been inspired and preserved. And, therefore, God's ultimate purpose for all things is on track. Because of his gracious sovereignty, and his redeeming work in Christ, and his quickening Spirit, and his written word, it is sure that in his time *God's infinite worth and beauty will be exalted in the everlasting, white-hot worship of the blood-bought bride of Christ from every people, language, tribe, and nation.*

The Supernatural Act of
Reading the Bible

We impart a secret and hidden wisdom of God, which God decreed before the ages for our glory. . . . And we impart this in words not taught by human wisdom but taught by the Spirit, interpreting spiritual truths to those who are spiritual.

1 CORINTHIANS 2:7, 13

Introduction to Part 2

One of the implications of part 1 was not listed in the six implications of the main proposal. It follows from all six of them and stands as the main point of this book—or we shall now see if it stands. That implication is this: *a proper reading of the Bible is a supernatural act.* What does that mean? And is it what the Bible itself really teaches? But first, let's restate the proposal of part 1 and how it gives rise to these questions. The proposal of part 1 was that

> the Bible itself shows that our ultimate goal in reading the Bible is that God's infinite worth and beauty would be exalted in the everlasting, white-hot worship of the blood-bought bride of Christ from every people, language, tribe, and nation.

In other words, God planned that the Bible—reading the Bible—would be an indispensable means of bringing about the ultimate purpose of creation and redemption. Working our way backward, we can describe the plan like this:

- Since the ultimate purpose of God is to be enjoyed and exalted in the *worship* of a beautiful bride, God's people must be *transformed* from glory to glory into the image of Christ.

- This transformation happens by means of *savoring* the glory of the Lord Jesus—that is, by being satisfied by Christ and supremely treasuring all that God is for us in him.

- This savoring of all that God is for us in Jesus happens by means of *seeing* the glory of Jesus for who he really is—more valuable and more beautiful than anything.

- This seeing is possible only because God reveals his peculiar glory to us through the inspired *Scriptures*.

- *Reading* these Scriptures—or hearing someone communicate them—is the means God has appointed for his word to have these glorious effects.

Therefore, reading the Bible is God's indispensable means of bringing about his ultimate purpose for creation and redemption.

God Intends That We Read His Word Supernaturally

In view of what we have seen in part 1, the implication staring us in the face is that God intends for us to read his word in a way that involves actions and experiences of the human soul that are beyond ordinary human experience. *Seeing* the glory of Jesus is not merely with our ordinary physical eyes, but with "the eyes of [our] hearts" (Eph. 1:18), and "comes from the Lord who is the Spirit" (2 Cor. 3:18). *Savoring* the glory of God is no ordinary human pleasure but is Christ's own joy in his Father, experienced in us by the presence of his Spirit (John 15:11). Our *transformation* is no ordinary moral rearmament or self-improvement but is brought about by the Holy Spirit (Rom. 8:13).

In other words, the act of reading that pursues God's purposes for reading is a profoundly supernatural experience. We will see in part 3 how *natural* the act of reading is in one sense. But, so far, it appears that reading is far more than natural. It appears that our entire encounter with the Bible, even if it involves our natural abilities, is a supernatural encounter.

This would seem to imply that whatever we meet in the Bible— historical facts, poetic praises, proverbial wisdom, promises of help, descriptions of God's nature, illustrations of God's ways, standards of holy living, procedures of church discipline, predictions, calamities, warnings of satanic opposition, summons to faith, analyses of human depravity, directions for husbands and wives, political insights, financial principles, and much more—all of it will be seen aright only when we see it illumined by, and in relation to, the peculiar glory of God. In other words, no matter how natural the process of reading is, and no matter how natural the objects discovered are, no reading and no discovery happen without dependence on God or without seeing all things in relation to his worth and beauty—*if* we are reading the way God means for his book to be read.

This part of the book—part 2—is intended to test whether this is, in fact, so.

He opened their minds to understand the Scriptures.

LUKE 24:45

To you has been given the secret of the kingdom of God, but for those outside everything is in parables.

MARK 4:11

Blessed are you, Simon Bar-Jonah! For flesh and blood has not revealed this to you, but my Father who is in heaven.

MATTHEW 16:17

11

The Necessity and Possibility of Reading the Bible Supernaturally

"He opened their minds to
understand the Scriptures."

How Is Reading the Bible Supernatural?

Why must reading the Bible be a supernatural act? By "supernatural act," I don't mean that humans are supernatural. We are not God, and we are not angels or demons. What I mean is that the act of reading, in order to be done as God intended, must be done in dependence on God's supernatural help. The Bible gives two decisive reasons: Satan and sin. That is, we have a blinding enemy outside and a blinding disease inside. Together these two forces make it impossible for human beings to read the Bible, as God intended, without supernatural help.

It is crucial that we realize this. It seems to me that thousands of people approach the Bible with little sense of their own helplessness in reading the way God wants them to. That's why I am writing part 2 of this book. This proverb applies as much to Bible reading as to anything else: "Trust in the LORD with all your heart, and do not lean on your own understanding. In all your ways acknowledge him, and he will make straight your paths" (Prov. 3:5–6). At every turn of the page, rely on God. That is a supernatural transaction. If more people approached the Bible with a deep sense of helplessness, and hope-filled reliance on

God's merciful assistance, there would be far more seeing and savoring and transformation than there is.

The Blinding Enemy Outside

Satan is real. His main identity is "a liar and the father of lies" (John 8:44). His way of lying is more by deception than bold-face falsehoods. He "is called the devil and Satan, the *deceiver* of the whole world" (Rev. 12:9). Therefore, he hates "the Spirit of truth" (John 15:26). He hates God the Father from whom the Spirit proceeds (John 15:26). He hates the Son of God, who is truth (John 14:6). And he hates the word of God because God's "word is truth" (John 17:17).

Therefore, he will do his best to take away the word, if he can, and twist it, if he can't—the way he did in the garden of Eden (Gen. 3:1) and in the temptations of Jesus (Matt. 4:6). Jesus described how Satan takes away the word: "When anyone hears the word of the kingdom and does not understand it, the evil one comes and snatches away what has been sown in his heart" (Matt. 13:19). How does that happen? It might be by sheer forgetfulness. Or Satan may draw a person from Bible reading to an entertaining video, with the result that any thought of Christ's worth and beauty is quickly lost in the flash of fire and skin.

Or Satan may simply blind the mind to the worth and beauty of Christ, which the Scriptures reveal. This is what Paul describes in 2 Corinthians 4:3–4:

> Even if our gospel is veiled, it is veiled to those who are perishing. In their case *the god of this world has blinded the minds of the unbelievers*, to keep them from seeing the light of the gospel of the glory of Christ, who is the image of God.

"The god of this world" is Satan. He is called "the ruler of this world" (John 12:31; 14:30), and John says that "the whole world lies in the power of the evil one" (1 John 5:19). It is this enormous blinding power that puts us in need of a supernatural deliverer. The thought that we could overcome this satanic force on our own is naïve.

No Opening of the Eyes without Divine Power

When the risen Christ sent Paul "to open their [the Gentiles] eyes, so that they may turn from darkness to light and from *the power of Satan* to God" (Acts 26:18), he did not mean that Paul could do this in human strength. Paul made that clear: "My speech and my message were not in plausible words of wisdom, but in *demonstration of the Spirit and of power*, so that your faith might not rest in the wisdom of men but in *the power of God*" (1 Cor. 2:4–5). That is what it takes to overcome the blinding effects of Satan.

Let it not be missed that the specific focus of Satan's blinding work is the gospel. That is, his focus is on our reading—or hearing—the heart of the message of the Christian Scriptures. Satan "has blinded the minds of the unbelievers, to keep them from seeing *the light of the gospel* of the glory of Christ." Satan would be happy for people to believe ten thousand true facts, as long as they are blind to "the light of the gospel of the glory of Christ." Let them make A's on a hundred Bible-fact quizzes as long as they can't see the glory of Christ in the gospel—that is, as long as they can't read (or listen) with the ability to see what is really there.

Bible Reading That Satan Leaves Alone

So Jesus (Matt. 13:19), Paul (2 Cor. 4:3–4), and John (1 John 5:19) warn that Satan is a great enemy of Bible reading that sees what is really there. Bible reading that only collects facts, or relieves a guilty conscience, or gathers doctrinal arguments, or titillates aesthetic literary tastes, or feeds historical curiosities—this kind of Bible reading Satan is perfectly happy to leave alone. He has already won the battle.

But reading that hopes to see the supreme worth and beauty of God—reading that aims to be satisfied with all that God is for us in Christ, reading that seeks to "taste and see that the LORD is good" (Ps. 34:8)—this reading Satan will oppose with all his might. And his might is supernatural. Therefore, any reading that hopes to overcome his blinding power will be a supernatural reading.

We Are Complicit in Satanic Deception

When we speak of the power of Satan over the human heart, we are not saying that all spiritual blindness is the sole work of Satan. We are not implying that Satan can take innocent people and make them slaves of deceit. There are no innocent people. "All have sinned and fall short of the glory of God" (Rom. 3:23). We are complicit in all our deception.

There is a terrible interweaving of satanic influence and human sinfulness in all our blindness to divine glory. You can see this inter-weaving in Ephesians 2:1–3:

> You were dead in the trespasses and sins in which you once walked,
> following the course of this world, following the prince of the power
> of the air, the spirit that is now at work in the sons of disobedi-
> ence—among whom we all once lived in the passions of our flesh,
> carrying out the desires of the body and the mind, and were by
> nature children of wrath, like the rest of mankind.

Notice *both* influences: first, "dead in sins," and, second, "following the prince of the power of the air." We are not innocent victims of this power. We are ready partners. Following the power of Satan and liv-ing "in the passions of our flesh" are two ways of describing the same path. We are, Paul says, "by nature children of wrath." So is "the rest of mankind." That is, our human nature is both corrupt and guilty. We deserve God's wrath. Therefore, no one will ever be able to scapegoat at the judgment, claiming, "Satan made me do it."

The Mind of the Flesh

Therefore, our own sinfulness is another source of our spiritual blind-ness that puts us in need of supernatural help, if we hope to see the glory of God in Scripture. Paul is overwhelmingly clear and strong on this point. For example, in Romans 8:4–9 he says there are two kinds of humans: "those who *are* according to the flesh" and "those who *are* according to the Spirit" (v. 5, literal translation). That is, one kind of person is deeply defined by the "flesh"—the merely human nature, apart of any transformation by the Spirit. And another kind of person is deeply defined by the "Spirit"—the supernatural invasion and trans-formation by the Holy Spirit.

Who are these two groups of humans? Paul says that the Christians are those who "are according to the Spirit." Verse 9: "You, however, are not in the flesh but in the Spirit, if in fact the Spirit of God dwells in you. Anyone who does not have the Spirit of Christ does not belong to him." The non-Christians, on the other hand, have "the mind of the flesh." This mind-set is "hostile to God, for it does not submit to God's law; indeed, it cannot. Those who are in the flesh cannot please God" (Rom. 8:7–8).

A Real *Cannot* in Our Heart

What then is the effect of this *flesh identity* of unbelievers on reading God's word? Paul tells us in verses 7–8: "The mind that is set on the flesh is hostile to God, for *it does not submit to God's law; indeed, it cannot.* Those who are in the flesh cannot please God." These are very strong words: "It *does* not submit to God's law [God's instruction, God's word]; indeed it *cannot.*" This is our rebellion prior to, and underneath, all satanic blinding. Before Satan adds his blinding effects, we are already in rebellion against God. And, Paul says, this rebellion makes it *impossible* ("cannot") for us to submit to the word of God.

That is, because of this flesh identity, we cannot acknowledge that the glory of God is more to be desired than anything else. Paul has already said that we "suppress" that knowledge (Rom. 1:18). We have "exchanged the glory of God for images" (Rom. 1:23). We prefer our own glory, and therefore cannot prefer God's. *Cannot.* That is what it means to prefer our own glory. This inability (this "cannot," v. 7) is *not* the inability of a person who prefers God but is not allowed to cherish him. No. This is the inability of a person who does *not* prefer God and therefore *cannot* cherish him. It is not an inability that keeps you from doing what you want. It is an inability to want what you don't want. You can't see as beautiful what you see as ugly. You can't embrace the glory of God as most valuable when you feel yourself to be more valuable.

Ignorance Is Not Our Deepest Problem

One of the implications of this pervasive human condition is that ignorance is not our deepest problem. There is a hardness of rebellion against God that is deeper than ignorance. That is why every natural attempt at enlightenment is resisted. This hardness of rebellion cannot submit to God's revelation.

Paul issues an urgent call to all Christians at Ephesus to decisively turn away from this condition, which, he says, is typical of their Gentile roots:

> Now this I say and testify in the Lord, that you must no longer walk as the Gentiles do, *in the futility of their minds.* They are *darkened in their understanding,* alienated from the life of God *because of*

the ignorance that is in them, *due to their hardness of heart.* (Eph. 4:17–18)

Notice the relationship between "ignorance" and "hardness of heart" as Paul describes it: "ignorance *due to* their hardness of heart." Hardness is more basic. Hardness is the cause. This is our deepest problem. Not ignorance.

The Impact of Our Hardness on Bible Reading

This is the condition of all mankind, apart from the saving work of the Holy Spirit (Rom. 8:9–10). And it makes reading the Bible impossible—if our aim is to read the way God wants us to read. We cannot submit to what we read. That is, we cannot let ourselves acknowledge that the glory of God is to be desired above all earthly treasures and pleasures. We must suppress this truth. We must exchange the glory of God for images. We cannot prefer the light when we love the dark. "This is the judgment: the light has come into the world, and people loved the darkness rather than the light" (John 3:19). Our problem is not that there is insufficient light shining from the Scriptures. Our problem is that we love the darkness.

The Bible Is Radiant with Divine Wisdom

The Scriptures are radiant with divine wisdom. This wisdom shines with the glory of God—and shows us the glory to come, which is the way Paul describes his own inspired teaching:

> We impart a secret and hidden wisdom of God, which God decreed before the ages for our glory. . . . We have received not the spirit of the world, but the Spirit who is from God, that we might understand the things freely given us by God. And we impart this in words not taught by human wisdom but taught by the Spirit, interpreting spiritual truths to those who are *spiritual.* (1 Cor. 2:7, 12–13)

But the problem is that apart from the supernatural work of the Holy Spirit, we are not "spiritual," but "natural." This makes the reading of Scripture impossible, if our aim is to grasp things "not taught by human wisdom" (1 Cor. 2:13). That's what Paul says next. "The natural person *does not* accept the things of the Spirit of God, for they are folly to him, and he is *not able* to understand them because they are spiritually discerned" (1 Cor. 2:14).

These words "does not accept" and "is not able to understand" are the very same "does not" and "cannot" that we saw in Romans 8:7 ("The mind that is set on the flesh *does not* submit to God's law; indeed, it *cannot*"). And who is it that cannot grasp what Paul teaches? The "natural person." That means all of us, until something *supernatural* happens to us (like the miracle of 2 Corinthians 4:6).

Therefore, reading the inspired Scriptures must be a supernatural act if we are to "accept the things of the Spirit of God," and if we are to "understand what is spiritually discerned." Without God's supernatural aid, we are merely natural and cannot see the glory of God for what it really is—supremely beautiful and all-satisfying. This peculiar, divine glory awakens no compelling affections in us, even though Paul shows that if it did, we would know it is "decreed before the ages *for our glory*" (1 Cor. 2:7). But instead, like the "rulers of this age," we do not cherish the "Lord of glory"; we crucify him (1 Cor. 2:8).

Any Hope to Read as We Ought?

And what is the supernatural act of reading? In essence it is a reliance on God, and the Spirit, and Christ to do for us what we cannot do for ourselves as we seek to *see* what is really there in Scripture, and as we seek to *savor* it and *be transformed* by it. There are several ways that the New Testament describes this divine assistance. We will look at five of them very briefly.

He Opened Their Minds

First, this miracle of divine help in reading is called the "opening" of our minds. After his resurrection from the dead, Jesus met two disciples on the Emmaus road. They did not recognize him, and so they told him, as if he didn't know, all about the crucifixion and resurrection and appearances of Jesus. They were baffled by all this. So Jesus said, "O foolish ones, and slow of heart to believe all that the prophets have spoken! Was it not necessary that the Christ should suffer these things and enter into his glory?" (Luke 24:25–26).

Jesus said that their failure to read the prophets perceptively was owing to *foolishness and slowness of heart*. He did not chalk it up to ignorance but to something in their hearts. Later, in their home, he was revealed to them and then vanished. They said to each other, "Did not our hearts burn within us while he talked to us on the road, while *he opened to us the Scriptures?*" (Luke 24:32). Then they ran to Jerusalem to find the eleven apostles and tell them what they had seen.

While they were gathered, Jesus stood among them and proved to them, by eating some fish, that he was not a ghost. Then he said, "These are my words that I spoke to you while I was still with you, that everything written about me in the Law of Moses and the Prophets and the Psalms must be fulfilled." Then, Luke writes, "*he opened their minds to understand the Scriptures*" (Luke 24:44–45).

So on the road to Emmaus, he "opened the Scriptures," and in the gathering of the eleven, he "opened their minds." Both are needed. One draws out the meaning of the text. The other enables the mind to see and savor the glory of what is really there. Christ took away the "foolishness" and "slowness" of heart. This is the supernatural help that every human needs if we are to read the Bible and see what Jesus expects us to see. It takes the supernatural *opening of our minds*.

He Shone in Our Hearts

Second, the miracle of divine help in reading God's word is compared to God's creation of light at the beginning of the world. We have seen the blinding effect of "the God of this world" in 2 Corinthians 4:4. Now comes the remedy for that blindness, in verse 6. After making clear in verse 5 that the miracle of verse 6 happens through the proclamation of Christ, Paul says, "God, who said, 'Let light shine out of darkness,' has *shone in our hearts* to give the light of the knowledge of the glory of God in the face of Jesus Christ."

The shining "in our hearts to give the light of the knowledge of the glory of God in the face of Jesus Christ" is compared to the divine act of creation: "Let light shine out of darkness." This means that a miracle of creation is needed for any of us to see the glory of God in the "knowledge" we gain in reading the Scriptures or hearing the gospel. Until the miracle of this new creation, we are all darkness—even if we have a PhD in biblical studies. The issue is "the glory of God" revealed in God's word—the worth and beauty of all that he is for us in Christ. That is what we cannot see until God says, "Let there be light."

He Enlightens the Eyes of Our Hearts

Third, the miracle of divine help in reading the Scriptures is called the enlightening of the eyes of our hearts:

> I do not cease to give thanks for you, remembering you in my prayers, that the God of our Lord Jesus Christ, the Father of glory, may give you the Spirit of wisdom and of revelation in the knowledge of him, *having the eyes of your hearts enlightened,* that you may know what is the hope to which he has called you, what are the riches of his glorious inheritance in the saints, and what is the immeasurable greatness of his power toward us who believe, according to the working of his great might. (Eph. 1:16–19)

When Paul prays that we would know our hope and the riches of God's inheritance and the greatness of God's power, he is not praying that God would inform us with *facts* we don't know. The facts have been taught. What he is asking is that we perceive—grasp, comprehend, assess truly, savor—the *glory* of our hope and the *riches* of our inheritance and the *greatness* of his power. This is a prayer not for the seeing of facts, but for the seeing of worth and beauty.

It is like the prayer in Ephesians 3:14–19, where Paul prays that we

> may have strength to comprehend with all the saints what is the breadth and length and height and depth, and to know the love of Christ that surpasses knowledge, that you may be filled with all the fullness of God. (vv. 18–19)

"Strength to comprehend" the incomprehensible! To know what surpasses knowledge. To feel the worth of the love of Christ—a love whose height and depth and length and breadth are immeasurable. That is what these prayers are about. They are about seeing and savoring the glory of God in its extremes of hope and riches and power and love and fullness. Paul is praying that mere awareness would become intense admiration and thankfulness and affection.

Christians Need Ongoing Supernatural Help

Don't miss the obvious here. Ephesians 1:16–19 is a *prayer.* This shows Paul's and our dependence on *God's* supernatural intervention in answer to prayer. And don't miss a second obvious and crucial thing: this prayer is for *believers*, not unbelievers. This means that the once-for-all creation of spiritual sight in our conversion to Christ (2 Cor. 4:6) does not exclude the need for ongoing supernatural help—"enlightening the eyes of the heart" (Eph. 1:18)—repeatedly in the Christian life.

The glory of Christ is not a steady-state brightness in the heart of a Christian. It has degrees. Not only do we "see in a mirror dimly" in this life (1 Cor. 13:12), but we see in varying degrees of dimness. The glory that we will see when we behold him face-to-face will be inexpressibly beyond what we see here with the "eyes of the heart." The apostle John had seen Jesus in the flesh. He had seen his "glory as of the only Son from the Father" (John 1:14). But when he saw him in his resurrection glory on Patmos, he fell down as if dead (Rev. 1:17).

Nevertheless, lest anyone think that what we can see of the glory of Jesus now is insignificant, do not forget that it is greater than the glory of all the things in this world, and it wakens in God's people "joy that is inexpressible and filled with glory" (1 Pet. 1:8). John Owen, who is as aware as anyone that the future glory will vastly outshine the present glory, nevertheless says—and I joyfully concur:

> There is no glory, no peace, no joy, no satisfaction in this world, to be compared with what we receive by that weak and imperfect view which we have of the glory of Christ by faith; yea, all the joys of the world are a thing of nought in comparison of what we so receive.[1]

But we all have our seasons of dimness. We all need to pray Paul's prayer for ourselves over and over. We all need to sing the prayer of the famous hymn "Spirit of God, Descend upon My Heart."

> I ask no dream, no prophet ecstasies,
>   No sudden rending of the veil of clay,
> No angel visitant, no opening skies;
>   But take the dimness of my soul away.[2]

The Gift of the Secret of the Kingdom

Fourth, this divine help in reading the Scriptures is also called a "blessing"—the giving of the secret of the kingdom of God. When the dis-

---

1. John Owen, *The Works of John Owen*, ed. William H. Goold, vol. 1 (Edinburgh: T&T Clark, n.d.), 415.
2. George Croly, "Spirit of God, Descend upon My Heart," 1854, accessed March 8, 2016, http://www.cyberhymnal.org/htm/s/o/sogdumyh.htm.

ciples wondered why Jesus spoke in parables, Jesus answered, "To you has been given the secret of the kingdom of God, but for those outside everything is in parables, so that 'they may indeed see but not perceive, and may indeed hear but not understand, lest they should turn and be forgiven'" (Mark 4:11–12). "But blessed are your eyes, for they see, and your ears, for they hear" (Matt. 13:16).

In other words, for some, the parables were part of God's judgment. He was handing them over to their pride and hardness of heart so that they might "see but not perceive." Or, as Jesus prayed in Luke 10:21, "I thank you, Father, Lord of heaven and earth, that you have hidden these things from the wise and understanding and revealed them to little children; yes, Father, for such was your gracious will."

But Jesus did not leave his disciples in the ignorance of human "wisdom and understanding." On the contrary, Jesus said, "To you has been given the secret of the kingdom of God" (Mark 4:11). The secret of the kingdom is the surprising reality that the Messiah has actually come but that he would not be the earthly king and victor over Rome that so many expected him to be. He would suffer first, and then, in an unexpected way, enter in to his glory. This "secret of the kingdom" was the same truth that Jesus criticized the disciples on the Emmaus road for not grasping from the Old Testament: "O foolish ones, and slow of heart to believe all that the prophets have spoken! Was it not necessary that the Christ should *suffer these things and enter into his glory?*" (Luke 24:25–26).

The point, for our purposes here, is that the disciples should have been able to read the Old Testament and see the terrible and wonderful reality of a suffering Messiah. They should have been prepared by the Old Testament to be open and receptive to the coming of God's kingdom in the way it came. First, it comes through suffering and death. Then through resurrection and reign from heaven. Then, at the second coming, in the establishment of Christ's earthly rule.

But they were "foolish and slow of heart." So a miracle of special illumination was needed for the disciples to see the pointers to these things in the Old Testament and in the teachings of Jesus. God gave that illumination, and Jesus thanked God that he had "revealed [these things] to little children" (Luke 10:21). He said, "To you has been given the secret of the kingdom of God" (Mark 4:11). "Blessed are your eyes, for they see" (Matt. 13:16).

My Father Revealed This to You

Fifth, this divine help in reading the Scriptures is also called God's revelation. When Peter recognized Jesus as the Messiah and Son of God, his understanding was not complete, but his breakthrough was so significant Jesus exulted in the miracle. Peter said, "You are the Christ, the Son of the living God" (Matt. 16:16). This insight was not native brilliance on Peter's part. It was not natural. It was supernatural. Jesus said, "Blessed are you, Simon Bar-Jonah! For flesh and blood has not *revealed* this to you, but my Father who is in heaven" (Matt. 16:17).

"Flesh and blood" refers to what Peter was by mere human nature. This was not the source of his breakthrough. The breakthrough was a gift from God. It was the sort of gift that all of us need if we are going to see Jesus for who he really is.

To be sure, by nature—by "flesh and blood"—we can know many facts about Jesus. The disciples and the Pharisees knew more facts about him than we do. But Jesus will not be seen as the treasure he is unless the Father in heaven does the miracle in our hearts and grants us to see.

Then it will be said over us what Jesus said over the disciples: "*Blessed* are the eyes that see what you see! For I tell you that many prophets and kings desired to see what you see, and did not see it, and to hear what you hear, and did not hear it" (Luke 10:23–24). If we are going to read the Scriptures about Jesus and see him and savor him and be transformed into his image, it will not be by mere human means. It will be a "blessing" that opens the eyes of our hearts to see his all-satisfying glory for what it really is.

God Keeps the Keys

If we aim to read the Bible with the goal of seeing and savoring the glory of all that God is for us in Christ, then reading must be a supernatural act. We must read in reliance on the miracle of God's help. In 1877, J. C. Ryle, Anglican bishop of Liverpool, wrote:

> Is the Bible the Word of God? Then be sure you never read it without fervent prayer for the help and teaching of the Holy Spirit. Here is the rock on which many make shipwreck. They do not ask for wisdom and instruction, and so they find the Bible dark, and carry nothing away from it. You should pray for the Spirit to guide you into all truth. You should beg the Lord Jesus Christ to "open your

understanding," as He did that of His disciples. The Lord God, by whose inspiration the book was written, keeps the keys of the book, and alone can enable you to understand it profitably. Nine times over in one Psalm does David cry, "Teach me." Five times over, in the same Psalm, does he say, "Give me understanding." Well says John Owen, Dean of Christ Church, Oxford, "There is a sacred light in the Word: but there is a covering and veil on the eyes of men, so that they cannot behold it aright. Now, the removal of this veil is the peculiar work of the Holy Spirit."[3]

We will see later that this deep dependence on the supernatural work of God to help us see the worth and beauty of God in Scripture does not diminish the necessity to use our minds in the process of construing textual meaning. It may, at times, feel like a paradox—to say that God gives the insight we need, and yet we must labor to see it. But the apostle Paul shows us the way. In 2 Timothy 2:7 he says, "Think over what I say, for the Lord *will give you understanding* in everything." So we are called to read the apostolic Scriptures rigorously, carefully, thoughtfully. Why? Not because this natural process of thinking attains the goal, but because, in that natural process of thinking, God acts supernaturally and *gives* a kind of sight we would not otherwise have. That is the supernatural act of reading the Scriptures.

---

3. J. C. Ryle, *Old Paths: Being Plain Statements of Some of the Weightier Matters of Christianity* (London: Charles J. Thynne, 1898), 33.

You know how to interpret the appearance of the sky, but you cannot interpret the signs of the times.

MATTHEW 16:3

The Father who sent me has himself borne witness about me. *His voice you have never heard.*

JOHN 5:37

How can you believe, when you receive glory from one another and do not seek the glory that comes from the only God?

JOHN 5:44

12

Why the Pharisees Couldn't Read

"Have you never read . . . the Scriptures?"

They Didn't Know What They Were Talking About

Probably in Jesus's day no one read the Bible more than the scribes and Pharisees. Jesus said, "The scribes and the Pharisees sit on Moses' seat, so do and observe whatever they tell you, but not the works they do" (Matt. 23:2–3). They carried more Bible in their minds, and in their mouths, than anyone else. They readily quoted the law of God (Matt. 19:7). They were meticulous in their attention to the details (Matt. 23:24). Yet Jesus repeatedly spoke to them as if they had not read the Scriptures!

This is amazing. Saying to the Pharisees, "Have you not read your Scriptures?" must have been highly offensive. He said it to them at least six times. The implication each time is that the most authoritative Bible readers of that day didn't know what they were talking about. Jesus was saying in effect that their words and actions showed that they did not know the Scriptures. How could that be? They *had* read the Bible. But something had gone wrong. Terribly wrong. Something hindered them from seeing what was really there. What went wrong? And what does this show us about the supernatural aspect of reading the Scriptures?

If You Read, You Would Not Have Condemned the Guiltless

One day Jesus and his disciples were walking through the grain fields. The disciples were hungry and plucked some grain to eat. It was the Sabbath. The Pharisees saw it and said to Jesus,

> "Look, your disciples are doing what is not lawful to do on the Sabbath." He said to them, *"Have you not read* what David did when he was hungry, and those who were with him: how he entered the house of God and ate the bread of the Presence, which it was not lawful for him to eat nor for those who were with him, but only for the priests? Or *have you not read* in the Law how on the Sabbath the priests in the temple profane the Sabbath and are guiltless? I tell you, something greater than the temple is here. And *if you had known what this means,* 'I desire mercy, and not sacrifice,' you would not have condemned the guiltless. For the Son of Man is lord of the Sabbath." (Matt. 12:1–8)

Jesus was not happy with the Pharisees' condemnation of his disciples. They should not have "condemned the guiltless" (v. 7). So there was a fundamental disagreement between Jesus and the Pharisees. They said the disciples were guilty of sin—"Your disciples are doing what is not lawful." But Jesus said they were "guiltless." Three times Jesus traced their mistaken condemnation back to misreading the Bible (vv. 3, 5, 6). And twice he traced it back to their misreading of him (vv. 6b, 8).

The Case of David and His Men

First, in Matthew 12:3–4 Jesus refers to 1 Samuel 21:1–6 where David and his men are fleeing from Saul and need food. He persuades Ahimelech the priest to give him the sacred bread of the presence.

> *Have you not read* what David did when he was hungry, and those who were with him: how he entered the house of God and ate the bread of the Presence, which it was not lawful for him to eat nor for those who were with him, but only for the priests?

In other words, Jesus implies, there are situations in which those on God's mission may sustain their lives and mission by breaking ceremonial laws. I don't argue that David and Jesus didn't really break such laws, because that is not the way Jesus defended his men. He did not say: "It *is* lawful to eat the bread of the Presence, and it *is* lawful to eat grain on the Sabbath." He said that David and his men ate what "was *not lawful* for him to eat" (v. 4).

Yes, Jesus is going to say in verse 7 that his disciples are "guiltless." This is not because no law was broken, but, first, because there are kinds of laws that may be broken in certain circumstances. He treats the Pharisees as if they had never read this story in 1 Samuel 6. "Have you not read?" He clearly finds fault with their Bible reading. They read, and they did not see. Something had gone wrong.

The Case of the Sabbath-Profaning Priests

Second, Jesus refers in verse 5 to the provision in the law that sacrifices and bread be prepared on the Sabbath by the priests so that offerings can be made (Num. 28:9–10; 1 Chron. 9:32). He calls this preparation "profaning" the Sabbath.

> Or *have you not read* in the Law how on the Sabbath the priests in the temple profane the Sabbath and are guiltless? I tell you, something greater than the temple is here.

Probably he uses the word "profane" as an ironical reference to what the Pharisees are accusing his disciples of doing. You say, my disciples are profaning the Sabbath. Well, if that is what is happening, then the priests not only did it too but were authorized to do it by the Bible itself. Jesus believes that the Pharisees should have been able to see that, when they read the Bible—"Have you not read?" But they didn't see it.

The Prophetic Case of Mercy over Sacrifice

Third, in verse 7 Jesus addresses a principle of Bible reading with huge implications. He says to the Pharisees, "And *if you had known what this means*, 'I desire mercy, and not sacrifice,' you would not have condemned the guiltless." That is a quote from Hosea where God chastises his people for cloaking their sinfulness with ceremonial show:

> What shall I do with you, O Ephraim? What shall I do with you, O Judah? Your love is like a morning cloud, like the dew that goes early away. Therefore I have hewn them by the prophets; I have slain them by the words of my mouth, and my judgment goes forth as the light. For *I desire steadfast love [or mercy] and not sacrifice*, the knowledge of God rather than burnt offerings. (Hos. 6:4–6)

These words from Hosea, "I desire mercy and not sacrifice" (which Jesus also spoke in Matt. 9:13), were not an isolated expression of God's heart. It was a common Old Testament refrain:

Has the LORD as great delight in burnt offerings and sacrifices,
    as in obeying the voice of the LORD?
Behold, to obey is better than sacrifice,
    and to listen than the fat of rams. (1 Sam. 15:22)

To do righteousness and justice
    is more acceptable to the LORD than sacrifice. (Prov. 21:3)

In sacrifice and offering you have not delighted,
    but you have given me an open ear.
Burnt offering and sin offering
    you have not required.
Then I said, "Behold, I have come;
    in the scroll of the book it is written of me:
I delight to do your will, O my God;
    your law is within my heart." (Ps. 40:6–8)

Not for your sacrifices do I rebuke you;
    your burnt offerings are continually before me.
I will not accept a bull from your house
    or goats from your folds. . . .
Offer to God a sacrifice of thanksgiving,
    and perform your vows to the Most High. (Ps. 50:8–9, 14)

With what shall I come before the LORD,
    and bow myself before God on high?
Shall I come before him with burnt offerings,
    with calves a year old?
Will the LORD be pleased with thousands of rams,
    with ten thousands of rivers of oil? . . .
He has told you, O man, what is good;
    and what does the LORD require of you
but to do justice, and to love kindness,
    and to walk humbly with your God? (Mic. 6:6–8)

Jesus was not nitpicking when he said, "If you had known what this means . . . you would not have condemned the guiltless." It was not as though the Pharisees had overlooked a tiny phrase. He was telling them that they were blind to a crucial teaching of the Scriptures—*God prioritizes mercy for people over ceremonial meticulousness.* They had read this. And they did not see what was there.

If You Believed Moses, You Would Believe Me

Besides tracing the Pharisees' mistaken condemnation back to their misreading of the Bible (Matt. 12:3, 5, 6), Jesus also traces it back to their misreading of him (vv. 6b, 8). This is not surprising, because Jesus saw a direct correlation between the misreading of the Scriptures and the failure to recognize him. "If you believed Moses, you would believe me; for he wrote of me" (John 5:46). "If they do not hear Moses and the Prophets, neither will they be convinced if someone should rise from the dead" (Luke 16:31). "You search the Scriptures because you think that in them you have eternal life; and it is they that bear witness about me, yet you refuse to come to me that you may have life" (John 5:39–40).

Something Greater than the Temple Is Here

Jesus's first connection between himself and the Pharisees' condemnation of the guiltless is in Matthew 12:5–6:

> Have you not read in the Law how on the Sabbath the priests in the temple profane the Sabbath and are guiltless? I tell you, *something greater than the temple is here.*

"Something greater than the temple is here." That is an oblique but staggering claim for his own significance. It's an argument from the lesser to the greater: if the temple with its sacrifices warrants the Sabbath-profaning "work" of the priests, how much more does *my presence* warrant the provision of my faithful disciples? If they condemn his disciples, the reason is not only that they didn't read the Bible the way God intended, but also that they couldn't interpret the acts and words of Jesus. Something was deeply wrong.

Lord of the Sabbath

Finally, in this encounter with the Pharisees, Jesus said, "For the Son of Man is lord of the Sabbath" (Matt. 12:8). This elevates the exalted claim of verse 6 to an unparalleled level. "I am the Lord of the Sabbath." To be the Lord of the Sabbath is to have the right to decide the meaning of the Sabbath. This puts Jesus in the place of the creator of the Sabbath. Jesus's actions and words with his disciples were the actions and words of God. The glory of God was shining—more brightly than if the temple itself had come down from heaven. Just as brightly as if the creator of the Sabbath had come down. But the Pharisees did not see the peculiar glory of God in the Scriptures and did not see it in Jesus. They could not read the Scriptures or recognize the Savior. Something had gone very wrong.

A Controversy over Divorce

On another occasion Jesus confronted the Pharisees with their inability to read concerning the issue of divorce:

> And Pharisees came up to him and tested him by asking, "Is it lawful to divorce one's wife for any cause?" He answered, "*Have you not read* that he who created them from the beginning made them male and female, and said, 'Therefore a man shall leave his father and his mother and hold fast to his wife, and the two shall become one flesh'? So they are no longer two but one flesh. What therefore God has joined together, let not man separate." They said to him, "Why then did Moses command one to give a certificate of divorce and to send her away?" He said to them, "Because of your hardness of heart Moses allowed you to divorce your wives, but from the beginning it was not so. And I say to you: whoever divorces his wife, except for sexual immorality, and marries another, commits adultery." (Matt. 19:3–9)

When Jesus said, "Have you not read" Genesis 1:27 and 2:24, he shows that he expected the Pharisees to draw out of the Scriptures what he is now making explicit. He expected them to see that the Mosaic provision for divorce, which they refer to from Deuteronomy 24:1–4, was not in accord with God's original plan for marriage. It was given as a temporary, inferior provision because of the hardness of their hearts (Matt. 19:8). And he did *not* draw the conclusion that, since people still have hard hearts, the provision still applies.

On the contrary. Something new has come into the world. The Messiah has come. The ransom has come (Mark 10:45). A new authority has come: "You have heard that it was said, . . . but I say to you" (Matt. 5:20–48). The standard is now raised for the followers of Jesus. The standard is returned to God's original design expressed in Genesis 1:27 and 2:24. Jesus has come to rescue the world both from the guilt and the power of sin. "What therefore God has joined together, let not man separate" (Matt. 19:6). This had been the ideal all along. That is why Jesus said to the Pharisees, "Have you not read?"

Just as Hosea 6:6 (with all its Old Testament parallels) should have kept the Pharisees from condemning his disciples for picking grain to eat on the Sabbath, so Genesis 2:24 should have kept them from treating divorce the way they did. But they were blind to the implications of Genesis 1:27 and 2:4. Jesus spoke to them as if they had not even read the text.

Confronting the Pharisees over the Praise of Children

After Jesus used a whip to drive the money-changers out of the temple and called it a "house of prayer," the blind and lame came to him for healing and the children were crying out, "Hosanna to the Son of David!"

> The blind and the lame came to him in the temple, and he healed them. But when the chief priests and the scribes saw the wonderful things that he did, and the children crying out in the temple, "Hosanna to the Son of David!" they were indignant, and they said to him, "Do you hear what these are saying?" And Jesus said to them, "Yes; *have you never read*, 'Out of the mouth of infants and nursing babies you have prepared praise'"? (Matt. 21:14–16)

Jesus treats the chief priests and scribes (like the Pharisees) as though they had not read Psalm 8. The psalm begins:

> O LORD, our Lord,
> how majestic is your name in all the earth!
> You have set your glory above the heavens.
> Out of the mouth of babies and infants,
> you have established strength because of your foes,
> to still the enemy and the avenger. (vv. 1–2)

"Have you not read this?" he asks them. Why did he say that? Because they were finding fault with what the children were saying. And they were finding fault with Jesus for not correcting them. The children were calling Jesus the Messiah, the Son of David. The chief priests and scribes did not believe Jesus was the Messiah. That's why they were so upset

204 The Supernatural Act of Reading the Bible

with the children. They were blind to who Jesus really was. They did not have eyes to see his glory.

The Peculiar Majesty They Could Not See

Why not? Jesus implies it's because they don't know how to read. They don't know what Psalm 8 is saying. It's as though they haven't read it. What did they miss in Psalm 8? The point of Psalm 8 is that God's majesty shines in meekness. I once preached two messages on this psalm,[1] one on Palm Sunday, one on Easter. One was about a donkey-riding King, and the other was about the majesty of the risen King.

The psalm begins and ends with the words, "O LORD, our Lord, how majestic is your name in all the earth!" That is the opening and closing assertion of the psalm. But the central truth of the psalm is not God's sheer majesty, but rather his majesty through weakness. Babies "establish strength" and "still the avenger." And mere men have dominion over the world—mere men who are scarcely noticeable in the magnitude of what God made with his fingers. So I summed up the psalm: *God defeats his foes with the weakness of children, he rules his world with the weakness of men.*

I think what Jesus means is that if the chief priests and the scribes had absorbed this mind-set from Psalm 8 and the rest of the Scriptures, they would have eyes to see the kind of Messiah Jesus was. But as it is, they don't know who he is. Which to Jesus looks as if they never read Psalm 8.

The Stone That the Builders Rejected

Again in Matthew 21:42 Jesus says to the chief priests and the Pharisees, "Have you never read in the Scriptures . . . ?" In this case, his point is virtually the same as the one he made from Psalm 8. The Pharisees did not see the peculiar glory of a weak and rejected Messiah when they read the Scriptures. Therefore, they could not see Jesus for who he really was.

Jesus had just told the parable of the tenants. In it, the owner of a vineyard sends his son to collect the fruit from the tenants. This represents the Son of God being sent to Israel to gather the fruit of repentance

---

1. "The Peculiar Marks of Majesty, Part 1 (April 1, 2007), and "The Peculiar Marks of Majesty, Part 2" (April 8, 2007), accessed March 10, 2016, http://www.desiringgod.org/messages/the-peculiar-mark-of-majesty-part-1#_ftnref1; http://www.desiringgod.org/messages/the-peculiar-mark-of-majesty-part-2.

and obedience. The result is that the tenants kill the son. Jesus asks his listeners what the owner in the parable will do to those tenants. They answer (with their own death warrant), "He will put those wretches to a miserable death and let out the vineyard to other tenants who will give him the fruits in their seasons" (Matt. 21:41).

To this response Jesus says, *"Have you never read in the Scriptures . . ."* And then he quotes, Psalm 118:22–23: "The stone that the builders rejected has become the cornerstone. This is the LORD's doing; it is marvelous in our eyes." In Psalm 8 the point was: *God defeats his foes with the weakness of children; he rules his world with the weakness of men.* In Psalm 118 the point is: *God establishes the glory of his Messiah through the pain of rejection.* This is the peculiar glory of God in Christ. In the mind of Jesus, the fact that the Pharisees do not see Jesus this way makes it look as though they had never read Psalm 118. But they *had* read it. They had read it in a way that we very much want to avoid. Something had gone wrong.

The Sadducees and the Resurrection of the Dead

Once more Jesus says—this time to the Sadducees—"Have you not read?" The Sadducees were a group who did not believe in the resurrection of the dead (Matt. 22:23). So they try to make Jesus look foolish by asking him whose wife a woman will be in the resurrection, having had seven husbands in this life. Jesus responds, "You are wrong, because you know neither the Scriptures nor the power of God. . . . As for the resurrection of the dead, *have you not read* what was said to you by God: 'I am the God of Abraham, and the God of Isaac, and the God of Jacob' [Ex. 3:6]? He is not God of the dead, but of the living" (Matt. 22:29, 31–32).

Jesus implies that the denial of the resurrection of God's covenant people (Abraham, Isaac, and Jacob) is like the admission that one has not read the Scriptures. "You are wrong, because you [do not] know . . . the Scriptures" (Matt. 22:29). Jesus assumes that God's declaration of his covenant commitment to his faithful people ("I am your God") carries in it a commitment to them forever—even through death. Jesus could have gone to a seemingly clearer Old Testament passage, like Psalm 49:15, "God will ransom my soul from the power of Sheol, for he will receive me." But he was talking about how to read the Scriptures.

He was showing that reading involves more than surface exposure. Reading the Scriptures includes thinking about what we read and penetrating to the implications, not just the surface statements.

Exodus 3:6 does not say explicitly, "My covenant people will be raised." So, evidently, when Jesus said, "Have you not read?" he meant, "Have you not read and pondered and drawn out of Exodus 3:6 the implications of what it means for God to be a person's God?" The answer is no, they had not read the Scriptures that way. Not the way Jesus expects us to read.

Reading, in the mind of Jesus, is not just seeing surface things—like the connection of words and phrases and clauses—but the things implied more deeply by the realities involved. Thus reading is thinking through what is said not just grammatically but—how shall we say it—essentially, or substantially. That is, reading includes asking about the implications of the realities signified. In this case God is a reality. And his relationship to the patriarch is a reality. And from the nature of God and the nature of the covenant relationship, there is an implication—resurrection! If we don't see it, Jesus says, "Have you read?" The Sadducees did not see it. Why not?

What Had Gone Wrong?

Over and over in this chapter so far, we have said, "Something had gone wrong. Terribly wrong." The experts in Bible knowledge could not read the Bible. Why not? What kept them from doing the kind of reading Jesus expected? What we will see is that the problem was not linguistic or grammatical or historical. It was moral and spiritual. What prevented the reading that Jesus expected was not skills they lacked, but sins they loved. The problem was not mental deficiencies, but misplaced desires.

Spiritual Adultery Made Reading the Bible Impossible

Jesus said to the Pharisees, "You know how to interpret the appearance of the sky, but you cannot interpret the signs of the times" (Matt. 16:3). Those signs were all the deeds and actions of Jesus. These were the signs that Jesus said they could not see because they were not able to read the Scriptures. Their Bridegroom, their Messiah, had come. But they did not want him. Their desires were for something else.

They were like an adulterous bride. So they kept demanding more signs, not because they wanted to believe Jesus was their husband, but because they had a love affair with the world. So Jesus called them what they were: "An evil and *adulterous* generation" (Matt. 16:4). This is why they could not "interpret." Their hearts were adulterous—they had other lovers besides Jesus. Their desires were misplaced. They loved their sins. And where truth stood in the way of those desires, it could not be seen as more desirable than the suitors they loved.

The Competing Lover: Human Glory

Probably at the top of the list of misplaced desires that blinded the Pharisees to Scripture and to Jesus was the desire for human praise. They loved the glory of man more than the glory of God. Astonishingly, Jesus said to the Jewish leaders, "The Father who sent me has himself borne witness about me. *His voice you have never heard*" (John 5:37). Never heard! In spite of all their reading in God's word! Their way of reading was so defective that everything was distorted. They never heard the true voice of God. In spite of all his wonders, they never saw the peculiar glory.

The result, Jesus said, is that "you do not have [God's] word abiding in you." And the evidence for that is that "you do not believe the one whom he has sent" (John 5:38). What is the root issue? We can see it in what follows:

> I know that *you do not have the love of God within you.* I have come in my Father's name, and you do not receive me. If another comes in his own name, you will receive him. *How can you believe, when you receive glory from one another and do not seek the glory that comes from the only God?* Do not think that I will accuse you to the Father. There is one who accuses you: Moses, on whom you have set your hope. For if you believed Moses, you would believe me; for he wrote of me. But if you do not believe his writings, how will you believe my words? (John 5:42–47)

I think this goes to the heart of the matter. The rhetorical question in verse 44 is a clear statement of the root problem: "How can you believe, when *you receive glory from one another and do not seek the glory that comes from the only God?*" Turn that rhetorical question into a statement: "You *cannot* believe in Jesus, when you love the glory of man more than the glory of God." Why? Because Jesus is the kind of Messiah that undermines self-exaltation.

Jesus said, "If another comes in his own name, you will receive him" (v. 43). Why is that? Because that kind of Messiah would be their kind of person. He would confirm their love affair with self-exaltation. But Jesus, as the truly human Messiah, loves God and God's glory above all things. This is not who the Pharisees want to be. They love their own glory. Therefore "you do not have the love of God within you." Therefore, you cannot believe. And you cannot read.

Misplaced Desires in Sync with Satan

Jesus links this love of self-exaltation to Satan. He says that these leaders cannot welcome the words of Jesus because their desires are in sync with the Devil:

> Jesus said to them, "If God were your Father, you would love me, for I came from God and I am here. I came not of my own accord, but he sent me. *Why do you not understand what I say? It is because you cannot bear to hear my word.* You are of your father the devil, and your will is to do *your father's desires.*" (John 8:42–44)

Why can't they understand? Because they cannot bear to hear. Why not? Because they are bent on other desires. It boils down to *desires.* It is a heart issue. Not a head issue. Misplaced desires, not mental deficiencies.

You Cannot See God's Glory If You Love Money

The love of human glory—the best seats in the synagogues (Matt. 23:6), greetings in the marketplaces (Luke 11:43), places of honor at feasts (Mark 12:39)—these were not their only adulterous desires. The Pharisees also loved money. They showed why such a misplaced desire blinds them from the truth of Jesus and the Scriptures. Jesus taught that "no servant can serve two masters, for either he will hate the one and love the other, or he will be devoted to the one and despise the other. You cannot serve God and money" (Luke 16:13). Luke comments, "The Pharisees, who were lovers of money, heard all these things, and they ridiculed him" (Luke 16:14).

Jesus taught the truth about money. But they could not hear these words as beautiful and compelling. They could only hear them as ridiculous, because they were *lovers* of money (Greek φιλάργυροι). Lovers! This is the issue. They were adulteresses. An adulterous generation. Their all-glorious, all-satisfying Bridegroom had come. He was full of spiritual truth and beauty. But they could not see it because they had other lovers—like the praise of man and the power of money. This is why they could not see Jesus, and it is why they could not read the Scriptures.

The problem was not that they lacked the light, but that they loved the darkness. "This is the judgment: the light has come into the world, and people *loved* the darkness rather than the light because their works were evil" (John 3:19). This results in a de facto hatred of the light. "Everyone who does wicked things *hates* the light and does not come to the light" (John 3:20).

The Greatest Obstacle: Sinful Hearts

By way of conclusion, perhaps the way to say it at this point is: those who love the darkness and hate the light may give their whole life to reading the Scriptures and yet never truly read them—never read them the way Jesus expects them to be read. You may read them day and night, yet hear Jesus say at every point, "Have you never read?" Or worse: "[God's] voice you have never heard" (John 5:37).

The greatest obstacles to reading the Scriptures are not intellectual. They are not lack of skill. Rigorous thinking and literary skills matter, as we will see in part 3. But *nothing creates as great a barrier to seeing what is really there in Scripture as a heart that loves other things more than God*. This, as we have seen in the case of the Pharisees, will nullify the greatest attention to Scripture. God's aim for us as we read the Scriptures is, above all, that we see and savor the glory of God as more desirable than anything. That aim will abort as long as our hearts are enslaved to the adulterous love of our own glory or money or any created thing.

Therefore, if we are going to succeed in reading, as God intends for us to read, it will have to be a supernatural act. God will have to take out the heart of stone, with its hardness and resistance to his glory, and put in a heart of flesh, with its living sensitivity to God's worth and beauty (Ezek. 11:19; 36:26). What will this supernatural reading be like? To that we turn in the next chapter.

You have been born again, not of perishable seed but of imperishable, through the living and abiding word of God. . . . Like newborn infants, long for the pure spiritual milk, that by it you may grow up into salvation.

1 PETER 1:23; 2:2

Of his own will he brought us forth by the word of truth. . . . Put away all filthiness and rampant wickedness and receive with meekness the implanted word, which is able to save your souls.

JAMES 1:18, 21

13

New Testament Pictures of Bible Reading as a Supernatural Act

"Receive with meekness the implanted word."

The Necessity of Reading the Bible Supernaturally

The previous two chapters have made clear that the Bible itself teaches that Bible reading is supposed to be a supernatural act. And it has become clear why that is. The Bible must be read supernaturally, not because the Bible is poorly written, but because our hearts are by nature "foolish . . . and slow" (Luke 24:25). We are in rebellion against what God has written and cannot submit to the truth that his worth and beauty are more to be desired than anything in this world (Rom. 8:7). On top of that, we have a supernatural enemy who exploits our rebellious nature and blinds us to "the light of the gospel of the glory of Christ" (2 Cor. 4:4). That is why reading the Bible must be a supernatural act—a human act in which God gives the decisive ability to see the all-surpassing worth of the glory of God.

In this chapter, the aim is *not* to show the necessity of reading the Bible supernaturally, but rather to examine how the Bible describes that act. My hope is that the biblical descriptions of interacting with the word of God supernaturally will make a deep impression on us and lead us to read the Bible in such a way that we see the glories of God and are changed by them.

New Birth and the Spiritual Act of Reading

The way we read the word of God is profoundly influenced by our understanding of how we were born again. Jesus said to Nicodemus, "Truly, truly, I say to you, unless one is born again he cannot see the kingdom of God" (John 3:3). He explained his meaning by saying,

> That which is born of the flesh is flesh, and that which is born of the Spirit is spirit. Do not marvel that I said to you, "You must be born again." The wind blows where it wishes, and you hear its sound, but you do not know where it comes from or where it goes. So it is with everyone who is born of the Spirit. (John 3:6–8)

All human beings are "born of the flesh." That is, we were born the first time naturally by ordinary human resources. In that natural condition, as we saw in chapter 11, we are spiritually lifeless (Eph. 2:5). We had no spiritual sensibilities. By *spiritual* we mean *created and sustained and formed by the Holy Spirit*. We were not spiritual in that sense. That is why we were blind to spiritual reality (2 Cor. 4:4), such as the compelling worth and beauty of the glory of God in Christ. We were only "natural," "born of the flesh," and, as Paul says, "the natural person does not accept the things of the Spirit of God, for they are folly to him, and he is not able to understand them because they are spiritually discerned" (1 Cor. 2:14). Which means we must be born again—we must be given spiritual life—in order to see the things of the Spirit as they really are—more beautiful and more precious than all earthly treasures.

The crucial thing to know for our purposes here is that the new birth happens *through the word of God*. This is why understanding the new birth is so important in shaping the way we read the Bible. Two key passages make the connection between the new birth and how we read the Bible: James 1:18–21 and 1 Peter 1:23–2:3. Let's look at these one at a time.

Brought Forth by the Word of Truth

James describes the new birth as a sovereign act of God, by which he gives us life "by the word of truth."

> Of his own will *he brought us forth by the word of truth*, that we should be a kind of firstfruits of his creatures. . . . Put away all

filthiness and rampant wickedness and *receive with meekness the implanted word*, which is able to save your souls. (James 1:18, 21)

The phrase "of his own will" emphasizes that this is God's sovereign act. He did this. We didn't. A newly conceived baby does not cause its own being. So we are supposed to think very consciously here, *This is a supernatural act*. God did it. But he did not do it without a secondary cause. He is the primary and decisive cause. But God uses a secondary cause, namely, "the word of truth." "He brought us forth *by the word of truth*" (v. 18).

The phrase "word of truth" probably has direct reference to the gospel of Jesus Christ (which we will see in a moment is the way Peter speaks of the regenerating word). But James does not emphasize any particular limited meaning of "the word of truth." What he makes explicit is that this "word" was God's agent in causing the new birth, and this word is true. He brought us forth by "the word of truth." We also know that a few verses later James exhorts us to be "doers of *the word*" (1:22), and he relates that "word" to "the perfect law of liberty" (1:25), which includes the command, "You shall love your neighbor as yourself" (2:8). Therefore, I am not inclined to treat "the word of truth" in James 1:18 narrowly. It is God's word, and it is true. This is the explicit focus. We owe our new life to the miracle of God's word.

Receive the Implanted Word, Again and Again

Then comes the decisive connection to the ongoing reading of God's word. James 1:21 says, "Receive with meekness the implanted word, which is able to save your souls." James sees "the word of truth," as "implanted" in us. In other words, the word that caused us to be born again did not come and then go. It came and remained. To use the words of Jesus, the word "abides" in us (John 15:7). With a modern analogy, we might say that God gave us life with the seed of his DNA, and now that word-borne DNA has become ours. It defines who we are as new creatures in Christ.

Then comes the amazing connection with reading. James says that this "implanted word" is to be "receive[d] with meekness." The word of God does not just come once at the moment of new birth. We are to receive it again and again. And this ongoing reception of the word "is able to save your souls." We are going to see this exact connection in

1 Peter 2:2—"long for the pure spiritual milk, that by it you may grow up *into salvation.*" Our final salvation is not owing simply to a spiritual vaccination we got at the new birth. Rather, it is owing to that *and* the spiritual life sustained by the ongoing reception of the word.

We will be "saved" at the last day because we are "alive." We have eternal *life.* And James is pointing out that this life is not only the gift of a past moment of birth, but an ongoing reality of vital communion with God sustained by the continual reception of God's word. Babies are born, and babies breathe. Christians are born, and Christians receive the word.

A Supernatural Receiving

Three traits mark this "receiving" of the word as supernatural. First, it "is able to save your soul"—which is not an effect of merely natural causes. Second, this word, even though from day to day we may hear it in the Bible or from various people, is nevertheless "implanted." And it is implanted because of the supernatural miracle of new birth. In a sense, the seed of all God's truth is rooted in our souls. So, even though we receive it from the Bible, we are receiving it as supernaturally implanted. Third, we are to receive it "with meekness." James uses this word one other time. In James 3:13, he refers to "the meekness of wisdom." And the wisdom he speaks of is contrasted with wisdom that is "earthly, unspiritual." The wisdom that is meek is "the wisdom that comes down from above" (James 3:15). Therefore, the meekness with which we receive the implanted word is a supernatural meekness. It is the fruit of the Spirit (Gal. 5:23).

Reading the Word Is Our Life

Therefore, the fact that we are "brought forth by the word of truth" is profoundly important in understanding how we read (and thus receive) the word of God. The word gave us eternal life. And the ongoing reception of the word sustains our eternal life—it saves our soul. This ongoing reception may happen in many ways—through preaching, mutual exhortation, Bible classes, and more—but common to all of them is the Scripture. Its root was planted in us indestructibly by regeneration. And for the rest of our lives, that implanted word draws us to the Scriptures as its fullest expression. And we receive it as our life.

Peter and James Speak as One

The parallels between James 1:18–21 and 1 Peter 1:23–2:3 are not the kind that prove James or Peter copied the other, or even that they used a common source. Rather, these parallels show that among the biblical writers we find a similar way of thinking about how new birth happens through God's word, and how the ongoing receiving of God's word sustains life. The parallels are remarkable. First, here is the relevant passage from 1 Peter 1:23–2:3:

> *You have been born again, not of perishable seed but of imperishable, through the living and abiding word of God*; for "All flesh is like grass and all its glory like the flower of grass. The grass withers, and the flower falls, but the word of the Lord remains forever." And *this word is the good news that was preached to you.* So put away all malice and all deceit and hypocrisy and envy and all slander. Like newborn infants, *long for the pure spiritual milk*, that by it you may grow up into salvation—if indeed you have tasted that the Lord is good.

Now the parallels:

James 1:18–21	Peter 1:23–2:3
He brought us forth	You have been born again
by the word of truth	through the living and abiding word of God.
Put away all malice	Put away all filthiness
In meekness	Like newborn infants
receive the implanted word	long for the pure spiritual milk
which is able to save your souls.	that by it you may grow up into salvation.

Go on Desiring and Drinking the Word

I am tempted to add one other parallel, but it is not as clear. In James the word we are to receive in an ongoing way is "the implanted word." In other words, it has entered into us and become part of us and gives us an ongoing readiness for God's word. Could this be parallel to 1 Peter 2:3, "if indeed you have tasted that the Lord is good"? Long for the pure milk of the word, because it has already entered into you, and you have tasted in it the goodness of the Lord. So just as the word in James 1:21 has been implanted, so the word in 1 Peter 2:3 has been tasted.

That may be a stretch. But what is not a stretch is that Peter, like James, connects the ongoing reception (drinking) of the word with the first awakening to the word in the new birth. This first experience of God's word is called an *implanting* in James 1:21, and it is called a *tasting* in 1 Peter 2:3. This implanting and tasting happened in the supernatural miracle of the new birth. And for both James and Peter, the miracle of that implanted and tasted word goes on. In James the word is to be "received." In Peter it is to be "longed for."

In both this receiving and drinking are God's means of final salvation. Receiving the implanted word "is able to save your souls" (James 1:21). Drinking the pure milk of the word causes you to "grow up into salvation" (1 Pet. 2:2). Which means that receiving and drinking the word are supernatural acts. Natural processes do not save the soul. Natural processes do not cause growth to salvation. But receiving the word and drinking the word do. They are not merely natural. It is a miracle when God's word is implanted in us, and it is a miracle when in it we taste the sweetness of God's goodness. From that moment on, all our reading of God's word is supposed to be an extension of that miracle in daily life—until we "grow up into salvation."

Receiving the Word Supernaturally at Thessalonica

Another example of the supernatural reception of the word of God is found in Paul's first letter to the Thessalonians. It is especially noteworthy because Paul goes out of his way to point out the wonderful, miraculous nature of this reception. It is, in this case, the reception of an *oral* word. But whether oral through hearing, or visual through reading, the point remains the same. A human word—through Christ's apostle—was received as the very word of God, which proved to be supernaturally alive and powerful:

> We . . . thank God constantly for this, that when you received the word of God, which you heard from us, you accepted it not as

the word of men but as what it really is, the word of God, which is at work in you believers. For you, brothers, became imitators of the churches of God in Christ Jesus that are in Judea. For you suffered the same things from your own countrymen as they did from the Jews. (1 Thess. 2:13–14)

A Word Supernaturally Given and Delivered

Note three supernatural aspects of what is happening here. First, the word delivered by Paul is called "the word of God." It is not any ordinary word. As he describes it in 1 Corinthians 2:13, it is "not taught by human wisdom but taught by the Spirit." Or as he says in Galatians 1:12, "I did not receive it from any man, nor was I taught it, but I received it through a revelation of Jesus Christ." This is a word supernaturally received from God and supernaturally delivered in the power of the Spirit (1 Thess. 1:5).

God, Not Man, Is Thanked

Second, Paul *thanks God* that the Thessalonians have received *his* word as the very word *of God*. He knows this does not always happen—Paul is the aroma of death to death for some of his listeners (2 Cor. 2:16). But it happened for these Christians in Thessalonica. And Paul is exultant with thankfulness. His thankfulness is not directed toward his own rhetorical gifts or to the spiritual discernment of the Thessalonians. He is exultant with thankfulness *to God*. "We . . . *thank God* constantly for this, that when you received the word of God, which you heard from us, you accepted it not as the word of men but as what it really is, the word of God." This was a miracle of sovereign grace. God granted the eyes of the Thessalonians to see the self-authenticating "light of the gospel of the glory of Christ" (2 Cor. 4:4). That is why they received the word of man as the word of God.

The Word Awakened Supernatural Joy and Courage

Third, this apostolic word, received as a divine word, was not a dormant word. It was not ineffective. The word itself, Paul says, "is at work in you believers" (1 Thess. 2:13). What does that mean? Paul explains in verse 14: "For you, brothers, became imitators of the churches of God in Christ Jesus that are in Judea. For you suffered . . ." Their readiness to suffer for Christ was the evidence that the word of God was at work in them.

How did this happen? Paul had already explained it in 1 Thessalonians 1:5–6: "Our gospel came to you not only in word, but also in power. . . . You became imitators of us and of the Lord, for you received the word in much affliction, with the joy of the Holy Spirit." How did the divine word enable them to suffer for Christ? By giving them "the joy of the Holy Spirit." The Spirit of God opened their eyes to see the glory of Christ in the word of God, and this sight of "the light of the gospel of the glory of Christ" filled them with joy. And this joy severed the root of fear and selfishness. It freed them to suffer rather than surrender the all-satisfying Christ that they had seen in the gospel.

This Pattern of Receiving the Word Goes On

In response to this, my question is: Is there any reason to think this pattern of receiving the apostolic word should stop? Can we really imagine that Paul would say, "At the beginning of your Christian life, my word came to you as God's word, in the power of God's Spirit. And because God was at work in you, you received my word as God's word. And by his Spirit, that word worked in you a great joy that transformed your life so deeply that you suffered for Christ, sustained by that joy. The whole experience was pervasively supernatural. But now, in the rest of your Christian life, the reading of my epistles can be done in a completely natural way." I ask you, can you imagine Paul thinking or saying anything like that? I cannot.

On the contrary. It seems clear to me that from that first day on, the Thessalonians—and every Christian with them!—should *thank God* that there is, in fact, a word from God. And we should *thank God* that we have received this word as the very word of God, even though it comes to us in human words. And we should *thank God* that it is at work in us by the Spirit, opening our eyes to the all-surpassing treasure of the glory of Christ and filling us with joy. And we should *thank God* that this divine word is so wonderfully powerful that we are willing to suffer the loss of anything in this world rather than lose Christ. In other words, from start to finish the Christian encounter with the word of God—which includes all of our reading of the Bible—is a work of

God. God is to be thanked. Reading the Bible is intended by God to be supernatural.

The Word of God Is Living and Active

Paul is not the only New Testament writer who draws our attention to the fact that the word of God "is at work in you believers" (1 Thess. 2:13). This verb "be at work" (Greek ἐνεργεῖται, *energeitai*) has a noun form that is used in Hebrews 4:12—"The word of God is living and active [Greek ἐνεργής, *energōs*]." Here's the context:

> The word of God is living and active, sharper than any two-edged sword, piercing to the division of soul and of spirit, of joints and of marrow, and discerning the thoughts and intentions of the heart. And no creature is hidden from his sight, but all are naked and exposed to the eyes of him to whom we must give account. (Heb. 4:12–13)

Where the Word Works, God Works

How pleasant and fruitful it would be to linger over the details of this text and draw out its wonders. But we are looking mainly for one thing: the way the Bible treats the reading of God's word as supernatural. Perhaps the most remarkable thing about this text is the shift from the "living," "working [active]," "piercing," and "discerning" work of the word in verse 12, to the action of God himself in verse 13. Verse 12 describes the way the word of God probes the depths and secrets of the human soul—to the division of soul and spirit, joints and marrow. It describes how the word of God exposes "the thoughts and intentions of the heart." And then, without a break, the writer says, "No creature is hidden from *his* sight." We are all "naked and exposed to the eyes of *him* . . ." *He* is the one to whom we will give an account. The writer shifts seamlessly from the work of the word to the work of God.

The implication is clear: where God's word is at work, God is at work. God is the one giving life to the word. God is the one making it active. God is the one who is using the word like a scalpel to pierce and divide and expose the secret intentions of the heart. Therefore, if we aim to encounter the word of God the way this writer means for us to, we will read the Bible with hope and faith and expectancy that

God himself will be encountered. And that means the encounter is supernatural.

The Word Wars against External Enemies

The working of the word of God in believers is, of course, not just for the exposure of the secrets of our hearts. To be sure, that is a great gift, and a great aid to repentance. And what is repentance but the returning from the vanities of the world to the treasure of all that God is for us in Jesus? And what is this returning but the great source of a transformed life? But the enemies of our soul are not just the self-deceptions inside of us that trick us into thinking the world is better than the Creator.

We have enemies—supernatural enemies—outside as well. And their aim is to ruin us by deceiving us into thinking and feeling that the glory of Christ is less satisfying than "the desires of the flesh and the desires of the eyes and pride of life" (1 John 2:16). Satan lured Adam and Eve with these in the beginning. And he still does.

These are the idols that destroy the soul. And John closes his first letter with the words, "Little children, keep yourselves from idols" (1 John 5:21). That is, "do not love the world or the things in the world" more than you love the Father (1 John 2:15). How are we to conquer a supernatural enemy who comes tempting us to love the world more than God?

The Word Abides in You, and You Conquer

John gives his answer in 1 John 2:14: "I write to you, young men, because you are strong, and *the word of God abides in you, and you have overcome the evil one.*" This is how the Evil One is overcome when he tries to deceive us that the things of the world are more satisfying than God—even the best things, even God's own creation and blessings. We overcome the lies of the Evil One by *the word of God abiding in us.*

Therefore, our aim in reading the Bible is that the word of God would abide in us and have this kind of effect. We read the word with the aim of overcoming the Evil One. That is a work of divine power, not our cleverness. The Devil does not flee before human willpower. He flees before the power of divine truth. And the word of God is the instrument of the Spirit in that warfare. Therefore, in all our Bible reading, we aim to have God's word abiding in us with that power. That is the kind of

Bible reading God calls us to—a supernatural engagement with a divine word and a demonic enemy.

The Sovereign Joy of the Holy Spirit

I draw this chapter to a close with one more glimpse into how the word of God overcomes the deceptions of the Evil One. Recall from 1 Thessalonians 1:6 and 2:13 the way the word of God was at work in the Christians of Thessalonica. It was producing in them an invincible joy that enabled them to suffer rather than give up the treasure of Christ for the sake of comfort and safety. That is how Satan is defeated. When he comes, telling us the lie that renouncing Christ is better than suffering, we resist him by faith in the word of God, which tells us the exact opposite. There is more joy, now and forever, in the glory of Jesus than anything this world can offer.

Jesus said that this is the reason he gave us his words. "These things I have spoken to you, that my joy may be in you, and that your joy may be full" (John 15:11). His aim, when we read his words, is that *his* joy would be in us. His aim is *not* that our joy would happen naturally in reading his words. His aim is that *his* own joy—divine, supernatural joy—would become our joy. This is not a merely natural joy. It is not a natural response to natural words. It is a miraculous effect of divine words. This is supernatural joy.

To the Thessalonians, Paul said it was "the joy of the Holy Spirit" (1 Thess. 1:6). This is the only joy that can counter the supernatural deception of Satan when he portrays the pleasures of the world in spectacularly attractive colors. Jesus said that this is why he gave us his words. This is why we should read them. It is not a merely natural act. It is supernatural.

The Path to Glory

God has given us his word and intends for us to read it supernaturally. We are to receive it again and again as a word that has given us life by being supernaturally implanted in us through the Spirit in new birth (James 1:18, 21). We are to desire it the way a baby desires milk because there is in us a Spirit-given taste for the all-satisfying goodness of God (1 Pet. 2:2–3).

Every time we read God's word we are to thank him that we have the God-given grace to welcome it as the word of God in the words of man (1 Thess. 2:13). We are to embrace the living, working, piercing, dividing, exposing effect of God's word as the very presence of God himself (Heb. 4:12–13). We are to store up God's words in us so that Satan's temptations fail as the word of God remains (1 John 2:14).

And we are to listen to Jesus as he speaks to us in the Scriptures so that his joy—the supernatural joy of the Son of God—might be our joy, and ours might be full (John 15:11). This is the path of change from glory to glory (2 Cor. 3:18). This is the path to the consummation of all things. And it is a supernatural path.

Transition to Part 3

We turn now, paradoxically, to the *natural* act of walking this supernatural path—the natural act of reading the Bible supernaturally. The supernatural act of seeing the glory of God through the glory of nature does not happen apart from the natural act of observing nature. During the life of Jesus Christ on earth, the supernatural act of seeing his divine glory did not happen apart from the natural act of observing his physical, historical presence. Today the supernatural act of seeing the peculiar glory of God, in and through the Scriptures, does not happen apart from the natural act of reading or hearing the Bible. The natural act of reading the Bible supernaturally is essential. What that looks like is the subject of part 3.

The Natural Act of Reading the Bible Supernaturally

Both these are from the Holy Ghost—namely, that we truly believe the Scripture to be the word of God, and that we understand savingly the mind of God therein.

JOHN OWEN

Introduction to Part 3

The aim of part 3 is to encourage a deep dependence on God and the fullest use of your natural powers in the supernatural act of reading the Bible. I will explain below what I mean by "natural powers." But first let me summarize briefly how we got here, and why I think our natural powers must be used supernaturally.

How We Got Here
The proposal I offered in part 1 was that, according to the Bible itself,

> our ultimate goal in reading the Bible is that God's infinite worth and beauty would be exalted in the everlasting, white-hot worship of the blood-bought bride of Christ from every people, language, tribe, and nation.

Implicit in the white-hot worship of a perfected people was the dramatic transformation of selfish sinners into God-centered, sinless saints. That transformation is at first a process of being changed incrementally through seeing the glory of the Lord (2 Cor. 3:18). Then it comes to a blazing consummation at the appearing of Christ at the end of the age. And, amazingly, even that final step of glorification happens by seeing his glory: "We know that when he appears we shall be like him, because we shall see him as he is" (1 John 3:2).

This sight of the glory of the Lord—as "in a mirror dimly" during this life, and then as "face to face" when the Lord comes (1 Cor. 13:12)—is no mere natural sight. It is not neutral or displeased. It is a sight of Jesus as he really is: supremely valuable and more satisfying than anything in the world (Phil. 1:21; 3:8). Thus it is a seeing *and* savoring of Christ. Together they are the key to the transformation that prepares the bride for her destiny of white-hot worship.

This seeing, which awakens this transforming savoring, happens through reading the Bible—either your reading, or someone else's reading who tells you what he read. God has ordained to gather and transform a people for his Son through the use of a book. This is amazing. And it is true. God has planned that the consummation of the ages hangs on the transforming power of the written word of God. This outcome is secure, because God is "watching over [his] word to perform it" (Jer. 1:12). The decisive cause of our seeing and savoring is God.

That's what part 2 of the book unfolded. The reading of the Bible that sees the glory of the Lord is a supernatural reading. It is a reading that depends on God for its necessary and decisive effect in accomplishing God's purposes. And this is the only kind of reading that prepares the people of God for their final destiny.

Now we come to part 3, titled, "The Natural Act of Reading the Bible Supernaturally." The aim in this final part of the book, as I said above, is to encourage a deep dependence on God in the fullest use of your natural powers in the supernatural act of reading the Bible.

What You Can Do Because You Are Human

By "natural powers," I mean your ability to see and hear, your ability to focus on spoken or written words, your ability to learn the meaning of words and phrases and clauses, your ability to construe an author's intention from what he has written, your ability to think and evaluate and relate what you learn to other things, your ability to remember things you've learned, your ability to write down your thoughts, your ability to get enough sleep and food and exercise so your powers are assisted by mental alertness and physical vigor, your ability to seek help from other people (dead or alive), and so on. In short, I mean everything you are capable of by virtue of having been born a human being and having received a basic education along with ordinary life experience.

As you can imagine, therefore, the possibilities for this part of the book are limitless. The possible intersections between the Bible and the variety of human powers are countless. The possible guidelines for helping someone read the Bible fruitfully are as many as there are people, circumstances, and groupings of words in the Bible. A discussion of how all of those variables relate to reading the Bible could go on forever. So I have to find a way to narrow down this part of the book into something useful but not exhaustive.

Limiting Our Discussion of the Act of Reading

When I get to chapter 20, I will explain more fully how I am narrowing my discussion of the actual, eyes-on-the-page, natural act of reading. But I will say in a nutshell here that I do not intend to discuss the different guidelines for reading different kinds of writing in the Bible, such as narrative, proverb, parable, poetry, and many more. There are good books that do this better than I could do it.[1] My approach is based on the simple observation that before anyone can discern from a text what *kind* of writing it is, one must be reading. Which means that there are important general strategies of reading that take place *before* you can let a certain kind of writing determine how you read.

I am going to focus in part 3 on what makes for good reading *before* you discover what kind of writing you are reading. This reading is, in fact, what enables you to discern what kind of writing you are dealing with and whether the author wants you to apply any unusual methods or expectations for understanding his writing. I choose this approach not only because the other approach would take too much space, but mainly because this way of thinking about reading has been so fruitful in my life. Most of what I have seen in Scripture has come not from learning rules for each kind of writing, but rather from the more basic discipline of looking long and hard at what is really there. I will explain this further in chapter 20.

The Natural Path to Supernatural Revelation

Now back to the first sentence of this introduction: my aim in part 3 is *to encourage a deep dependence on God and the fullest use of your*

---

1. For instance, among many, see *The Literary Guide to the Bible*, ed. Robert Alter and Frank Kermode (Cambridge, MA: Belknap Press, 1990); *A Complete Literary Guide to the Bible*, ed. Leland Ryken and Tremper Longman (Grand Rapids, MI: Zondervan, 1999); Leland Ryken, *A Complete Handbook of Literary Forms in the Bible* (Wheaton, IL: Crossway, 2014); Andreas J. Köstenberger and Richard D. Patterson, *For the Love of God's Word: An Introduction to Biblical Interpretation* (Grand Rapids, MI: Kregel, 2015); Robert H. Stein, *A Basic Guide to Interpreting the Bible: Playing by the Rules*, 2nd ed. (Grand Rapids, MI: Baker Academic, 2011); as well as Jason S. DeRouchie, *How to Understand and Apply the Old Testament: Twelve Steps from Exegesis to Theology* (Phillipsburg, NJ: P&R, 2017); and Andrew David Naselli, *How to Understand and Apply the New Testament: Twelve Steps from Exegesis to Theology* (Phillipsburg, NJ: P&R, 2017).

natural powers in the supernatural act of reading the Bible. I do not mean that we should read the Bible in a natural way and then hope that it has some spiritual, supernatural effect *at a later time.* That, I'm afraid, is the way many people read the Bible. They read it in a merely human way, and then hope—even pray—for some more-than-human impact. Rather, I want to encourage you to take every step of your natural reading in a supernatural way. I want you to read the Bible in a way that is only possible because God himself is in you, by his Spirit, creating a supernatural encounter with the Bible.

When Peter uttered the perfectly human sentence to Jesus, "You are the Christ, the Son of the living God" (Matt. 16:16), Jesus said, "Flesh and blood has not revealed this to you, but my Father who is in heaven" (Matt. 16:17). That means this recognition of Jesus was supernatural—beyond what flesh and blood (human nature) can do. Evidently Peter needed to be told this. Jesus was helping him understand how he arrived at this wonderful declaration. If Peter had gone out in the woods alone seeking a voice from heaven, and God had said in a thundering voice: "Jesus is the Christ, and my divine Son," Peter would not need to be told, "My Father revealed this to you."

But Peter had not received the revelation that way. He had *watched* Jesus. He had *listened.* He likely had *prayed* for wisdom—perhaps Psalm 119:18, "Open my eyes." The result was that he saw the irrefutable marks of Jesus's reality. *That* is what needed explanation. At one level, it all had felt fairly natural. Peter needs an explanation for what has really happened. So Jesus says, in effect, "Peter, in all your watching and listening and praying, my Father has been at work. And he has caused you to see what is really here: my self-authenticating glory. Your watching and listening and praying have not been *merely* natural. They *also* have been supernatural. My Father has been in your watching and in your listening and in your praying. What you saw and heard and received through natural means, has, in fact, been seen and heard and received supernaturally."

That is what I mean by "the fullest use of your *natural* powers in the *supernatural* act of reading the Bible." That is what part 3 is about—the fullest use of your natural abilities in the act of reading the Bible, but in such a reliance on God that you see and savor the glory of God in ways you otherwise never could.

Do not be children in your thinking. Be infants in evil, but in your thinking be mature.

1 CORINTHIANS 14:20

By the grace of God I am what I am, and his grace toward me was not in vain. On the contrary, I worked harder than any of them, though it was not I, but the grace of God that is with me.

1 CORINTHIANS 15:10

Work out your own salvation with fear and trembling, for it is God who works in you, both to will and to work for his good pleasure.

PHILIPPIANS 2:12–13

14

God Forbid That We Despise
His Natural Gifts

*"Think over what I say, for the Lord will
give you understanding in everything."*

A Barren Womb and a Blind Mind

When Abraham was a hundred years old, and his wife Sarah was not only beyond the years of childbearing but also barren, God promised him a son by Sarah. This is analogous to our condition when we want to read the Bible and see the glory of God. There is no hope that it can happen without God's supernatural intervention. But, in fact, God did intervene for Abraham. And he does for us.

When we stare blankly at the word of God and feel no supreme worth and beauty in it, God acts supernaturally. He shines "in our hearts to give the light of the knowledge of the glory of God in the face of Jesus Christ" (2 Cor. 4:6). He enlightens the eyes of the heart (Eph. 1:18). He gives understanding (1 John 5:20). He opens the mind (Luke 24:45). He reveals what flesh and blood can't perceive (Matt. 16:17). He turns an impossibility into a supernatural reading.

Fully Convinced God Could Do What He Promised

How does this happen? Note carefully that this promised child was, in one sense, wholly natural. Abraham and Sarah had sexual relations.

We know this because the Scripture says, "Sarah conceived and *bore Abraham* a son" (Gen. 21:2). This was not a virgin birth like that of Jesus, whom Mary conceived supernaturally. Abraham and Sarah had sexual relations. Sarah conceived. She carried the child for nine months. And she gave birth. And all of this was perfectly natural. Except there would have been no child without God's supernatural intervention in the natural process.

That is the way it is with the supernatural act of reading the Bible. In one sense, it is perfectly natural. We use our ordinary natural powers. But without God's supernatural intervention, we would have no motivation to read the Scriptures in the hope of treasuring Christ above all things (1 Kings 8:58; Ps. 119:36). Without God's supernatural illumination, we would not see and savor what is really there—the all-satisfying glory of all that God is for us in Christ. In one sense, the act of reading is natural—in another, supernatural. This is why I call it "the natural act of reading the Bible supernaturally."

We Act the Miracle of Supernatural Bible Reading

Another way of describing this "natural act of reading the Bible supernaturally" is to say that God does a miracle of granting sight, but we act the miracle of seeing.[1] God does not see for us. God enables *us* to see. We do the seeing. And the supernatural act of seeing "the light of the gospel of the glory of Christ" is by means of the natural act of seeing the story of the gospel written (or spoken) in natural human words.

If you want to see the glory of a master painting, you don't take your eyes off it and look at your email. The seeing of the glory happens in seeing the painting. So it is with the glory of God in the Scriptures. We don't take our eyes off the natural words and phrases and clauses that the biblical writers wrote. We don't disengage our minds from the natural process of construing meaning in the text. We stay focused on the natural object of the text. Our natural powers of observation and thinking stay fully engaged. That is where the miracle of seeing the beauty of Christ happens.

---

1. For more on this idea of acting the miracle, see *Acting the Miracle: God's Work and Ours in the Mystery of Sanctification*, ed. John Piper and David Mathis (Wheaton, IL: Crossway, 2013). In this chapter, I have used some of the material from my essays in that book.

Seeing Glory in the Natural Man Jesus

It is, as we have seen, similar to the way people saw the divinity of Christ. They looked at the natural man Jesus. They saw him with natural eyes. They heard him with natural ears. They touched him with natural hands. They construed his words with natural processes of thinking. But some saw nothing that attracted them. The glory of Christ was there. It was not above or below or beside the man Jesus. It was *in* him. It was *in* all he said and did. You would not discover it by taking your eyes off Jesus and looking at the sky and asking God to write it in the clouds. God had written it in the miracle of the incarnation. Those who had eyes to see saw it. The apostle John was one of those. He wrote, "The Word became flesh and dwelt among us, and we have seen his glory, glory as of the only Son from the Father, full of grace and truth" (John 1:14).

But others had no heart and no taste and no mind for this. "None of the rulers of this age understood this, for if they had, they would not have crucified the Lord of glory" (1 Cor. 2:8). The chief priests and elders of Jesus's own people wanted him dead (Matt. 26:4). Judas had no heart for a Messiah who planned suffering for his followers and not riches in this life (John 12:6). They did not see "the Lord of glory." They saw a weak pretender to messiahship. To them, he was a stumbling block—a barrier between them and their deepest desires. They could not see his glory because that would have eclipsed their own—which they loved supremely (John 5:44).

Incarnate Christ, Inspired Bible

The Scriptures are similar to Jesus in this way. Their language is natural, the way Jesus's body and mind and voice were natural. Jesus could be seen. The Bible can be read. Jesus was more than natural. The Bible is more than natural. Jesus was the Son of God. The Bible is the word of God. Jesus was incarnate. The Bible is inspired. Jesus spoke in ordinary human language. The Bible is written in ordinary human language.

To know Jesus, people had to look and listen to what was presented to their natural senses. To know the Scriptures, we must look and listen to what is presented to our natural senses. To look for the glory of God in Christ apart from his natural presence was useless. To look for the glory of God in Scripture apart from its natural presence is useless.

Jesus was seen by many as weak and pretentious. Many see the Bible as weak and pretentious. It took a supernatural miracle to see the glory of God in Jesus. "No one knows the Father except the Son and anyone to whom the Son chooses to reveal him" (Matt. 11:27). And it takes a supernatural miracle to see the glory of God in Scripture. "He opened their minds to understand the Scriptures" (Luke 24:45).

The Miracle Is *in* the Reading

So when you think about reading the Bible supernaturally, do not think the urgency and effort of reading the Bible naturally will be less than with any other book. All the human effort and skill that you can muster to construe the meaning of biblical passages will be called for. The glory is seen through the *meaning* of the text. And the meaning is found by reading and thinking. God is united to the man Jesus. The glory of God is united to the meaning of biblical texts.

Therefore, when the miracle of seeing and savoring the glory of God happens, it is *in* the act of reading and thinking. We read. God reveals. God *gives* the supernatural miracle. We *act* the supernatural miracle.

All of Life Is to Be Lived Supernaturally

This tension, or paradox, between God's *performing* the miracle of our reading supernaturally and our *acting* the miracle of reading supernaturally may be a new thought for you. Let me try to illustrate it more widely, and show it from Scripture, and then apply it to reading the Bible. Here are some other examples of what I mean by saying that God *gives* the miracle and we *act* the miracle:

- *God* opens the eyes of the blind, but it is the *blind* who see.
- *God* gives strength to shriveled legs, but it is the *lame* who do the walking.
- *God* touches the ears of the deaf, but it is the *deaf* who do the hearing.
- *God* calls Lazarus from the grave, but it is *Lazarus* who walks out on his own two feet.
- *God* gives you merciful humility, but it is *you* who turns the other cheek.
- *God* gives you courage and love, but it is *you* who shares Christ with your neighbor.

- *God* puts a generous spirit in you, but it is *you* who writes the check.
- *God* gives you a patient confidence in his timing, but it is *you* who drives the speed limit and stops at stop signs and buckles your seatbelt.
- *God* makes his glory more satisfying than lust, but it is you who turns away from pornography.
- *God* inclines your heart to his word, but it is *you* who gets out of bed early in the morning to read your Bible.

So you can see how reading the Bible supernaturally is only one instance of how all of life is to be lived. The Bible makes plain that Christian living is pervasively supernatural—meaning, it is pervasively sustained and shaped by God in ways that lead to final salvation. We are not talking about the *common* grace of divine providence that controls all things. We are talking about God's special new-covenant work (Jer. 31:33), purchased for the elect by the blood of Christ (Luke 22:20), that by the Spirit enables God's people to see the glory of Christ and live in a way that shows his supreme worth.

For example, the Scriptures tell us that we "live by the Spirit" (Gal. 5:25). That is, we have "begun [our Christian life] by the Spirit" (Gal. 3:3). We are "led by the Spirit" (Rom. 8:14; Gal. 5:18). We "walk by the Spirit" (Gal. 5:16). We put sin to death "by the Spirit" (Rom. 8:13). We "worship by the Spirit" (Phil. 3:3). And all of this is summed up in saying that God works our "sanctification by the Spirit" (2 Thess. 2:13). This is why I say that all of life is to be lived supernaturally. In the Christian life, every moment of reliance on the Spirit to produce his Christ-honoring fruit of holiness and love is a miracle.

We Are Still the Actors of the Miracle

But notice that *we* remain the actors of this miracle. It is we who act "by the Spirit." We do not turn into the Spirit. And the Spirit does not turn into us. We are human. And we act as humans. The Spirit decisively inclines, and we act. We see this over and over in the Bible. For example:

- Romans 7:6: We "died to that which held us captive, so that we serve in the new way of the Spirit and not in the old way of the written code." Notice that *we* serve. To be sure "in the new way of the Spirit"! But it is *we* who do the serving. Note also, lest it go unsaid and unnoticed, that our "death" with Christ happened once for all when he died (Gal. 2:19–20). We experience this by faith alone when we are united to Christ through the work of the Spirit (Gal. 3:26). Thus the penalty for all our sins is paid in full, once and for all (Heb. 7:27; 9:12, 26; 10:10). Christ's righteousness is counted as ours forever because of this union with Christ (Phil. 3:9), who was "made . . . sin . . . so that in him we might become the righteousness of God" (2 Cor. 5:21). This means that our subsequent serving, obedience, and good deeds are *not* the *ground* of our acceptance with God, but the *fruit* of it. We are not made right with God because of them. God works them in us because we were made right with him, once for all, through faith in Christ. This is crucial to stress, lest my emphasis on "acting the miracle" give the impression that this *acting* in any way *earns* or *grounds* the fact that God is 100 percent for us. That total acceptance with God is grounded in Christ alone, by grace alone, through faith alone.

- Galatians 2:20: "I have been crucified with Christ. It is no longer I who live, but Christ who lives in me. And the life I now live in the flesh I live by faith in the Son of God, who loved me and gave himself for me." Notice that "*I* now live in the flesh." To be sure, the old self-reliant *I* has died. To be sure, Christ is living in me. But I—the new *I* of faith—am the one living my life. And the key is "faith in the Son of God."

- 1 Peter 4:11: "Whoever serves, [let him do it] as one who serves by the strength that God supplies—in order that in everything God may be glorified through Jesus Christ." Notice that *I* am serving. But I am serving "by the strength that *God* supplies." God is supplying the supernatural help. I am acting the supernatural miracle.

- 1 Corinthians 15:10: "By the grace of God I am what I am, and his grace toward me was not in vain. On the contrary, I worked harder than any of them, though it was not I, but the grace of God that is with me." Notice that *I* worked hard. But my work was not decisive. God's work was decisive. It was the grace of God with me. Grace was the supernatural miracle. But the miracle did not replace me. It empowered me. By that grace "I am what I am." By that grace "I worked harder than any."

In every case it is I, the human Christian, who is serving, living, working, willing. But in every case, my will is empowered by another will— the will of the Spirit, the will of Christ, the will of God, the will of grace. Here's the way Jonathan Edwards describes the paradox of God's grace and power in our lives:

> We are not merely passive in it, nor yet does God do some and we do the rest, but God does all and we do all. God produces all and we act all. For that is what he produces, our own acts. God is the only proper author and fountain; we only are the proper actors. We are in different respects wholly passive and wholly active.[2]

Work, Because God Is at Work in You

Perhaps the most explicit passage in the Bible that tells us to "act the miracle"—including the miracle of reading the Bible supernaturally—is Philippians 2:12–13:

> Therefore, my beloved, as you have always obeyed, so now, not only as in my presence but much more in my absence, work out your own salvation with fear and trembling, for it is God who works in you, both to will and to work for his good pleasure.

To feel the amazing force of this passage, consider three observations.

1) The verb translated "*work out* your salvation" (Greek κατερ-γάζεσθε, *katergazesthe*) means "produce it," or "bring it about," or "effect it." As doctrinally dangerous as this language may seem, it is biblical. "Bring about your salvation." "Produce your salvation." "Effect your salvation by continuous, sustained, strenuous, effort." I say "dangerous" because Paul also teaches that salvation "is the gift of God, not a result of works, so that no one may boast" (Eph. 2:9). But there is no contradiction here, because the works that can't save are the works that try to produce a saving relationship with God. That is hopeless (Rom. 3:20). The works that "effect" our salvation are works that

---

2. Jonathan Edwards, *Writings on the Trinity, Grace, and Faith*, ed. Sang Hyun Lee, vol. 21, *The Works of Jonathan Edwards* (New Haven, CT: Yale University Press, 2003), 251.

God himself brings about because there *already is* a saving relationship. That's what Paul goes on to show.

2) The *salvation* that Paul tells us to "work out" is not only the great reality of total deliverance from condemnation and hell; it is also the more narrow, specific reality of daily deliverance from the soul-destroying works of the flesh (1 Pet. 2:11)—things like anger and self-pity and greed and lust. "Work out your salvation—your deliverance—from those deadly enemies." In other words, we are to use our mind and our will to actively oppose these sins as we see them rising in our hearts. And this active opposition, Paul says, is really *our* acting. But what we see next is that we are acting a miracle, because *God* is performing this willing in us. "For it is *God* who works in you, *to will.*"

3) Besides telling us to work—that is, to make effort and actively bring about our deliverance from the looming sin—Paul also says we should do this "*with fear and trembling*, for it is God who works in you, both to will and to work for his good pleasure." Why should there be "fear and trembling" as I attack my sin and "bring about salvation" from anger or self-pity? The reason given for our trembling is not a threat. It's a gift.

Paul says to fight your sin *with fear and trembling*, because God Almighty, maker of heaven and earth, redeemer, justifier, sustainer, Father, lover is so close to you that *your* working and willing are *his* working and willing. Tremble at this breathtaking thought! God Almighty is in you. God is the one in you willing. God is the one in you working. Your "continuous, sustained, strenuous" effort is not only being carried out in the *presence* of God, but is the very work of *God* himself. *God* is at work in you. And what he is working is *your* working. Therefore, we are not *waiting* for a miracle. We are *acting* a miracle.

Read the Bible, Act the Miracle

This is how we are supposed to read the Bible. We will and work because God is willing and working in us. We work with all our natural powers to see the meaning of the inspired writings, because God is at work in us to open our minds to see the glory that is really there. Here is the way the writer of Proverbs puts it (note all the human activity in italics and God's provision in bold):

> My son, if you *receive* my words
> > and *treasure up* my commandments with you,
> making your ear attentive to wisdom
> > and inclining your heart to understanding;
> yes, if you *call out* for insight
> > and *raise your voice* for understanding,
> if you *seek* it like silver
> > and *search* for it as for hidden treasures,
> then you will understand the fear of the LORD
> > and find the knowledge of God.
> **For the LORD gives wisdom;**
> > from his mouth come knowledge and understanding;
> he stores up sound wisdom for the upright. (Prov. 2:1–7)

Verses 1–4 exhort us to use all our powers to gain wisdom and insight—to see into the mind of God, receive God's words, treasure up his commandments, listen to wisdom, call out for insight, raise our voice for it, seek it like silver, search for it like treasure. This is the writer's way of saying, Bend every effort. Exert all your energy. Focus all your desires. Use all your powers. To what end? God's wisdom!

Then comes the surprising ground for all this effort. "For the LORD *gives* wisdom." He *gives* it. We seek it with all our might. God gives it. Our labor is *essential*. But God's giving is *decisive*. If God does not "give," we do not find. We "work out our deliverance" from blindness to God's wisdom—reading carefully with all our might. For God is at work in us "to will and to work" the discovery of his light. He creates the miracle of giving spiritual sight. We act the miracle of seeing.

Seek Light with All Your Strength, for God *Gives* Sight

The apostle Paul showed us over and over in his writing that he expected his readers, or listeners, to use their full powers of mental focus and thinking in order to see the light of the gospel of the glory of Christ. For example, at least ten times in the book of Acts, we see Paul's strategy to "reason" with people in his effort to show people the truth and beauty of Christ (Acts 17:2, 4, 17; 18:4, 19; 19:8, 9; 20:7, 9; 24:25). This was the oral version of the book of Romans. His assumption is that his listeners and readers would use their minds as fully in listening and reading as he did in speaking and writing.

So he told the Corinthians, "Do not be children in your thinking. Be infants in evil, but in your thinking be mature" (1 Cor. 14:20). Even more forcefully he said that he would rather speak five understandable words with his mind to instruct others than ten thousand unintelligible words with the miracle of tongues (1 Cor. 14:19). And Paul expected all of that "thinking" to reach its maximum fervor and focus in the act of reading his inspired letters. "When you *read* this, you can *perceive* my insight into the mystery of Christ" (Eph. 3:4). In other words, engaging the mind in the mental task of reading is God's appointed pathway into the glories of God. *We* do the thinking—the rigorous effort to read with understanding; *God* creates the miracle of supernatural light in processes of our thought.

Think Over Revelation, for God Gives Illumination

The apostle Paul makes the point most clearly and forcefully with these simple words: "*Think over* what I say, for the Lord will *give* you understanding in everything" (2 Tim. 2:7). We think. God gives. Both-and. Not either-or. So many people swerve off the road to one side of this verse or the other. Some stress the first part: "Think over what I say." They emphasize the indispensable role of reason and thinking and then minimize the supernatural role of God in making the mind able to see and embrace the glory of truth. Others stress the second half of the verse: "for the Lord will give you understanding in everything." They emphasize the futility of reason.

But Paul will not be divided that way. For Paul it was not either-or, but both-and. "*Think over* what I say, for *the Lord will give you understanding* in everything." Notice the little word "for." It means that the will of God to give us understanding is the *ground* of our thinking, not the *substitute* for it. Paul does not say, "God gives you understanding, so don't waste your time thinking over what I say." He does not encourage us to substitute prayer for thinking, but to saturate thinking with prayer. Nor does he say, "Think hard over what I say because it all depends on you, and God does not illumine the mind." No. He emphatically makes God's gift of illumination the ground of our deliberation. He makes God's giving light the reason for our pursuing light. "Think over what I say, *for* the Lord will give you understanding."

Reading in Another's Power

The point of this chapter is that the supernatural reading of the Bible does not minimize the urgency or effort of using all our natural powers in that process. Or, to put it positively, the Bible itself encourages the fullest use of our body and our will and our reason in the supernatural act of reading the Scriptures. Reading the Bible, in reliance on God, is one particular act among thousands of acts that, in the Christian life, are supernatural in this way. Our life is to be lived "in the Spirit" and "by the Spirit" (Rom. 8:9; 1 Cor. 12:3; Gal. 5:16, 18, 25; Eph. 6:18; Phil. 3:3; 2 Thess. 2:13). That is true, whether we are roasting a turkey, running for office, or reading the Bible.

God does not intend to replace us when we are united to Christ; he intends to renew us and empower us and guide us. He intends for us to be able to say, "I worked hard," and also to say, "Nevertheless, it was not I but the grace of God with me" (see 1 Cor. 15:10). He means for us to say, "I exerted my will and my mind and my body with all my might," and also to say, "Because God was willing and working in me" (see Phil. 2:12–13). He means for us to use our mind to "discern what is pleasing to the Lord" (Eph. 5:10) and also to joyfully confess that God is "working in us that which is pleasing in his sight" (Heb. 13:21).

We will have more to say about how the natural act of reading and the supernatural gift of light in reading intersect. But for now, the all-important point is: the God-appointed aim of reading the Bible will not happen without a supernatural intervention. And the normal way God intervenes is through the natural act of reading supernaturally. God forbid that believing in the God-given supernatural would make us despise the God-created natural.

The question, then, that presses on us now is, How do we read the Bible, if the great effects of seeing and savoring and being transformed through reading are decisively in the power of another, not ourselves?

Apart from me you can do nothing.

JOHN 15:5

Receive with meekness the implanted word.

JAMES 1:21

15

Humility Throws Open a Thousand Windows

"He leads the humble in what is right,
and teaches the humble his way."

How Do I Act the Miracle of Supernatural Reading?

One of the most important, persistent, all-pervading questions of my adult life has been, How do you go about living the Christian life in such a way that *you* are actually doing the living, and yet *another*—the Holy Spirit—is decisively doing the living *in and through* your living? The previous chapter showed us that this is, in fact, what it means to live the Christian life. "I worked harder than any of them, though it was not I, but the grace of God that is with me" (1 Cor. 15:10). But the question is, How? What do you actually do in order to obey 1 Peter 4:11, "[Let] whoever serves [do so] as one who serves *by the strength that God supplies"?* How do you serve, or live, or read in the strength of another? That is, how do I *act* the miracle that God causes?

I found that I needed a simple strategy to help me live this way hour by hour as I moved from one challenge to another. It seems to me that the biblical answer to the question of how to live this way can be summed up in five steps, which stay in my memory with the help of the acronym A.P.T.A.T. Most often I have used it when reading or preaching the Bible. I knew that I needed God's help to overcome my dullness and see the glory that is really there in God's word (Eph. 1:18). And I knew that I needed divine power in preaching, if Christ-exalting changes were to happen in people's lives (1 Cor. 2:4). So the question about how to read and preach *in the strength of another* became especially urgent at those points in my life.

Summary of A.P.T.A.T.

What I aim to do, therefore, in this chapter is give a brief overview of what I mean by A.P.T.A.T. Then I'll try to show how the first letter, A (*admit* the need for help), relates to the natural act of reading the Bible supernaturally. Then in subsequent chapters we will deal with the other letters.

Living the acronym A.P.T.A.T. is how I seek to "walk by the Spirit" (Gal. 5:16). Or, to be specific, it's how I seek to *read the Bible* "by the Spirit," that is, read it supernaturally.

A—*Admit*

I *admit* that without Christ I can do nothing.

> I am the vine; you are the branches. Whoever abides in me and I in him, he it is that bears much fruit, for apart from me you can do nothing. (John 15:5)

P—*Pray*

I *pray* for God's help, whatever form of help I need.

> Ask, and it will be given to you; seek, and you will find; knock, and it will be opened to you. (Matt. 7:7)

> You do not have, because you do not ask. (James 4:2)

> Call upon me in the day of trouble. (Ps. 50:15)

T—*Trust*

I *trust* a specific promise of God that is tailor-made for my situation, or a general promise that covers lots of situations. For example, before I stand up to preach, I might trust this promise:

> My word . . . shall not return to me empty. (Isa. 55:11)

Or:

> It is not you who speak, but the Spirit. (Matt. 10:20)

Or, more generically, I might call to mind this favorite verse and put my trust here:

> I am your God;
> I will strengthen you, I will help you,
>   I will uphold you with my righteous right hand. (Isa. 41:10)

Or:

> God is able to make all grace abound to you, so that having all sufficiency in all things at all times, you may abound in every good work. (2 Cor. 9:8)

Or:

> My God will supply every need of yours. (Phil. 4:19)

A—*Act*

I *act* in obedience to God's word, expecting God to act under and in and through my acting, so that the fruit is decisively from *his* acting. I act the miracle, but God is the decisive cause:

> I planted, Apollos watered, but *God* gave the growth. So neither he who plants nor he who waters is anything, but only *God* who gives the growth. (1 Cor. 3:6–7).

> *Work* out your own salvation with fear and trembling. (Phil. 2:12)

> *I worked* harder than any of them, though it was not I, but the grace of God that is with me. (1 Cor. 15:10)

> If by the Spirit *you put to death* the deeds of the body, you will live. (Rom. 8:13)

T—*Thank*

I *thank* God for whatever good comes. I give him the glory.

> Giv[e] thanks always and for everything to God the Father in the name of our Lord Jesus Christ. (Eph. 5:20)

> The one who offers thanksgiving as his sacrifice glorifies me . . . ! (Ps. 50:23)

I was thrilled to find, long after I began to use A.P.T.A.T., that J. I. Packer commended an almost identical process of living the Christian life. He was writing about the pursuit of holiness—which is what Christian living is. He calls it *Augustinian* holiness, because the great African theologian Augustine struck the note so well:

> The activity Augustinian holiness teaching encourages is intense, as the careers of such prodigiously busy holy men as Augustine, himself, Calvin, Whitefield, Spurgeon, and Kuyper show, but is not in the least self-reliant in spirit. Instead, it follows this four-stage sequence. First, as one who wants to do all the good you can, you observe what tasks, opportunities, and responsibilities face you. Second, you pray for help in these, acknowledging that without Christ you can do nothing—nothing fruitful, that is (John 15:5). Third, you go to work with a good will and a high heart, expecting to be helped as you asked to be. Fourth, you thank God for help given, ask pardons for your own failures en route, and request more help for the next task. Augustinian holiness is hard-working holiness, based on endless repetitions of this sequence.[1]

Packer's first and last steps (see what needs to be done; ask for pardon for failures) are in addition to my five steps. I took his first step for granted. His last is good counsel. (Feel free to create a new acronym if you can make it work!) But the other suggestions Packer makes are the same as my five: (1) Acknowledge you can't do anything without Christ. (2) Pray for help. (3) Go to work. (4) Expect to be helped. (5) Thank God.

The *A*: Admit We Can Do Nothing without Divine Help

Another way to describe this first step in reading the Bible in the power of another is to say it begins with *humility*. It begins with the renunciation of pride. It begins with a real sense of how depraved and distorted our minds are, and how readily our hearts desire other things more than we desire God. If the Holy Spirit does not work in us the fruit of humility and meekness and teachability (Gal. 5:23; James 3:17), we will either deny or distort the truth of Scripture. For all of Scripture exalts God above us.

---

1. J. I. Packer, *Keep in Step with the Spirit* (Grand Rapids, MI: Baker, 2005), 105.

Jonathan Edwards quotes Psalm 25:9 ("He leads the humble in what is right, and teaches the humble his way") and says, "Pride is a very great obstacle to the entering of divine light, yea, and such an obstacle as will eternally prevent it, till it be mortified."[2] What a wonderful promise: "He . . . teaches the humble his way"! If we hope to see God act supernaturally as our teacher when we read the Bible, this is how we will begin. We will humble ourselves under the mighty hand of God (1 Pet. 5:6). We will take to heart the refrain of Scripture: "The LORD lifts up the *humble*" (Ps. 147:6). "The LORD . . . adorns the humble with salvation" (Ps. 149:4). "Receive with *meekness* the implanted word" (James 1:21). "This is the one to whom I will look: he who is *humble* and contrite in spirit and trembles at my word" (Isa. 66:2). If God will not "look to" a proud person who reads the Scriptures, it is certain that the proud reader is not going to receive his help. John Owen sums up the point, "The Spirit of God never did nor ever will instruct a proud, unhumbled soul in the right knowledge of the Scripture, as it is a divine revelation."[3]

The Childlikeness of Happy Need

If we hope to read the Scriptures supernaturally, we must be done with all pretenses of self-sufficiency. This is what Jesus meant by the necessity of childlikeness. "Truly, I say to you, unless you turn and become like children, you will never enter the kingdom of heaven. Whoever humbles himself like this child is the greatest in the kingdom of heaven" (Matt. 18:3–4). The humility of a child is not his freedom from vanity. Children are naturally selfish (as are adults). The humility of a child, rather, is his free and willing awareness that he cannot provide for his own needs and must have an adult to meet all his needs.

No child mopes because he is not able to earn his own living. He accepts this as his station in life, and he trusts his parents to take care of him. That is the way we are supposed to approach life, including the way we read the Bible. We are like children, who will do all we can to understand what our Father has written for us, but who also will admit freely we will not see his glory without the gift of light.

---

2. Jonathan Edwards, "A Spiritual Understanding of Divine Things Denied to the Unregenerate," in *Sermons and Discourses, 1723–1729*, ed. Harry S. Stout and Kenneth P. Minkema, vol. 14, *The Works of Jonathan Edwards* (New Haven, CT: Yale University Press, 1997), 87.
3. John Owen, *The Works of John Owen*, ed. William H. Goold, vol. 4 (Edinburgh: T&T Clark, n.d.), 186.

So Peter tells us to long for the milk of the word "like newborn infants" (1 Pet. 2:2). That comparison probably carries not only the meaning of hearty craving, but also the unashamed sense that the nutrition of this milk is utterly undeserved. It is a free gift. And I am helpless to taste it apart from God's quickening grace.

Humility as the Opposite of Self-Glorification

In chapter 12, we saw the blinding effects of the proud love of our own glory over the glory of God. This was at root why the Pharisees could not see the meaning of the Old Testament or the meaning of Jesus's own ministry. Jesus put it so plainly:

> I have come in my Father's name, and you do not receive me. If another comes in his own name, you will receive him. How can you believe, when you receive glory from one another and do not seek the glory that comes from the only God? (John 5:43–44)

The human heart by nature prefers images of God's glory (especially the one in the mirror) above the glory of God himself (Rom. 1:18–23). That preference is the essence of sin and the root of our pride and of the corruption that keeps us from seeing the glory of God in Scripture. The most central work of the Holy Spirit in assisting us in reading the Scriptures is not to add new information to our minds that is not in the Bible, but rather to humble us so that we relish the glory of Christ more than we relish our self-exaltation.

This is the role Jesus promised for the Holy Spirit: "When the Spirit of truth comes . . . he will glorify me" (John 16:13–14). We know the Spirit is working when the exaltation of Christ is cherished. For "no one can say 'Jesus is Lord' except in the Holy Spirit" (1 Cor. 12:3). When the Spirit works in the reading of Scripture, we are humbled, and Christ is exalted. Our old preference for self-exaltation is replaced with a passion for Christ-exaltation. This new passion is the key that throws open a thousand windows in Scripture to let in the brightness of God's glory.

Humility Has Eyes

Jesus approaches the need for humility still another way. He says:

> My teaching is not mine, but his who sent me. If anyone's will is to do God's will, he will know whether the teaching is from God or

whether I am speaking on my own authority. The one who speaks on his own authority seeks his own glory; but the one who seeks the glory of him who sent him is true, and in him there is no falsehood. (John 7:16–18)

The idea of humility is expressed here in two ways. One is to say that our will must be so humbled that we are ready and eager for God's will to be our will. We are not bent on proudly saying his will must conform to ours. Rather, "our will is to do his will." That is who we are. That is the miracle that the Holy Spirit has done. He has given us an eagerness for our will to conform to God's. Jesus says that his humble, God-exalting disposition "knows" divine teaching when it sees it. A "seeing" comes with this self-renouncing joy in God's will.

The other way humility is expressed here is by emphasizing Jesus's commitment to living for the glory of the Father: "The one who speaks on his own authority seeks his own glory; but the one who seeks the glory of him who sent him is true, and in him there is no falsehood." The reason a person can recognize that kind of Messiah as true is that the person is eager to join Jesus in that self-denying exaltation of the Father's glory. So humility is at the root of recognizing the truth. Humility is a key ingredient in the eye salve that gives supernatural sight in reading Scripture. That's why Jesus said to the church at Laodicea, "I counsel you to buy from me . . . salve to anoint your eyes, so that you may see" (Rev. 3:18). The main ingredient in that supernatural salve is the humbling of self.

Humility Leads to Prayer

This admission of our helplessness—this humility—is the root of *prayer.* This next step in A.P.T.A.T. grows from the first. The five steps of this acronym are not merely sequential; they are organically related. Prayer grows in the soil of humility. None of us would pray as we ought without the humility to admit helplessness. So we turn now, in the next two chapters, to the absolutely indispensable role of prayer in the natural act of reading the Bible supernaturally.

You do not have, because you do not ask.

JAMES 4:2

Ask, and it will be given to you; seek, and you will find; knock, and it will be opened to you.

MATTHEW 7:7

16

The Indispensable Place of Prayer in Reading the Bible Supernaturally: Wakening Our Desire for the Word

"Incline my heart to your testimonies,
and not to selfish gain."

At the beginning of chapter 15, I summarized the meaning of the acronym A.P.T.A.T., which is my practical and biblical attempt to help us serve "by the strength that God supplies" (1 Pet. 4:11). It is a way of "walk[ing] by the Spirit" (Gal. 5:16). It's a way of fleshing out what it means to say, "I worked hard," but "it was not I, but the grace of God" (1 Cor. 15:10). This means it is also a pathway into the natural act of reading the Bible supernaturally. We turn in this chapter and the next to the *P* in A.P.T.A.T.—the indispensable place of *prayer*.

Prayer Is the Path of Perception

God has made plain that the path to seeing his peculiar glory is prayer. "Open my eyes, that I may behold wondrous things out of your law" (Ps. 119:18). How much light have we forfeited by failure to pray over the word we are reading! "You do not have, because you do not ask" (James 4:2). The longest chapter in the Bible is an extended meditation on the preciousness of the word of God. It is punctuated with explicit prayers, and the entire psalm is written as in the presence of God. Seven times the psalmist prays, "Teach me!":

> Blessed are you, O LORD;
>   teach me your statutes! (Ps. 119:12)
>
> When I told of my ways, you answered me;
>   teach me your statutes! (Ps. 119:26)
>
> Teach me, O LORD, the way of your statutes;
>   and I will keep it to the end. (Ps. 119:33)
>
> The earth, O LORD, is full of your steadfast love;
>   teach me your statutes! (Ps. 119:64)
>
> Teach me good judgment and knowledge,
>   for I believe in your commandments. (Ps. 119:66)
>
> You are good and do good;
>   teach me your statutes. (Ps. 119:68)
>
> Deal with your servant according to your steadfast love,
>   and teach me your statutes. (Ps. 119:124)

These prayers do not mean, "Show me which sayings among the world's wisdom are yours." The psalmist knows where God's word is found. The Jewish people were not adrift wondering where to find God's word. These prayers mean, "Open my eyes to the full and glorious meaning of your word." We have treasures in God's word that the merely natural mind cannot see (1 Cor. 2:14). There is a divine "teaching" that enables us to see the truth and beauty of God's mind. It is the opening of our minds to see the supreme desirability of all that God is for us in Christ. And so it is the work of God that enables us to come to Christ. So Jesus says, "It is written in the Prophets, 'And they will all be *taught by God.*' Everyone who has heard and *learned from the Father* comes to me" (John 6:45). This ongoing miracle of divine teaching, in and through God's written word, is a gift in answer to prayer.

With slightly different words, the psalmist prays five times that God would give him understanding:

Make me understand the way of your precepts,
   and I will meditate on your wondrous works. (Ps. 119:27)

Give me understanding, that I may keep your law
   and observe it with my whole heart. (Ps. 119:34)

Your hands have made and fashioned me;
   give me understanding that I may learn your commandments.
      (Ps. 119:73)

I am your servant; *give me understanding,*
   that I may know your testimonies! (Ps. 119:125)

Let my cry come before you, O LORD;
   give me understanding according to your word!
      (Ps. 119:169)

What God Has Joined, Don't Separate

We saw in chapter 14 that the divine gift of understanding does not nullify our natural effort to understand the Bible. We saw this in 2 Timothy 2:7: "*Think over* what I say, for the Lord will *give* you understanding in everything." True understanding of the apostolic word is a free gift of God. We do not find it on our own. It is given. That is why we pray, "Give me understanding." But it is also the fruit of thinking—indeed, rigorous thinking. So as we talk about the necessity of prayer in the process of reading, don't slip into thinking that this creates a shortcut around the natural act of wrestling with words and phrases and clauses—the natural act of reading.

Benjamin Warfield (1851–1921), the great Princeton professor of theology, was rebuked by an unsympathetic saint of his day for Warfield's emphasis on study: "Ten minutes on your knees will give you a truer knowledge of God than ten hours over your books." Warfield's response captured the biblical marriage of thinking and praying. He said, "What! [More] than ten hours over your books, on your knees?"[1] He would not accept the implied either-or. Nor should we. Pray *and* study. Study *and* pray. What God has joined together, let no intellectual (thinker) or charismatic (pray-er) separate!

---

1. Benjamin Warfield, "The Religious Life of Theological Students," in *The Princeton Theology,* ed. Mark Noll (Grand Rapids, MI: Baker, 1983), 263.

"Incline My Heart to Your Testimonies"

There is a more basic prayer than the prayer for God's teaching and understanding. We should pray this prayer continually. It grows out of the admission of our helplessness at the most fundamental level. Without God's supernatural help, we do not even want to read the Bible, let alone cry out for full and deep understanding.

The most basic prayer we can pray about reading the Bible is that God would give us the desire to read this book. Not just the *will*—that would be next best—but the *desire*. That is what the apostle Peter said we should have: "Like newborn infants, *long for* the pure spiritual milk" (1 Pet. 2:2). Similarly, the psalmist said that the righteous person *delights* in the law of the Lord (Ps. 1:2). And why wouldn't we, since God's words are "more to be *desired* . . . than gold" and "*sweeter* . . . than honey and drippings of the honeycomb" (Ps. 19:10)? Why wouldn't we? Because our hearts tend to become cold and dull and hard and blind.

That's the most basic reason we need to pray about our Bible reading. We drift away from the desire to do it. We even sing about this dreadful tendency:

> Prone to wander, Lord, I feel it,
> Prone to leave the God I love;
> Here's my heart, O take and seal it;
> Seal it for Thy courts above.[2]

That's exactly right. "O, Lord, here's my heart—my drifting, cooling, wavering, fickle, hardening heart. Take it! Do whatever you must do to seal it for yourself forever. Keep it alive and yearning and loving and delighting and treasuring." Few prayers have I prayed more often than this—*Lord, keep me from drifting away from your word!*

In fact, I have another acronym I use: I.O.U.S. I pray these four prayers when it is time to read the Bible:

I—*Incline.* "*Incline* my heart to your testimonies, and not to selfish gain" (Ps. 119:36).
O—*Open.* "*Open* my eyes, that I may behold wondrous things out of your law" (Ps. 119:18).

---

2. Robert Robinson, "Come Thou Fount of Every Blessing," 1757.

U—*Unite.* "Teach me your way, O LORD, that I may walk in your truth; *unite* my heart to fear your name" (Ps. 86:11).

S—*Satisfy.* "*Satisfy* us in the morning with your steadfast love, that we may rejoice and be glad all our days" (Ps. 90:14).

"I Know I Should, but I've Lost the Desire"

Let's linger here on the prayer for desire. "*Incline* my heart to your testimonies." Over the years in my pastoral ministry, many people have complained to me that they do not have motivation to read the Bible. They have a sense of duty that they should, but the desire is not there. It is remarkable how many of those people feel that the absence of the desire is the last nail in the coffin of joyful meditation on God's word.

When I ask them to describe to me what they are doing about it, they look at me as if I had misunderstood the problem. What can you do about the absence of desire, they wonder. "It's not a matter of *doing*. It's a matter of *feeling*," they protest. The problem with this response is that these folks have not just lost desire for God's word, but they have lost sight of the sovereign power of God, who gives that desire. They are acting like practical atheists. They have adopted a kind of fatalism that ignores the way the psalmist prays.

Evidently, the psalmist too felt this terrible tendency to drift away from the word of God. Evidently, he too knew the cooling of desire and the tendency of his heart to incline more to other things—especially money. Otherwise why would he have cried out, "Incline my heart to your testimonies, *and not to selfish gain*"? He is pleading with God to give him desire for the word. He knows that ultimately God is sovereign over the desires of the heart. So he calls on God to cause what he cannot make happen on his own. This is the answer to fatalism. This is the answer to acting like an atheist—as if there were no God who rules the heart, and can restore what we have lost.

We Are Fighting for Our Lives

I cannot stress enough how our real spiritual helplessness (A—*Admit*) should be accompanied by the daily cry to God that he would sustain and awaken our desire to read his word (P—*Pray*). Too many of us are passive when it comes to our spiritual affections. We are practical fatalists. We think there is nothing we can do. "Oh, well, today I have no desire to read. Maybe it will be there tomorrow. We'll see." And off to work we go.

This is not the way the psalmists thought or acted. It is not the way the great saints of church history have acted either. Life is war. And the main battles are fought at the level of desires, not deeds. When Paul said, "Put to death . . . what is earthly in you," he included in the list "passion, evil desire, and covetousness" (Col. 3:5). These are the great destroyers of desire for the word of God. What did Jesus say takes away our desire for the word? "The cares of the world and the deceitfulness of riches and *the desires for other things* enter in and *choke the word*" (Mark 4:19). Paul tells us to kill those "desires for other things" before they kill us! He does not encourage us to be passive or fatalistic. He encourages us to fight for our lives. That is, fight for your desire for God's word.

And the first and most decisive blow we can strike against "the desires for other things" that "choke the word," and take away our desire for God's word, is the daily cry to God that he would "incline" our hearts to his word and "not to selfish gain." Don't wait until you have lost the desire before you start praying for this desire. If the desire is present, give thanks and ask him to preserve it and intensify it. If you sense that it is cooling, plead that he would kindle it. And if it is gone, and you do not feel any desire to pray, do what you can. Repent. Tell him you are sorry that your desire for his word is dead. Tell him just how you feel. He knows already. And ask him—this is possible without hypocrisy because of the "imperishable seed" (1 Pet. 1:23) that remains in his children—ask him to give you the desire that right now you can barely even muster the will to ask for. He is merciful.

Christ Died So Your Prayer for Desire Would Be Answered

The reason we can pray like this, expecting mercy with confidence, is that this desire for the word of God is what Jesus died to purchase. He died for you so that this prayer would be answered. God promised, through the prophets Moses and Jeremiah and Ezekiel, that one day he would make a "new covenant" with his people. Jesus said that the shedding of his blood was the purchase of that new covenant for all who would trust him as their Savior and Lord and supreme treasure. At the Last Supper he explained, "This cup that is poured out for you is *the new covenant in my blood"* (Luke 22:20). By the shedding of his own blood, Jesus obtained the new covenant for his people. It secured the forgiveness of sins for all who trust him (Acts 10:43). "This is my blood of the covenant, which is poured out for many for the forgiveness of sins" (Matt. 26:28).

On the basis of this forgiveness, the other blessings of the new covenant flow to God's people. And these blessings relate mainly to the change of our desires—particularly our desires for God and his word. Here are the key promises of the new covenant:

> The LORD your God will circumcise your heart and the heart of your offspring, so that *you will love the LORD your God* with all your heart and with all your soul, that you may live. (Deut. 30:6)

> This is the covenant that I will make with the house of Israel after those days, declares the LORD: *I will put my law within them, and I will write it on their hearts.* And I will be their God, and they shall be my people. (Jer. 31:33)

> I will give them one heart, and a new spirit I will put within them. I will remove the heart of stone from their flesh and give them a heart of flesh, that they may walk in my statutes and keep my rules and obey them. And they shall be my people, and I will be their God. (Ezek. 11:19–20)

> I will give you a new heart, and a new spirit I will put within you. And I will remove the heart of stone from your flesh and give you a heart of flesh. And I will put my Spirit within you, and cause you to walk in my statutes and be careful to obey my rules. (Ezek. 36:26–27)

Jesus died so that our prayers for renewed love to him and his word could be mercifully answered. We are not asking him for fresh desires for his word on the basis of our merits. We are asking him on the basis of Christ's blood and righteousness. We don't argue with God that he owes us anything in ourselves. He doesn't. Everything we receive is a free gift of grace.

When we pray, "Incline my heart to your testimonies" (Ps. 119:36), we are admitting we deserve nothing—a cool heart toward infinite beauty is an infinite sin. We are confessing our helplessness and sinfulness. And we are looking away from ourselves to Christ. Our plea is: O God, for Christ's sake! For the sake of your dear Son! For the sake of his infinitely precious blood (1 Pet. 1:19), hear my cry and restore to me the joy of my salvation (Ps. 51:12) and the delight I once had in your word (Ps. 1:2). Restore to me the fullness of my love for you (Deut. 30:6). Grant me to say again from the bottom of my heart, "Oh how I love your law!" (Ps. 119:97).

Surrendering Your Identity to God

Don't miss how radical it is to pray this way about your Bible reading. The prayer contains an absolute surrender of yourself to God. You are saying, in effect, I am happy for you to have the most basic control of my heart. I am happy for you to go beneath my conscious willing and control the roots of my desires and my longings and, therefore, all that flows from my innermost being. This is radical. This is a surrender to God of your identity. Our very being as individual persons is who we are at the depths.

Our deepest identity is not the mere outward acts of religious performance, or charitable efforts, or skillful achievement. All of that is downstream from the spring of our identity. We are who we are in the hidden place, where desires and longings and passions and affections are born. When we pray, "Incline my heart," we are surrendering the control of those depths. We are looking to Christ, and his death for sinners, and we are seeing a person worthy of the deepest trust. For his sake we are saying to God, "I believe you are good. I believe you can be trusted. I believe you will not obliterate me but will make me what I was created to be. So I surrender to you the roots of my being—the spring of my very identity. I ask you to take control of that and give me the desires that accord with your worth and my greatest joy in you.

I suspect that many who pray for God to help them with their Bible reading do not get the answer because they really are not willing to make the surrender involved in crying out, "Incline my heart." They are saying deep inside, "I am not sure I really want to have a desire for God's word that is greater than my desire for sex or money or popularity or marriage or family or life itself." They are not really saying, "Your steadfast love is *better* than life" (Ps. 63:3). They are holding back. A deep cherishing of some sin or some "desire for other things" prevents the surrender of the whole heart. But such negotiations with God—such half measures—are not accepted. "If I had cherished iniquity in my heart, the Lord would not have listened" (Ps. 66:18).

God's Word Is Himself Revealed

Self-deception is likely happening here. The deception is that they are dealing only with God's word and not with God. They don't let themselves think that shrinking back from the fullest desire for the word of God is a shrinking back from God. They allow themselves the illusion that one can have a long-term relationship with God while cultivating quiet idolatries in their heart. God sees through such subterfuges. Jesus made plain what we all know in our deepest heart. The word of God is, as Derek Kidner says, "thyself revealed."[3] Jesus said, "If anyone loves me, he will keep my word" (John 14:23). That's how close the relationship is between Christ and his word. Loss of interest in the word of God is loss of interest in God.

Therefore, here at the outset of answering the question, "How do we read the Bible in the strength of another?" we have encountered the deepest demand of all. Reading the Bible is something we should *desire* to do (Ps. 1:2; 1 Pet. 2:2), but the desires of our sinful hearts are fickle. Therefore, everything begins with this test: do we really *want* to desire and enjoy the word of God above all created things? Are we willing to surrender the spring of our desires—our identity—into the hands of God? Are we willing to pray, "Incline my heart to your testimonies," and not hold anything back? In other words, the question about how to read the Scriptures is a question of radical Christian surrender of our deepest self into the hands of God to do as he pleases. It is a question about what it means to be a Christian.

Prayer for the Opening of Our Eyes

After we have prayed for God to incline our heart to his testimonies (Ps. 119:36)—the *I* of I.O.U.S.—we are now looking at the book. We are reading. We will see shortly what natural processes are involved in that act. But what needs to be stressed here is that when God gives us the desire for his word, the task of prayer has just begun. Before and

---

3. Derek Kidner, *Psalms 73–150* (London: Inter-Varsity Press, 1975), 462.

during our reading, we are offering up the prayer, "*Open my eyes*, that I may behold wondrous things out of your law" (Ps. 119:18). These eyes are what Paul calls the eyes of the heart (Eph. 1:18). His prayer is essentially the same as the psalmist's, only he is praying for others. He asks that "*the eyes of your hearts* [may be] enlightened."

All of us know what it is like to read without seeing "wondrous things." We have stared at the most glorious things without seeing them as glorious. We have seen marvels without marveling. We have put God's sweet kindness on the tongue of our soul without tasting sweetness. We have seen unspeakable love without feeling loved. We have seen the greatest power and felt no awe. We have seen immeasurable wisdom and felt no admiration. We have seen the holiness of wrath and felt no trembling. Which means we are "seeing without seeing" (see Matt. 13:13). This is why we must continue to weave the thread of God-dependent prayer into our reading: "Show me your glory" (Ex. 33:18).

If we do not feel the value of what we see, we are not seeing it as it really is. We are seeing it the way Satan sees it—except that even the demons tremble (James 2:19). We are seeing it the way the natural man sees. Before the supernatural "enlightenment" of our hearts at conversion (Eph. 1:18; Heb. 10:32), we look at the story of Jesus and are blind to "the light of the gospel of the glory of Christ" (2 Cor. 4:4). And even after that initial enlightenment (2 Cor. 4:6), we must pray repeatedly, the rest of our lives, that God would continue to give us eyes to see.

We know this because Paul is praying for *Christians* when he asks that "the eyes of your hearts" be enlightened. We know it, too, because the writer of Hebrews is writing to *Christians* when he says, "You have become dull of hearing" (Heb. 5:11). Until Jesus comes back, we "see in a mirror dimly" (1 Cor. 13:12), and that mirror has various degrees of mist to make things blurry. God has ordained that prayer be an indispensable means of wiping that mirror clean so that we can see the wonders of the word for what they really are.

Pray without Ceasing

That is not a once-for-all prayer. Not even a once-a-day prayer, or a once-at-the-beginning-of-devotions prayer. I have spent most of my forty-five-year ministry looking at biblical texts. I can testify that "pray[ing] without ceasing" (1 Thess. 5:17) has a special relevance for

Bible reading and Bible study. How many hundreds of times have I hit a wall in my effort to understand a text. Often I have had a sense of desperation because I must preach on this text in two days. I have used the original languages. I have used the books of other scholars. I have begun my work with prayer. But I am still perplexed. I pause—again!— and plead with the Lord to lead me into the truth and beauty of this text. It is a wonderful thing how many times, within the next half hour or so, something opens up that I had not seen before. I bow my head in wonder at his mercy and patience. Charles Spurgeon put it like this:

> We may hammer away at a text sometimes in meditation, and strike it again and again, and yet it may not yield to us, but we cry to God, and straightway the text opens, and we see concealed in it wondrous treasures of wisdom and of grace. . . . To read only is unprofitable: to pray without reading is not so soul-enriching; but when the two run together, they are like the horses pulling the chariot, and they speed along right merrily.[4]

Getting Ahead of Ourselves for a Reason

Implied in my last paragraph, and in Spurgeon's quote, is a fact that we have not made explicit yet. God answers our prayers not only by enabling us to see glory and beauty and worth where we would otherwise be dull and unresponsive, but also by enabling us to see the basic meaning of texts through which that glory shines. I am getting ahead of myself here, because we have not yet talked specifically about what the *meaning* of a text is. That comes later. But I need to draw that into our view now, because otherwise we won't know the full effect of prayer. I will pick this up in the next chapter as we complete our consideration of the indispensable place of prayer in reading the Bible supernaturally.

---

4. C. H. Spurgeon, *The Metropolitan Tabernacle Pulpit Sermons*, vol. 58 (London: Passmore & Alabaster, 1912), 427.

Sanctify them in the truth; your word is truth.

JOHN 17:17

Lead me in the path of your commandments,
    for I delight in it.

PSALM 119:35

17

The Indispensable Place of Prayer in Reading the Bible Supernaturally: To See, Savor, and Love with a United Heart

"Open my eyes, that I may behold wondrous things out of your law."

Meaning and Glory

In the first part of our treatment of prayer (chapter 16), I ended by referring to my experience of hitting a wall in trying to understand a biblical text, then pausing to pray for help, and finally getting a breakthrough. Then I commented that this personal experience introduced an aspect of prayer that I had not yet mentioned. Up till then, the focus was on the power of prayer to open the eyes of our hearts to see the glory of God where we otherwise would be dull and unresponsive. But the new point is that prayer has an effect not only on the heart's spiritual perception of God's glory, but also on the mind's intellectual grasp of the *basic meaning* of the text through which the glory shines.

I pleaded guilty of getting ahead of myself because, in using the phrase *basic meaning*, I am assuming things that I am going to discuss later (in chapter 20) about what we actually *mean* by "meaning." But I pleaded that I need to get ahead of myself for the sake of showing the fullness of what prayer is meant to do for us in reading the Bible.

When we pray for God to show us his glory in the Scripture, we are not asking him to bypass the meaning of the text, but to open the fullness of the author's meaning. Therefore, in our quest to see and savor the glory of God in Scripture, we pray for his help to grasp the basic meaning of the words. Glory does not hover over the text like a cloud to be seen separately from what the authors intended to communicate. It shines in and through what they intended to communicate—their *meaning*.

Illustration from Philippians

Even this is not quite the way to say it, because the glory is *part of* what they intended to communicate. But I think it is helpful to distinguish the *basic meaning* of a passage, on the one hand, and the *worth and beauty of the message*, on the other hand. I know they are not really separable. And both are part of what the author wants us to experience. Perhaps an illustration will help us see why I think the distinction is important, and how it relates to prayer.

In Philippians 1:23, Paul says, "My desire is to depart and be with Christ, for that is far better." Suppose some careless reader knew that Paul was in Rome and assumed Paul meant that his desire was to depart *from Rome* and be *with Christ* in a more rural, peaceful place than the dangerous urban center of the empire. And suppose the reader feels that this is a wonderful thought, full of sweet implications about the value of nature and peacefulness for the soul's refreshment.

Well, he would be wrong. First, this careless reader got the *basic meaning* wrong. Paul did not intend to say anything about departing from Rome to the countryside, or about the value of rural peacefulness. He intended to say that he desired to depart this life and be with Christ in heaven. So our reader simply missed Paul's intention. But it gets worse. On the basis of the wrong meaning, this careless reader also saw a kind of glory that was not there. He felt a sweetness about peaceful, rural living for the refreshment of the human soul. That feeling has no basis in this text. He has seen something he would call glorious or wonderful. But the glory and the wonder are not there.

The point of that illustration is this: when the psalmist prayed, "Open my eyes, that I may behold *wondrous things* out of your law" (Ps. 119:18), he did not mean that the sight of wonders could skip the natural process of careful reading. Therefore, prayer does not take the place of careful interpretation. Prayer serves careful interpretation. This is what I was getting at in the previous chapter when I said that sometimes I hit a wall in trying to understand a text, then I pray for help, and often a breakthrough comes. My prayer is not just for the sight of glory, but for the help in grasping the meaning through which the glory shines.

Pray about All, Because God Governs All

However we describe the levels of a text's meaning, prayer is fruitful at every level. God not only opens the eyes of our heart to see his glory; he also guides us providentially in the whole process of interpretation—even the most natural parts. He is sovereign over all of it. He governs every part of our textual observation or thinking or research. Jesus said that not a sparrow falls to the ground apart from our heavenly Father (Matt. 10:29). So it is with Bible reading. We do not make the smallest discovery without God's providential guidance. Of course, this is true for the unbelieving scholar as well. God's governance is not thwarted by the self-assertions of unbelief.[1] But in the case of believers, the mystery of believing prayer is operating.

As incredible as it may seem, God mysteriously weaves the prayers of his people into the way he runs the world. Things happen because we pray that would not happen if we did not pray. That is what James means when he says, "You do not have, because you do not ask" (James 4:2). And it is what Jesus means when he says, "Ask, and it will be given to you; seek, and you will find; knock, and it will be opened to you" (Matt. 7:7). This does not make us God—as if our will were the final arbiter of what happens in the world. But it does mean that our requests, made to God in faith, are part of the way God causes his will to happen. That includes his gracious will in helping us see the fullness of the meaning of his word—its basic message and its glory.

---

1. If you would like to join me in pondering more extensively the sovereignty of God over the sinful actions of man and Satan, see John Piper, *Spectacular Sins: And Their Global Purpose in the Glory of Christ* (Wheaton, IL: Crossway, 2008).

That We Prayed Does Not Make Us Infallible

This does not mean that we can ever make a case for our interpretation by saying, "I prayed for God's help, and so my interpretation is the right one." That kind of argument is not compelling, for at least three reasons. First, the person making the case may not be telling us the truth. Maybe he prayed; maybe he didn't. Second, God sometimes withholds the fullness of his illumination for wise and holy reasons, even when we ask him for help in interpreting a text. If he didn't withhold some insight, one hearty prayer might turn a reader into an infallible commentator on Scripture. God evidently does not think that is a good idea. Just as he wills to sanctify us gradually rather than perfecting us overnight, so he also wills to lead us to the full meaning of biblical texts gradually rather than making us infallible overnight. Infallible interpretation awaits the coming of Christ (1 Cor. 13:12).

Third, and most importantly, we cannot make a case for our interpretation by claiming divine illumination in answer to prayer, because the way God illumines the text is by *showing what is really there*. This means that when we want to make a case for how we understand a text, we must show what is really there. One good, solid grammatical argument for what the text means outweighs every assertion that the Holy Spirit told me the meaning. The reason that statement is not irreverent is that it takes more seriously the glorious work of the Holy Spirit in inspiring the grammar than it does the subjective experiences of an interpreter who ignores it.

Pray for Help to Pay Attention to What Is Written

Therefore, even though the guidance of the Holy Spirit in Bible reading does not give us an argument that our interpretations are true, his guidance and illumination are essential. So we should be praying for them repeatedly during the entire process of reading and studying the Bible. We should pray, for example, that he would help us pay close attention to all the features of the text. Oh how frustrating and defeating is the tendency of our minds to wander! Indulge me in a personal example from my journal:

> Just this morning—it could have been any morning—I was reading Exodus 34 as part of my morning devotions. I neglected to pray for

this help as I began. I was at a motel and out of my usual routine of time and place (excuses, excuses), and plowed right into reading without praying my trusty I.O.U.S.[2] I was paying attention when I started reading. Moses was recounting the words of God as he went up on the mountain to receive the Ten Commandments for a second time. I got through verse 4, but in a few minutes (yes, whole minutes!) I "woke up" and was reading verse 9 without the slightest recollection of what was in verses 5–8. I didn't fall asleep. My mind wandered. It wandered to a meeting my wife and I were going to have with someone at a restaurant in about an hour—a meeting that might prove very difficult.

I apologized to the Lord. Yes, I think it is an insult not to pay attention when someone is talking to you. We need to apologize, the same as if we were daydreaming at a restaurant when someone across the table is talking to us. Then I prayed that he would help me pay attention and that he would give me something to help me at this meeting. I went back and reread the verses. Here is what I saw: "The LORD passed before him and proclaimed, 'The LORD, the LORD, a God merciful and gracious, slow to anger, and abounding in steadfast love and faithfulness, keeping steadfast love for thousands, forgiving iniquity and transgression and sin, but who will by no means clear the guilty.'" (Ex. 34:6–7)

Glorious. Glorious! Do you hear the way God identifies himself after being rejected by his people who made the golden calf? The Lord. The Lord. God. Merciful. Gracious. Slow [not quick!] to anger. Abounding in love. Abounding in faithfulness. Forgiving iniquity. Forgiving transgression. Forgiving sin. Punishing the guilty who won't embrace grace.

It doesn't get much sweeter in the New Testament or Old Testament than those two verses from Exodus 34. That is what Satan did *not* want me to see. I believe it was God who graciously woke me up at verse 9 and rebuked me and sent me back to see the glory I missed because my mind simply glazed over.

And here is where it is all going. I called my wife over to sit on the bed and listen. I read these verses to her. Then we prayed. We specifically applied those verses to ourselves and the meeting we were about to have at the restaurant. We were strengthened. We were given hope. And God moved. The conversation took a turn at

---

2. For the I.O.U.S. acronym, see chap. 16.

one point that was simply amazing, and hearts opened and candor happened and love flowed.

I almost missed that gift. And if I had, I think the Lord would have been fully warranted in saying, "You did not have, because you did not ask. You just dutifully plowed ahead in your reading, and you jumped right over the glory that was waiting there for you to see." But, as the text says, he is merciful. So merciful. So forgiving. So willing to start over with us—at verse 9.

So ask the Lord to help you pay attention. If you tend to fall asleep while reading the Bible, ask him to give you the discipline you need to go to bed early enough to get the rest you need. Or ask him to teach you when the optimal time is when you will not be so sleepy. Or ask him to give you the motivation to get up and pace back and forth in your room while you read your Bible, because it's harder to fall asleep while walking. Or, if your conscience will allow it, ask him to make you caffeine-tolerant; then put your coffee to work for the glory of God!

God Makes Every Method More Fruitful—If You Ask

The number of things you could pray for to help you see what is in the Scripture is as great as the number of strategies for getting insight. God can make all of them more fruitful, if we ask him. This would include:

- Prayer to guide you to notice parts of the text that are especially illuminating.
- Prayer to lead you to other passages in the Bible that would shed light on the one you are reading.
- Prayer to lead you to other books or sermons or lectures that would be useful in shedding light on some problem you have run into.
- Prayer for experiences, or a reminder of experiences you've had, that would make what you are reading more real.
- Prayer for friends who could study the Bible with you and help you see things you haven't seen.
- Prayer against any sinful habits or inclinations that might blind you to a part of Scripture you would find uncomfortable.
- Prayer that as you write the text down in your journal, you would notice things you missed in simply reading.

Anything that helps you pay closer attention to what is actually written, pray about this. Ask God to make it more illuminating than it would be without his help.

"Unite My Heart" as I Read Your Word

So, in our use of the acronym I.O.U.S. to guide our prayer for help in reading the Bible supernaturally, we have now considered I—*Incline*. "*Incline* my heart to your testimonies, and not to selfish gain" (Ps. 119:36). And we've looked at O—*Open*. "*Open* my eyes, that I may behold wondrous things out of your law" (Ps. 119:18). The next letter in the acronym is U—*Unite*. "Teach me your way, O LORD, that I may walk in your truth; *unite* my heart to fear your name" (Ps. 86:11).

The difference between this prayer—"unite my heart"—and the prayer for focus is that this one concerns the heart, not just the mental attentiveness to the text. It reveals a deep human problem. Our hearts are prone to be divided, not united. Søren Kierkegaard wrote a book titled with the astonishing claim *Purity of Heart Is to Will One Thing*.[3] Behind that claim is a powerful biblical support: "Draw near to God, and he will draw near to you. Cleanse your hands, you sinners, and *purify your hearts, you double-minded*" (James 4:8). To be impure is to be divided in your heart. Part of your heart is cleaving to God, and part of it is cleaving to something that competes with God for your desires.

The Universal Experience of a Divided Heart

This is the universal experience for every person who has been invaded by the Spirit of God and brought to faith in Jesus. Jesus is now the supreme treasure. "Whoever loves father or mother more than me is not worthy of me, and whoever loves son or daughter more than me is not worthy of me" (Matt. 10:37). But until we die, or until Jesus comes again, the battle rages. We Christians must daily reassert our allegiance to Jesus as supreme. We must, as Paul says, "Consider [ourselves] dead to sin and alive to God in Christ Jesus" (Rom. 6:11). We must actively "consider" or "reckon" ourselves as belonging to God. We *do* belong to him. We *are* dead to sin. We *are* alive to God. And therefore, we

---

3. Søren Kierkegaard, *Purity of Heart Is to Will One Thing* (New York: Harper Brothers, 1948).

must *reckon* it to be so, because daily there are other forces at work to drag us the other way. Paul describes Christian reality when he says, "I do not understand my own actions. For I do not do what I want, but I do the very thing I hate" (Rom. 7:15).[4] He cries out, "Wretched man that I am!" (Rom. 7:24). That is what it is like to be double-minded (James 1:8).

This is why, when we read the Bible, we must pray with the psalmist, "Unite my heart." If the meaning and the glory of Scripture is to be seen and savored with our whole heart, we must have a whole heart for God. This is the first and great commandment: "You shall love the Lord your God with *all* your heart and with *all* your soul and with *all* your mind" (Matt. 22:37). How shall this command be obeyed by a divided heart? The great, central, all-pervading message of the Bible is that God is to be loved above *all* things, and with *all* that we are. He is supreme in worth and beauty. There is little hope, therefore, that the central message of the Bible—and all it touches—will be rightly seen and savored where the heart is divided. Let us pray, therefore, with Thomas Ken,

> Direct, control, suggest, this day,
>   All I design, or do, or say,
> That all my powers, with all their might,
>   In Thy sole glory may *unite*.[5]

The Prayer for Savoring the Glory of God

The fourth letter in my acronym of prayer (I.O.U.S.) is S—*Satisfy*. "*Satisfy* us in the morning with your steadfast love, that we may rejoice and be glad all our days" (Ps. 90:14). Recall the proposal from part 1:

> The Bible itself shows that our ultimate goal in reading the Bible is that God's infinite worth and beauty would be exalted in the everlasting, white-hot worship of the blood-bought bride of Christ from every people, language, tribe, and nation.

---

4. I know some good scholars do not think Romans 7 describes Christian experience, but I do. I have tried to make the case in a six-part sermon series, "Who Is This Divided Man?," accessed March 23, 2016, http://www.desiringgod.org/scripture/romans/7/messages.

5. Thomas Ken, "Awake, My Soul, and with the Sun," 1674, accessed March 23, 2016, http://cyberhymnal.org/htm/a/w/awakemys.htm; emphasis added.

All our Bible reading is aiming toward this end—the exaltation of God's glory in the white-hot worship of his people. Therefore, we devoted three chapters (3–5) to the implication that God's glory must be *seen* in the word, and two chapters (6–7) to the implication that God's glory must be *savored* in the word.

The present chapter is about the necessity of praying that God would cause these implications to happen. The acronym I.O.U.S. comes to its highest point in the prayer that God would cause us to *savor* him—or be satisfied in him—above all things: "*Satisfy* us in the morning with your steadfast love." This is what I mean my *savoring* the glory of God. It means we find him to be more *satisfying* than any created reality. We say with the psalmist, "When I awake, I shall be *satisfied* with your likeness" (Ps. 17:15).

The Psalmist Needs Divine Help to Love God

Is it not comforting and inspiring that the psalmists felt the need to pray this way? "Satisfy me with your love!" Why would they pray this? Because their hearts were divided like ours. Every day they needed to lay hold on the supremacy of God's worth. Every day they had to acknowledge that yesterday's love does not suffice for today. We need new mercies every morning. We need fresh grace. We need for God to reveal his beauty and worth to us again. This is why we read our Bible every day. And this is why we pray, "Open my eyes to your glory," and, "Satisfy me with all you are for me in Jesus."

David models for us in Psalm 63 the progress of his soul from *seeking* to *seeing* to *savoring*:

> O God, you are my God; earnestly I *seek* you;
>   my soul thirsts for you;
> my flesh faints for you,
>   as in a dry and weary land where there is no water.
> So I have *looked* upon you in the sanctuary,
>   *beholding* your power and glory.
> Because your steadfast love is better than life,
>   my lips will praise you.
> So I will bless you as long as I live;
>   in your name I will lift up my hands.

My soul will be *satisfied* as with fat and rich food,
    and my mouth will praise you with joyful lips. (vv. 1–5)

When David and the other psalmists (such as Asaph) saw and savored the Lord above all things, they loved to tell him so:

Whom have I in heaven but you?
    And there is nothing on earth that I desire besides you.
My flesh and my heart may fail,
    but God is the strength of my heart and my portion forever.
        (Ps. 73:25–26)

I say to the LORD, "You are my Lord;
    I have no good apart from you." (Ps. 16:2)

I.O.U.S.—L.?

Now, if you have been tracking with me, you realize that I.O.U.S. is incomplete. The aim of reading the Bible does not terminate on my personal satisfaction in God without reference to other people and the end of history. So in part 1, I devoted two chapters (8–9) to the fact that seeing and savoring God leads to a beautiful transformation from self-ish behavior to radical, risk-taking, loving behavior. The key text was 2 Corinthians 3:18 ("Beholding the glory of the Lord, [we] are being transformed into the same image from one degree of glory to another"). *Seeing* God's glory for what it really is—all-*satisfying*—transforms the root of all our actions, and leads to love.

Therefore, we need to mess up our neat little acronym with another letter—L for *Lead*. We should move from "*Satisfy* me with your love," to "*Lead* me in paths of love and righteousness" (see Ps. 23:3). "*Lead* me in the path of your commandments, for I delight in it" (Ps. 119:35). "*Lead* me in your truth and teach me" (Ps. 25:5). "Lead me, O LORD, in your righteousness" (Ps. 5:8). "Lead us not into temptation, but deliver us from evil" (Matt. 6:13).

Beware of thinking that this "leading" is different from the deep inner transformation we saw in 2 Corinthians 3:18. Jesus and the psalmists do not mean, "Lead us by external force the way you would lead a mule with a whip." They mean, "Lead us by showing us the glory of your grace, and satisfying us to the depths of our being so that we

are freed to risk our lives in the cause of love." We know this because
of the way David describes God's leading in Psalm 32:8–9:

> I will instruct you and teach you
>> in the way you should go;
> I will counsel you
>> with my eye upon you.
> Be not like a horse or a mule,
>> without understanding,
> which must be curbed with bit and bridle,
>> or it will not stay near you.

If you need a bit and bridle, you have not seen the glory of God. "Whoever
does good is from God; whoever does evil *has not seen God*" (3 John 11).

Paul shows us how to pray for transformation. To be sure, he prays
for the eyes of our hearts to be opened (Eph. 1:18) and for our hearts
to be ravished by the immeasurable love of Christ (Eph. 3:14–19). But
he also prays for the practical, visible fruit of righteousness and good
works. "We have not ceased to pray for you . . . that you . . . walk in a
manner worthy of the Lord, fully pleasing to him: bearing fruit in every
good work and increasing in the knowledge of God" (Col. 1:9–10). "It
is my prayer that [you might be] filled with the fruit of righteousness that
comes through Jesus Christ, to the glory and praise of God" (Phil. 1:11).

"Sanctify Them in the Truth—Your Word"

We know that these prayers for God's leading and God's gift of right
living and good deeds are prayers for the *fruit of Bible reading*, because
the Bible makes clear that God gives us his word precisely to bring
about these changes in our lives. Reading God's word and being led by
God's Spirit are not separable. Jesus prayed explicitly that his Father
would lead us into holy living by means of God's word. "Sanctify them
in the truth; your word is truth" (John 17:17). He had explained earlier
that our liberation from sin comes by the truth of God's word. "You
will know the truth, and the truth will set you free" (John 8:32). And
when the apostle Paul affirmed the inspiration of Scripture, he too made
the connection between God's word and our good deeds explicit:

> All Scripture is breathed out by God and profitable for teaching,
> for reproof, for correction, and for training in righteousness, that

the man of God may be complete, equipped for every good work. (2 Tim. 3:16–17)

So when we pray that God would lead us in paths of righteousness (Ps. 23:3), and that he would cause us to bear fruit in every good deed (Col. 1:10), and that he would fill us with the fruit of righteousness (Phil. 1:11), we are praying that *Scripture* would have this effect on us. We are praying about the way we read *the Bible*.

But we are not praying that we would become legalists—doing good just because the Bible says to do good, whether we are changed on the inside or not. That's the way the Pharisees handled the word of God. And Jesus told them they acted as if they never read it (see chapter 12). No. We are praying that the word reveal the worth and beauty of all that God is for us in Christ, so that we would *see* it as all-satisfying, and *savor* it above all other desires, and *be changed* by it from selfish to self-giving, so that people might see our good deeds and *give glory to God* (Matt. 5:16).

God at Work in Our Reading

We have spent two chapters on the indispensable place of prayer in reading the Bible supernaturally. This act is represented by the P in the acronym A.P.T.A.T., "P"—Prayer. Under the banner of prayer we drilled more deeply into the specificity of praying with the help of another acronym, I.O.U.S.—Incline, Open, Unite, Satisfy. The aim was not only to help us pray about reading the Bible, but also to pray the way the Bible itself prays about that.

A.P.T.A.T. is a guide for how to live life—including reading the Bible—by the power and leading of the Holy Spirit. It is an attempt to answer what *we* are to do if we hope to say with Paul: I worked hard, but it was not I but God's grace (1 Cor. 15:10). I read my Bible, but it was not I but God at work in me. A.P.T.A.T. is an effort to describe what it means to *act the miracle* of the Christian life. We must begin with humility. That is, we begin our Bible reading by *admitting* (A) that we cannot do anything apart from God's grace. Then we must *pray* (P) for new desires, and open eyes, and united hearts, and satisfied souls, and a life of love.

And now we turn to the first T of A.P.T.A.T.—*Trust*. If we are going to experience the supernatural reality of God's intervention in our Bible reading, we must not only ask for his help, but trust his promises to give it. That is the focus of chapters 18 and 19.

We walk by faith, not by sight.

2 CORINTHIANS 5:7

Does he who supplies the Spirit to you and works miracles among you do so by works of the law, or by hearing with faith?

GALATIANS 3:5

18

Reading the Bible by Faith
in the Promises of God

"I live by faith in the Son of God,
who loved me and gave himself for me."

At the beginning of chapter 14, we looked at Abraham and Sarah as an example of the natural act of experiencing supernatural help. They were both old. Sarah was barren. God promised that Sarah would conceive a child by Abraham and bear a son. It was humanly impossible. That's the point of the story. God does supernatural things to fulfill his promises. The fulfillment of divine promises doesn't just happen. God makes it happen. "I am watching over my word to perform it" (Jer. 1:12). But Abraham and Sarah still do the *natural* thing: they have sexual relations. So it all still seems very natural. In one sense it *is* natural. But there would have been no Isaac without God's supernatural intervention.

That's the way it is with reading the Bible. The seeing and savoring and transformation that God has promised to give through Scripture will not happen in the minds and hearts of sinful human beings unless there is a supernatural intervention. That was the point of chapters 11–13. God must perform a new creation (2 Cor. 4:6), enlighten the eyes of the heart (Eph. 1:18), open the mind (Luke 24:45), and reveal what is really there (Matt. 16:17). In all of that, he turns an impossibility into supernatural reading.

Finally to the First T of A.P.T.A.T.

I asked in chapter 14, How does this happen? How did Abraham and Sarah act the miracle of bearing a son of promise? How do we act the miracle of seeing the beauty of God in Scripture? The answer I gave simply focused on the fact that God does his supernatural work without nullifying the natural processes of begetting children or reading Scripture. He ordinarily works *through* them, not *around* them. Therefore, as the chapter title said, "God Forbid That We Despise His Natural Gifts."

But what I entirely passed over in chapter 14 was an absolutely essential part of the Abraham and Sarah story—and an equally essential part of reading the Bible supernaturally. I passed over Abraham's *faith*—his *trust* in the promise of God. I am returning to Abraham's trust now as we take up the first T in A.P.T.A.T.

A.P.T.A.T., you recall, is a practical and biblical guide to help us live supernaturally—to "serve by the strength that God supplies" (1 Pet. 4:11). It is a way of "walk[ing] by the Spirit" (Gal. 5:16), and fleshing out what it means to say, "I worked hard," yet "it was not I, but the grace of God" (1 Cor. 15:10). So A.P.T.A.T. is the path we walk into the natural act of reading the Bible supernaturally. In this chapter, we focus on the first T—*Trust*. "*Trust* in the LORD with all your heart, and do not lean on your own understanding. In all your ways [including reading the Bible!] acknowledge him, and he will make straight your paths" (Prov. 3:5–6).

Fully Convinced God Could Do What He Promised

Abraham is given as our example in acting the miracle—receiving and performing the supernatural. Like us, he was standing before a human impossibility. What did he do? What should we do? Paul focuses on Abraham's God-glorifying *trust* in God's word. "No unbelief made him waver concerning the promise of God, but he grew strong in his faith *as he gave glory to God*, fully convinced that God was able to do what he had promised" (Rom. 4:20–21). It is remarkable that the glory of God is shown in two ways at this point in Abraham's life—both in the God-glorifying miracle of *Isaac's birth*, and in the God-glorifying *faith* of Abraham in believing God would do it.

This is the way it is with reading the Bible. Our aim is to see and savor and be changed by the glory of God in and through the meaning of what we read, and that corresponds to the miracle of Isaac's birth. On the way to that end, there is a God-glorifying way to seek that meaning and that glory, namely, by trusting God's promise to help us—which corresponds to Abraham's faith. "He grew strong *in his faith.*" He was "*fully convinced* that God was able to do what he had promised." And in this "faith" and this "full conviction," Abraham "gave glory to God." That is, he showed by his trust that God is gloriously strong and trustworthy. God can give a son to a hundred-year-old man and a barren woman. And God can cause a once–spiritually dead human heart, like ours, to see the glory of God in the Bible.

Walk and Live—and Read—by Faith

Reading the Bible is part of the normal Christian walk through life. As such we are to read the Bible the way we are to *walk* and *live*. And the biblical answer is that we are to "walk *by faith*" (2 Cor. 5:7) and "live *by faith*" (Gal. 2:20). Or, as the whole eleventh chapter of Hebrews draws out, we are to understand by faith (v. 3), obey by faith (v. 8), change places by faith (v. 9), receive power by faith (v. 11), make sacrifices by faith (v. 17), stand against tyrants by faith (v. 24), and so on. In other words, everything we do should be done "by faith."

The most important reason for the necessity of doing everything by faith—including reading the Bible—is that this is the only way God will receive the glory he should have from us in every action. Abraham is our example of this: "No unbelief made him waver concerning the promise of God, but he grew strong in his faith *as he gave glory to God*, fully convinced that God was able to do what he had promised" (Rom. 4:20–21). Trusting God for his help in what we do draws attention to his power and trustworthiness. Faith in God's promised help turns every act into a God-exalting virtue. And if you believe that all God's promises are purchased for us only through Christ (2 Cor. 1:20; Rom. 8:32), then faith in God's promised help turns every act into a Christ-exalting virtue.

And since everything should be done for the glory of God (1 Cor. 10:31), therefore, every act should be by faith in the promised help of God. Therefore, without faith it is impossible to please God (Heb. 11:6), since God wills to be glorified in all things, and we do not glorify him if we do not trust him. Which means that "whatever does not proceed from faith is sin" (Rom. 14:23). For it is a sin to treat the promised help of God as untrustworthy.

Of course, this assumes that we are utterly dependent on God for the simplest acts of life, as well as the difficult ones. Which is true, even though most people do not believe this, and many of those who do believe it theoretically don't pray and trust and act like they do. Nevertheless, Jesus said, "Apart from me you can do nothing" (John 15:5). And the apostle Paul said, "[God] himself gives to all mankind life and breath and *everything*" (Acts 17:25). "What do you have that you did not receive? If then you received it, why do you boast as if you did not receive it?" (1 Cor. 4:7). "From him and through him and to him are *all things*. To him be glory forever" (Rom. 11:36). We cannot even go from one town to the next without God's sustaining power.

> Come now, you who say, "Today or tomorrow we will go into such and such a town and spend a year there and trade and make a profit"—yet you do not know what tomorrow will bring. What is your life? For you are a mist that appears for a little time and then vanishes. Instead you ought to say, "If the Lord wills, we will live and do this or that." As it is, you boast in your arrogance. All such boasting is evil. (James 4:13–16)

What is the opposite of this boasting in arrogance? The opposite is faith, that is, happily admitting we are not in ultimate control of our lives—not even in the most incidental things—and therefore should gladly trust in the promised help of God to live every minute of our days, including the minutes we spend reading the Bible. We cannot turn from one page to another without God. We cannot think one thought without God. We cannot feel one feeling without God. And we certainly cannot see the most glorious wonders in the word without God. Therefore, we must read by faith in the blood-bought promise that God will help us.

How Do We Read "by the Spirit"?

What is the relationship between living *by the Spirit* and living *by faith*? I ask this, because I have argued that A.P.T.A.T. is a strategy for living "by the strength that God supplies" (1 Pet. 4:11) and "walk[ing] by the Spirit" (Gal. 5:16). We now are dealing with the first T of A.P.T.A.T., and the T says, "walk by *faith* [*=trust*]"—that is, by *trusting* God's promised help. So there is an implicit relationship between reading the Bible "by the Spirit" and reading the Bible "by faith." What is that relationship?

The answer is found in Paul's letter to the Galatians where he tells us that we "live *by faith*" (Gal. 2:20) and that we "live *by the Spirit*" (Gal. 5:25)—and that we are to "walk *by the Spirit*," and be "led *by the Spirit*," and "keep in step *with the Spirit*" (Gal. 5:16, 18, 25). The connection between living by faith and living by the Spirit is found in Galatians 3:5. Paul makes a point by asking a rhetorical question: "Does he who supplies the Spirit to you and works miracles among you do so by works of the law, or by hearing with faith?" He expects the answer to be obvious. The Spirit does *not* do his work "by works of the law." In other words, law keeping is not the channel through which the Spirit flows as he does his powerful work. Rather the channel through which the Spirit flows is *faith*. When we *trust* the promises of God, the Spirit moves to do his powerful work.

The reason I refer to "trusting *the promises of God*" rather than referring simply to a generic trust is that Paul used the phrase "*hearing with faith.*" "Does he who supplies the Spirit to you and works miracles among you do so by works of the law, or *by hearing with faith?*" This is not generic faith. This is faith in response to the *word* of God. God has *said* something that needs to be *heard* (or read) and trusted. Most basically, this is the gospel of Jesus with the promise of forgiven sins and eternal life. But the principle is not limited to any single promise or group of promises. Wherever God promises any help, of any kind—from the most eternal to the most immediate and practical—faith in that promise is the channel through which the Holy Spirit acts. That is the point of Galatians 3:5.

Trust a Specific Promise for Help

So the connection between reading the Bible *by the Spirit* and reading the Bible *by faith* is that faith in God's promised help is the channel through which the help of the Spirit comes. The implication of this connection for using A.P.T.A.T. is that when we *admit* (A) our need, and *pray* (P) for help, we must pray in faith. We must *trust* (T) the promises of God to help us find the meaning of Scripture, especially the beauty and worth of God shining through that meaning. In this way, the supernatural work of God comes into action, and we find ourselves reading supernaturally—that is, by the Spirit.

What I have found over the years is that the most common breakdown in the pattern of life described in A.P.T.A.T. is the failure to trust a specific promise from the Lord as we move into our *action* (A)—in this case, our Bible reading. Even people who are familiar with this biblical pattern of living by the Spirit by faith often experience a kind of mental and spiritual haze between P and T. They *pray* for help, but they have no specific promise of God in mind that they are praying about, and so their trust floats in the air instead of fastening onto a solid promise. Promises are meant to be believed. Specifically believed. Faith is meant to fasten firmly and unshakably on one or more of those promises. But when promises are not in view, faith dangles in the air. This does not establish the soul, or honor God, as if we took hold of a promise and joyfully trusted that God would keep it as we work.

Trusting a Person to Keep His Word

I know that our faith is ultimately in a *person*. But trust in a person who makes no promises is meaningless. To say, "I trust Joe, but I don't know what Joe might do," is not a tribute to Joe. It's a sign of your folly. Joe is worthy of trust, or not, because you know something about his character, his ability, and his intentions toward you. Good intentions are called "promises." The evidence that you trust Joe as a *person* is your trust in his word.

So part of living by faith, and thus walking by the Spirit, is that we keep God's good intentions before us. When we start to pray for God's help in reading the Bible, we put those intentions before us in the form of promises, and we trust them. Then, in that trust, we *act* (A). That is what makes that action "by the Spirit." The Spirit moves through that trust (Gal. 3:5). Or to put it another way, by that trust in the promise of God to help us, Bible reading becomes the human acting of a miracle. God works by the Spirit to help us, according to his promise. We act by faith in that promise and thus receive the help.

What Promises?

The question, therefore, that presses to be answered is this: What divine promises do we have for help in reading the Bible? Are they only general promises for help? Or are there specific promises relating directly to the task of seeking God's mind in the Scriptures? That is the question we take up in chapter 19.

He who did not spare his own Son but gave him up for us all, how will he not also with him graciously give us all things?

ROMANS 8:32

If any of you lacks wisdom, let him ask God, who gives generously to all without reproach, and it will be given him.

JAMES 1:5

19

Reading the Bible by Faith in His Promise to Instruct Us

*"Good and upright is the LORD;
therefore he instructs sinners in the way."*

In chapters 18 and 19, we are focusing on the first T in A.P.T.A.T.—
Trust. This acronym is a way of describing how we go about living a
supernatural life naturally—or how you perform the *natural act of reading the Bible supernaturally*. What we have seen is that walking "by the
Spirit" happens in and through walking "by faith." Faith—or trust—is
the channel through which the supernatural work of God flows into our
natural tasks. We saw that this trust is most effective when it attaches
to specific promises of God, rather than dangling vaguely in the air of
God's goodness. Which leads us now to ask what these promises are.

"How Will He Not Give Us All Things?"
What divine promises do we have for help in reading the Bible? We
start with the broad and wonderfully all-encompassing promises and
their connection to the cross of Christ. Many Christians would start
with one of the greatest and most inclusive promises God ever made to
his children, Romans 8:28: "We know that for those who love God all
things work together for good, for those who are called according to his
purpose." In other words, if we love God, we can approach every task

with a strong confidence that God will turn it for our good—including the task of reading the Bible.

I prefer to begin with Romans 8:32, because this verse embraces Romans 8:28 but goes even further by connecting it with the rock-solid foundation of the cross of Christ: "He who did not spare his own Son but gave him up for us all, how will he not also with him graciously give us all things?" This is a rhetorical question. That means it needs to be expressed as a statement to see its plain meaning. It is, in fact, an amazing promise. "Since God did not spare his own Son, but gave him up on the cross for us all, therefore he will most certainly graciously give us all things with him." There is no greater foundation (God's sacrifice of his Son in our place) and no greater structure built on that foundation—the promise that God will give his children all things.

"All things" means "all things that are good for us." That's why I said that Romans 8:32 embraces Romans 8:28. "All things working together for our good" is virtually the same as "graciously give us all things." We know the promise does not include every comfortable thing in this life. Three verses later, Paul includes in the *all things* "tribulation, distress, persecution, famine, nakedness, danger, and sword," and then he adds, "For your sake we are being killed all the day long; we are regarded as sheep to be slaughtered" (Rom. 8:35–36). But these horrors that Christians may expect do not separate us from the love of Christ, but in fact work for our eternal good—especially conformity to the Son of God (Rom. 8:29).

So the most foundational promise that we can trust at every moment of the day is, *God will give us what we need in order to do his will and reach the goal of likeness to Jesus.* "My God will supply every need of yours according to his riches in glory in Christ Jesus" (Phil. 4:19). Not every "want" or "desire." But every *need*. Whatever we need *to do his will*. "I know how to be brought low, and I know how to abound. In any and every circumstance, I have learned the secret of facing plenty and hunger, abundance and need. I can do *all things* through him who strengthens me" (Phil. 4:12–13). "I can do *all things*." I can be *brought low* for the glory of God. I can *go hungry* for the glory of God. I can *be in need* for the glory of God. And in it all, we can be joyfully confident that God is for us and is working *all things* for our good. Whatever we need to that end, he promises to supply.

All-Embracing Promises

It is crucial that we fasten our faith to two or three clear expressions of this all-embracing promise in Scripture. I say this because, even for longtime followers of Jesus, the content of our hope can become hazy. Hazy hope provides weak motivation. A nebulous sense that God is somehow working to help us is not such a clear channel for the Holy Spirit's power as when we have a clear, sharp sight of a specific promise. So it is good to memorize a few definite promises that are so all-encompassing that they cover every situation. For example:

> The eyes of the LORD run to and fro throughout the whole earth, to give strong support to those whose heart is blameless toward him. (2 Chron. 16:9)

> Fear not, for I am with you;
> be not dismayed, for I am your God;
> I will strengthen you, I will help you,
> I will uphold you with my righteous right hand. (Isa. 41:10)

> Goodness and mercy shall follow me
> all the days of my life. (Ps. 23:6)

> The LORD God is a sun and shield;
> the LORD bestows favor and honor.
> No good thing does he withhold
> from those who walk uprightly. (Ps. 84:11; cf. 34:9–10)

> Seek first the kingdom of God and his righteousness, and all these things will be added to you. (Matt. 6:33)

> All things are yours, whether Paul or Apollos or Cephas or the world or life or death or the present or the future—all are yours, and you are Christ's, and Christ is God's. (1 Cor. 3:21–23)

> All the promises of God find their Yes in him. That is why it is through him that we utter our Amen to God for his glory. (2 Cor. 1:20)

With these sweeping promises, we should come to the task of reading our Bibles (as to every other task) greatly encouraged that God will help us. He gave his Son to give us life. Will he not give us help to know him, and understand his ways, and see his glory? Whenever we think of the obstacles hindering our understanding and our spiritual sight, we should remember the promises that God is for us and not against us. "No good thing does he withhold from those who walk uprightly."

Fasten Your Faith on Focused Promises

But not only should we nail to the wall of our mind several specific all-encompassing promises of God's help; we also should call to mind at various times even more focused promises that relate directly to the task at hand. If we are facing the temptation of covetousness or financial difficulty, we should call to mind God's promises about money (Heb. 13:5–6). If we are facing sexual temptation, we should call to mind God's promises to the pure in heart (Matt. 5:8). If we are tempted with pride and boasting, we should call to mind the promises made to the humble (1 Pet. 5:6–7). If we are tempted to take revenge, we should remember the promises that God himself will settle accounts (Rom. 12:19). If we are facing death, we should recall God's promises to the dying (John 11:25–26). This is what it means to walk by faith—moment by moment trusting God to do what he has promised to do in every situation of our lives. All the promises are yes in Christ. They are the blood-bought birthright of every born-again person. That's what the logic of Romans 8:32 secures.

He Instructs Sinners in the Way

Therefore, when we come to read our Bible, we should not only glance at the all-encompassing promises nailed to the wall of our mind—"I will strengthen you, I will help you, I will uphold you" (Isa. 41:10)—but we should also call to mind more focused promises that relate to our present need, the need to understand the mind of God in Scripture, and to see his glory. For example, from my seminary days forty-five years ago up to this very day, Psalm 25 has been a close friend in my effort to understand the Scriptures.

> O my God, in you I *trust*;
>   let me not be put to shame. . . .
> Good and upright is the LORD;
>   therefore he *instructs* sinners in the way.
> He *leads* the humble in what is right,
>   and *teaches* the humble his way. . . .

Who is the man who fears the LORD?
> Him will he *instruct* in the way that he should choose.
>> (Ps. 25:2, 8–9, 12)

I suppose, to be honest, the reason this promise is so precious to me is that I so easily qualify for it. "He instructs *sinners* in the way." What a relief! It is usually sin that makes our task of seeing glory in the Scripture so hard. So we might fear that we have utterly disqualified ourselves from God's help because we have blinded ourselves by our own sinning. But God comes to us in Psalm 25 and reminds us of his mercy. He will help *sinners* understand. He will instruct *sinners*! Not cavalier sinners. Not arrogant, self-exalting, impenitent sinners. But broken and humble sinners. "He leads the *humble* in what is right." Not the self-sufficient who think they can find the meaning of Scripture on their own—or who don't feel any need for Scripture at all. But the sinners who *trust* and *fear* the Lord. "O my God, in you I *trust*. . . . Who is the man who *fears* the LORD? Him will he instruct."

Blood-Bought Promises for Bible Reading

So we open our Bibles with a sweet sense that even though we don't deserve it, God will *lead* us and *instruct* us. Our very reading is the experience of gospel grace. Christ died for sinners so that the promise would come true: *God helps sinners understand the Bible.* These blood-bought promises are given to us so that we might believe them. Not just hear them. Believe them. Trust them. Because, remember from Galatians 3:5, God "supplies the Spirit to you . . . by hearing *with faith*." We stand before the Bible ready to read. We hear a promise. "I will instruct you and teach you." We put our faith in it. The Spirit moves in the channel of faith, and we "act the miracle." We read supernaturally. So it is good to gather some of these precious promises and store them up:

> The LORD gives wisdom;
>> from his mouth come knowledge and understanding;
>> he stores up sound wisdom for the upright. (Prov. 2:6–7)

> Trust in the LORD with all your heart,
>> and do not lean on your own understanding.
> In all your ways acknowledge him,
>> and he will make straight your paths. (Prov. 3:5–6)

I will instruct you and teach you in the way you should go;
  I will counsel you with my eye upon you. (Ps. 32:8)

You guide me with your counsel,
  and afterward you will receive me to glory. (Ps. 73:24)

Do not be anxious about . . . what you should say, for *the Holy Spirit will teach* you in that very hour what you ought to say. (Luke 12:11–12)

Jesus said to the Jews who had believed him, "If you abide in my word, you are truly my disciples, and *you will know the truth*, and the truth will set you free." (John 8:31–32)

If any of you lacks wisdom, let him ask God, *who gives generously* to all without reproach, and it will be given him. But let him ask in faith, with no doubting, for the one who doubts is like a wave of the sea that is driven and tossed by the wind. For that person must not suppose that he will receive anything from the Lord; he is a double-minded man, unstable in all his ways. (James 1:5–8)

Infallibility Is Not Promised

God's promise to help us and instruct us and give us wisdom as we read the Bible is not a promise that we will become infallible in this life. I argued in chapter 17 that we should never make a case for the correctness of our interpretation by saying, "I prayed for help, I trusted God to help me; therefore, I know my interpretation is true." Whether an interpretation is true depends on whether it is really there in the words and phrases and clauses of the text. Others who also have prayed may see things differently. The conversation that you have with each other is not an argument about who prayed more earnestly or who trusted more deeply. It's a mutual effort to show what is really there in the text for the other to see.

Whether we can explain it fully or not, the fact is that God has planned to sanctify us and enlighten us *gradually*, not instantaneously. Otherwise, one prayer ("Thy will be done") could make me impeccable, and one prayer ("Instruct me") could make me infallible. But Jesus taught us not only to pray, "Thy will be done," every day, but also to pray, "Forgive us our sins," every day (see Matt. 6:9–13). And just as sin dogs us every day, to the day of our death (1 John 1:8–10), so also shortcomings in biblical interpretation burden us to the end of our days. This is why James warned us not to become Bible teachers without serious consideration:

> Not many of you should become teachers, my brothers, for you know that we who teach will be judged with greater strictness. For we all stumble in many ways. And if anyone does not stumble in what he says, he is a perfect man, able also to bridle his whole body. (James 3:1–2)

This proneness to "stumble in many ways" in our effort to see and teach the truth is one of the reasons God put his children in churches. We are not supposed to be isolated interpreters of God's word. We are supposed to "exhort one another" (Heb. 3:13), and "encourage one another" (1 Thess. 5:11), and "admonish one another" (Col. 3:16), and "instruct one another" (Rom. 15:14), and "stir up one another to love" (Heb. 10:24), and "confess [our] sins to one another" (James 5:16). In other words, there is a profound and God-designed interdependence within the body of Christ. Where one person sees things poorly in a passage of the Bible, another person may see them clearly. Christ would not have given *teachers* (Eph. 4:11) to the church if he intended us to be so individualistic that we could not learn from others how better to see what is in the Bible.

If Not Infallibility, Then What?

That leaves this final question: When God promises to give us wisdom and to guide us, what may we trust him for, if not infallible interpretation? The first part of my answer is to remind us that God guides us into truth in ways that are not always immediate and solitary, so the guidance may not be readily apparent. He may lead us over time. He may lead us by gradually bringing people into our lives with insights that we did not have on our own. He may lead us by giving us experiences without which some texts remain dark. "It is good for me that I was afflicted, that I might learn your statutes" (Ps. 119:71). And he may lead us by the repetition of looking at the text so that the tenth time we look, we finally see what we had missed the previous nine times. So we must not conclude quickly, when we lack understanding, that God is not at work. He may be preparing the affliction, or the sermon, or the alertness that will bring us light. None of our efforts will have been wasted. God weaves even the seemingly failed hour of study into the fabric of illumination.

The second part of my answer is that the assurance of our salvation through faith in Christ includes, by implication, the assurance that God will help us see in the Bible all we need to see in order to arrive safely in his presence at the end of our lives, or at the day of his coming. There is a holiness without which we will not see the Lord (Heb. 12:14). God creates and sustains that measure of holiness by means of the word of God (John 17:17). Therefore, the faithfulness of God in keeping us secure in Christ (Phil. 1:6; Rom. 8:30; 1 Cor. 1:8) includes this commitment to keep his promises to guide us into enough truth and obedience to confirm our faith and union with Christ at the last day (Phil. 1:10–11). In his typically complex sentence structure, John Owen expresses this part of my answer:

> I shall, therefore, fix this assertion as a sacred truth: Whoever, in the diligent and immediate study of the Scripture to know the mind of God therein so as to do it, doth abide in fervent supplications, in and by Jesus Christ, for supplies of the Spirit of grace, to lead him into all truth, to reveal and make known unto him the truth as it is in Jesus, to give him an understanding of the Scriptures and the will of God therein, *he shall be preserved from pernicious errors*, and *attain that degree in knowledge as shall be sufficient unto the guidance and preservation of the life of God in the whole of his faith and obedience.*[1]

The last part of my answer to the question—When God promises to give us wisdom, what may we trust him for?—is that there are gifts of understanding and glimpses of glory that no one can predict or quantify ahead of time. God loves his people and very often wants to give them special help from his word. To that end, he may give unusual insight to a pastor or teacher or small-group leader or father of a family that he never would have had, except that God wanted that understanding to be given as a gift to his people. Which means that whenever we read

---

1. John Owen, *The Works of John Owen*, ed. William H. Goold, vol. 4 (Edinburgh: T&T Clark, n.d.), 204; emphasis added.

the Bible, we should desire that all our insights would serve others, not just ourselves. And then we should pray for God's help, and *trust* him, that he would give us not only what we need for our own perseverance, but also for the strength and beauty of his people—whether we are encouraging a friend or preaching to thousands.

How Holy Help Flows

We have been unfolding the "Natural Act of Reading the Bible Supernaturally." The acronym A.P.T.A.T. has been our guide. To read the Bible supernaturally, we must *admit* (A) that without divine intervention we will neither see nor savor nor be changed by the truth and beauty of Scripture as it really is. From this sense of dependence on God, we must, then, *pray* (P) for God's help in our reading. In this praying and in the subsequent *acts* (A) of interpretation (which we will turn to next), we must *trust* (T) the promises of God for Christ's sake. Through these three movements of our heart (admitting, praying, trusting), the supernatural work of the Holy Spirit flows.

Without this divine intervention, our spiritual eyes would not be opened (Eph. 1:18); our hearts would not be softened (Ezek. 11:19; Eph. 4:18); our minds would not be enlightened (2 Cor. 4:6); our souls would not be receptive (1 Cor. 2:14); and our wills would not be submissive to the word of God (Rom. 8:7). Therefore, our reading would see and savor nothing as it really is. Many meanings would be distorted at their basic level, and all meaning would be stripped of its most important aspect—the relationship to God and his glory. God's purpose to transform his people through beholding glory (2 Cor. 3:18) would pass us by.

We turn now to the most natural aspect of reading supernaturally— the second A of A.P.T.A.T. Admit. Pray. Trust. *Act.* The work of the Holy Spirit is decisive. But the work of the reader is essential. The words of Paul concerning his own ministry apply to all fruitful Bible reading: "I toil, struggling with all [Christ's] energy that he powerfully works within me" (Col. 1:29). Christ's energy is decisive. But do not underestimate what is expected of you: "I toil. I struggle." That is the natural act of reading supernaturally.

They read from the book, from the Law of God, clearly, and they gave the sense, so that the people understood the reading.

NEHEMIAH 8:8

Do you understand what you are reading?

ACTS 8:30

20

The Ordinary Aim of Reading:
The Meaning of Meaning

"We are not writing to you anything other
than what you read and understand."

Reading to Know What We Are Reading

In the introduction to part 3, I said that in chapter 20 I would explain
more fully how I am limiting my treatment of the actual eyes-on-the-page
act of reading. I gave a glimpse of my limited focus in saying that I was
not going to deal with the different guidelines for reading various kinds of
writing in the Bible (sometimes called *genres*, with a fancy French pronun-
ciation)—narrative, poetry, proverb, parable, and many more. Rather, I
am going to focus on the general habits of good reading that need to be in
place *before* you can even discern what kind of writing you are reading. I
said that the main reason for this limited focus is that these basic, general
habits of good reading have been very fruitful in my life. Most of what I
have seen in Scripture (and preached) was seen not because I learned rules
for reading each genre. It was owing to the more basic discipline of looking long and hard at what is really there—whatever the genre.

Hundreds of Thousands of Unique Word Combinations

Let's go further now in explaining why I think this more basic approach will be helpful. The Bible itself offers innumerable challenges of

interpretation. I mean that literally. Innumerable. The challenge is not simply that there are a few dozen kinds of writing—as if we needed to learn how to read those kinds and then our problems would be solved. There are, in fact, an enormous number of kinds of writing.

For starters, we find historical facts, poetic praises, proverbial wisdom, parables and riddles, ceremonial prescriptions, extended stories, vigorous debates, promises of help, descriptions of God's nature, illustrations of God's ways, standards of holy living, procedures of church discipline, predictions, calamities, warnings of satanic opposition, summons to faith, analyses of human depravity, directions for husbands and wives, political insights, financial principles, and more. In one sense, it is pointless to try to count the kinds of writing in the Bible, because the distinctions blur and you can't be quite sure whether you are dealing, for example, with a piece of poetry or just a momentary flare of figurative prose. So the kinds of writing are more like endless points on a continuum than distinct boxes with their own rules of interpretation.

But the situation is much more complex than that. Virtually every word and every group of words in the Bible is a unique challenge for the reader. For example, there are 783,137 words in the King James Version of the English Bible. Each of them occurs in a context (smaller or larger) that is not exactly like the context of that word in other places. To be sure, words can carry a *similar* meaning in different contexts. But we all know that the same word can have slightly different meanings in different contexts. The word *set* has 464 definitions in the *Oxford English Dictionary*. *Run* has 396.

The glory and the vexation of language is that it is incalculably flexible. Authors and speakers (you included) regularly put words into combinations that never existed before. Thus there is a constant tension between the *stability* of language and its *adaptability*. My point here is simply that, besides a typical list of genres in the Bible, there are hundreds of thousands of unique word combinations that call for special attention. It would be impossible to develop methods or rules of interpretation for each genre, or each word grouping.

We Read Before We Know What We Are Reading

So we have seen two reasons why I find it futile and discouraging to give Bible readers the impression that they need to learn lots of rules for lots of genres in the Bible in order to understand the text. The first reason is that genres are fluid and overlapping. The second is that unique word groupings offer unique challenges—and these are innumerable. The third reason for not focusing on genres, and the supposed rules that guide us in reading them, picks up on the first paragraph in this chapter: a reader must start reading the Bible *before* he knows what sort of word grouping or genre his text is. He has to be able to read the text first, *so that he can find out what sort of text he is reading.* This basic, primal strategy of reading is my focus.

Sometimes scholars give the impression that there is a set of rules for how to read a particular genre in the Bible—say parables, or poetry, or proverbs, or that slippery one called "apocalyptic" (like locusts that have the appearance of horses with gold crowns and human faces, Rev. 9:7). But here's the catch: in order to know which genre you have, you have to read. And if you must read first to discover the genre you are reading, then good reading cannot be defined only as what you do *after* you know the genre of what you are reading.

It's not good reading to start with a preconceived notion of genre, and a preconceived set of expectations of how the genre works, and then make the text fit your expectations. You have to read words and construe them *before* you know whether you are reading poetry or parable or whatever. Which means that good reading must *precede* the awareness of what the genre is so that one can make a judgment about what it is, by means of reading. That's one of the things that reading is for!

Or picture this. Suppose you approach a chapter of the Bible, and someone tells you it is proverbial or casuistic or apodictic or parabolic, or apocalyptic (you don't have to know what any of those words mean to get my point—I'm not even sure I do). And suppose you've read up on your "rules of interpretation" for this genre. If you start pressing the text to fit the expectations you have for that genre, *how would an author let you know if he is mixing it up*? How would he let you know that he is intentionally using only some of the usual rules of that genre but breaking out of the usual pattern to make a point?

Humble Skepticism

I know that some study Bibles and commentaries tell you, before you read, what genre you are dealing with. My own suggestion is to be humbly skeptical about those labels. Not because they are wrong (they might be, or might not be), but for three reasons, in ascending order of importance: (1) They might be wrong, and you need to decide if they are *by reading.* (2) Genres are not airtight categories with rigid rules of interpretation; they are flexible, and you should be too. (3) This is the most important: the mind-set that usually sees the most in a text, and sees it with the most transformative authenticity and confidence, is the mind-set that lets the text itself dictate as much as possible, while we scrutinize the text with all our might. That is the mind-set I want to encourage.

My approach, therefore, is to avoid the abundant (and important!) discussion of the various kinds of biblical writing. There are many good books that discuss this better than I could (I footnoted a few in the introduction to part 3). I want to focus on what a serious reader of the Bible would have to do with any part of the Bible before he knows what kind of genre it is. In other words, what makes for good reading that could find out what the genre is by reading? I believe there are helpful habits of mind and heart that really are that basic, and are amazingly fruitful.

Personal Testimony

I freely confess that my approach is influenced by my own pilgrimage in learning to read fruitfully. I am sure that I bring to the task of Bible reading many weaknesses. I am a slow reader, for example. So I have not been able to read lots of books on how to read the Bible. I am not a widely read scholar. That is one of the reasons I left academia after six years of college teaching. I knew my limitations would not make me a great scholar—slow reader, weak memory, impatient with certain academic protocols.

I accepted my weaknesses as God's blessing, sought to discern what they implied for my life, and then did my best to maximize what I *could* do, rather than be paralyzed with discouragement about what I *couldn't* do. (I recommend this approach to life.) What I *could* do was read and think carefully. I did not have the speed or the recall to benefit from looking at *much.* So I decided to make the most of looking at *little.* Under God's gracious helpfulness, I think I owe most of what I have seen and savored in the Bible to the attentive, reflective, prayerful wrestling with passage after passage. There are habits of mind and heart that I think are stunningly fruitful with life-changing insight. That is what I want to focus on.

From Ultimate Aim to Ordinary Aim

In order to talk about the habits of mind that form the basic task of actual eye-on-the-page reading, we must, at last, clarify what the ordinary aim of reading is. I say "at last" because, at certain points up till now, we have *assumed* what that ordinary aim is, without clarifying it or defending it. For example, we have referred at times to the "*meaning* of a text" without explaining what the meaning of a text includes. And I refer to the "*ordinary* aim of reading" to distinguish this aim from the "*ultimate* aim of reading Scripture" discussed in part 1.

In part 1, I proposed that the Bible itself shows that our ultimate goal in reading the Bible is that God's infinite worth and beauty would be exalted in the everlasting, white-hot worship of the blood-bought bride of Christ from every people, language, tribe, and nation. I unpacked this ultimate goal of reading Scripture by focusing on its implications—especially that we should (1) always read the Bible in order to see God's supreme worth and beauty, and (2) savor his excellence above everything else, and (3) be transformed into Christ's likeness by seeing and savoring this glory.

Now the question is this: How does the *ultimate* aim of reading the Bible relate to the *ordinary* aim of actual, eyes-on-the-page reading? Hence the need to finally clarify what that ordinary aim is. I said in chapter 5 that God's glory does not float over the Bible like a gas. It does not lurk in hidden places separate from the meaning of words and sentences. *It is seen in and through the meaning of texts.* In chapter 17, I said that when we pray for God to show us his glory in the Scripture, we are not asking him to bypass *the meaning of the text.* In our quest to see and savor the glory of God in Scripture, we don't just pray for the miracle of supernatural light; we also pray for his help to grasp *the basic meaning of the words.* God's glory does not hover over the text like a cloud to be seen separately from what the authors intended to communicate. It shines in and through what they intended to communicate—their *meaning.* I illustrated this with an example from Philippians 1:23.

The point I was making was this: when the psalmist prayed, "Open my eyes, that I may behold *wondrous things* out of your law" (Ps. 119:18), he did not mean that the sight of wonders could *skip the natural process of careful reading*. He did not mean that the *ordinary* aim of reading could be neglected. Our prayer, therefore, is not just for the sight of glory, but for the help in grasping *the meaning of the text* through which the glory shines.

The Definition of *Meaning* Is (in One Sense) Arbitrary

So here and there I have used the phrases "meaning of the text," "basic meaning of the words," and "ordinary aim of reading." The time has come to clarify what these phrases refer to, and to show from the Scripture itself what this *ordinary aim* of Bible reading is. To be more precise, when I say that the ordinary aim of reading is to *grasp* the *meaning of the text*, what does that include?

In one sense, all definitions are arbitrary. There is nothing intrinsic in the word *boot* that makes it the rear compartment of a car in Britain and a kind of footwear in America. Or the removal of someone from the team. Or lots of other meanings—to boot. Meanings grow up around words by usage, and the main task we have in communication is making sure, when we talk to someone, that both of us are using the same definitions. Lots of supposed disagreements would go away if the folks who are disagreeing would pause to make sure they are defining their terms in the same way.

So my decision to assign a definition to the term *meaning* in relation to biblical texts is, in one sense, arbitrary. You could say that the term *meaning* is something else. Definitions are not right or wrong until you attach a mean-er. Once you speak of "*John's* definition of meaning," then you can be wrong about it. You could tell someone my definition is *x* when, in fact, it is *y*. So in one sense, there is not much point arguing that one definition is better than another in the abstract. We just need to be sure that when we talk to each other, we know whose definition we are using.

However, definitions rarely, if ever, exist in the abstract. And there are arguments that can be made for why it is wise to use one definition rather than another. That is what I am going to do. I'm going to give you my definition of *meaning in relation to biblical texts*, and then give five reasons why I think it is wise to think of *meaning* this way.

The Definition of *Meaning* I Encourage

The meaning of a biblical text is *what the author intended to communicate by his words.* This is how most people use the word when correcting someone. We correct someone by saying, "I didn't mean that." What we are saying is, "What you are saying is not what I intended to communicate." So in this book, I am using a very ordinary definition of *meaning*—what an author intended to communicate. I use the word *communicate* to keep open the possibility that the author may intend to communicate an *emotion* that he wants us to share. I might have said, the meaning of a biblical text is what the author intended us *to understand.* The word *understand,* for most people, would have limited the author's intention to ideas. And of course emotions can, in one sense, be *understood.* But the author's intention may be that we not only understand his emotion, but *experience* it. I am defining the meaning of a text to include that intention as well as the transfer of thoughts from one mind to another.

But I want to make clear that the communication of the author's *thoughts* to our *understanding* is foundational. Emotions that have any Christ-honoring worth are rooted in truth. Therefore, the emotions that a biblical author aims to share with his readers are transmitted through understanding—that is, through thinking the author's thoughts after him. He uses language in such a way that truth in *his* mind can be communicated to *our* minds. We then may discern from those thoughts whether part of the author's intention is that we also share the emotion he expresses about this truth.

Two More Questions That Need Answering

I know that this definition of *meaning* calls for at least two other questions to be answered. First, how does the human author's intention relate to God's intention as the one who inspired the text (2 Tim. 3:16–17)? Second, can the human author intend things of which he is not conscious at the moment? I will try to answer these questions in chapter 22. But the next thing that needs to be done, in chapter 21, is to give the five reasons that I encourage us all to use this definition, namely, that *the meaning of a text is what the author intended to communicate.* This is the burden of the next chapter.

Meaning is an affair of the consciousness not of words. A word sequence means nothing in particular until somebody either means something by it or understands something from it. To banish the original author as the determiner of meaning was to reject the only compelling normative principle that could lend validity to an interpretation.

E. D. HIRSCH

21

The Ordinary Aim of Reading:
Five Reasons to Define *Meaning*
as What the Author Intended
to Communicate

"I wrote to you in my letter . . .
not at all meaning . . ."

The ultimate aim of reading the Bible is to be a glad part of the glorious purpose of God, namely, that his infinite worth and beauty would be exalted in the everlasting, white-hot worship of the blood-bought bride of Christ from every people, language, tribe, and nation. But to be a glad part of that great purpose, we must first see and savor the God that the Bible reveals. That sight of glory happens not by ignoring the words and phrases and clauses of the Bible, but by reading them carefully and understanding their meaning. And I am arguing that the most helpful way of defining the meaning of a text is to say that a text's meaning is what the author intended to communicate. Finding that is the ordinary aim of reading. And through that discovery, the beauty and glory of God and his ways shine.

I have at least five reasons for advocating for this understanding of what a text means and what our ordinary aim in reading should be.

First Reason for This Definition: The Bible Assumes It

The Bible itself assumes that when we read, we are seeking to understand *what the author intended to communicate by his words*. For example, 1 Corinthians 5:9–11:

> I wrote to you in my letter not to associate with sexually immoral people—not at all *meaning* the sexually immoral of this world, . . . since then you would need to go out of the world. But now I am writing to you not to associate with anyone who bears the name of brother if he is guilty of sexual immorality.

Paul had written to the Corinthians at least once *before* 1 Corinthians and told them not to associate with sexually immoral people. Some in the church had *misunderstood* what he wrote. That is, they did not construe his *meaning* correctly. That is, they did not see what he really *intended*. They thought he meant "all immoral people," even unbelievers outside the church. So Paul corrects their misunderstanding by saying that is "not at all what I *meant*."[1] The most natural way to construe Paul's words is to understand that his meaning is what he "intended to communicate." They did not see his *meaning*. They imputed something to his *intention* that was not there.

Another biblical example of textual meaning as *what the author intended to communicate by his words* is John 21:20–23:

> Peter . . . saw the disciple whom Jesus loved [John] following them. . . . When Peter saw him, he said to Jesus, "Lord, what about this man?" Jesus said to him, "If it is my will that he remain until I come, what is that to you? You follow me!" So the saying spread abroad among the brothers that this disciple was not to die; yet Jesus did not say to him that he was not to die, but, "If it is my will that he remain until I come, what is that to you?"

Here again we have words that in the author's (Jesus's) mind carry a clear and certain meaning. But others misconstrue those words and say Jesus meant something he did not say or mean—that is, did not *intend to communicate*. What he said to Peter about John was, "If it is my will

---

1. In the original Greek, Paul assumes the word for "meaning," rather than using it. His word for "I wrote to you" in verse 9 governs the action of verse 10: "I wrote to you in my letter [expressing the intention for you] not to associate with sexually immoral people—not at all [referring in my intention to] the sexually immoral of this world, or the greedy and swindlers, or idolaters, since then you would need to go out of the world" (1 Cor. 5:9–10).

that he remain until I come, what is that to you? You follow me!" The rumor spread that Jesus had said, "John will remain alive until I come back." That is not what Jesus said or meant or intended. To correct them, he simply repeats his words.

What a lesson this interchange provides! Jesus really does intend for us to pay close attention to his words in order to hear what he really intends to communicate. The difference between what Jesus meant to communicate and what they misunderstood him to communicate is a single two-letter word in English (if), and a three-letter word in Greek (ἐὰν, *ean*). Leave that out, and Jesus says, "It is my will that he remain until I come." Which is not what he meant—not what he intended.

Here is one more example to show that the Bible itself assumes that when we read, we are seeking to understand *what the author intended to communicate by his words*:

> [Jesus] said to them, "Our friend Lazarus has fallen asleep, but I go to awaken him." The disciples said to him, "Lord, if he has fallen asleep, he will recover." Now Jesus had spoken of his death, but they thought that he meant taking rest in sleep. Then Jesus told them plainly, "Lazarus has died." (John 11:11–14)

Jesus spoke metaphorically about Lazarus's death. He intended that the disciples would understand that Lazarus was literally dead. Perhaps Jesus intended by the metaphor of sleep to communicate that for him it is as easy to raise someone from the dead as it is to wake someone from sleep. The disciples do not understand Jesus's intention. They think he means Lazarus is "taking rest in sleep." So Jesus corrects them with clearer language. "Jesus told them plainly, 'Lazarus has died.'" That was his intention the first time. That was his meaning.

So my first reason for encouraging us to think about the meaning of texts this way is that the Bible does. There is little good that will come if we bring a definition of meaning to the Scriptures that they themselves do not assume. The meaning of a biblical text is *what the author intended to communicate by his words*.

Second Reason for This Definition: The Golden Rule

We should use this definition of meaning (what an author intends to communicate) because it helps us treat others the way we would like to be treated. Specifically, treat *authors* the way we would like to be treated, namely, courteously.

Read an author of any important communication the way you would like to be read if you wrote an important communication. We are not talking here about playful language games. You might not care how someone reads something like that. We are talking about matters of life and death. Suppose you wrote a note to a friend to tell him you were being held captive by kidnappers. And suppose you describe how the police could find you. How would you want your friend to read this note? Would you feel loved and respected if he said, "The author's intention doesn't matter. What matters is how creative I can be in finding my own meaning in this note." No. You would not feel loved. You would feel abandoned.

When we write important things, we want our readers to make every effort to see and honor our intentions as we wrote. If you put your intentions in a letter, or a contract, or a sermon, you expect others to try to draw out what you put in. So this is what we should do for authors—especially Bible authors.

Third Reason for This Definition: Humility

To read in search of an author's intention is a humble way to read.

When we labor to find what another person thinks, we are admitting that there are things we don't know, and that others probably do. So we want to learn by reading. We want to grow. We are willing for others to be the means of making us less ignorant. We are not reading merely to see a reflection of what we already know. Only pride reads like that. We are reading to learn about reality outside ourselves that we don't already know. We are assuming a receptive demeanor. We are willing to be dependent on others. This is a humble act. Of course, there are other goals in reading besides learning, such as the pleasure of a good story or a well-crafted poem or essay. But I'm not talking about that just now.

Fourth Reason for This Definition: Objective Reality Outside of Us

When we read in order to find what authors intended to communicate, our way of reading corresponds to the way the universe really is.

We live in a time when people do not prize the life-shaping reality that is not themselves. Of course, people have always refused to submit to ultimate and absolute reality (Ps. 14:1; Rom. 1:18–23). They have always leaned toward the claim that "man is the measure of all things" (Protagoras). But in our time, there is an even more radical claim by many that not only will we not submit to ultimate reality outside ourselves, but we do not believe there is any.

The longer I live, the more impressed I am with the magnitude of the impact on our lives by the simple conviction that there is a life-shaping, objective reality outside of us that we cannot control and that we need to know and adapt to. Anyone who takes God seriously knows that this view of reality is true. God is absolute reality. We are not. God has spoken, and his word exists as an objective reality outside of us. Human authors existed. They were objectively inspired by God to write certain words with certain meanings. Those words and those intentions of those authors are objective realities outside of us.

When we read to find what those authors intended to communicate, we are affirming this view of reality. It is a glorious view. The other view can never rise above vanity and narcissism. To read with the aim of creating your own meaning, instead of finding the author's meaning, leaves you trapped in the tiny world of self. But to read with the hope and aim and expectation that you might actually be able to see more of reality through the eyes of another and know more of what God and the world are like—that is a glorious thing.

C. S. Lewis was a great lover of objective reality outside of us. He believed it was a great tragedy of modern man that so many have given up on "the doctrine of objective value, the belief that certain attitudes are really true, and others really false, to the kind of thing the universe is and the kind of things we are."[2] Lewis was once asked by a person who did not share his (or my) aim in reading:

> Why should I turn from a real present experience—what the poem means to me, what happens to me when I read it—to inquire about the poet's intentions or reconstructions, always uncertain of what it may have meant to his contemporaries?

Lewis responded:

2. C. S. Lewis, *The Abolition of Man* (New York: Macmillan, 1947), 29.

308 *The Natural Act of Reading the Bible Supernaturally*

There seem to be two answers. One, is that the poem in my head which I make from my mistranslations of Chaucer or misunderstandings of Donne, may not be so good as the work Chaucer or Donne actually made.

Secondly, why not have both? After enjoying what I made of it, why not go back to the text this time looking up the hard words, puzzling out the allusions and discovering that some metrical delights in my first experience where due to my fortunate mispronunciations, and see whether I can enjoy the poet's poem, not necessarily instead of, but in addition to my own.[3]

This answer exposes the superficiality and ingrown vanity of many modern readers. They are content with their misunderstandings (because they don't believe there are such things) and so content to remain in their tiny orbit around themselves as the sun.

But if Lewis had been dealing with authoritative texts (like the Bible), he would not have merely called attention to the laziness and self-absorption of the readers, but also to the mortal danger they are in. If I am content with the meaning in my head that I make from my own misreadings, then I do not live under the authority of God, and I am lost.

We are dealing not with small things. Giving yourself to the task of finding an author's intention is a way of reading that corresponds to the way things really are. God is. God has spoken. Human authors have imparted their God-given intention to words. Those words exist, and those meanings exist. They are objective realities outside of us. It is our glory to seek them and find them—by reading.

Fifth Reason for This Definition: God's Authority Is Possible

If the meaning of a text is what the author intended to communicate, it can have authority over us.

If the meaning of a biblical text can be anything inside our own head, triggered by the text, then God ceases to have any authority in our lives. But if the meaning of a text is what the author intended, then it is objective and fixed. It cannot change. Not even an author can later turn his past intention into a nonpast intention. If he changes his mind about

---

3. C. S. Lewis, *An Experiment in Criticism* (Cambridge, UK: Cambridge University Press, 1965), 100–101.

what he meant, he would be wrong to say, "I did not mean that," when in fact he did mean that. That's what changing your mind means. Once, you intended to communicate one thing. And now you don't think that intention is true anymore. Instead he must say, "I *did* mean that, and I was wrong to mean that. I have now changed my mind. Here is the new thing I intend to communicate." So meanings, once they are written down, are fixed in that writing. The meaning of a text never changes. That is, what the author intended to communicate is a once-for-all historical event, and the past cannot be changed. That meaning can have constantly changing *applications* in different times and cultures. But the meaning—the intention of the author—stays the same.

This is why God, through the Bible, can have authority over us. We can't impute meanings to the Bible as a way of escaping the teachings that we don't like. They are what they are. It is precisely their unchangeability that lets their divine authority endure from age to age.

Life-Changing Implications of Seeing Meaning This Way

For these five reasons, I encourage you to think this way about reading and about the meaning of texts. The meaning of a biblical text is *what the author intended to communicate by his words*. And *reading* is what you do to find that intention. The *ordinary aim* of reading is to grasp what the author intended to communicate by his words.

The implications of this are life changing. You will never go to the Bible again simply to see if you can feel inspired by whatever comes to your mind. You will never be content in a group Bible study where the aim is for everyone to say "what the text means to you." You will not be excited about a pastor who tells you interesting stories and talks about history and politics and psychology and personal experience but never shows you what the biblical authors intended to communicate in particular texts.

Instead you will make every effort to read the Bible in a way that opens the intentions of the authors and inspires you with *that*. You will seek to see and savor God through *that*. You will love small-group Bible studies where everyone is helping each other see aspects of the text that bring out more and more of what the author really meant. You will give God thanks for every sermon that shows you what the biblical authors actually meant. And, yes, in your personal reading and group study and sermon listening, you will seek to apply the meaning to your life and your circumstances and your world. And the power of that application will increase with the confidence that it is based on real, objective, unchanging meaning that is really there.

Turning to Answer Our Lingering Questions

There are more implications of viewing the ordinary aim of reading as the discovery of what the author intends to communicate. We will see some of these in the next chapter as we try to answer the two questions posed at the close of chapter 20. First, how does the human author's intention relate to God's intention as the one who inspired the text? Second, can the human author intend things of which he is not conscious at the moment?

Concerning this salvation, the prophets who prophesied about the grace that was to be yours searched and inquired carefully, inquiring what person or time the Spirit of Christ in them was indicating when he predicted the sufferings of Christ and the subsequent glories.

1 PETER 1:10–11

No prophecy of Scripture comes from someone's own interpretation. For no prophecy was ever produced by the will of man, but men spoke from God as they were carried along by the Holy Spirit.

2 PETER 1:20–21

22

The Ordinary Aim of Reading: God's Intention through Man's Intention

"The things I am writing to you
are a command of the Lord."

The ordinary aim of reading that I am commending is that we read to discover *what the author intended to communicate*. Which implies that meaning is outside of us. It is discovery, not creation. We do not bring it to the Bible. It is already there because the authors, with God's guidance, put their words together so as to communicate what they intended. When we read the Bible, its meaning is not the ideas that come into our head that may be "meaningful" to us. Those ideas may or may not be part of what the author meant. Rather, when we read the Bible we are digging for the gold of what inspired writers wanted to communicate. We are not creating meaning. We are seeking it.

> If you seek it like silver
> and search for it as for hidden treasures,
> then you will understand the fear of the LORD
> and find the knowledge of God. (Prov. 2:4–5)

What would we think of a person who started mining for gold and one day brought some of his own nicely carved stones with him into the mine, then took them out of his pocket, and came running to us crying,

"Look what I found in the mine! Look. I found these in the mine! They must be really valuable!" We would say he is a fool.

The Bible's meaning is not something already in our head. It is what was in the author's head and is now imbedded, by the wonder of language, in the words and their structure on the page. The ordinary aim of reading is to dig it out. It is a glorious work. The rewards are inestimable.

> More to be desired are they than gold,
>   even much fine gold;
> sweeter also than honey
>   and drippings of the honeycomb. (Ps. 19:10)

Inspiration and God's Intention in Biblical Texts

I mentioned at the end of the previous chapter that there are at least two questions that this view of meaning raises. The first one we will deal with is, How does the human author's intention relate to God's intention as the one who inspired the text? My assumption in this book is that God inspired the Bible in such a way that he guided the writers of Scripture to express his intentions through their own.[1] Texts that point toward this assumption include:

> All Scripture is breathed out by God and profitable for teaching, for reproof, for correction, and for training in righteousness, that the man of God may be complete, equipped for every good work. (2 Tim. 3:16–17)

> No prophecy of Scripture comes from someone's own interpretation. For no prophecy was ever produced by the will of man, but men spoke from God as they were carried along by the Holy Spirit. (2 Pet. 1:20–21)

> We have received not the spirit of the world, but the Spirit who is from God, that we might understand the things freely given us by God. And we impart this in words not taught by human wisdom but taught by the Spirit, interpreting spiritual truths to those who are spiritual. (1 Cor. 2:12–13)

---

1. I have tried to show how the Scriptures reveal themselves to be completely true, in John Piper, *A Peculiar Glory: How the Christian Scriptures Reveal Their Complete Truthfulness* (Wheaton, IL: Crossway, 2016).

If anyone thinks that he is a prophet, or spiritual, he should acknowledge that the things I am writing to you are a command of the Lord. (1 Cor. 14:37)

Comparing the Islamic View of the Qur'an with the Christian View of the Bible

The doctrine of the inspiration of Scripture can be misunderstood in such a way that the human authorship is virtually canceled out. This is a serious mistake. We can see how serious the mistake is by comparing the historic Muslim view of the Qur'an and the historic Christian view of the Bible. For Muslims, "the Qur'an is understood as the *ipsissima verba* [the very words] of God himself, given in *Tanzil* [the "sending down"] to Muhammad, in Arabic, as a transcribing of the Divine Book in heaven."[2] In other words, the Qur'an actually exists in heaven in Arabic, and the claim is that when it was delivered to Muhammad, it was simply delivered in a wording already set in heaven that did not take Muhammad's authorship into account.

By contrast, consider this insightful comparison by Andrew Walls between the Christian Scriptures and the Islamic Qur'an:

> Christian faith must go on being translated, must continuously enter into vernacular culture and interact with it, or it withers and fades. Islamic absolutes are fixed in a particular language, and in the conditions of a particular period of human history. The Divine Word is the Qur'an, fixed in heaven forever in Arabic, the language of original revelation. For Christians, however, the divine Word is translatable, infinitely translatable. The very words of Christ himself were transmitted in translated form in the earliest documents we have, a fact surely inseparable from the conviction that in Christ, God's own self was translated into human form. Much misunderstanding between Christians and Muslims has arisen from the assumption that the Qur'an is for Muslims what the Bible is for Christians. It would be truer to say that the Qur'an is for Muslims what Christ is for Christians.[3]

Jesus Christ, the incarnate God-man, has a personal, physical, psychological, cultural, ethnic identity that does not change. People may paint

---

2. Kenneth Cragg, "Contemporary Trends in Islam," in *Muslims and Christians On the Emmaus Road*, ed. J. Dudley Woodberry (Monrovia, CA: MARC, 1989), 28.

3. Andrew F. Walls, "Christianity in the Non-Western World," in *The Cross-Cultural Process in Christian History* (Maryknoll, NY: Orbis, 2002), 29.

pictures of him as a blond-haired, blue-eyed Anglo-Saxon or Scandi-navian man, or as African, or as Chinese, but that is quite wrong. He was not, is not, and never will be other than the God-man, who was incarnated by the Holy Spirit in Mary's womb and lived his life as a Jewish carpenter and teacher and prophet and Messiah.

The incarnation of the Son of God fixes him in history in a way that the inspiration of the Scriptures does not fix them. To be sure, God inspired them in Greek and Hebrew, and it is these original writings that we affirm as infallible as a reflection of God's truthfulness. But this divine act of inspiration imparted to the words of the human authors meanings that God intended to be put into other languages and cultures. We can see this happen already in the New Testament as the Christian faith moves from a dominantly Jewish milieu to a dominantly Gentile one. New terms are picked up and made to serve the truth.

God's Intentions Communicated through Human Intentions

So when we consider the inspiration of Scripture, we are navigating our way between two misuses of the doctrine. One turns the original writings into the dictation of God so that the words of Scripture do not reflect the thinking of the human authors and are not truly transferable to other languages. The other mistake treats the human authors as untethered from God's special guidance so that we have *only* human intentions, and not the intention of God. The historic view, and the one I am assuming here, is that God's intentions are present in all of Scripture, and they are mediated to us through a proper understanding of what the human authors intended to communicate when they wrote.

Underlying this conviction is the view that God humbled himself not only in the incarnation of the Son, but also in the inspiration of the Scriptures. He bound his divine Son to human nature, and he bound his divine meaning to human words. The manger and the cross were not sensational. Neither are grammar and syntax. But that is how God chose to reveal himself. A poor Jewish peasant and a prepositional phrase have this in common: they are both human and both ordinary. That the poor peasant was God and the prepositional phrase is the word of God do not change this fact. Therefore, if God humbled himself to take on human flesh and to speak human language, woe to us if we presume to ignore the humanity of Christ and the grammar of Scripture.

Not Just Human Language, but the Language of These Humans

But it is not enough to say that God's revelation in Scripture comes to us in human language. It comes in the language of particular human authors in particular times and places. There are no distinctively divine language conventions. This is where the Christian view of Scripture departs profoundly from the Islamic view of the Qur'an. Muslims think there is an Arabic original of the Qur'an in heaven. This means that the wording reflects not the vocabulary or style of any human author, but only of God. But Christians see in the Scriptures that this is not the way God inspired the Bible. When God spoke through human authors, he did not always use the same language or the same style or the same vocabulary. Rather, all the evidence points to the fact that God availed himself of the language, style, vocabulary, and peculiar usages of individual biblical writers. Even in the prophetic speeches where God is directly quoted, we find language traits that distinguish one human author from another.

The implications of this for how we will go about reading the Bible are enormous. Let me illustrate. In view of this conception of inspiration, suppose we want to understand what God intends by the word *wisdom* in James 1:5: "If any of you lacks *wisdom*, let him ask God, who gives generously to all without reproach, and it will be given him." We do not assume God's use of the word *wisdom* will always be the same, as if there is a fixed divine meaning for that word *wisdom* in heaven. Therefore, we do not jump to Proverbs 8 for a definition of *wisdom* in James 1:5 with the assumption that, since the word *wisdom* is used there, it must have the same meaning it has here in James 1— since God inspired both.

Rather, we recognize that when God inspired the Scriptures, he spoke *through the vocabulary and communication patterns of the inspired human authors*. And so we realize that it would be wiser to let James himself give us guidance about what *he* means by "wisdom" in James 1:5. Thus we would do better to look at the other three uses James himself makes of the word *wisdom*. In carefully discovering James's intention, we will know the mind of God better than if we gave no special role to James's vocabulary, but instead assumed that there is a trans-biblical divine vocabulary.

My conclusion, therefore, is that God's meaning—*what God intends to communicate*—in Scripture is only accessible through the particular vocabulary and communication patterns of the various human authors. My belief in inspiration, therefore, is a belief that *to grasp what these human authors intended to communicate in their particular historical situation is also to grasp God's own intention for that situation.* Consequently, the basic, ordinary aim of reading the Bible is to understand what the biblical authors intended to communicate in their situation.

Can an Author Mean More Than He Is Conscious Of?

This leads to another question about how divine and human intentions relate: Does our definition of meaning, as what the author intended to communicate, imply that God was never referring to more, with the words he inspired, than the human authors intended to communicate?

Before answering this, I need to insert my answer to the second question I asked at the end of the previous chapter: Can the human author of Scripture intend things of which he is not conscious at the moment? I answer this here because the answer I give is really part of how I answer the other question about whether God means more in texts than the human authors.

So, can the human author intend things of which he is not conscious at the moment? The answer is yes. I know this sounds contradictory, since I have defined meaning as what the author *intends* to communicate. And now I am saying he can *intend* something he is not conscious of. What does that mean?

It really is not that strange. You do this every time you use the little abbreviation *etc.* Or when you say, "and so forth." Suppose you say, "Any green vegetable that you can buy at the grocery store is good for you, including lettuce, broccoli, cucumbers, etc." At that moment, those are the only three green vegetables that come to your mind. You are *not conscious* of any others at the moment you speak. But the term *etc.* is designed to carry your intention beyond what you are conscious of.

Etc., in your sentence, can't mean just anything. You have given it boundaries. You said, "Any green vegetable," and you said, "that you can buy at the grocery store." These two traits limit the meaning of *etc.* So if someone said, "Do you *mean*—that is, do you intend—to include asparagus?" you would say, "Yes." You meant asparagus even though you were not conscious of asparagus. Another way of saying this is to point out that *necessary implications* of our conscious meaning are included in our meaning, even if we are not conscious of all of them. We will see in what follows a specific biblical illustration of this from Colossians 3:17.

God Can Mean More Than Human Authors

Now I return to the question about God's intention in Scripture and man's. Does our definition of meaning, as *what the author intended to communicate*, imply that God never meant more, with the words he inspired, than the human authors intended to communicate?

No. It does not imply that. We know, for example, from 1 Peter 1:10–12 that God is, at least sometimes, referring to more than the human authors were aware of:

> Concerning this salvation, the prophets who prophesied about the grace that was to be yours searched and inquired carefully, *inquiring what person or time the Spirit of Christ in them was indicating* when he predicted the sufferings of Christ and the subsequent glories. *It was revealed to them that they were serving not themselves but you,* in the things that have now been announced to you through those who preached the good news to you by the Holy Spirit sent from heaven, things into which angels long to look.

Note several things. First, God did not intend to communicate to the prophets or their hearers in their own day the specifics about the identity or the timing of the Messiah. Rather, God intended that a later generation would see things in these prophecies that the authors themselves could not see, and *knew they could not see*. We know this from the words, "It was revealed to them that they were serving not themselves but you." In other words, Peter's contemporaries should be able to read the prophecies and see the person and ministry *of Jesus*. The prophets could not see the glories and suffering of Jesus the way later Christians can.

The second thing to notice is that these later generations of readers must still come to terms with the particular prophet's own way of writing. Even when God has more to communicate to a later generation than a prophet is aware of, that revelation is not couched in a special divine vocabulary or style. The only access to it is through the prophet's particular way of writing. So the contemporaries of Peter hundreds of years later had to read and understand what the human prophet wrote. Without this understanding, they would not have been able to see how the words fit the life of Jesus.

The Unwitting Prophecy of Caiaphas

The same can be said of the prophecy of Caiaphas the high priest concerning the death of Jesus. The chief priests and Pharisees come to Caiaphas and fret aloud that if something does not stop Jesus, "the Romans will come and take away both our place and our nation" (John 11:48). Caiaphas responds:

> "You know nothing at all. Nor do you understand that it is better for you that one man should die for the people, not that the whole nation should perish." He did not say this of his own accord, but being high priest that year he prophesied that Jesus would die for the nation, and not for the nation only, but also to gather into one the children of God who are scattered abroad. (John 11:49–52)

They key prophetic words are "it is better for you that one man should die for the people, not that the whole nation should perish" (v. 50). Caiaphas's immediate intention was to communicate that it would be better that Jesus be killed than that the Jewish nation be wiped out by the Romans. God communicated to John that God had a different intention with the same words, namely, that Christ's death would indeed, by a substitution, save his people, but that salvation would be greater, both in depth and scope. Christ's death would not just save from the Romans, but also from sin. And not just Jews would be saved, but all "the children of God" scattered around the world.

What is similar here to 1 Peter 1:10–12 is that God did not intend to communicate the fullness of this meaning to the scribes and Pharisees in that moment. He gave words to Caiaphas that later, according to John's divine insight, readers could see fit perfectly with the deeper and wider effect of Jesus's death. But again, the point remains, God's greater intention is not communicated by a special God-language. It is communicated through the vocabulary and ordinary way of speaking that Caiaphas used. There was no hidden divine code in the sentence that told the reader to switch off the ordinary aim of reading and switch on some new method of discerning God's intention.

God *Always* Means More

So I conclude that God can and does have more in mind to communicate through the inspired Scriptures than the human authors are fully aware of. I think it would be safe to say that in one sense, God *always* has more in mind to communicate than the human authors are fully aware of. I say this for at least two reasons.

One is the point we already made in this chapter, namely, that *necessary implications* are part of an author's meaning as I use the term. Yet no author, except God, sees all the necessary implications of what he writes. But God does. And therefore God always means consciously what human authors mean only implicitly. For example, when Paul says, "Whatever you do, in word or deed, do everything in the name of the Lord Jesus" (Col. 3:17), God sees every single one of the billions of acts included in "everything" and intends for us to do each of them in the name of Jesus. Paul, however, cannot see the specific implications of the word *everything* for every Christian who ever lives. Therefore, God, in this sense, always intends a fuller, more specific, meaning than the human authors.

A second reason I say that God always has more in mind to communicate by the words he inspires is that God saw all the connections between everything the biblical authors wrote. They could not see all those connections because, for the most part, they were not even aware of what others would write. But now that we have all the inspired books of the Bible, we can spend a lifetime exploring these connections. There are tens of thousands of connections among the various books of the Bible. It is fully possible that as you ponder something Paul said and something John said, you may get a glimpse of reality that neither of them saw. Of course, God saw it, and he saw that you would see it. God intended all these connections. He inspired them. The authors and the readers—to this very day—see only a fraction of these connections. They are worth a lifetime of searching.

The point here is, God always has more in mind to communicate than the human authors do. But that does not disconnect the intentions of God from the vocabulary and habits of writing used by the human authors. We have no other sure and certain access to the mind of God than through the way the human authors use language to communicate their intentions.

Glory in the Meaning of the Text

Therefore, when we think about the natural act of reading the Bible supernaturally, we must not ignore the urgency of pursuing the human authors' intention with all our might. This calls for all the human effort and skill we can muster. To be sure, our ultimate aim is to glorify God by seeing and savoring and being changed by his beauty and worth in the Scripture. But what we have seen is that his glory is revealed to us in and through the meaning of the text—*what the author intended to communicate*. And the meaning is found by reading and thinking. As God is united to the man Jesus in the incarnation, similarly the glory of God is united to the meaning of biblical texts.

Therefore, when the miracle of seeing and savoring the glory of God happens, it is *in* the act of reading and thinking. We read. God reveals. God *gives* the supernatural miracle. We *act* the supernatural miracle. The practical procedures for doing this are where we turn next.

I will meditate on your precepts
and fix my eyes on your ways.

PSALM 119:15

Scholarship is first to see, second to see, third to see, and ever and ever again to see.

ADOLF SCHLATTER

23

The Power of Patience and
Aggressive Attentiveness

"If you seek it like silver and search
for it as for hidden treasures . . ."

Bible Reading and the Purpose of the Universe

The astonishing fact is that reading the Bible is one of the indispensable means by which God brings about his ultimate purpose for the universe. Ponder that word *indispensable*. It means that this great purpose will not be reached if the ordinary aim of reading is not achieved among God's people. The ordinary aim of reading is *to grasp what the biblical authors intend to communicate*. This is indispensable because the *ultimate* aim of reading comes about through the act of pursuing this *ordinary* aim of reading.

The ultimate aim of reading (which we proposed in part 1) is that God's infinite worth and beauty would be exalted in the everlasting, white-hot worship of the blood-bought bride of Christ from every people, language, tribe, and nation. The exaltation of God's worth and beauty in white-hot worship depends on God's worth and beauty—his peculiar glory—being seen and savored in Scripture as the supreme treasure of the universe. Seeing God's glory in Scripture is a supernatural work of God's grace, because by nature we are hardened against it, and blind to it. But the miracle happens in and through the natural act of reading the Bible supernaturally.

That is, the miracle happens as we read, by faith, with the *ordinary* aim of grasping what the biblical authors intended to communicate. Just as the glory of the Son of God can be seen only by looking at the incarnate Son of Man, so the glory of the word of God can be seen only by looking at the inspired word of man. Divine illumination happens through human observation. The beauty of divine truth is seen in beholding human words—that is, in reading. "When you *read* this you can perceive my insight into the mystery of Christ" (Eph. 3:4).

I Learned to Read at Twenty-Two

The most fundamental task of this natural act of reading is to see what is really there. My aim in this chapter is to persuade you and encourage you that, as you read the Bible, you can see more than you ever thought you could. And I am going to argue that this will happen not mainly because you learn Greek and Hebrew, or get a seminary education (though these can be valuable), but rather because you form the habit, and develop the patience, to look longer and more carefully than you ever have. Most failures to see what authors intended to communicate are not owing to insufficient education or inadequate intelligence but to passive reading that is not aggressively attentive to what is there.

I speak with great conviction and hopefulness for you because of my own experience. When I was twenty-two years old, I learned how to read. Actually, I suppose, that's not fair to my parents or the excellent teachers I had up till that time. It would be more accurate to say that my understanding of what reading is, and my commitment to do it well, was given a life-changing booster shot when I was twenty-two. That is what I hope happens to you in reading this book. I learned the difference between passive and active reading (with the help of Mortimer Adler[1]). I saw the wonder of the ordinary aim of reading—to think another person's thoughts after him (with the help of E. D. Hirsch[2]). And I learned the kinds of questions to ask (with the help of Daniel Fuller[3]). I had never read anything by these men before age twenty-two.

---

1. Mortimer Adler and Charles van Doren, *How to Read a Book* (New York: Simon & Schuster, 1972).
2. E. D. Hirsch, *Validity in Interpretation* (New Haven, CT: Yale University Press, 1967).
3. Daniel P. Fuller, *Hermeneutics*, unpublished paper, Fuller Theological Seminary.

Seeing by Looking, Really Looking

The first thing that Professor Daniel Fuller insisted upon in those life-changing seminary days was that we believe in the possibility and fruitfulness of actually *seeing by looking*—specifically, looking at the text of the Bible. That may sound strange to you. But think how much of your waking life your eyes are open, but passive. You are seeing the world but hardly noticing anything. You are hearing all the time but hardly noticing any particular sounds.

Dr. Fuller was not the only one who was pushing me to actively see and hear. One day in a class on preaching, the professor was making the point that pastors should get their illustrations from real life, not from books of illustrations. He paused for about 30 seconds of silence. We didn't know what he was doing. Then he said, "Did you hear that?" We didn't know what he was talking about. He said, "The siren! Down on Colorado Avenue. That's an ambulance. Someone is probably seriously hurt or seriously ill right now as we sit here." That moment made an indelible impression on me. The fact that I remember it now, forty-eight years later, shows what an impact it made. *Wake up*, I thought. *You are sleepwalking through life. You see and hear, but you don't notice. Wake up!*

Most people read half asleep. We read the Bible pretty much like we watch television—passively. What I mean by passively is that we expect the TV program to affect us. Entertain us, or inform us, or teach us. Our minds are almost entirely in the passive mode as impulses come into our minds. The opposite is when our minds go on alert and watch carefully. We become aggressively observant. When we see TV or the world actively, we see layers and dimensions and aspects of reality that before were totally unnoticed. The difference is that now the mind is engaged. You have issued a command to the brain: *Look! Listen! Think about what you are seeing. Spot clues. Be aggressively observant. Be unremitting in your attentiveness. Be unwaveringly watchful. Make connections. Notice patterns. Ask questions.*

Another unforgettable inspiration in my growing desire to see, as I had never seen before, was the story of Agassiz and the fish. As I read this story for the first time, I was riveted. It was like a bright explosion on the horizon of my new life of Bible study. The brightness made all the details of the Bible light up. Suddenly, I was seeing patterns and interrelationships and lines of thought that I had never seen before. And all of this was happening not because a teacher was telling me what to see, but because someone was telling me, *Look, look, look.*

Louis Agassiz (1807–1873) was the founder of the Harvard Museum of Comparative Zoology and a Harvard professor. One of his students, Samuel Scudder, wrote about how this amazing professor showed him what he could see if only he would form the habit and patience of looking long and hard at the object of his study.

"Agassiz and the Fish, by a Student"
It was more than fifteen years ago that I entered the laboratory of Professor Agassiz, and told him I had enrolled my name in the scientific school as a student of natural history. He asked me a few questions about my object in coming, my antecedents generally, the mode in which I afterwards proposed to use the knowledge I might acquire, and finally, whether I wished to study any special branch. To the latter I replied that while I wished to be well grounded in all departments of zoology, I purposed to devote myself specially to insects.

"When do you wish to begin?" he asked.

"Now," I replied.

This seemed to please him, and with an energetic "Very well," he reached from a shelf a huge jar of specimens in yellow alcohol.

"Take this fish," he said, "and look at it; we call it a Haemulon; by and by I will ask what you have seen."

With that he left me, but in a moment returned with explicit instructions as to the care of the object entrusted to me.

"No man is fit to be a naturalist," said he, "who does not know how to take care of specimens."

I was to keep the fish before me in a tin tray, and occasionally moisten the surface with alcohol from the jar, always taking care to replace the stopper tightly. Those were not the days of ground-glass stoppers, and elegantly shaped exhibition jars; all the old students will recall the huge, neckless glass bottles with their leaky, wax-besmeared corks, half-eaten by insects and begrimed with cellar dust. Entomology was a cleaner science than ichthyology, but the example of the professor who had unhesitatingly plunged to the bottom of the jar to produce the fish was infectious; and though this alcohol had "a very ancient and fish-like smell," I really dared not show any aversion within these sacred precincts, and treated the alcohol as though it were pure water. Still I was conscious of a passing feeling of disappointment, for gazing at a fish did not commend itself to an ardent entomologist. My friends at home, too, were annoyed, when they discovered that no amount of eau de cologne would drown the perfume which haunted me like a shadow.

In ten minutes I had seen all that could be seen in that fish, and started in search of the professor, who had, however, left the museum; and when I returned, after lingering over some of the odd animals stored in the upper apartment, my specimen was dry all over. I dashed the fluid over the fish as if to resuscitate it from a fainting-fit, and looked with anxiety for a return of a normal, sloppy appearance. This little excitement over, nothing was to be done but return to a steadfast gaze at my mute companion. Half an hour passed, an hour, another hour; the fish began to look loathsome. I turned it over and around; looked it in the face—ghastly; from behind, beneath, above, sideways, at a three-quarters view—just as ghastly. I was in despair; at an early hour, I concluded that lunch was necessary; so with infinite relief, the fish was carefully replaced in the jar, and for an hour I was free.

On my return, I learned that Professor Agassiz had been at the museum, but had gone and would not return for several hours. My fellow students were too busy to be disturbed by continued conversation. Slowly I drew forth that hideous fish, and with a feeling of desperation again looked at it. I might not use a magnifying glass; instruments of all kinds were interdicted. My two hands, my two eyes, and the fish; it seemed a most limited field. I pushed my fingers down its throat to see how sharp its teeth were. I began to count the scales in the different rows until I was convinced that that was nonsense. At last a happy thought struck me—I would draw the fish; and now with surprise I began to discover new features in the creature. Just then the professor returned.

"That is right," said he, "a pencil is one of the best eyes. I am glad to notice, too, that you keep your specimen wet and your bottle corked."

With these encouraging words he added—"Well, what is it like?"

He listened attentively to my brief rehearsal of the structure of parts whose names were still unknown to me; the fringed gill-arches and movable operculum; the pores of the head, fleshly lips, and lidless eyes; the lateral line, the spinous fin, and forked tail; the compressed and arched body. When I had finished, he waited as if expecting more, and then, with an air of disappointment: "You have not looked very carefully; why," he continued, more earnestly, "you haven't seen one of the most conspicuous features of the animal, which is as plainly before your eyes as the fish itself. Look again; look again!" And he left me to my misery.

I was piqued; I was mortified. Still more of that wretched fish? But now I set myself to the task with a will, and discovered one new thing after another, until I saw how just the professor's criticism had been. The afternoon passed quickly, and when, towards its close, the professor inquired,

"Do you see it yet?"

"No," I replied. "I am certain I do not, but I see how little I saw before."

"That is next best," said he earnestly, "but I won't hear you now; put away your fish and go home; perhaps you will be ready with a better answer in the morning. I will examine you before you look at the fish."

This was disconcerting; not only must I think of my fish all night, studying, without the object before me, what this unknown but most visible feature might be, but also, without reviewing my new discoveries, I must give an exact account of them the next day. I had a bad memory; so I walked home by Charles River in a distracted state, with my two perplexities.

The cordial greeting from the professor the next morning was reassuring; here was a man who seemed to be quite as anxious as I that I should see for myself what he saw.

"Do you perhaps mean," I asked, "that the fish has symmetrical sides with paired organs?"

His thoroughly pleased, "Of course, of course!" repaid the wakeful hours of the previous night. After he had discoursed most happily and enthusiastically—as he always did—upon the impor-tance of this point, I ventured to ask what I should do next.

"Oh, look at your fish!" he said, and left me again to my own devices. In a little more than an hour he returned and heard my new catalogue.

"That is good, that is good!" he repeated, "but that is not all; go on." And so for three long days, he placed that fish before my eyes, forbidding me to look at anything else, or to use any artificial aid. "Look, look, look," was his repeated injunction.

This was the best entomological lesson I ever had—a lesson whose influence was extended to the details of every subsequent study; a legacy the professor has left to me, as he left it to many others, of inestimable value, which we could not buy, with which we cannot part.

A year afterwards, some of us were amusing ourselves with chalking outlandish beasts upon the blackboard. We drew prancing star-fishes; frogs in mortal combat; hydro-headed worms; stately craw-fishes, standing on their tails, bearing aloft umbrellas; and grotesque fishes, with gaping mouths and staring eyes. The professor came in shortly after, and was as much amused as any at our experiments. He looked at the fishes.

"Haemulons, every one of them," he said; "Mr. _____ drew them."

True; and to this day, if I attempt a fish, I can draw nothing but Haemulons.

The fourth day a second fish of the same group was placed beside the first, and I was bidden to point out the resemblances and differences between the two; another and another followed, until the entire family lay before me, and a whole legion of jars covered the table and surrounding shelves; the odor had become a pleasant perfume; and even now, the sight of an old six-inch worm-eaten cork brings fragrant memories!

The whole group of Haemulons was thus brought into review; and whether engaged upon the dissection of the internal organs, preparation and examination of the bony framework, or the description of the various parts, Agassiz's training in the method of observing facts in their orderly arrangement, was ever accompanied by the urgent exhortation not to be content with them.

"Facts are stupid things," he would say, "until brought into connection with some general law."

At the end of eight months, it was almost with reluctance that I left these friends and turned to insects; but what I gained by this experience has been of greater value than years of later investigation in my favorite groups.[4]

---

4. Horace E. Scudder, ed., *American Poems: Longfellow: Whittier: Bryant: Holmes: Lowell: Emerson; with Biographical Sketches and Notes*, 3rd ed. (Boston: Houghton, Osgood, 1879), 450–54.

I Cannot Thank God Enough for This Lesson

As I look back now, I cannot thank God enough for a similar testimony—a professor who did not tell me what the Bible meant, but every day, in eight classes over three years, said, "Look. Look. Look."—and showed me how to ask questions about what I saw. He would come into class and set up his overhead projector with the text on it, and we would proceed to test whether what we had seen was really there. And in the process, oh, how much more we would see! There was no bluffing. If it was not there, you couldn't get away with any nice, spiritual wishful thinking, or any plea that, even if it's not here, it surely is in another text. Right. But not here. Our aim was to see what was here, and we would look at it for hours.

And just like Agassiz said, even on the days when others saw much, and I saw little, the "next best thing" to seeing much is to "see how little you had seen." That taught us there was always more to see than we had seen. And, I can say after forty-eight years of looking at the Book, that is true. The barrier to seeing the riches of the Scriptures is not owing to the fact that more people don't know Greek and Hebrew, but that more people don't have the patience to look, look, look.

A Misery That Is Totally Worth It

Scudder said that Agassiz told him, "Look again; look again." And then he said, "He left me to my misery." Ah, yes. But this misery is not long-lived. But we must be honest. The aggressive, patient, rigorous discipline of looking is indeed costly. Seeing does not happen casually. It happens with effort—the effort to see. And this effort can be as hard a work as any you've ever done. You will sometimes feel, "He left me to my misery." I have often groaned to my wife, "I can't see it. I can't figure it out. I've been wrestling with this text for four hours, and it won't yield." So I do not want to give the impression that the treasures of a text give themselves up to passive, laid-back, casual, easygoing reading. They may not give themselves up quickly to the most focused, aggressive reading.

> If you call out for insight
> and raise your voice for understanding,
> if you seek it like silver
> and search for it as for hidden treasures . . . (Prov. 2:3–4)

Call out! Raise your voice! Seek! Search! As if you knew that ten million dollars was hidden in this house. Yours for the finding. How would you look? You would look, look, look. And if you got tired and found the task miserable at times, you would press on. Well, by God's grace, you will know and feel that the treasures of God's word are "more to be desired, than gold, even much fine gold" (Ps. 19:10). They are like a "treasure hidden in a field, which a man found and covered up. Then in his joy he goes and sells all that he has and buys that field" (Matt. 13:44).

A Kindred Spirit in Germany

After seminary, I spent the next three years in Germany looking at Jesus's teaching about loving our enemies. That was the topic of my doctoral dissertation. The pressure of scholarship to read *about* texts, rather than look *at* texts, was enormous. But what a joy it was to find a German scholar from the previous generation who gave voice to what I was feeling. Adolf Schlatter (1852–1938) had been a kind of academic maverick in biblical scholarship at the University of Tübingen. He was highly respected because of his immense erudition in first-century Semitic backgrounds. But he was eccentric when it came to his published scholarship, since he scorned the use of footnotes as a parading of the wideness of his reading. His famous motto was, "Scholarship is first to see, second to see, third to see, and ever and ever again to see."[5] This was "Agassiz and the Fish" all over again. It was a great confirmation to me at the time. And I was encouraged to press on with my passion to see what was there in the text rather than speculate about how it might have come about.

Agassiz among the Arts

In the November–December 2013 issue of *Harvard* magazine, Jennifer Roberts, the Elizabeth Cary Agassiz Professor of the Humanities at Harvard, published an article titled "The Power of Patience: Teaching Students the Value of Deceleration and Immersive Attention."[6] As you can imagine, I loved this title. "Agassiz" is in her professorship title.

---

5. Adolf Schlatter, "Atheistische Methoden in der Theologie?," in *Zur Theologie des Neuen Testaments und zur Dogmatik: Kleine Schriften*, ed. Ulrich Luck (Munich: C. Kaiser, 1969), 142. The German original reads: "Wissenschaft ist erstens Sehen un zweitens Sehen und drittens Sehen und immer und immer wieder Sehen."

6. Jennifer Roberts, "The Power of Patience," *Harvard* magazine, Nov.–Dec. 2013, accessed March 29, 2016, http://harvardmagazine.com/2013/11/the-power-of-patience.

And the spirit of Agassiz is in her article title. Indeed, he is in all her work. What she does in this article is inspire us again with the possibilities of seeing more than we thought we could. She is not a zoologist like Agassiz. She is an art historian. So instead of looking at fish, she wants us to look at a painting—and then look at everything. She teaches a course at Harvard called "The Art of Looking."

Her strategy with her students is the same as Agassiz's. They will have to look and look and look. Her aim is to help students develop the patience to "decelerate" and "immerse" themselves in attention. To feel the full import of her assignment and her art-related illustration of Agassiz's principle, you may want to go to the Internet and look at the painting she refers to.[7]

> Every external pressure, social and technological, is pushing students in the other direction, toward immediacy, rapidity, and spontaneity. . . . I want to give them the permission and the structures to slow down. . . . The first thing I ask them to do in the research process is to spend a painfully long time looking at that object.
>
> Say a student wanted to explore the work popularly known as *Boy with a Squirrel*, painted in Boston in 1765 by the young artist John Singleton Copley. Before doing any research in books or online, the student would first be expected to go to the Museum of Fine Arts, where it hangs, and spend three full hours looking at the painting, noting down his or her evolving observations as well as the questions and speculations that arise from those observations. The time span is explicitly designed to seem excessive.

At first many of the students resist being subjected to such a remedial exercise. To help the students over this hump Roberts tells them she did the same discipline herself—three hours looking, looking, looking at *Boy with a Squirrel*. She reports what happened in her experience:

> Just a few examples from the first hour of my own experiment: It took me 9 minutes to notice that the shape of the boy's ear precisely echoes that of the ruff along the squirrel's belly—and that Copley was making some kind of connection between the animal and the human body and the sensory capacities of each.

---

7. See John Singleton Copley's "A Boy with a Flying Squirrel" (1765), Museum of Fine Arts Boston, accessed October 27, 2016, http://www.mfa.org/collections/object/a-boy-with-a-flying-squirrel-henry-pelham-34280.

It was 21 minutes before I registered the fact that the fingers holding the chain exactly span the diameter of the water glass beneath them.

It took a good 45 minutes before I realized that the seemingly random folds and wrinkles in the background curtain are actually perfect copies of the shapes of the boy's ear and eye, as if Copley had imagined those sensory organs distributing or imprinting themselves on the surface behind him. And so on.

What this exercise shows students is that just because you have *looked* at something doesn't mean that you have *seen* it.

What turns access into learning is time and strategic patience.[8]

You might want to try your eye at this (to view the painting, see note 7). Did you notice that the bend of the inside of the squirrel's tail forms a curve virtually identical to the curve formed by lower edge of the boy's bottom lip? Or did you notice that one of the white ruffles protruding at the boy's left hand is identical to the outline of the white fur of the squirrel's belly? And, of course, did you notice there is a squirrel sitting on this boy's desk? A squirrel! And he (or she?) appears to be on a chain leash! What is he or she doing there? What is the meaning (intention!) of all this weaving together of human and animal?

The Power of Patience in Looking

You may be among those who are too impatient to look at a fish or a painting for this length of time. But what about the Bible? Are the possible rewards great enough that you might exert the effort to keep looking? Professor Roberts makes a telling point about why she calls patience a kind of power:

> The virtue of patience was originally associated with forbearance or sufferance. It was about conforming oneself to the need to wait for things. But now that, generally, one need *not* wait for things, patience becomes an active and positive cognitive state. Where patience once indicated a lack of control, now it is a form of control over the tempo of contemporary life that otherwise controls us. Patience no longer connotes disempowerment—perhaps now patience is power.

---

8. Roberts, "The Power of Patience."

If "patience" sounds too old-fashioned, let's call it "time management" or "temporal intelligence" or "massive temporal distortion engineering." Either way, an awareness of time and patience as a productive medium of learning is something that I feel is urgent to model for—and expect of—my students.[9]

The Bible Beckons Us to Look for a Long Time

When the Bible calls us to meditate on the Lord's instruction "all the day" (Ps. 119:97), indeed "day and night" (Ps. 1:2), and to "fix [our] eyes" on it (Ps. 119:15), is this not a call to look and look and look? Or to listen and listen and listen (which is the same thing), as we speak the words to ourselves day and night? What might you see? Vastly more than you think.

I close this chapter with one example from the Scriptures. Suppose a wise teacher handed you Proverbs 6:16–19 and told you to find a quiet place and look at it with aggressive attentiveness for one hour. A modest suggestion. What would you see?

> There are six things that the LORD hates,
>   seven that are an abomination to him:
> haughty eyes, a lying tongue,
>   and hands that shed innocent blood,
> a heart that devises wicked plans,
>   feet that make haste to run to evil,
> a false witness who breathes out lies,
>   and one who sows discord among brothers.

The first thing you might do—since Agassiz told Scudder, "A pencil is one of the best eyes"—is write the text and put the list of things the Lord hates in a column rather than side by side in a paragraph. This way you might be able to see the relationships better. And seeing relationships is one of the most illuminating things about a text. So here they are. What do you see?

1. haughty eyes,
2. a lying tongue,
3. hands that shed innocent blood,
4. a heart that devises wicked plans,

---

9. Ibid.

5. feet that make haste to run to evil,
6. a false witness who breathes out lies,
7. one who sows discord among brothers.

Here we are an hour later! Did you see that of these seven things the Lord hates, the middle one (4) refers to the innermost organ, the heart, and seems to function like a fulcrum for the three on either side? As we move out from the heart, as the root of our behavior, it appears that (3) and (5) correspond to each other: hands and feet. Specifically, hands shedding blood and feet running to do evil. Then it appears that (2) and (6) correspond: tongue and breath—both of them telling lies. So the heart devises wickedness, then that inner intention comes out through hands and feet that hurt others, and through mouths that deceive others.

Now, in view of this pattern (3 = 5; 2 = 6), we expect that (1) and (7) will correspond. Haughty eyes corresponding with sowing discord. Or do they? What do you make of that? I think they do correspond and that the writer wants us to dig in and figure out how. I will leave that with you. And there is so much more to see as well. Patience, prayer, time, and a pencil. They all have eyes.

What Does the Mind of the Active Observer *Do*?

The question before us now is: What does the mind do while patiently looking and looking and looking? When we speak of *active* reading and *aggressive* attentiveness, what are we implying? Are there kinds of tasks that the looking mind performs? How intentional are those tasks? That is where we turn in the next chapter.

Resolved: To study the Scriptures so steadily, constantly, and frequently, as that I may find, and plainly perceive, myself to grow in the knowledge of the same.

JONATHAN EDWARDS

People only truly think when they are confronted with a problem. Without some kind of dilemma to stimulate thought, behavior becomes habitual rather than thoughtful.

JOHN DEWEY

24

Active Reading Means
Asking Questions

"Think over what I say, for the Lord
will give you understanding."

The Brain Is Like a Muscle

If God gives us the desire and the patience to look at one paragraph of the Bible for several hours, what would we actually do? What does it mean to give a passage of Scripture "aggressive attentiveness"? What does it mean to pursue *active* reading rather than passive? It means that we treat our minds like a kind of muscle the way we do the muscles of our arm. When we want a glass of water, we say to our arm (quite unconsciously), "Arm, stretch yourself out and take that glass of water and bring it to my lips." And amazingly the muscles in our arm do exactly as they are told. There is a great mystery in how an act of immaterial will is transfigured into an act of physical matter.

In the same way, we can say to our minds, "Mind, get focused. Pay attention. Look closely at this paragraph. Examine it. Ask questions. Think about it. Read it again and again. Don't coast. Don't drift. Don't be passive. Don't just wait for an idea to pop into your head. Search. Explore. Examine. Pursue. Ransack these words. Squeeze them until they drip their meaning into your mind." In the Scriptures, this kind of Bible reading is compared to tracking down treasure with vehemence.

It is not compared to lying down and waiting for a grape to fall in our mouth.

Thinking Means Asking and Answering Questions

But can we be more specific? Yes, we can. When we are aggressively attentive and mentally active, *the mind asks questions and tries to answer them* by looking at what is in this paragraph and related writings. "People only truly think when they are confronted with a problem," said John Dewey. "Without some kind of dilemma to stimulate thought, behavior becomes habitual rather than thoughtful."[1] I think Dewey was right about this. Reading becomes a passive habit of drifting through texts unless we form the habit of asking questions, that is, unless we habitually spot things that at first don't make complete sense, feel a disturbance in our minds, and then dig our way down to the beauty of truth.

I think the apostle Paul confirms this when he says to Timothy, *"Think over what I say,* for the Lord will give you understanding in everything" (2 Tim. 2:7). What does it mean *to think something over?* It means that we ask questions about it and try to answer them by seeing connections and relationships. Most of us do this so intuitively that we don't realize that is what we are doing. But to read actively is to turn this intuitive habit into a conscious and vigorous one.

Illustrating with a Text Message

Let me illustrate how we all think, as we read, by asking and answering questions. Suppose you got a text message from your friend that said, "I need you to come quickly. I'm trapped at the mill. Bring the bar."

That's all it said. What does your mind do with these words and phrases? The first thing you do is ask, "Is this urgent?" You answer by comparing, in a split second, these words to what you know about your friend. You know he never uses words like, "I *need* you to come." Ordinarily he would say, "I would like you to come." Or, "Please come." The words he is using now are unusual. They are more desperate. And the word *quickly* confirms your answer. It's urgent.

Then you ask, "Why does he need me to come so urgently?" And to

---

1. No source.

answer this question, you intuitively insert a "because" between the first two sentences. "I need you to come quickly. [Because] I'm trapped at the mill." You needed an answer to the question, "Why the urgency?" and he gave it to you. "I'm trapped at the mill." You intuitively saw this sentence as a *reason* or a *ground* for the first one. He could have said, "*Because* I'm trapped at the mill." But he knew you would supply that in your mind because of the context.

Third, you ask, "Where is he?" You answer by noticing the phrase "at the mill." You ask, "What does *mill* refer to?" You recall that you and he had hiked into the woods last week to find an old abandoned mill on the creek that runs through your father's property. There are no other serious contenders in your mind for what *mill* might refer to. You hope that some automatic spell checker did not correct a mistyped "mall" to "mill."

Then you ask, "What's wrong, and how can I help?" You don't know what he means by *trapped*. How could you be trapped at the mill? There weren't any buildings or rooms. You ask, "Does the last sentence shed light on this uncertainty?" "Bring the bar." You ask, "What bar? What does he intend to communicate by *bar*?" And how does that relate to his being trapped at the mill?

You wrack your brain. You think. You run the word *bar* through your memory bank. You are *not* passive. Your mind is not just coasting or drifting, waiting for some idea to come out of the blue about the meaning of "bar." Your mind has gone on high alert (aggressive attentiveness). You are commanding your mind to search its data bank of words and conversations and experiences with your friend. Bingo. You recall that last week, as you were leaving the mill, he said, "Next time we come out here, we should bring a crowbar and see what's under some of these stones." "That's it," you say. There are lots of other questions you could ask about this message. But that's enough under these circumstances. You get the crowbar, hop in the car, and head to the rescue—still thinking. Still asking questions.

That is the way we all read. We ask and answer questions. Almost all those we asked in that little story were intuitive. They took only seconds to answer. They were immediately answered by familiar word usage. We do this sort of reading so spontaneously that we don't realize how skilled we really are in answering our questions with the clues of language. We have been practicing this skill since we were in the first year of our lives. Most of our questions are answered before they can get on our lips. It would be wonderful, perhaps, if that were the case with *all* interpretation. But it's not.

Active reading and aggressive attentiveness turn this intuitive habit into a conscious, vigorous discipline. In other words, active readers form the habit of asking questions of what they read. This is what it means to have an active mind. It is what Paul wants us to do when he says, "Think over what I say" (2 Tim. 2:7).

Humble Asking, Not Arrogant

Admittedly, this is temporarily an uncomfortable task, and even a dangerous one. Ignorance is bliss. And as long as we are not asking questions, we will not be perplexed by not having answers. And our reading will be comfortably shallow and powerless. But if we habitually spot things that demand effort to understand, we will experience seasons of discomfort between the spotting and the resolution.

The danger lies in the possibility that our querying the text may become arrogant and skeptical. We may start to put ourselves in the position of judge over the text and ask our questions like a prosecuting attorney, not like a hope-filled seeker. Remember that Zechariah, the father of John the Baptist, and Mary, the mother of Jesus, both asked the angel questions. But Zechariah's question was met with indignation and the penalty of not being able to speak (Luke 1:18–20), while Mary's question was met with approval and a profound answer (Luke 1:34–35). The difference was that Zechariah was skeptical, and Mary was humble and trusting.

When I say that the key to understanding is the habit of asking questions, I am not urging skepticism or distrust or arrogance. This is a hopeless approach to Scripture. I am urging childlike, humble, but insistent and vigorous sightings of things that you don't at first understand fully, the humble query of what they might mean, and the patient, even painful effort to find the answers.

Martin Luther Would Not Let Go of the Text

God has had mercy on many readers at this point to give them the help they need, even when their attitudes were not completely exemplary.

For example, Martin Luther was angry at God because he could not understand the meaning of the gospel in Romans 1:16–17, where Paul writes:

> I am not ashamed of the gospel, for it is the power of God for salvation to everyone who believes, to the Jew first and also to the Greek. For in it the righteousness of God is revealed from faith for faith, as it is written, "The righteous shall live by faith."

Luther could not get beyond the negative implications of the term "righteousness of God" from his philosophical training. But in God's great mercy, Luther kept looking and looking and looking. He was desperate to have an answer to this question about how the revelation of the righteousness of God could be good news instead of judgment:

> I hated that word "righteousness of God," which *according to the use and custom of all the teachers, I had been taught to understand philosophically* regarding the formal or active righteousness, as they called it, with which God is righteous and punishes the unrighteous sinner.
>
> I was angry with God, and said, "As if, indeed, it is not enough, that miserable sinners, eternally lost through original sin, are crushed by every kind of calamity by the law of the Decalogue, without having God add pain to pain by the gospel and also by the gospel threatening us with his righteous wrath!" Thus I raged with a fierce and troubled conscience. Nevertheless, *I beat importunately upon Paul at that place, most ardently desiring to know what St. Paul wanted.*
>
> At last, by the mercy of God, *meditating day and night,* I gave heed to the context of the words, namely, "In it the righteousness of God is revealed, as it is written, 'He who through faith is righteous shall live.'" There *I began to understand* [that] the righteousness of God is that by which the righteous lives by a gift of God, namely by faith. And this is the meaning: the righteousness of God is revealed by the gospel, namely, the passive righteousness with which [the] merciful God justifies us by faith, as it is written, "He who through faith is righteous shall live." Here I felt that I was altogether born again and had entered paradise itself through open gates. Here a totally other face of the entire Scripture showed itself to me. *Thereupon I ran through the Scriptures from memory. . . .*

> And I extolled my sweetest word with a love as great as the
> hatred with which I had before hated the word "righteousness of
> God." Thus *that place in Paul* was for me truly the gate to paradise.[2]

I can hardly think of a better illustration of vigorousness of "aggressive attentiveness" and "active reading." He was desperate to see how
two parts of a text fit together: good news and righteousness of God.
He says that the breakthrough was virtually his new birth: "I felt that I
was altogether born again and had entered paradise itself through open
gates." God was wonderfully merciful toward the anger and struggles
Luther endured. And we may hope that he will be to us as well. But
under God, here was the key: in spite of all his confusion and anger he
said, "Nevertheless, I beat importunately upon Paul at that place, most
ardently desiring to know what St. Paul wanted." This is "aggressive
attentiveness." This is "thinking over what I say." This is the vigorous
habit of asking and answering questions. This is active reading.

Is Asking Questions Disrespectful of God's Word?

I realize that for some people my plea may seem disrespectful—we form
the habit of spotting things that at first don't make complete sense,
and feel a disturbance in our minds, and then dig our way down to the
beauty of truth. This misgiving is understandable: asking questions is
the same as posing problems, and many of us have been discouraged all
our lives from finding problems in God's word. There is a good instinct
here. I do not want to cultivate a habit of suspicion.

It is impossible to respect the Bible too highly. But it is possible to
respect it wrongly. If we do not ask seriously how the parts of a text fit
together, then we are either superhuman (and see all truth at a glance),
or indifferent (and don't care about seeing the coherence of truth). But
how can anyone who is indifferent, or who pretends to be superhuman,
have a proper respect for the Bible? Reverence for God's word demands
that we ask questions and pose problems. A humble seeker after God's
truth realizes that these are *our* questions and *our* problems. They are
no sign of the defectiveness of God's word. And if he has inspired his
Scriptures so that "there are some things in them that are hard to un-

---

2. John Dillenberger, ed., *Martin Luther: Selections from His Writings* (Garden City, NY: Double-
day, 1961), 11–12; emphasis added.

derstand" (2 Pet. 3:16), this is good for us, and we should receive the challenge as humbling and challenging rather than irritating. He wants us to ask our questions like a man on a quest to find gold, for he has promised that there are treasures new and old (Matt. 13:52).

We Are All Children

Surely God wants his children to ask questions about what we don't understand in his word. I did not accuse my six-year-old daughter of disrespect when she could not make sense out of a Bible verse and asked me about it. She was just learning to read. And in a sense, we are all just learning to read. When Paul said that in this age "we see in a mirror dimly, but then face to face" (1 Cor. 13:12), he compared it to the stage of a man's life when he is a child: "When I was a child, I spoke like a child, I thought like a child, I reasoned like a child. When I became a man, I gave up childish ways" (v. 11). He is comparing childhood ways of seeing to seeing in a mirror dimly. And he is comparing adult ways of seeing to seeing face-to-face. Which means that Paul knows that in this age we are all, in a sense, like children in our abilities to discern divine truth. We can see and know. But, oh, how vastly more there is that we will one day see and know.

So we are all like my daughter at six. Our abilities to read have not been perfected. None of us grasps the logic of a paragraph and sees instantly on the first reading how every part of a sentence or the paragraph fits together. How much less do we see how an entire epistle, or the whole of the New Testament, or all the Bible fits together! Therefore, if we love the Bible and care about truth, we must relentlessly query the text and form the habit of spotting things that at first don't make complete sense, and then be willing to feel a disturbance in our minds, and then dig our way down to the beauty and unity of truth.

The Opposite of Irreverence

Asking questions of what we see there is just the opposite of irreverence. It is what we do if we crave the mind of Christ. Nothing sends us deeper into the counsels of God than seeing puzzling things in the Bible and then pondering them day and night until they grow into an emerging vision of unified truth. These puzzles may be at the micro level of words and phrases and how they fit together. Or they may be at the macro level of how statements in one part of the Bible fit together with statements in another part. What I am pleading for is that with the profoundest respect for God's word, and with great confidence in its unity, we spot these puzzles and spare no effort to dig down till we find the unity.

See the Paradoxes and Pour All Your Energy into Seeing the Unity

Jonathan Edwards once formed this resolution: "Resolved, when I think of any theorem in divinity to be solved, immediately to do what I can towards solving it, if circumstances don't hinder."[3] "Theorem in divinity to be solved" means any biblical or theological puzzle that he does not at first understand. What an amazing resolution! No wonder he was such a deep and fruitful thinker and preacher. What we can learn from this resolution is that the effort to press down into the Scriptures to answer the questions we have is what lovers of God and his word do. And it is incredibly fruitful.

I spend a lot of time working my way through biblical paradoxes on my way to deeper and more intense worship. I have little empathy for those who say their worship is greater when they have their hands full of nothing but mysteries. I think the biblical approach is to say there is a direct correlation between what we understand of God and how intensely we admire him. You can muster only so much admiration for someone you don't know. God is not honored by such admiration.

So this is the sort of thing I spend a lot of my time thinking about:

- How can Paul say, on the one hand, "Do not be anxious about anything" (Phil. 4:6), but, on the other hand, say that his "anxiety for all the churches" was a daily pressure on him (2 Cor. 11:28)?

- How can he say, "Rejoice always" (1 Thess. 5:16), and also say, "Weep with those who weep" (Rom. 12:15)?

- How can he tell us to give thanks "always and for everything" (Eph. 5:20) and then admit, "I have great sorrow and *unceasing* anguish in my heart" (Rom. 9:2)?

---

3. Jonathan Edwards, *Letters and Personal Writings*, ed. George S. Claghorn and Harry S. Stout, vol. 16, *The Works of Jonathan Edwards* (New Haven, CT: Yale University Press, 1998), 754.

- What does it mean that Jesus said in Matthew 5:39 to turn the other cheek when struck, but said in Matthew 10:23, "When they persecute you in one town, flee . . ."? When do you flee, and when do you endure hardship and turn the other cheek?

- In what sense is it true that God is "slow to anger" (Ex. 34:6), when it is also true that "his wrath is quickly kindled" (Ps. 2:12)?

I'm not going to solve these puzzles for you. But I am going to testify that I have dug my way down to the common root of these paradoxes. And I have discovered over the years that the fruitfulness of this effort for life and worship is incalculable. There are hundreds of such paradoxical teachings in the Scriptures. We dishonor the word of God not to see them and not to think them through to the root of their unity and beauty. God is not a God of confusion. His tongue is not forked. There are profound and wonderful resolutions to all such puzzles—whether we see them in this life or not. He has called us to an eternity of discovery so that every morning for ages to come we might break forth in new songs of praise.

Aggressively Ask Questions

Amazing things happen when you form the rigorous habit of querying the text—when you *aggressively ask questions* to yourself and to the text. Little by little, thread by thread, you begin to see the intricately woven fabric of God's revelation. Over time you will be changed.

- You become a *Sherlock* tracking down clues with ever greater excitement as the plot of the passages thickens.

- You become a *lover* wanting to see and savor more and more of the message your God has sent you.

- You become your own *cross-examining attorney* forcing yourself to answer the questions others may ask you.

- You become a *tree* planted by living streams, and you find yourself growing and becoming strong.

- You become a *teacher* ready with questions and answers for others who want to discover with you.

- You become a *new person* according to the truth laid down in 2 Corinthians 3:18, "Beholding the glory of the Lord, [we] are being transformed into the same image from one degree of glory to another."

- You become a *worshiper* moving ever closer to the white-hot intensity we will know when we see face-to-face and know even as we are known.

Aggressive attentiveness, expressed in habitual and humble questions, with zealous efforts to answer them from the text itself, will bear more fruit than you ever dreamed. So what kinds of questions should we form the habit of asking? That is what we turn to next.

How sweet are your words to my taste,
  sweeter than honey to my mouth!

PSALM 119:103

How precious to me are your thoughts, O God!
  How vast is the sum of them!

PSALM 139:17

25

Asking Questions about
Words and Phrases

"The unfolding of your words gives light;
it imparts understanding to the simple."

Query the Text for the Author's Intention

We turn now to ask what kinds of questions we should be asking when we humbly and habitually query the text of Scripture. If asking questions is the key to understanding, what should we ask? Let the *ordinary aim* of reading help us answer. I argued in chapter 20 that the ordinary aim of reading is *to grasp what the author intended to communicate* when he wrote the text we are reading. Therefore, the questions that should fill our minds as we read should mainly be various forms of, *What did the author intend by that?*

What did he intend by *that* selection and arrangement of words? Those are the two main tasks of composition or writing: selecting which words to use, and then putting them in various groupings and connections. So we should ask mainly about what the author intends to communicate by choosing *those* words. And what does he intend to communicate by the way he arranged and connected the words and phrases and clauses and paragraphs of his composition?

Which English Translation to Use

Before I give specific examples of the kinds of questions I have in mind, and how to go about answering them, I need to make an observation about our English Bible translations. I am assuming that most people who read this book do not know Greek and Hebrew. That means you need a faithful English translation of the original inspired documents. I do believe that the Greek and Hebrew texts that our translations are based on are essentially the same as what the inspired writers wrote in Greek and Hebrew all those centuries ago. I argue for this in chapter 4 of *A Peculiar Glory: How the Christian Scriptures Reveal Their Complete Truthfulness.*[1] From this, I also conclude that careful, faithful English translations of those Greek and Hebrew texts are a reliable presentation of God's word.

Some English versions are better than others for the kind of close reading that I am commending in this book. Translators have different philosophies about what a translation should be. Some lean more toward making the text as understandable as possible. Their approach is sometimes called *dynamic equivalence*, or thought-for-thought translation. Others lean more toward making the text as similar in wording to the original as possible. Their approach is sometimes called *formal equivalence*. Both of these are worthy goals. I am happy to tell you my preference below, but the main message I want you to hear about Bible translations is that *whichever* translation you use, aggressive attentiveness and active reading will yield a bounty of fruit for your soul and your life that will make the issue of which translation pale by comparison.

My own recommendation, nevertheless, is that for this kind of Bible reading you use a translation that leans toward *formal equivalence*. That means the effort has been made, wherever possible in understandable English, to preserve the *forms* or structures of the Greek and Hebrew. This is often simply not possible because the forms and structures of the language are different. Greek and Hebrew have kinds of language structures we simply do not have in English. But where formal correspondence can be preserved, the *formal equivalence* approach generally tries to do it.

Given those convictions, the two translations I recommend are the *English Standard Version* (ESV) and the *New American Standard Bible*

---

1. John Piper, *A Peculiar Glory: How the Christian Scriptures Reveal Their Complete Truthfulness* (Wheaton, IL: Crossway, 2016), 69–86. "The Greek and Hebrew texts on which our modern language translations are based today are essentially the same as what the inspired authors wrote" (86).

(NASB). Both of these translations seek to capture the wording of the original. Further, they have both accomplished a solid degree of readability and literary excellence in conjunction with their more precise adherence to the originals. The ESV especially stands out in this regard. It seeks to uphold precision and accuracy, while achieving an even greater degree of clarity of expression than the NASB. The NASB, on the other hand, probably has more of the precise wording that makes the most careful textual analysis possible. As you have noticed, I am using the ESV in this book, as I do in my own personal reading. I think the ESV has found a good balance that will make it the most faithful and useful English translation for decades to come—for Bible memory, personal devotion, liturgical church use, and for preaching.[2]

Why Does an Author Choose the Words He Does?

Now that we have our English translation in front of us, the most basic cluster of questions we want to ask has to do with the words that the author used. Why did he choose these words, and why did he relate them to other words the way he did? Why this word? Why here among these other words? It may be that one of the reasons the author chose a particular word is the way it *sounds*. We all realize this when an author is writing poetry. He may want certain words to rhyme. But he may not be writing poetry and may simply want his words to sound a certain way with a certain consonance or assonance or cadence. His aim may simply be to make the reading more enjoyable. We all love certain cadences and rhythms and sounds. Some are more pleasing than others. But the author may also signal by similar sounds that we should link two words together.

Far more often, authors choose their words and put them in a certain arrangement in order to communicate certain thoughts or ideas or truths. This is especially true when we are dealing with documents that claim high degrees of authority—like a contract, or the US Constitution, or the Bible. So as we read the Bible, we are mainly looking for the truth that the author intends to communicate by this selection of words in their arrangement.

---

2. I have given more thoughts on Bible translations at http://www.desiringgod.org/articles/good -english-with-minimal-translation-why-bethlehem-uses-the-esv; and http://www.desiringgod.org /interviews/what-do-you-think-about-paraphrased-bible-translations (accessed March 30, 2016).

The most obvious answer to why an author chose a particular word is that he knows from the way the word is used that it can carry his meaning. I say, it *can* carry his meaning. Whether it *will* carry his meaning depends on what he does with it. Words don't have intrinsic meaning. They get their meaning from usage. We noticed in chapter 20 that the English word *set* has 464 definitions in the *Oxford English Dictionary*, and the word *run* has 396. What that means is that a word like *set* can be used in 464 different ways. It gets its particular meaning from the specific way an author *uses* it—whether John *set* the book on the table, or played a tennis *set*. So an author does not choose a word because he knows the word, all by itself, will carry his meaning, but because he knows from his experience that it *can* carry his meaning. Then he gives it his particular meaning by the way he uses it with other words. So one early task of active reading is to ask about what meanings a word ordinarily carries, and then the way the author uses it in relation to other words—all with a view to finding *what the author intended to communicate.*

Coming to Terms with an Author

Since any word may carry more than one meaning, our task is to determine precisely which meaning an author intends a given word to have. Mortimer Adler helpfully distinguishes between *words* and *terms*. He suggests that we call a word a "term" when an author uses it with a definite and particular meaning in a given context.[3] He calls this specific aspect of reading "coming to terms." We "come to terms" with an author when we figure out how he is using his words. What definite meaning is he giving his words so that they don't have 464 meanings but only one—or two, if he wants to suggest to us a double entendre (double understanding or double intention)?

We cannot *come to terms* with a biblical author by looking up his words in a dictionary, not even a Greek dictionary. Dictionaries give a list of possible meanings but do not specify with certainty which meaning a word has in any given text. The only way to discover *the author's* meaning of a word is by asking the question about its relation to other words in its context. And you have to ask about those *other* words

---

3. Mortimer Adler and Charles van Doren, *How to Read a Book*, rev. ed. (New York: Simon & Schuster, 1972), 66–113.

in the same way. This is true, Adler says, no matter how "merry-go-roundish" it may seem at first.[4]

One of the reasons Adler calls this method "merry-go-roundish" is that, at this point in coming to terms, we find ourselves going around in the notorious *hermeneutic circle*—which means words can only be understood from their context, and a context is made up of words that also need to be understood. Catch-22—like the paradox: to read this text, you need to experience reading, but to get experience reading, you need to read texts. However, the fact that we all communicate with words every day, with a great deal of success, shows that the *hermeneutic circle* is not as vicious as it sounds. You can get off a merry-go-round in a different place than you got on. It can take you where you need to go. When you combine the limited possible uses of most words, with (1) the added limitations laid down by grammatical structures, and (2) the added limitations of an author's own habits, with (3) the added limitations of a particular paragraph, the circle regularly gives way to clarity. E. D. Hirsch tackles the problem of the hermeneutic circle head-on in *Validity in Interpretation* and shows that "it is less mysterious and paradoxical than many in the German hermeneutical tradition have made it out to be."[5]

It may be helpful to consider three biblical examples of how the same word can become different "terms"—that is, have different particular meanings—when used in different ways.

Circumcision

In Ephesians 2:11–12, Paul uses the word *circumcision* to refer to the Jewish people in general, over against the Gentiles:

> Therefore remember that at one time you Gentiles in the flesh, called "the uncircumcision" by what is called the *circumcision*, which is made in the flesh by hands—remember that you were at that time separated from Christ.

But in Philippians 3:2–3, he uses the same word in a radically different way, to refer to Christians, including Gentiles, who had not even received the physical act of circumcision:

---

4. Ibid., 107.
5. E. D. Hirsh, *Validity in Interpretation* (New Haven, CT: Yale University Press, 1967), 76–77.

Look out for the dogs, look out for the evildoers, look out for those who mutilate the flesh. For we are the *circumcision*, who worship by the Spirit of God and glory in Christ Jesus and put no confidence in the flesh.

This unexpected use of the word *circumcision* should provoke in us several questions. If he wants to refer to Christians, why use a word that ordinarily refers to Jews? What connection is he trying to make between Christians and Israel? What actually are the marks of the true circumcision if not the physical act of cutting away the foreskin? Are there other places where Paul uses the term *circumcision* in this same way that might shed light on any of these questions? These are the kinds of questions that make up serious, active Bible reading.

You can see from that last question (Are there other similar uses in Paul?) that a good concordance will become one of the most helpful partners in this kind of active reading. A concordance is a book that has lists of all the words of the Bible and where they are used. So with a concordance, you can find all the places where *circumcision* is used. This proves to be immensely fruitful.

For example, *circumcision* turns up in Colossians 2:11: "In him also you were circumcised with a *circumcision* made without hands, by putting off the body of the flesh, by the circumcision of Christ." And in Romans 2:29: "A Jew is one inwardly, and *circumcision* is a matter of the heart, by the Spirit, not by the letter." These verses go a long way to answering how Paul was thinking about the relationship between Christians and Israel. But the main point here is how essential it is to base the meaning of words on how they are used, not on any dictionary definition. In this process I have found that besides the text of Scripture itself and the discipline to look and look and look, no other tool has been of more help to me than the concordance.[6]

When you look up the other uses of a word, I recommend that you consider those other uses, as they occur, in concentric circles starting with the paragraph or chapter you are studying. Then consider uses of the word in the same biblical book. Then consider uses in other books

---

6. Unless you have no access to a smartphone or tablet or computer, Bible software provides the most helpful tools for concordance usage. There are many good programs. Be sure to get one with a feature to search the whole Bible for any word. And it is really helpful if the search feature can limit the search to particular authors and books of the Bible. This feature is your virtual concordance.

by the same author. Then in the New Testament or Old Testament as a whole, and finally the whole Bible. The reason for this suggestion is that our aim in reading is to grasp what *the author* intends to communicate. It makes sense, therefore, that we would not consult first the way *another* author uses the word. That may, in fact, shed light on Paul's use in the case of *circumcision*. But we prioritize Paul's uses of the word, because our aim is to know *what Paul intended to communicate*.

Called

Consider an example in which the same word is used by two different authors in similar doctrinal contexts but with very different meanings. The apostle Paul loves to use the word *called* to refer to Christians. In his thinking, the word ordinarily refers to the act of God that effectively creates the faith it commands. For example, he distinguishes the "called" from Jews and Greeks who have heard the *general call* of the gospel, but have refused it:

> We preach Christ crucified, a stumbling block to Jews and folly to Gentiles, but to those who are *called*, both Jews and Greeks, Christ the power of God and the wisdom of God. (1 Cor. 1:23–24)

So the "called," in Paul's way of thinking, are not merely those who have been called in an evangelistic meeting by a preacher. The Jews and Greeks had indeed been called in *that* way. Rather, the "called" in Paul's meaning are those who have experienced an act of God like Jesus's call to Lazarus when he was dead. "Lazarus, come out" (John 11:43). The call created the life. It created what it commanded.

You can see this meaning, perhaps, most clearly in Romans 8:30 where Paul says that all the called are justified and glorified: "Those whom he predestined he also *called*, and those whom he *called* he also justified, and those whom he justified he also glorified." So, just as in 1 Corinthians 1:23–24, the called are not just offered the inviting call of God, which they may or may not accept. Rather, the called are those whom God pursues decisively and effectively and by his call makes alive—forever.

But then we turn to Matthew's Gospel and find a very different use of the word *called*. Jesus has just told the parable of the wedding feast. A king gave a wedding feast for his son. But the people invited did not want to come. "They paid no attention and went off, one to his farm, another to his business, while the rest seized his servants, treated them shamefully, and killed them" (Matt. 22:5–6). So the king said that his servants should go and call everyone they can find. "Go therefore to the main roads and invite [call] to the wedding feast as many as you find" (Matt. 22:9). At the end, the wedding feast is full of people, but some came in without the proper clothing—probably representing that they had little respect for the king and that their lives had not been changed by his grace. Such a person is thrown out "into the outer darkness." The parable ends, "In that place there will be weeping and gnashing of teeth. For many are *called*, but few are chosen" (Matt. 22:13–14).

You can see how different this meaning of *called* is from Paul's. For Paul, all the called are glorified (Rom. 8:30). But for Matthew, the called are thrown into outer darkness. What a great mistake it would be to think that Paul and Matthew have contradictory views of salvation. They don't. But they do use words in different ways. Here is the way Leon Morris puts it in his commentary on Matthew:

> This is an expression of the doctrine of election that we find in one form or another throughout the New Testament. . . . The gospel invitation goes far and wide, but not everyone who hears it is one of God's elect. We know those who are elect by their obedient response. Perhaps it is worth noticing here that this doctrine is also found in Paul, but that he expresses it differently. For him the "call" is the effectual call, so that it is enough for him to speak of people as being called by God. "Call" in his writings means much the same as "chosen" here.[7]

Of

Oh, how many times we fly over words in our reading without slowing down to ask, with patience and care, what does the author intend to communicate by this word? Some of the most common words carry some of the weightiest meanings and some of the greatest challenges. This is surely true concerning the little word *of*, which can be used in so many different ways. As a preposition, it always occurs with another word, and together they create a phrase—such as "of faith." Then we

---

7. Leon Morris, *The Gospel according to Matthew*, Pillar New Testament Commentary (Grand Rapids, MI: Eerdmans, 1992), 553.

face the same challenges with the *phrase* as we did with the individual words. Phrases can have different meanings depending on how they are used in a sentence and paragraph. So whenever we see the word *of*, we need to determine which one of its many possible meanings the author intends.

Consider Paul's use of this phrase "of faith." By itself, the phrase carries no clear or definite meaning. We need to see it in connection with other words. Two times in the letter to the Romans, Paul connects the phrase with the word *obedience*—"obedience of faith."

> Through [Christ] we have received grace and apostleship to bring about the *obedience of faith* for the sake of his name among all the nations. (Rom. 1:5)

> The mystery . . . has been made known to all nations, according to the command of the eternal God, to bring about *the obedience of faith* . . . (Rom. 16:25–26)

What does the three-word phrase "obedience of faith" mean? It depends on the meaning of the word *of* (or, in Greek, the meaning of the genitive case). This is not easy because the possibilities are many. Paul uses the word *of* in numerous ways:

- Work of faith (1 Thess. 1:3; 2 Thess. 1:11), probably meaning "produced by" faith.
- Shield of faith (Eph. 6:16), probably meaning "composed of" faith.
- Household of faith (Gal. 6:16), probably meaning "characterized by" faith.
- Word of faith (Rom. 10:8), probably meaning "about" faith.
- Righteousness of faith (Rom. 4:13), probably meaning "declared through" faith.

The most likely candidates for "obedience of faith" seem to be (1) "obedience that *consists in* faith"—that is, the believing is the obeying. Or (2) "obedience that *springs from* faith"—that is, the faith gives rise to and empowers the obedience. I don't want to rob you of your own privilege of "looking at the fish" (Agassiz!). But when you have looked as closely as you can in the immediate context for clues as to which of these two Paul means, your concordance will lead you to Romans

10:16, which says, "They have not all *obeyed* the gospel. For Isaiah says, 'Lord, who has *believed* what he has heard from us?'" That connection between obedience and belief might incline us to say that Paul uses them interchangeably here, and therefore, perhaps in Romans 1:5 and 16:26.

But then the concordance also leads you to an even closer parallel to Romans 1:5, namely, 15:18: "I will not venture to speak of anything except what Christ has accomplished through me to bring the Gentiles to *obedience—by word and deed.*" This looks like it might settle the matter. If the obedience he is pursuing among the Gentiles is "by word and deed," then it is more than faith. It includes other concrete "deeds" of obedience. So the phrase "obedience of faith" would probably mean "obedience that comes from faith." But there's a possible glitch. What does the phrase "by word and deed" modify? I just assumed that it modifies "obedience." But does it? Most commentators say, no, it modifies *Paul's* ministry. He led them to obedience by *his own* word and deed.

A Method That Forces Us to "Look at the Fish"

I'm going to leave it there with you, and simply draw out one more implication for the kinds of questions we ask when we read actively. We have seen that coming to terms with an author means figuring out how he uses his words to give them definite meanings. And we have just now seen that we must also discern the relationship between the various parts of his sentences, like the relationship that the phrase "by word and deed" has to the other words in Paul's sentence. Does it modify Paul's ministry, or the obedience of the Gentiles?

There is a method of analyzing biblical sentences that forces us to take all these relationships seriously and to decide how we think an author is using all his words and phrases. You may have used this method, as I did, in the seventh grade. It's called *sentence diagramming.* Not everyone had my experience. But I do not cease to thank God for Mrs. Adams, who made us diagram sentences all year long—at least that's what my memory says. I found it as exciting as watching detective stories. Trying to figure out how all the pieces of a sentence fit together to make one coherent whole was a very satisfying task for me. Of course, not everyone is wired this way.

My aim is not to teach you the skill of diagramming sentences, but to commend it to you as extremely helpful in forming a habit of observation that puts every part of a sentence into its author-intended relationship to the others. This must be done, if not on paper, then intuitively in your own mind. Otherwise, the pieces of the sentence simply dangle with no clear purpose. You can be the judge whether you see these relationships intuitively or whether some practice with sentence diagramming would help.

One of the places where the method of sentence diagramming is laid out fully and helpfully is in chapter 5 of Thomas Schreiner's *Interpreting the Pauline Epistles*.[8] Schreiner concedes that one can see the meaning of a text without diagramming the sentences. But he is right to insist that you cannot see that meaning if you don't know the grammatical habits that guided an author to arrange his words the way he did. Why then should you consider the practice of sentence diagramming? Schreiner answers:

> I began to see that diagramming forced me to think through the syntactical relationship of every word, phrase, and clause in the sentence. Diagramming compelled me to ask and answer questions that I would not always ask otherwise, such as . . . What word or words does the prepositional phrase modify?
>
> One of the great values of diagramming, then, is that it compels the interpreter to slow down and to think carefully through every element of the text. . . . Diagramming is also helpful because it lays out the text visually. Such a schematic immediately shows the main clause, main verb, direct object(s), indirect object(s), modifiers, subordinate clauses (if any), and other key grammatical parts.[9]

In other words, sentence diagramming forces us to be aggressively attentive. It forces us to stay at the table with Agassiz's fish, and stay at the art museum looking at *Boy with a Squirrel* (see chapter 23).[10]

---

8. Thomas Schreiner, *Interpreting the Pauline Epistles*, 2nd ed. (Grand Rapids, MI: Baker Academic, 2011), 69–96.

9. Ibid., 69–70.

10. Most of the major computer Bible programs have a sentence-diagramming module so that you can do it on your computer. Accordance, Bible Works, and Logos all provide help for using their sentence-diagramming features. I want to mention one online resource that is of special interest to me because I was involved indirectly in its birth and because it is owned by Bethlehem College & Seminary, where I serve as the chancellor: Biblearc.com (https://biblearc.com) enables you to learn diagramming with the help of instructional videos and then provides the means of doing the diagramming online and saving your work. I am especially eager to commend this website because, in

Careful Observation, Not Memorizing Rules

Examples of words and phrases of the sort we have been considering could be multiplied by the hundreds. And with each one, something slightly different would present itself to challenge our minds. This is why it is impractical to give rules for every challenge of interpretation. They are all different in some small or large way, and the key lies in becoming a very careful observer, not in memorizing countless rules. The more texts we analyze with aggressive attentiveness, the more adept we will become at interpreting others.

My main aim in this chapter, therefore, has been to point you toward some of the kinds of questions to ask about an author's words and phrases. My hope is to encourage you to form and deepen the habit of mind and heart that loves to look long and hard at the Scriptures, and to be joyfully confident that such aggressive attentiveness is worth the effort.

In the next chapter, we move beyond words and phrases to the kinds of questions to ask about how clauses or propositions are related to each other. In my own experience, this is the level of observation and analysis that has proved explosive with life-changing insight.

---

the next chapter, we will see a method, which I have found immeasurably helpful and which I still use today, of relating the propositions of a paragraph, and Biblearc is the best online resource for helping you use this particular method.

This meant, for me, a whole new approach to Bible reading. No longer did I just read and memorize verses—collect nuggets. I also sought to understand and memorize and apply arguments.

JOHN PIPER

Here is where the lights went on for me most brightly. Paul was not stringing pearls. He was forging links.

JOHN PIPER

26

Propositions: Collections of Nuggets or Links in a Chain?

"He spoke boldly, reasoning and persuading . . ."

How Did I Learn to Read at Age Twenty-Two?

In chapter 23, I began to tell the story of how the years 1968 through 1971 were explosive in my discovery of what it means to read. In one sense, I said, I learned to read when I was twenty-two. My encounters with Daniel Fuller, Mortimer Adler, and E. D. Hirsch were life changing. Hirsch convinced me that interpretations can claim validity only if meaning is defined in terms of what an author willed to communicate through his words. Adler showed me how passive my reading was and what it means to put my mind in gear as I read so that I am constantly asking questions and trying to answer them. Fuller took my hand, as it were, for three years, and guided me through dozens of biblical texts, forcing me to put into practice the disciplines of aggressive attentiveness.

Did I really learn to read when I was twenty-two? Did I really have to wait until my first year in seminary to discover what it means to read the Bible? You judge. The most fruitful discovery I made about how to read was that the authors of Scripture *argue*. They develop arguments—trains of interlinking thoughts that lead somewhere. Until those days, I read the Bible mainly to collect precious *nuggets*. Doctrinal nuggets. Devotional nuggets. Pearls. These were wonderful. I don't begrudge the years of collecting and stringing pearls. They served me well. I loved them. I think they probably would have led me faithfully to heaven.

But within a matter of days, in a hermeneutics course based on the book of Philippians, I was startled to see that *Paul does not string nuggets; he forges chains.* This is what was new. I don't blame anyone in my past for not showing me this. They may have shown me, and I was simply not ready to receive it. So it may not have registered. This is not about blame at all. It is about the joy of discovery. Or maybe I should call it awakening. Paul's thoughts are not nuggets. They are links. If this has always been obvious to you, and you are saying, "Duh," then I say, praise God. But for me, it came at age twenty-two with the force of a hurricane. I was caught up into a way of reading that was new, and arduous, and rewarding beyond all hopes. We called it "arcing."

Daniel Fuller developed this procedure of identifying the clauses or propositions of a text, figuring out how they relate to each other in the emerging argument, and then labeling them with abbreviations under the arcs that we connected with ever-enlarging arcs as we saw how the pieces of the argument fit together. I will come back and illustrate this shortly, since you may be having a hard time visualizing what I mean.

The Roots of Arcing

But first it seems only fair, and also encouraging, to point out that Fuller too had undergone his own hermeneutical awakening in the late 1940s at Princeton Seminary under Howard T. Kuist. Justin Taylor tells this story in his doctoral dissertation.

> One of their teachers at Princeton was Howard T. Kuist (1895–1964), Charles T. Haley Professor of Biblical Theology for Teaching of English Bible, a pioneering advocate of the inductive Bible study method. (The index to his manuscript collection at Princeton can be viewed online at http://manuscripts.ptsem.edu/collection/195 [accessed July 16, 2014]). Kuist emphasized *observation*, defined as "the art of seeing things as they really are." Preachers, he argued, have only a limited amount of time for sermon preparation, and therefore a majority of the preacher's time should be spent in the text itself, not in secondary literature. Commentaries should be consulted only for *facts*, not conclusions.

Kuist sought to convince his students to put aside all hermeneutical systems and presuppositions—including any sermon, creeds, or lesson they had heard before—and let the Bible speak for itself, as if they were approaching it for the first time. "Such talk," Fuller recounts, "was a life-changing moment for me. I tend to construe my whole life since then as this idea's playing a crucial role in what I did and how I thought thereafter." (Daniel Fuller to Justin Taylor [January 1, 2011]; in author's possession. My own view is that Kuist's effort to "put aside all hermeneutical systems and presuppositions—including any sermon, creeds, or lesson they had heard before," is not possible. The way I would put it is to say that, all readers of Scripture should seek to be aware of their preconceptions and should pray and work toward a kind of teachability that makes one willing to change our views if the Scriptures call for it.) Kuist devoted the bulk of his classroom time "to coaching students in how to grasp an author's intended meaning from the verbal symbols in a text." (Daniel P. Fuller, "How I Became a Berean," http://documents.fuller.edu/ministry/berean/i_became.htm [accessed October 30, 2013]). The English Bible was their main text. Kuist also had his students read two short readings. The first was Mortimer Adler's chapter on "Coming to Terms" from *How to Read a Book*. (Mortimer J. Adler, *How to Read a Book: The Art of Getting a Liberal Education*, 1st ed. [New York: Simon and Schuster, 1940], 185–208). The second reading was a testimony from entomologist and paleontologist Samuel Scudder (1837–1911) about his student days in the classroom of Louis Agassiz (1807–1873), founder of the Harvard Museum of Comparative Zoology. . . .

Fuller recounts, "This story produced a most profound change in my strategy for studying the Bible. It made me realize how diligently I must scrutinize a Bible passage to see just what is there and try to forget what I had previously heard or read about that passage." (Fuller, "How I Became a Berean.")[1]

The Birth of the Method

In 1953, as a new professor at Fuller Seminary, Daniel Fuller began to convert all he had learned about inductive Bible study from Kuist

---

1. Justin Gerald Taylor, "John Piper: The Making of a Christian Hedonist," PhD diss., the Southern Baptist Theological Seminary, 2015.

into the procedure that has become known as arcing. Taylor continues the story:

> From March through May of that spring semester [1953], Fuller taught the NT Survey class for Wilbur Smith, who was on sabbatical (the seventh year of the school's existence). This course required teaching the whole of the New Testament in thirty-eight sessions, 50 minutes per class. So a book like Romans would have to be summarized in just three sessions.
>
> As Fuller studied the book inductively to prepare for class, the beginning of the process of "arcing" was born. He would see certain units being embraced by larger units, and began to employ a system of representing units of thoughts by drawing an arc over a set of propositions. Eventually all of Romans 1–8 was encompassed under one arc, from which an outline could be constructed. The students would receive an outline, with space for notes, instead of a lecture. The students responded quite positively to Fuller's teaching, which eventually led to him getting hired full-time. Fuller would go on to develop the arcing method as a means of keeping track of an author's train of thought by discerning the relationship between the various propositions in a passage. (For explanations of arcing, see Thomas R. Schreiner's chapter on "Tracing the Argument" in his book, *Interpreting the Pauline Epistles*, 2nd ed. [Grand Rapids: Baker Academic, 2011], 97–124; John Piper, *Biblical Exegesis: Discovering the Meaning of Scriptural Texts* [Minneapolis: Desiring God, 2002], and the website http://biblearc.com).[2]

I find myself deeply moved, and filled with thankfulness, because of the faithfulness and providence of God to put me in a generational line marked by this kind of rigorous attention to the Scriptures.

Propositions: Basic Building Blocks of Thought

In this chapter, I would like to simply give you a taste of what for me was so revolutionary about arcing.[3] In doing this, I hope to underscore again that *asking questions is the key to understanding*, and that some of the most fruitful questions are those about how propositions relate

---

2. Ibid.
3. I am borrowing in this chapter from my unpublished paper that Justin Taylor referred to: John Piper, *Biblical Exegesis: Discovering the Meaning of Scriptural Texts*.

to each other. Implicit in the previous chapter was the fact that words and phrases do not convey a clear and definite meaning until they are seen as parts of a proposition. For example, the phrase "for sinners" has no definite meaning by itself. Neither does "died." Nor "Jesus." But when you put them together to form a proposition according to the rules of English grammar, all of them take on their distinct meanings: "Jesus died for sinners." Therefore, propositions are the basic building blocks of a train of thought.

A proposition is an assertion about something. "Jesus wept" is a proposition. It has a subject and a predicate (a verb and its modifiers), and they are in the order that makes a point. In order to understand propositions, we must know at least the rudiments of grammar and syntax of the language we are reading—even if the knowledge is intuitive rather than self-conscious. Propositions have meanings only because they are composed of words and phrases put together according to established rules. You cannot communicate if you disobey all the rules. "Paul carried the basket" and "The basket carried Paul" are two propositions that use *exactly the same words* but convey very different meanings. There is a syntactical rule in English that says the subject of such a sentence (which does the acting) typically *precedes* the verb. That's why these two propositions with the very same words have different meanings. A new set of rules has to be learned when we want to read Greek or Hebrew. Whether you are reading Greek or Hebrew or English (or any other language), you must pay attention to the appropriate rules of grammar if the meaning of an author's propositions is to be understood.

The Relationship between Propositions

So far I have only said what I already knew when I was reading the Bible to collect nuggets. Now comes the new insight—plain though it may be. After understanding the grammatical structure of a proposition, and coming to terms with the words and phrases in it, *we still may not understand its meaning*. Why? Because just as words and phrases derive meaning from their use in a proposition, so a proposition derives its precise meaning from its use in relationship to other propositions. Links in a chain depend on the other links in a way that nuggets in a sack do not.

For example, in Colossians 2:21, Paul says, "Do not handle, Do not taste, Do not touch." Taken alone, these three propositions would suggest that Paul is prescribing certain rules of behavior. That would be a complete misunderstanding. The preceding proposition—the rhetorical question of verse 20—says, "Why . . . do you submit to regulations?" (Rhetorical questions are questions left without an expressed answer, because the author assumes we can see what is being asserted—"Don't submit to such regulations!") So what Paul really means is the very opposite of what the three propositions of verse 21 say when isolated from their context. He means, beware of regulations such as, "Do not handle, do not taste, do not touch."

The All-Important Word *For*

Another example would be Philippians 2:12: "Work out your own salvation with fear and trembling." This proposition will not be properly understood unless it is viewed in relation to the clause that follows: "For it is God who works in you, both to will and to work for his good pleasure" (Phil. 2:13). A whole theology hangs on the way you relate these two propositions. If you make the second clause the *result* of the first, you would be saying, "Work out your own salvation with fear and trembling, *so that* God will be at work in you both to will and to work for his good pleasure." You would be saying that God's action in sanctification is dependent on our working first.

But if you make the second clause the *ground* of the first, you would be saying, "Work out your own salvation with fear and trembling, *because* God is at work in you both to will and to work for his good pleasure." You would be saying *our* efforts toward holiness are initiated by *God*, and possible only because God is already at work in us. Paul leaves no room for doubt which of these he intends to communicate. He makes it explicit by joining the two clauses by the conjunction *for* or *because*. "Work out your own salvation with fear and trembling, *for* it is God who works in you, both to will and to work for his good pleasure" (Phil. 2:12–13). God's work in us is the *ground* and empowering of our working. Theologically, few things are more important than getting this line of argument correct.

The Flow of an Author's Thought

The point of seeing propositions in relationship to each other is not merely to elucidate the meaning of each proposition, but also to help us grasp the flow of an author's argument. Here is where the lights went on for me most brightly. Paul was not stringing pearls. He was forging links in a chain. I remember the very point in the hermeneutics class where it hit me. We were working our way through Philippians 1:6–8, where Paul writes:

> I am sure of this, that he who began a good work in you will bring it to completion at the day of Jesus Christ. It is right for me to feel this way about you all, because I hold you in my heart, for you are all partakers with me of grace, both in my imprisonment and in the defense and confirmation of the gospel. *For God is my witness, how I yearn for you all with the affection of Christ Jesus.*

I had read the book of Philippians many times since I was a child. My King James Version of the Bible that my parents gave me on my fifteenth birthday (which I have here in front of me) is marked heavily in red and blue pencil. The words "Key Joy" are written beside the title. But seven years later, when I was twenty-two, someone asked me for the first time, "Did you notice the word *for* at the beginning of verse 8?" Yes. I see that. "What does it tell you about the relationship between verses 7 and 8?" It tells me that verse 8 is a ground or cause or basis of verse 7. "Right. Now, *how* does that argument work? *How* is Paul's yearning for the Philippians with the affection of Christ a *ground* for Paul's justified confidence that God would complete in them the work he began?" That question stumped me totally. That is the sort of question I have been asking myself for the last forty-eight years. That is the most fruitful kind of question: How do the arguments work?

The conclusion of that discussion was something like this: If Paul really loves the Philippians with the very affection of Christ—that is, if Christ's own affection for them is what Paul feels for them—then Paul's commitment to them is really Christ's commitment to them, and it is a sure sign that Christ will preserve them to the end. They will persevere. I had never had a thought like that. And the reason I hadn't is that I had never asked that question about how the argument of verses 7 and 8 works. Asking that question forced me to think in ways I had never thought. Multiply this kind of discovery hundreds of times, and you may see why I felt as though I had just learned to read.

From Collecting Nuggets to Finding Chains

This meant, for me, a whole new approach to Bible reading. No longer did I just read and memorize verses—collect nuggets. I also sought to understand and memorize and apply *arguments*. This involved finding the main point of each literary unit and then seeing how each proposition fit together to unfold and support the main point.

To carry out this kind of analysis of propositions in an extended way, we need two things. First, we need to know the kinds of relationships that can exist between propositions. If we don't know how thoughts relate to each other, it is a great hindrance to understanding how propositions form complex units of meaning. If we have only a vague idea of how two propositions are related, we are hindered because, even if we do intuit the right relationship, we won't know how to put our understanding into words. We need a list of possible logical relationships, with descriptive names, so that we can use them when we discuss a text's meaning.

Second, we need some kind of method or device to help us hold a long or complex argument in our mental view. For most of us, it is impossible to keep before our mind the complex interrelationships of an argument developed at the beginning of a paragraph while we are struggling to see how the propositions ten verses later fit into that argument. It may be that the earlier argument holds the key to the later one. So we must find a way to preserve, in a brief space, the interrelationships of an author's line of argument. Otherwise, it will be nearly impossible to grasp the totality and unity of what he intends for his paragraph to communicate.

That's What Arcing Is For

These two things, which we need in order to follow the thread of an author's thought, are what *arcing* is designed to provide. It is a means of *seeing* and *preserving* the intricate development of an author's thought in its complexity and unity. In the appendix, I give a more detailed explanation and illustration of the process of arcing. The best way to learn this method of reading the Bible is in partnership with others who are ahead of you. This is why Bethlehem College & Seminary has created the website biblearc.com.[4] This is the go-to place to learn and to

---

4. See chap. 25, note 10.

practice arcing. I use it for my own study, and I use it in teaching book studies at Bethlehem College & Seminary.

If you don't have the computer resources to visit and use this website, the introduction I give in the appendix of this book is sufficient to get started. I did arcing for forty years with pencil and paper before the computer opportunities were developed. So don't let anything stop you. The key is not in the technology, or even in the technique. The key is in rigorous observation, good questions, hard thinking, and getting your answers from the connections in the text—all of it soaked in prayer for God's illumination (chapters 11–13).

Query the Text

The point of this chapter has been that words and phrases get their definite meaning by the way they are used in a proposition, and propositions get their meaning from the way they are connected to other propositions in the building of a train of thought. Therefore, the mental habit of asking questions about how propositions work in relation to each other has been the most fruitful kind of reading for me. But we are not finished with our suggestions about what questions to use when querying the text. Questions about propositions and their relationships are paramount. But questions about paradoxes, pleasures, and transformed lives are also crucial. That is what we turn to next.

As soon as God's Word becomes known through you, the devil will afflict you, will make a real doctor of you, and will teach you by his temptations to seek and to love God's Word. For I myself . . . owe my papists many thanks for so beating, pressing, and frightening me through the devil's raging that they have turned me into a fairly good theologian.

MARTIN LUTHER

How sweet are your words to my taste,
   sweeter than honey to my mouth!

PSALM 119:103

27

Querying the Text about Paradoxes, Pleasures, and a Transformed Life

"The sum of your word is truth, and every
one of your righteous rules endures forever."

I Didn't Get the Job

In the previous chapter, I commended the method of serious active reading called *arcing* (see also the appendix). It is a way of identifying the propositions of a text, discerning their relationships, and preserving them in a schematic form that helps us identify the main point of a text and how all the parts fit together to clarify and support that point. My aim was not to convert you all into arcers, but to persuade you that seeing the text this way and asking these kinds of questions is worth all the effort you can give. You may be so sharp that you can intuitively do what some of us must depend on arcing to do for us. There are eyes in arcs.

In fact, I was being interviewed for a teaching job once, and one of the professors on the committee considering me asked, "Isn't that arcing stuff just a crutch?" I had no hesitation and said, "Absolutely, and I am mentally crippled and need all the help I can get. And I assume most of my students need the same help." I didn't get the job. Which was probably one of the sweetest denials the Lord ever performed on my behalf.

But I do concede that it is the principles and questions and hard thinking that surround arcing that make the difference, not the actual technique of creating the schematic form. Developing the mental habits that arcing demands is the point.

Asking about Relationships across the Whole Bible

If we extend the principle of arcing over a whole book in the Bible, or over the whole Bible, we see what kinds of questions we need to be asking. The aim, if we live long enough, is to grasp what all the biblical authors intended to communicate. So we keep asking questions about how each paragraph relates to the others until we grasp the main point of each book. The *main point* is the point supported by all the other points but supporting nothing. It's the ultimate aim of the author in what he wrote. All the other parts of the text serve to explain and argue for the main point. And as we see the main points of the books, we ask questions about how the messages of the books relate to each other. In this way, we move toward the main message of the whole Bible.

Since we believe that God is the ultimate author, inspiring the human authors with what God intends to communicate, we also believe that the Bible will prove to be coherent. It will not contradict itself. People who believe they are constantly stumbling onto contradictions in the Bible cut themselves off from much insight. Insight is the fruit of dogged searching and digging down into the texts to find what it is that makes the apparent contradiction—the paradox—a profound unity. Cutting short this process of digging by disbelief in the unity of Scripture is a tragic loss to those who give up so quickly.

But for those who hold fast to the inspired unity of Scripture, rooted in a God of truth, who does not speak an ultimate and contradictory yes and no (2 Cor. 1:17–22), the labor is long and the fruit is glorious. One of the most fruitful habits when asking questions is to ask how the meaning of a passage fits together with other passages that seem contradictory or inconsistent. I never assume the Bible is inconsistent. My assumption is I am not seeing all I need to see. Here's an example of the kind of questions I have in mind—and an example about how pondering paradoxes is one of the most fruitful acts of meditation on the Scriptures.

Does God Love or Hate the Wicked?

In Romans 5:8, Paul says, "God shows his *love* for us in that while we were still *sinners*, Christ died for us." But Psalm 11:5 says, "The LORD tests the righteous, but *his soul hates the wicked.*" So, on the one hand, God *loves* us while we are sinners. And on the other hand, God *hates* the wicked.

This is good. We have been looking with enough aggressive attentiveness that we have seen the tension between Romans 5:8 and Psalm 11:5—God's love for sinners and his hate for sinners. So we start asking questions. Ultimately, our question is, How do these fit together in such a way that God is revealed as glorious and not schizophrenic? We believe there is unity here and that both texts are true. Now we need to see *how* they are both true in relation to each other. You can see that this is the kind of question that *arcing* trained us to ask, even though we are not drawing any arcs on a page, or on a computer screen, between Romans and the Psalms. Rather, we are thinking a certain way, trained by the discipline of asking questions about how texts relate to each other.

To give you an idea of how this may work, here are some of the questions I asked myself as I pondered how God's love for sinners relates to his hate for sinners. These questions are like trial balloons that you send up to see if any of them may prove illuminating.

- Are two different groups being talked about in "sinners" and "wicked"?
- Are the sinners whom God loves not included in the sinners whom God hates?
- Is there a difference between "sin" and "wickedness" so that he really doesn't love the wicked or hate the sinners?
- Did something change between the Old Testament and the New Testament so that God does not hate the wicked today but did then?
- What, more specifically, does God's hate involve?
- What, more specifically, does God's love involve?
- Does the hate he has for the wicked exclude the possibility that he might also love them?
- What different kinds of hate might he have?
- Is one kind of hate the intense loathing of a person's wicked heart?
- Is another kind of hate the purpose to destroy?
- Could the loathing be present without the purpose to destroy?

- If so, could he love those whom he loathes by aiming to rescue them from their loathsomeness and from his hate?
- What other texts should I look at to help answer these questions?

These kinds of questions pour into the mind when two passages in tension are brought together with the aim of figuring out how they fit. This process of asking questions and trying to answer them is what I call *thinking*. When done humbly and with trust in God's promised help, it is an act of obedience to Paul's words, "*Think over* what I say, for the Lord will give you understanding in everything" (2 Tim. 2:7). That command applies to all biblical revelation.

It's not my aim here to solve the problem of God's love and hate. I am only trying to illustrate the way the discipline of *arcing* trains our mind to seek coherence across the whole Bible. So it trains us to ask questions about how everything relates to everything. So we wind up spotting the tension between Romans 5:8 and Psalm 11:5.

But I will suggest this much by way of a solution. God's hate of the wicked has two meanings, depending on the context. One is a strong disapproval of the ugly condition of the wicked soul. The other is a just and holy resolve to punish. His love, on the other hand, has the same two kinds of meaning, only in a positive sense. On the one hand, it means a strong approval of the beautiful condition of the righteous soul. On the other hand, it means a gracious and merciful resolve to save. (Those insights have come from pondering many biblical texts about God's love and hate.) Noticing these kinds of love and hate raises the possibility that God's love and hate may *both* be true toward the same person at the same time. I will leave it with you to think this through to the end.

My point is that it is amazing how much we learn by means of this habit of asking questions about paradoxes in various parts of the Scriptures. Few things make a person deeper and richer in their knowledge of God, and his ways, than this habit of humbly asking how texts cohere in reality when at first they don't look like they do.[1]

---

1. The apostle Peter commented on some things in Scripture that are "hard to understand" (2 Pet. 3:16). John Owen steps back and puts this fact in the light of God's larger intentions: "There are in the Scripture . . . some things that are 'hard to be interpreted;' not from the nature of the things revealed, but from the manner of their revelation. Such are many allegories, parables, mystical stories, allusions, unfulfilled prophecies and predictions, references unto the then present customs, persons,

When Is Application Part of Interpretation?

The aim of biblical writers is not only that we know things, but that we do things and do them in a certain way. So part of our response to Scripture is to form the habit of asking questions concerning application—to ourselves, to our church and other Christians, to our relationships, to our culture, to the unbelievers and institutions of the world. This means that the task of application is never done. There are millions of ways a text can be applied to millions of situations and relationships.

Ordinarily questions about application are not viewed as part of the process of *finding* a text's meaning but *using* a text's meaning in life. There is a difference between a text's *meaning* and its *significance*. I have been treating a text's meaning as *what an author intended to communicate*. Its significance is the use that gets made of it in the hundreds of ways it may affect life and culture. The *meaning* of a text may be: show mercy. And the *significance* downstream culturally may be a 30-mph speed limit in a neighborhood with lots of children.

However, I want to make a point that is often overlooked—that posing questions of application, and the actual effort to put a text into practice, often sheds light back on the *meaning* of the text, not just its significance. This again is merry-go-roundish. We need to see the meaning before we can make any claim to apply or obey it. On the other hand, once we make the attempt to apply or obey it, we may discover aspects of the meaning that we failed to see. Real-life experience is not just a crucible for application, but a school for deeper understanding.

Martin Luther's Seminary of Suffering

The biblical basis for this is found in Psalm 119:71, "It is good for me that I was afflicted, that I might learn your statutes." The experience of suffering does not just call for the application of God's statutes, but also

---

and places, computation of times, genealogies, the signification of some single words seldom but once used in the Scripture, the names of divers birds and beasts unknown to us. . . . Whatever is so delivered in any place, if it be of importance for us to know and believe, as unto the ends of divine revelation, it is in some other place or places unveiled and plainly declared; so that we may say of it as the disciples said unto our Savior, 'Lo, now he speaketh plainly, and not in parables.' There can be no instance given of any obscure place or passage in the Scripture, concerning which a man may rationally suppose or conjecture that there is any doctrinal truth requiring our obedience contained in it, which is not elsewhere explained. . . . Some things are in the Scripture disposed on purpose that evil, perverse, and proud men may stumble and fall at them, or be farther hardened in their unbelief and obstinacy." John Owen, *The Works of John Owen*, ed. William H. Goold, vol. 4 (Edinburgh: T&T Clark, n.d.), 196–98.

offers insights into those statutes. Martin Luther has written perhaps more forcefully than anyone about the necessity of affliction in becoming a good interpreter of the Bible. He said:

> I want you to know how to study theology in the right way. I have practiced this method myself. . . . Here you will find three rules. They are frequently proposed throughout Psalm [119] and run thus: *Oratio, meditatio, tentatio* (prayer, meditation, trial).[2]

And trials (*Anfechtungen*) he called the "touchstone." Trials, he writes, "teach you not only to know and understand but also to experience how right, how true, how sweet, how lovely, how mighty, how comforting God's word is: it is wisdom supreme."[3] He proved the value of trials over and over again in his own experience:

> As soon as God's Word becomes known through you, the devil will afflict you, will make a real doctor of you, and will teach you by his temptations to seek and to love God's Word. For I myself . . . owe my papists many thanks for so beating, pressing, and frightening me through the devil's raging that they have turned me into a fairly good theologian, driving me to a goal I should never have reached.[4]

On the outside, to many, Luther looked invulnerable. But those close to him knew the *tentatio*. He wrote to Melanchthon from the Wartburg castle on July 13, 1521, while he was supposedly working feverishly on the translation of the New Testament,

> I sit here at ease, hardened and unfeeling—alas! praying little, grieving little for the Church of God, burning rather in the fierce fires of my untamed flesh. It comes to this: I *should* be afire in the spirit; in reality I am afire in the flesh, with lust, laziness, idleness, sleepiness. It is perhaps because you have all ceased praying for me that God has turned away from me. . . . For the last eight days I have written nothing, nor prayed nor studied, partly from self-indulgence, partly from another vexatious handicap [constipation and piles]. . . . I re-

---

2. Ewald M. Plass, comp., *What Luther Says: An Anthology*, vol. 3 (St. Louis, MO: Concordia, 1959), 1,359. I am borrowing these thoughts about Luther from John Piper, *The Legacy of Sovereign Joy: God's Triumphant Grace in the Lives of Augustine, Luther, and Calvin* (Wheaton, IL: Crossway, 2000).
3. Plass, *What Luther Says*, 1,360.
4. Ibid.

ally cannot stand it any longer. . . . Pray for me, I beg you, for in my seclusion here I am submerged in sins.[5]

These were the trials that he said made him a theologian. These experiences were as much a part of his exegetical labors as was his Greek lexicon. How often I am tempted to think that the pressures and conflicts and frustrations are simply distractions from the business of study and understanding. Luther (and Psalm 119:71) teaches us to see it all another way.

Obeying the Text Showed Me What I Missed in the Text

I will give one example from my own ministry. Along with the elders of our church, I had studied Matthew 18:15–17. This passage deals with how to respond in the church when one member sins against another:

> If your brother sins against you, go and tell him his fault, between you and him alone. If he listens to you, you have gained your brother. But if he does not listen, take one or two others along with you, that every charge may be established by the evidence of two or three witnesses. If he refuses to listen to them, tell it to the church. And if he refuses to listen even to the church, let him be to you as a Gentile and a tax collector.

I thought I had a clear idea about how to proceed and how to treat people all along the way in this process. But then we entered into the painful and messy reality of putting the text into practice. In the midst of this process of *application*, I realized I had not noticed that some period of time may pass between taking two or three witnesses to confront an unrepentant brother and the next step of taking his case to the whole church. This was simply a question I had failed to ask in reading the text: How much time may go by between these steps toward reconciliation or discipline? Therefore, I also failed to ask how an unrepentant brother should be treated between confronting him with two friends and when his case goes to the church.

Simply put, the effort to apply and obey biblical texts regularly (I think I would say *usually*) sheds light back on the *meaning* of those texts. The effort to apply the meaning of a text often helps us ask

---

5. E. G. Rupp and Benjamin Drewery, eds., *Martin Luther: Documents of Modern History* (New York: St. Martin's Press, 1970), 72–73.

questions about the text that we had failed to ask. And these questions reveal things we had not seen.

One of the implications of this fact for how we read the Bible is that we not become artificial in distinguishing the processes of interpretation, on the one hand, and application, on the other. They are interwoven. Another implication is that as we read, one of the ways to see more of an author's intention is to imagine ourselves putting the text into practice. In other words, go ahead and live out the application in your mind, and the result will be that you ask a lot of questions to the text that otherwise you would not have asked. And this will bear much fruit in seeing what is really there.

How Does Meaning Relate to Pleasure—and Other Emotions?

Another kind of question to ask when trying to grasp what an author intended to communicate is, What sort of emotions should we be experiencing in response to his revelation? Even before we inquire into the kinds of emotions the authors of Scripture may call forth by what they write, we are told that the writings themselves are a delight. "His *delight* is in the law of the LORD, and on his law he meditates day and night" (Ps. 1:2). "Blessed is the man who fears the LORD, who greatly *delights* in his commandments!" (Ps. 112:1). "More to be *desired* are they than gold, even much fine gold; *sweeter* also than honey and drippings of the honeycomb" (Ps. 19:10). "How *sweet* are your words to my taste, *sweeter* than honey to my mouth!" (Ps. 119:103).

Therefore, I conclude that part of God's intention for his word is that it be our pleasure. If we come to the word and, over time, as a whole, do not find it to be our delight, we are not seeing what is really there for what it is—better than gold, sweeter than honey. Is this part of the meaning of the text?

I proposed in chapter 20 that we should define the *meaning* of a text to include the author's intention that we *feel* a certain way about what he is revealing. I emphasized that an author's *thoughts* and our effort to *understand* them are foundational. Emotions that have any Christ-honoring worth are rooted in truth. Therefore, the emotions that a biblical author aims to share with his readers are transmitted through our understanding of what the author thinks—through thinking the author's thoughts after him. We then may discern from those thoughts whether part of the author's intention is that we also share the emotion he expresses about this truth.

It is clear from dozens of texts that the intention of the authors of Scripture is that we not only *understand* what they say, but also *repent* and *believe* and *hope* and *rejoice*. In fact, it seems clear to me that biblical authors are *never* indifferent to the way their readers feel in response to what they say. If we asked them, they would never say, "It is no part of my intention in this book that people feel brokenhearted for sin, or thankful for mercy, or confident in promises, or peaceful in justification, or hopeful for heaven." Rather, they would always say that their intention is to communicate truth in such a way that the *mind* would understand and the *heart* would respond with the appropriate emotion.

Therefore, as we try to *grasp what the authors intended to communicate,* we should always ask questions about the kind of emotions the author is trying to awaken. The most forthright evidence that authors intend to stir up the affections of our hearts is that they *command* us to have them. For example, all of these emotions are commanded:

- gratitude (Ps. 100:4)
- hope (1 Pet. 1:13)
- joy (Phil. 4:4)
- sorrow (James 4:9)
- compassion (Col. 3:12)
- fear (Rom. 11:20)
- contentment (Heb. 13:5)
- tenderheartedness (1 Pet. 3:8)
- anger (Eph. 4:26)
- shock (Jer. 2:12)

It would not be surprising, therefore, that the authors of Scripture intend for us to feel appropriate emotions in response to everything they reveal about God and man and sin and salvation and holiness and heaven. The Bible deals with the greatest realities in the universe. Nothing is insignificant when related to God. Therefore, everything is meant to move us. Being moved is part of what Scripture intends.

What If We Do Not Feel What We Should?

But, oh, how many readers of Scripture come up short at this point. They see, to some degree, the worth and beauty of God and his ways in Scripture, but their hearts lag far behind. They do not feel anything close to the affections warranted by what they see. What is to be done? Is there any way, without becoming hypocrites, that we can move our hearts to respond appropriately? I think there is. It seems to me that there is a section in the book of Proverbs that aims to address this very problem and give us help.

The section runs from Proverbs 22:17 down to 24:22. In 22:20, this section is identified as "thirty sayings" ("Have I not written for you thirty sayings?"). These *thirty sayings* are found in Proverbs 22:17–24:22 in groupings of verses. Some translations break the groupings out for us. So every time a new theme starts, there is a new saying, and there are thirty of them in this unit. Verse 17 is where they start, and it says, "Incline your ear, and hear the words of the wise." So these are often entitled "The Words of the Wise."

What is so relevant for our present concern is that the first two verses in this section are written precisely to answer the question, How do you hear the proverbs and appropriately feel the reality behind them?

> Incline your ear, and hear the words of the wise,
>   and *apply your heart* to my knowledge,
> for it will be pleasant if you keep them within you,
>   if all of them are ready on your lips. (Prov. 22:17–18)

Notice two things: The first line says, "Incline your ear, and hear the words of the wise." So clearly the point is: Words are being spoken, and you should *lean in*. You should *pay attention. Focus! Incline* your ear. If we can't hear, we lean forward. We press in closer. But we do that with our attention as well. If we are reading words, or hearing words, and the words are just going by, the wise man is saying to us: Don't let them go by. Don't let any of the words go by. Catch them with your consciousness. Focus! Pay attention! These words are going to shape the knowledge of your mind.

The second line says—and this is the key to our question—"*Apply your heart* to my knowledge." Words of the wise are about to be spoken. These will communicate knowledge of something valuable or precious or important—something wise and helpful and beautiful. Then we read that the effect of this knowledge "will be *pleasant*." And I assume that the heart, which he just referred to, is the organ of pleasantness or pleasure. So he is now addressing the issue before us. How can I experience pleasure in this knowledge? How can I experience an appropriate admiring and valuing and treasuring and loving and embracing and enjoyment and satisfaction in what I perceive through the words of the wise? And to answer, he says that the way you do it is *apply your heart.*

So the wise man is answering our question. We are asking, When we do not feel what we should in response to biblical knowledge, is there anything we can do? His answer is yes. He says: *Apply your heart* to what your ear has heard and the knowledge that is forming in your mind. What does that mean?

The Hebrew word for *apply* simply means to "put" or "set" or "place." So you take your heart and you *put* it. You *place* it into what you have seen with your eyes or heard with your ears. You rub the nose of your heart in the beauty of the knowledge. If the heart is not feeling anything, you say to your heart: *Heart, wake up!* And you take hold of the heart, and you *apply.* You *push* it. You *place* it in the knowledge. If you have no experience of doing such an intentional thing with your emotions, learn from this a new thing. That's why it is here.

Tasting Steak and Seeing Leaves

Here is an analogy. Suppose you would like to taste a steak. You can *hear* it sizzling on the grill outside. So you go outside, and then your eyes *see* the steak sizzling on the grill. And if you get close enough, your nose may *smell* the steak sizzling on the grill, and yet there is still no taste in your mouth of that steak. Is there anything you can do?

That is the question. Is there anything you can do with the steak of God's word? You know what the answer is. You take a knife and you cut off a piece and you put it in your mouth and you chew slowly, and then you swallow, and you taste. In the same way you say to your heart: Eat, heart. Eat! Taste and see that the Lord is good (Ps. 34:8).

Another illustration: I am walking to church. It is October in Minneapolis—the most beautiful month of the year. The leaves on the trees in my neighborhood are unbelievably bright with yellow and orange, and the sun is shining, and it is more mild than usual, around 60 degrees. The leaves are flickering, and it is absolutely stunning. But I am walking to a prayer meeting, and I am a bit late. I am not noticing anything. My eyes are seeing, but I am not seeing.

This is the way we often read the Bible. What has to happen? I pause. God's grace causes me to pause. I look at a tree in the yard at Augustana Apartments. I keep looking. I lean in and say: "Heart, that is orange. That is yellow. They were green, and now they are orange and yellow and gold, and the sun is making them bright. And they are waving at you with the breeze, and God is trying to get your attention. Heart, the glory of God is shining here. *Look*, heart! Taste! Feel!" And you push the nose of your heart up into the beauty of the tree.

You do the same thing with the word of God. A diamond is offered you. You see the diamond, but you don't see the diamond, and you say to your heart, "Heart, move around this diamond. Look at the diamond from that side, and look at the diamond from this side. Heart, this is beautiful!"

Talking to the Heart and to God

When a born-again person does this—that is, applies his heart to knowledge according to Proverbs 20:17—he can't help but turn it into prayer. When we are preaching to our heart and we are saying to our heart, "Come on, heart, wake up. Come on, heart, look at this. Feel this! This is beautiful! Wake up!" we instinctively find ourselves not only speaking to our heart, but also speaking to God. But you do talk to your heart (Ps. 42:5)! You are *putting* it, *placing* it, *applying* it, *telling* it where to go and what to do. And you are also praying, "God, help me. God, open my eyes. God, cause me to feel the worth and beauty of your truth."

Some of you may sigh and respond, "I have tried that, and it doesn't work." Or someone else may say, "That is so foreign to me, I don't even know what you are talking about." May I urge you—even plead with you—don't say that you are beyond the capacity to feel the beauty of the knowledge of God in the Bible. Proverbs 22:17 is God's word to you. "*Apply* your heart!"

I conclude, therefore, that we should always be asking as we read the Bible, "What kind of emotional response does this author want his readers to have to the truth he is presenting?" God's word is honored not just by being *understood* rightly, but also by being *felt* rightly. A blank response of the heart to glorious truth is a defective response to the Bible. It is a failure to *grasp what the author intended to communicate.*

Am I Being Changed by This Meaning?

As we come near to the end of this book, it will be good to remind ourselves of the big picture. I proposed in part 1 that the ultimate aim of reading the Bible is *that God's infinite worth and beauty would be exalted in the everlasting, white-hot worship of the blood-bought bride of Christ from every people, language, tribe, and nation.* I unfolded some of the implications, namely, that such white-hot worship will come about only through *seeing,* and *savoring,* and *being transformed* by the glory of God in Scripture. I argued in part 2 that this seeing and savoring and being changed are humanly impossible. Only a supernatural work of God in and through our reading will bring that about.

In part 3, I have been commending and describing *the natural act of reading the Bible supernaturally.* The heart of this natural act of reading has been an aggressive attentiveness fed by relentless questions and vigorous mental effort to answer them from the texts themselves. Those questions have dealt with words, phrases, propositions, paradoxes, and pleasures. If you are a really aggressive reader, you may have noticed that these questions have been leading us in the sequence from *seeing* to *savoring* to *being changed.* That is where we are now at the end of this chapter, and almost at the end of the book—questions about if and how we are being changed by what we read.

You may also notice that as soon as we touched on emotions and affections and pleasures in response to what we read, we have already entered the territory of personal change. The awakening of emotions for God—fear, love, admiration, delight, hope, treasuring, exulting—are the greatest changes that can happen in the human soul. And I have argued that these are part of what the authors of Scripture intended for us to experience when they wrote.

But it is good to make explicit here at the end that part of active reading, when reading *the word of God,* must be the habit of asking: Am I being changed by these texts the way the authors intend for me to be? Recall the all-important text of Scripture on how our transformation comes about, 2 Corinthians 3:18:

> We all, with unveiled face, beholding the glory of the Lord, are being transformed into the same image from one degree of glory to another. For this comes from the Lord who is the Spirit.

There are many ways the Bible describes the process of becoming holy as God is holy. There are many biblical ways of describing how motives for godliness work. But basic to all of them is this verse from 2 Corinthians: "*Beholding the glory of the Lord, [we] are being transformed.*" Beholding is the essence. Seeing. Not just any seeing. But seeing that comes from the lifted veil of sinful blindness (2 Cor. 3:14–17). Seeing that sees the glory of God in the face of Christ for what it really is (2 Cor. 4:6). Seeing that knows and feels intuitively the infinite worth and beauty of the glory of God. Therefore, a seeing that is *inseparable from savoring.* And this seeing and savoring of God above all other pleasures is what changes us in a deep and everlasting way—"from one degree of glory to another." And this emerging brightness of Christlike glory, in turn, shines as a light in a dark place "so that [others] may see your good works and give glory to your Father who is in heaven" (Matt. 5:16; 1 Pet. 2:12).

Therefore, as we read the Bible, we should always be asking, *Am I being changed in a way that conforms to what this author intended to communicate?* Perhaps more than all the other questions we must ask as we read, this one will put us on our faces in prayer for the supernatural work of God. Which, of course, is where every hour spent reading the Bible should begin and end.

Then the LORD said to me, "You have seen well, for I am watching over my word to perform it."

JEREMIAH 1:12

Conclusion

My prayer is that our great and merciful God would use this imperfect book to lead many into the glories of his perfect book, the Bible. You may wonder how a book written over so many centuries, with so many different kinds of literature, by so many authors, could be called *perfect*. Sometimes when we read it, we might desire that it were written differently,. according to our own preferences, with more of this and less of that.

But pause and think how God intended his book to be the book of all the peoples of the world, not just us. He meant for it to be understood and lived in every culture and every ethnic group in the world, during all the ages of history. If we have our preference for the kind of literature in the Bible that is most helpful for us, think how a tribe ten thousand miles and ten centuries away might have different preferences and different needs. Could it be that God knew exactly what he was doing when he inspired all of these diverse authors and diverse writings that we have in this one inspired book? That is what I believe.

Let John Owen express it wonderfully. He is responding to some in his day who complained that the Bible was not systematic enough in its presentation of divine truth. Owen's answer begins with a criticism of such desires and then exults in what God gloriously offers us in the Scriptures:

> God puts no such value upon men's *accurate methods* as they may imagine them to deserve. . . . Yea, ofttimes when, as they suppose, they have brought truths unto the *strictest propriety of expression*, they lose both their power and their glory. Hence is the world filled with so many *lifeless, sapless, graceless*, artificial declarations of divine truth in the *schoolmen* and others. We may sooner squeeze water out of a pumice-stone than one drop of spiritual nourishment out of them.

But how many millions of souls have received divine light and consolation, suited unto their condition, in those occasional occurrences of truth which they meet withal in the Scripture, which they would never have obtained in those wise, artificial disposals of them which some men would fancy! . . .

In the writing and composing of the holy Scripture, the Spirit of God had respect unto the various states and conditions of the church. It was not given for the use of one age or season only, but for all generations—for a guide in faith and obedience from the beginning of the world to the end of it. . . .

The principal end of the Scripture is of another nature. It is, to beget in the minds of men faith, fear, obedience, and reverence of God—to make them holy and righteous; and those such as have in themselves various weaknesses, temptations, and inclinations unto the contrary, which must be obviated and subdued. Unto this end every truth is disposed of in the Scripture as it ought to be. . . .

In those very fords and appearing shallows of this river of God where the lamb may wade, the elephant may swim. Everything in the Scripture is so plain as that the meanest believer may understand all that belongs unto his duty or is necessary unto his happiness; yet is nothing so plain but that the wisest of them all have reason to adore the depths and stores of divine wisdom in it.[1]

Amen. "Every truth . . . in the Scripture [is] as it ought to be." The lambs may wade, and the elephants may swim. Each may know his duty. And the wisest explore God's depths for eternity.

So, yes, my prayer is that many would turn from my book to God's book with new zeal for aggressive attentiveness and active reading. And I pray that this zeal would be rooted in a deep biblical understanding of the glorious calling to pursue *the natural act of reading the Bible supernaturally*. God performed a supernatural act by inspiring natural language. We act the miracle in reverse when we trust God for supernatural help in the natural act of reading. To help you experience this supernatural encounter with God's word has been the subordinate goal of this book.

The reason for that subordinate goal is that God's ultimate goal depends on it. God has made the natural act of reading the Bible su-

---

1. John Owen, *The Works of John Owen*, ed. William H. Goold, vol. 4 (Edinburgh: T&T Clark, n.d.), 189–93.

pernaturally the indispensable means of achieving the ultimate goal of the universe. This was the point of part 1. The ultimate goal of reading the Bible is *that God's infinite worth and beauty would be exalted in the everlasting, white-hot worship of the blood-bought bride of Christ from every people, language, tribe, and nation.* The Bible is not incidental or marginal or optional in God's ultimate purpose for redemptive history. It is essential. It is necessary. If it does not accomplish its designs, then the ultimate purpose of God will abort.

But God's purposes will not abort. For he has not set his word to drift aimlessly on the sea of human caprice. Rather, as he said through the prophet Jeremiah, "I am watching over my word to perform it" (Jer. 1:12). God does not watch his word to see if it will come true. He watches it to make it come true. Therefore, there is no doubt about the outcome.

> I am God, and there is no other;
>   I am God, and there is none like me,
> declaring the end from the beginning
>   and from ancient times things not yet done,
> saying, "My counsel shall stand,
>   and I will accomplish all my purpose." (Isa. 46:9–10)

The purpose of God for the Bible cannot fail. And that purpose is *to reveal* God's infinite worth and beauty as the ultimate value and excellence in the universe, to open the eyes of his people *to see* that glory in the Scriptures, so that we *savor* the excellence of God above all created treasures, and, by beholding and being satisfied with God, *be changed* from glory to glory, until the bride of Christ—the family of God across all centuries and cultures—is complete in number and beauty for the white-hot worship of God forever and ever.

God purchased and secured this great salvation through the incarnation of the Son of God, so that he might live a perfect life, die in the place of sinners, and rise from the dead to rule the world. To preserve and perform this great plan of salvation, God inspired and preserved the Christian Scriptures. And now he is carrying out his plan as millions of people pursue *the natural act of reading the Bible supernaturally.* I invite you to join us. It is the only way for your life to be of lasting service to the world, and for your work to show forth the glory of God, and for your soul to be fully satisfied forever.

Appendix

Arcing

In chapter 26, I suggested that Biblearc.com is the go-to place for learning and practicing the method of textual analysis called "arcing." Bethlehem College & Seminary maintains this website as a ministry to encourage, explain, and facilitate the kind of Bible reading I have been commending in this book. Everything you see below is more fully explained and interactively illustrated with videos at Biblearc.com.

What Arcing Provides

I am including a summary of the process of arcing here so that at least you can have a quick resource for what you need to do it if you don't have computer access. I mentioned in chapter 26 that we need two things to follow an extended argument by a biblical author. First, we need to know the kinds of relationships, with some descriptive names, that can exist between propositions so we can recognize them and talk about them.

Second, we need some kind of schematic way of visually representing the author's emerging line of thought so that as its length and complexity increase, we can remember, and see at a glance, what the main point of the text is and how all the other parts explain and support it. By "main point," I don't mean the most important reality in the paragraph. I mean the point that everything else supports but itself does not support anything in that unity. This may not be the most important reality.

For example, I might say, "I took my Bible to school, because it is the word of God." We have two propositions: "I took my Bible to school" and "it is the word of God." What is the most important reality in that pair of propositions? Clearly the assertion that the Bible is the word of

God is infinitely more important than the fact that I took it to school. But what is the main point? The main point is, "I took my Bible to school." Why? Because it is *supported* by the ground clause, "because it is the word of God."

This is often the case in Scripture—that the grounds or causes or foundations for statements refer to greater realities than the assertions or actions they support. There is no disrespect implied in saying that the greater reality is supporting a less great assertion—not any more so than to disrespect a priceless heirloom pedestal that you used as a place to put your tea when serving guests. The tea has no comparison in worth to the pedestal. But the pedestal is supporting the tea.

Two Large Groupings of Relationships between Propositions

So a unit of biblical text has a "main point," and the rest of the propositions in the unit are either *coordinate* with it and with one another, or are *subordinate* to it and possibly to others. *Coordinate* relationships are not usually seen as explaining or arguing for one another. They each make their own contribution but without explanatory or argumentative relation to the others.

However, within the *subordinate* relationships, propositions do *explain* or *argue*. We usually call this "supporting." Thus a proposition can support another proposition by explaining it in some way or arguing for it in some way. As I illustrate the kinds of relationships that exist under each of these groupings, I will give the names of the relationships and the abbreviations we generally use to label them when drawing the "arcs" that represent the propositions.

Coordinate Relationships (Propositions That Do Not Support)

Series

Definition: Each proposition makes an independent contribution to a whole.

Conjunctions: and, moreover, furthermore, neither, nor, etc.

Example: "The sun will be darkened, and the moon will not give its light, and the stars will fall from heaven, and the powers of the heavens will be shaken" (Matt. 24:29; see also Matt. 7:8; Rom. 12:12).

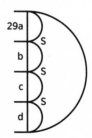

Progression

Definition: Like series, but each proposition is a further step toward a climax. There is some kind of advance in the series.

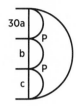

Conjunctions: and, moreover, furthermore, etc.

Example: "Those whom he predestined he also called, and those whom he called he also justified, and those whom he justified he also glorified" (Rom. 8:30; see also Mark 4:28; 1 Pet. 1:5–7).

Alternative

Definition: Each proposition expresses a different possibility arising from a situation.

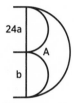

Conjunctions: or, but, while, on the other hand, etc.

Example: "Some were convinced by what he said, but others disbelieved" (Acts 28:24; see also Matt. 11:3; John 10:21, 22).

Subordinate Relationships (Propositions That Support)

Support by Restatement

ACTION-MANNER

Definition: The relationship of a statement of an action and another statement that indicates the way or manner in which this action is carried out.

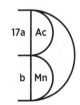

Conjunctions: in that, by, etc.

Example: "God has not left himself without a witness *in that* he gave you from heaven rains and fruitful seasons" (Acts 14:17 author's translation; see also Acts 16:16; 17:21; Phil. 2:7).

COMPARISON

Definition: The relationship between two statements expressing an action or idea or state of affairs more clearly by showing what it is like.

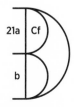

Conjunctions: even as, as . . . so, like, just as, etc.

Example: "As the Father has sent me, even so I am sending you" (John 20:21; see also 1 Cor. 11:1; 1 Thess. 2:7).

NEGATIVE-POSITIVE

Definition: The relationship between two alternatives, one of which is denied so that the other is enforced. It is also the relationship implicit in contrasting statements.

Conjunctions: not . . . but, etc.

Example: "Do not be foolish, but understand what the will of the Lord is" (Eph. 5:17; see also 5:18; Heb. 2:16; see also 1 Cor. 4:10 for an example of contrast: "We are fools for Christ's sake, but you are wise in Christ").

IDEA-EXPLANATION

Definition: The relationship between an original statement and one clarifying its meaning. The clarifying proposition may define only one word of the previous proposition.

Conjunctions: that is, etc.

Example: "Jacob supplanted me these two times; he took away my birthright and now he has taken away my blessing" (Gen. 27:36 author's translation; see also 1 Cor. 10:4).

QUESTION-ANSWER

Definition: Statement of a question and the answer to that question.

Conjunction: (question mark or grammatical structures that signify a question)

Example: "What does the Scripture say? 'Abraham believed God . . .'" (Rom. 4:3; see also Ps. 24:3–4; Rom. 6:1).

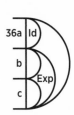

Support by Distinct Statement

GROUND (MAIN CLAUSE–CAUSAL CLAUSE)

Definition: The relationship between a statement and the argument or reason for the statement (supporting proposition follows).

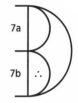

Conjunctions: for, because, since, etc.

Example: "Blessed are the poor in spirit, for theirs is the kingdom of heaven" (Matt. 5:3; see also 1 Cor. 7:9; Phil. 2:25–26).

INFERENCE (MAIN CLAUSE–INFERENTIAL CLAUSE)

Definition: The relationship between a statement and the argument or reason for the statement (supporting proposition precedes).

Conjunctions: therefore, wherefore, consequently, accordingly, etc.

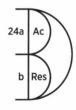

Example: "The end of all things is at hand; therefore be . . . sober-minded for the sake of your prayers" (1 Pet. 4:7; see also Matt. 23:3; Rom. 6:11–12; 1 Pet. 5:5b–6).

ACTION-RESULT (MAIN CLAUSE–RESULT CLAUSE)

Definition: The relationship between an action and a consequence or result that accompanies that action.

Conjunctions: so that, that, with the result that, etc.

Example: "There arose a great storm on the sea, so that the boat was being swamped by the waves" (Matt. 8:24; see also John 3:16; James 1:11).

ACTION-PURPOSE (MAIN CLAUSE–PURPOSE CLAUSE)

Definition: The relationship between an action and the one that is *intended* to come as a result.

Conjunctions: in order that, so that, that, with a view to, to the end that, lest

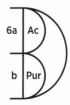

Example: "Humble yourselves, therefore, under the mighty hand of God *so that* at the proper time he may exalt you" (1 Pet. 5:6; see also Mark 7:9; Rom. 1:11).

CONDITIONAL (MAIN CLAUSE–CONDITIONAL CLAUSE)

Definition: This is like Action-Result except that the existence of the action is only potential or conditional.

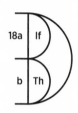

Conjunctions: if . . . then, provided that, except, etc.

Example: "If you are led by the Spirit, you are not under the law" (Gal. 5:18; see also John 15:14; Gal. 6:1).

TEMPORAL (MAIN CLAUSE–TEMPORAL CLAUSE)

Definition: The relationship between a proposition and the occasion when it occurs.

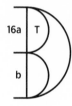

Conjunctions: when, whenever, after, before, etc.

Example: "When you fast, do not look gloomy" (Matt. 6:16; see also Luke 6:22; James 1:2).

LOCATIVE (MAIN CLAUSE–LOCATIVE CLAUSE)

Definition: The relationship between a proposition and the place where it happens or is true.

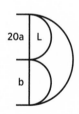

Conjunctions: where, wherever, etc.

Example: "Where two or three are gathered in my name, there am I among them" (Matt. 18:20; see also Ruth 1:16; 2 Cor. 3:17).

BILATERAL

Definition: A bilateral proposition supports two other propositions, one preceding and one following. (It is a judgment call whether the middle supporting proposition may first be arced together with the following proposition if, for example, it is an Action-Purpose relationship, and then those two arcs, now united as one, would be arced with the first of the three as a support.)

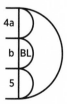

Conjunctions: for, because, therefore, so, etc.

Example: "Let the nations be glad and sing for joy, for you judge the peoples with equity and guide the nations upon earth. Let the peoples praise you, O God" (Ps. 67:4–5; see also Rom. 2:1b–2).

Support by Contrary Statement

Concessive

Definition: The relationship between a clause and a statement that stands *in spite of* a contrary statement. (The Concessive symbol [Csv] labels the statement that is overcome so that the other will stand. It is the "even though" proposition, not the "nevertheless" proposition.)

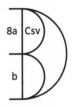

Conjunctions: although . . . yet, although, yet, nevertheless, but, however, etc.

Example: "Although he was a son, he learned obedience through what he suffered" (Heb. 5:8; see also 1 Cor. 4:15; 9:13–15).

Situation-Response

Definition: The relationship between a situation in one clause and a response in another. (This relationship is included under "Support by Contrary Statement" because when a person responds in a way not intended by the situation that another creates, the situation behaves like a concessive clause. I suggest that you use this relationship in your arcing of non-narrative literature only sparingly. The reason is that almost any relationship can be seen as a response to a situation in some sense, and it tells you very little about the relationship. Use the possible relationship that communicates the most to the understanding of the text.)

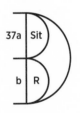

Conjunctions: and, etc.

Example: "How often would I have gathered your children together as a hen gathers her brood under her wings, and you were not willing" (Matt. 23:37; see also John 7:21).

An Illustration from Romans 12:1–2

Let's illustrate the process of relating propositions with each other by using Romans 12:1–2. First, here is my translation of the text:

> Therefore, I beseech you by the mercies of God, brothers, to present your bodies to God as a living, holy, acceptable sacrifice, which is your spiritual service of worship. And do not be conformed to this age but be transformed by the renewing of your mind, in order that you might approve what the will of God is, namely, the good, the acceptable, and the perfect.

I see four individual propositions or assertions in this paragraph. Note that it is crucial to number the propositions so that each one gets a number, even when a single verse has several propositions as verse 2 does here.

12:1   I beseech you by the mercies of God, brothers, to present your bodies to God as a living, holy, acceptable sacrifice which is your spiritual service of worship.

12:2a   *And* do not be conformed to this age

12:2b   *but* be transformed by the renewing of your mind,

12:2c   *in order that* you might approve what the will of God is, namely, the good, the acceptable, and the perfect.

We may symbolize each of these propositions with an arc as follows:

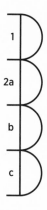

The easiest relationship to see is between 2a and b. They command virtually the same thing, one negatively and the other positively. "Don't be conformed, but be transformed." We can symbolize this relation with a larger arc as follows:

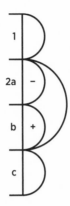

When a larger arc is drawn, we regard what is under it as asserting one main thing, in this case, "Be a transformed person with a new mind and thus different from this age!"

Then Paul makes very plain to us how 2ab relates to 2c because he connects them with the conjunction "in order that" (in Greek, *eis to* + the infinitive). Therefore, 2c is the *purpose* of 2ab, which is the *action* or means. This relationship we can symbolize as follows:

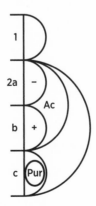

I circle the Pur (= purpose) because that is primary in Paul's mind; it is the goal, the main point of Romans 12:2. (The only relationships in which one symbol has to be circled are Ac-Pur, Ac-Res, and Sit-R.) Verse 2ab is simply the necessary means to accomplish the purpose of 2c. To paraphrase: "Be transformed so that with your new mind you can think like God thinks and approve what he approves. The necessary prerequisite to knowing and embracing the holy is a renewed mind."

Now comes the final relationship. How does the main point of verse 2 (2c) relate to the proposition of verse 1? To answer this, we must have some idea of what verse 1 is asserting. As it stands, Paul says, "I beseech you by the mercies of God, brothers, to present your bodies to God as a living, holy, acceptable sacrifice, which is your spiritual service of worship."

What this image of presenting ourselves as a sacrifice means is illumined by a parallel thought in Romans 6:13 (author's translation): "Do not present your members as weapons of unrighteousness to sin but present yourselves to God as those alive from the dead and your members as weapons of righteousness of God" (see 6:19). There is no reason to think Paul means anything very different in 12:1 when he says, "Present your bodies to God," than he did in 6:13 when he said, "Present your members to God." This makes very good sense in the context of Romans 12:1–2, and the same word for "present" is used in both places. Romans 12:1 is not a command to the unconverted to submit to God, but rather a command to believers to honor God in their bodies.

Paraphrased, Romans 12:1 means something like this: "In view of how merciful God has been to you, make it your aim in all your daily, bodily existence to do what honors God; worship God by doing his will with your body" (see 1 Cor. 6:20). Now we are prepared to relate verses 1 and 2. Knowing and approving the will of God (v. 2c) is a means of doing God's will with your body (v. 1). The link between verse 1 and verse 2c is evident in the repetition of the word "acceptable." *Approving* what is acceptable (v. 2c) is the prerequisite of *offering the body in daily life* as an acceptable sacrifice (v. 1). Therefore, I symbolize the relationship as Purpose (v. 1) to Action [means] (v. 2).

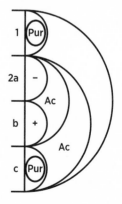

In this way, we arrive at an interpretation of Romans 12:1–2: The most basic change that must occur in the believer is that he ceases to think the way this age thinks, and thinks instead with a new mind, with new sentiments, priorities, and values. With this new mind, he then is able to judge and assess what is holy and good and acceptable. Not only can he assess it properly with his new mind, but he now approves of it and delights in it. This leads necessarily to a bodily life given up to God for his purposes. The daily deeds of the body become acts of worship in that they demonstrate the great worth we ascribe to God's mercy. By this is fulfilled the command of our Lord that we should let our light shine that men may see our good deeds and give glory to our Father in heaven.

Notice the structure of the final arcing. There is now one arc over the whole, which means that we have gotten a glimpse of the main thesis of this unit. Under this one arc are two arcs related as action-purpose. Under the larger of these are another two arcs related as action-purpose. Under the larger of these are two arcs related as negative-positive. In other words, the smallest arcs are gradually grouped together into larger units that then are related to other units until there is one arc over the whole. We then can see how each of the smaller propositions functions to help communicate one main point. It cannot be determined in advance which units to arc together first. This comes from guided practice.

Special Problems in Finding the Propositions

Before we can do any arcing, we must divide a text into its significant propositions. This is not always easy, since a sentence can have several propositions, and since propositions can be concealed in different kinds of phrases. We previously discussed the nature of propositions and defined a proposition as an assertion (having a subject and a predicate).

This, of course, is oversimplified. Language can be very complex, and writers can make assertions in a great variety of ways. These may not always look like the standard proposition: "Jesus wept." At these points, a keen, sometimes delicate, sensitivity to the author's intention is needed to tell whether a certain grammatical construction should be construed as a proposition. There are no rigid rules for making these decisions. There are only general guidelines. Note the following examples.

Questions

Are we to continue in sin that grace may abound? By no means!
How can we who died to sin still live in it? (Rom. 6:1–2)

The principle to follow in handling questions is that when an answer
is given, let the question and the answer stand as separate propositions
and relate them as Q-A. Together they make one assertion, usually
found in the answer. In Romans 6:1–2, the first question is answered
with, "By no means!" The second question is not answered. When
questions are not answered, the author is indirectly asserting something. He expects us to provide the answer in such a way that we
know he is asserting something. Therefore, you should always restate
such questions as indicative statements. The question "How shall we
who died to sin still live in it?" is really asserting that it is unthinkable
for us who have died to sin to still live in it. The relationship between
the first question-answer and the second question then becomes plain.
The second is a ground for the first. We would set out the propositions like this:

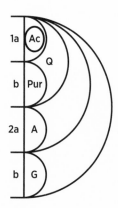

1a   Are we to continue in sin

b   *in order that* grace may
abound?

2a   *Answer*: Absolutely not!

b   *The reason is that* we who died
to sin cannot still live in it.

Note: The first question is really two propositions, each having its own
subject and its own predicate. 1a relates to 1b as action to purpose; that
is, 1b is the purpose of 1a.

Relative Clauses

A relative clause usually begins with *who, which,* or *that.* It usually
functions to define some person or thing in the sentence. Therefore,

as a modifier, a relative clause is not usually construed as a distinct proposition, even though it has a subject and a predicate. (Note how the relative clause was handled back in Romans 12:1.)

For example, notice in Romans 6:2 the proposition "How can we who died to sin still live in it?" Within this proposition is a relative clause: "who died to sin." Its predicate is "died to sin." Its subject is "who." The function of this relative clause is to modify "we," the subject of the main clause. Therefore, I have not given it the status of a separate proposition.

But when you stop to ponder the logic of Romans 6:2b, it becomes evident that this relative clause could be given a separate status. Paul is really saying that *since* we died to sin, the *result* is that we cannot go on living in it. Logically, that is, the relative clause is functioning as the cause of our not continuing in sin. If we choose to set out the propositions this way, it would look like this:

1a   Are we to continue in sin

  b   *in order that* grace may abound

2a   *Answer*: No!

  b   The reason is that we have died to sin

  c   *with the result that* we can't continue to live in it

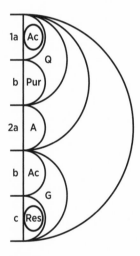

The difference between this arcing and the first one we did of Romans 6:1–2 is that this is more detailed. Both are right. In the end, you must decide whether a relative clause is so crucial that it demands its own proposition. An example of a relative clause that almost certainly should be given its own status as a proposition is found in John 1:12–13, "But to all who did receive him, who believed in his name, he gave the right to become children of God, *who were born, not of blood nor of the*

will of the flesh nor of the will of man, but of God." In this verse, the means of becoming children of God is given in a relative clause: "who were born, not of blood nor of the will of the flesh nor of the will of man, but of God." This is crucial to the argument and should be arced as a distinct proposition.

Note: the one thing Romans 6:1–2 is saying in verse 2a is "Don't go on sinning" (imperative). This imperative, then, is supported by the indicative 2c, "You can't continue in sin," which is in turn supported by 2b, "you died to sin." The whole aim of arcing is to find the one main thing each literary unit is saying and to discover how the rest of the unit functions to support or unfold it.

Participial Clauses

A common way of making an assertion (especially in New Testament Greek) is by using a participle. An example of this is Romans 5:1: "*Having been justified by faith*, we have peace with God through our Lord Jesus Christ" (NASB). "Having been justified by faith" is a participial clause. We call it a clause even though it has no expressed subject, because it makes an assertion. You can express it as an assertion: "We have been justified by faith." So it is up to you, the interpreter, to discover how this assertion is related to the other assertion in Romans 5:1, "We have peace with God." I would suggest the following relationship:

5:1a *Since* we have been justified by
       faith

   1b *the result is that* we have peace
       with God through our Lord
       Jesus Christ.

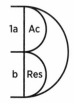

Infinitives

Sometimes infinitives, with their objects and modifiers, function as propositions. For example, John 14:2: "I go to prepare a place for you." Here the words "to prepare a place for you" could be paraphrased, "*in order that* I might prepare a place for you." This infinitive, with its object, makes an assertion about Christ's going. It tells the purpose. Thus we would set out the propositions like this:

14:2a   I go

  2b   *in order that* I might prepare a
       place for you.

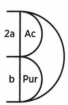

Note: Not all infinitives make crucial and distinct assertions like this, and so not all will be given the status of separate propositions. But be alert to those that do assert something crucial.

You will often find peculiar problems in trying to determine the propositions of a text. But I hope these few examples will give you an idea of what is involved. It is an extremely rewarding job, because in the struggle to untangle the logic of a passage in this way, its meaning becomes clearer and clearer.

Type	Name/Symbol	Definition	Some Key Words	Examples	Notes	Symbol
COORDINATE — (one proposition does not support the other, but each makes its own contribution in the whole)	Series (S)	Each proposition makes its own independent contribution to the whole.	and, moreover, furthermore, neither, nor, etc. (καί, δέ, τε, οὔτε, οὐδέ, υήτε, υηδέ)	The sun will be darkened, and the moon will not give its light, and the stars will fall from heaven, and the powers of the heavens will be shaken. (Matt. 24:29; also 7:8; Rom. 12:12)	Arcing: A schematic way of representing the kinds of relationships between all propositions in any coherent writing, leading to a summary of the argument which shows the role of each part in play in the argument.	main clauses coexisting
	Progression (P)	Like series, but each proposition is a further step toward a climax.	and, moreover, furthermore, etc. (καί, δέ, τε, οὔτε, οὐδέ, υήτε, υηδέ)	Those whom he predestined he also called; and those whom he called he also justified, and those whom he justified he also glorified. (Rom. 8:30; also Mark 4:28; 1 Pet. 1:5–7)		main clauses climaxing
	Alternative (A)	Each proposition expresses a different possibility arising from a situation.	or, but, while, on the other hand, etc. (ἀλλά, δέ, ἤ, μέν ... δέ)	Some were convinced... but others disbelieved. (Acts 28:24; also John 10:21, 22; Matt. 11:3)	General Notes: 1. Never cross arcs; some other option is always possible. 2. There will inevitably be some overlap in categories. Try hard to get the category which best fits. 3. Do your arcing in pencil or on the computer; you will inevitably erase and change things as you go along. 4. How do you know when to join two arcs together instead of two others? Remember that the supporting arc (in subordinate relationships) should modify the supported arc as a whole, including everything in it.	main clauses contrasting
SUBORDINATE RELATIONSHIPS — SUPPORT BY RESTATEMENT	Action-Manner (Ac/Mn)	The statement of an action, and then a statement which indicates the way or manner in which this action is carried out.	in that, by, etc. (In Greek this relationship is often introduced by an adverbial participle of means or manner.)	God has not left himself without a witness in that he gave you from heaven rains and fruitful seasons. (Acts 14:17; also Phil. 2:7; Acts 16:16; 17:21)		main clause / modal clause
	Comparison (Cf)	The relationship between a statement and one showing what it is like.	even as, as ... so, like, just as (ὡς, καφώς, οὕτως, ὥσπερ)	As the Father has sent me, even so I am sending you. (John 20:2; also 1 Cor. 11:1; 1 Thess. 2:7)		main clause comparative clause
	Negative-Positive (-/+)	The relationship between two alternatives, one of which is denied so that the other is enforced. It is also the relationship implicit in contrasting statements.	not ... but (οὐ, μή, ἀλλά, δέ)	Do not be foolish, but understand what the will of the Lord is. (Eph. 5:17; also Heb. 2:16; Eph. 5:18) Cf. 1 Cor. 4:10 for an example of contrast: "We are fools for Christ's sake, but you are wise in Christ."	Ask: "How does this proposition relate to that one?" 1. Divide 2. Assign 3. Summarize	main clause adversative clause
	Idea-Explanation (Id/Exp)	The relationship between a statement and one clarifying its meaning. The clarifying proposition may define only one word of the previous proposition.	that is (τοῦτ, ἐστίν)	Jacob supplanted me these two times; he took away my brithright and now he has taken away my blessing. (Gen. 27:36; also 1 Cor. 10:4)	Used when clarifying the meaning of a word, phrase, or sentence; however, if author is speaking of an action and giving details about it, use Ac-Mn instead.	main clause epexegetical clause
	Question-Answer (Q/A)	Statement of question and answer to that question.	look for the question mark	What does the Scripture say? "Abraham believed God ..." (Rom. 4:3; also Rom. 6:1; Ps. 24:3, 4)	Note: rhetorical questions can be rephrased into statements and arced as statements.	interrogative clause / main clause

Type	Name/Symbol	Definition	Some Key Words	Examples	Notes		Symbol
SUBORDINATE RELATIONSHIPS — SUPPORT BY DISTINCT STATEMENT	Ground (G)	The relationship between a statement and the argument or reason for the statement (supporting proposition follows).	for, because, since, etc. (γάρ, ὅτι, ἐπεί, ἐπειδή, διότι)	Blessed are the poor in spirit, for theirs is the kingdom of heaven. (Matt. 5:3; also 1 Cor. 7:9; Phil. 2:25–26)	BE CAREFUL NOT TO MIX THESE TWO UP! In Ground, the conclusion comes first.	main clause / causal clause	3a
	Inference (I)	The relationship between a statement and the argument or reason for the statement (supporting proposition precedes).	therefore, wherefore, consequently, accordingly, etc. (οὖν, διό, ὥστε)	The end of all things is at hand; therefore be sensible and sober in prayer. (1 Pet. 4:7; also Rom. 6:11–12; Matt. 23:3; 1 Pet. 5:5b–6)	In Inference, the conclusion comes second.	main clause / result clause	7a
	Action-Result (Ac/Res)	The relationship between an action and a consequence or result which accompanies that action.	so that, that, with the result that (ὥστε)	There arose a great storm on the sea, so that the boat was being swamped by the waves. (Matt. 8:24; also John 3:16; James 1:11)		main clause / result clause	20a
	Action-Purpose (Ac/Pur)	The relationship between an action and the one that is intended to come as a result.	in order that, so that, that, with a view to, to the end that, lest (ἵνα, ὅπως, ἵνα ... μή)	Humble yourselves under God's mighty hand that he may lift you up. (1 Pet. 5:6; also Rom. 1:11; Mark 7:9)		main clause / purpose clause	18a
	Conditional (If/Tn)	This is like Action-Result except that the existence of the action is only potential.	if ... then, provided that, except, etc. (εἰ, ἐάν)	If you are led by the Spirit, you are not under the law. (Gal. 5:18; also Gal. 6:1; John 15:14)		main clause / conditional clause	
	Temporal (T)	The relation between the main proposition and the occasion when it occurs.	when, whenever, after, before, etc. (ὅτε, ὅταν)	When you fast, do not look gloomy. (Matt. 6:16; also James 1:2; Luke 6:22)	The author chooses to emphasize the occasion rather than the cause even though the occasion may be the cause.	main clause / temporal clause	
	Locative (L)	The relationship between a proposition and the place where it is true.	where, wherever, etc. (ὅπου, οὗ)	Where two or three are gathered together in my name, there am I in the midst of them. (Matt. 18:20; also 2 Cor. 3:17; Ruth 1:16)		main clause / locative clause	
	Bilateral (BL)	A bilateral proposition supports two other propositions, one preceding and one following.	See conjunctions for other relationships that support.	Let the nations be glad and sing for joy, for you judge the peoples with equity and guide the nations upon the earth. Let the peoples praise you, O God. (Ps. 67:4–5; also Rom. 2:1b–2)	Note that "BL" tells that there is a relationship in each direction and that the "G" and ∴ specify exactly what the relationships are.		
SUPPORT-CONTRARY STATEMENT	Concessive (Csv)	The relationship between a main clause and a contrary statement.	although ... yet, although, yet, nevertheless, but, however (καίπερ, εἰ, καί, ἐάν, καί)	Although he was a Son, he learned obedience from what he suffered. (Heb. 5:8; also 1 Cor. 4:15; 9:13–15)	The concessive clause "supports" the main clause because it highlights the strength of the main clause which stands despite the obstacle of the concessive clause.	main clause / concessive clause	
	Situation-Response (Sit/R)	The relationship between a situation in one clause and a response in another.		How often would I have gathered your children together as a hen gathers her brood under her wings, and you were not willing. (Matt. 23:37; also John 7:21)	The relationship between the two clauses can either be what would be expected or a surprise, depending on the response of one's will.		

A Word of Thanks

The kind of thanks one feels at age seventy is not entirely the same as when one was forty. It is more obvious now that every minute of life is a gift. Every pain-free moment is a gift. Every memory of something read or thought, one more year's gainful employment, each day's renewal of energy, friends who have not yet died or moved away, hearing the doorbell, seeing words on a page, one more spectacular October maple in Minneapolis just outside my window—all gifts.

Of course, they have always been gifts. But the closer you are to saying good-bye to a friend, the more precious he feels. Don't get me wrong. My thoughts are indomitably future-oriented. I'm not dead yet. In fact, nearing the end makes me feel more alive, not less. That could be owing to the smell of heaven blowing back into this world. For heaven is a very alive place. Or it could be the adrenaline of urgency with less and less time left to do more and more.

In any case, I am thankful for every day, and every gift. I love being alive. And I love writing. Some things you just feel made to do. I suppose that's what Eric Liddell meant when he said, "God made me fast. And when I run, I feel his pleasure." I'm not fast. In fact, the list of competencies that I don't have is painfully long. Writing is not about being great. It's about making something. Writing is my carpentry, my masonry, my culinary arts, my painting and sculpting and carving, my gardening, my knitting and crocheting and needlepoint, my coin collecting.

Writing is about the joy of creating—as Dorothy Sayers would say, sharing "the Mind of the Maker." What an amazing thing: to make much of the Maker by making like the Maker. So I am thankful for the calling and the freedom and the pressure to write. I am thankful for Desiring God, where I work full-time, and where they expect me to write. They pay me to write. And they expect me to write what is true and what is beautiful. They hold me to it.

What a gift! The whole team is precious to me. And David Mathis, executive editor, stands out, because he reads everything I write, and his suggestions make it better. I thank God for David's leadership of a great team of writers at Desiring God—Jon Bloom, Tony Reinke, and Marshall Segal. How can one not write with joy when surrounded by such thinkers and writers?

In one sense, publishing is secondary to my writing. If nobody wanted to read what I write, I would still write, because it's how I see things, and how I savor reality. It's how I learn. But the fact is that God has blessed me with an amazing partnership with Crossway. I love their vision, and they have been willing to publish my books. This is a gift to me. It's much more than a business arrangement. It's a camaraderie in Christ and in his global cause of glorifying the Father.

On the home front, the children are all grown and gone their ways. So only Noël and I (and the dog) are left. That leaves only Noël to celebrate in this paragraph. And what a gift she is! She has supported this calling to write from the beginning. She is a good writer herself. She is working on a biography of a missionary to China. God has been good to me in such a wife. I can't imagine what life would have been without her. I said to her the other day, "I'm really glad you're here to come down to from my study at the end of the day."

Of course, behind all these gifts is the Giver. I thank God for Jesus, and for loving me in him, and for giving me his Holy Spirit, and covering all my sins. Noël and I look to him and say,

The Lord, our God, shall be our strength,
And give us life, whatever length
On earth he please, and make our feet
Like mountain deer, to rise and cleat
The narrow path for man and wife
That rises steep and leads to life.

General Index

Abraham: Abraham and Sarah as an example of the natural act of experiencing supernatural help, 231–32, 277; Abraham's trust in God's word, 278–79; God's promise to, 166

Acting the Miracle: God's Work and Ours in the Mystery of Sanctification (ed. Piper and Mathis), 43n1, 232n1

Adler, Mortimer, 326, 354–55, 365; "Coming to Terms," 367

affections: affections that are not godly, 96; as essential, 119–20; as not physical, 118–19; true illumination precedes, warrants, and shapes the affections, 100–101

Agassiz, Louis, 328, 367. *See also* "Agassiz and the Fish, by a Student" (Scudder)

"Agassiz and the Fish, by a Student" (Scudder), 328–31, 332, 367

Alcorn, Randy, *Happiness*, 105–6

Alford, Henry, 92

Alter, Robert, *The Literary Guide to the Bible* (with Kermode), 227n1

A.P.T.A.T., 243–44, 246, 251, 274, 278, 280–81, 285, 293; A—Admit, 244, 255, 274, 281, 293 (*see also* humility); P—Pray, 244, 255, 274, 282, 293 (*see also* prayer); T—Trust, 244–45, 274, 278, 282, 285, 293 (*see also* trust); A—Act, 245–46, 282, 293; T—Thank, 245

arcing, 375; and biblearc.com, 361n10, 372–73; birth of the method, 367–68; and the flow of an author's thought, 370–71; illustration (Rom. 12:1–2), 402–5; as a means of seeing and preserving the intricate development of an author's thought in its complexity and unity, 372–73; propositions as basic building blocks of thought, 368–69; the relationship between propositions, 369–70; roots of, 366–67; what arcing provides, 395–96. *See also* arcing, and coordinate relationships (propositions that do not support); arcing, and special problems in finding the propositions; arcing, and subordinate

relationships (propositions that support), support by contrary statement; arcing, and subordinate relationships (propositions that support), support by distinct statement; arcing, and subordinate relationships (propositions that support), support by restatement

arcing, and coordinate relationships (propositions that do not support): alternative, 397; progression, 397; series, 396

arcing, and special problems in finding the propositions, 405; infinitives, 408–9; participial clauses, 408; questions, 406; relative clauses, 406–8

arcing, and subordinate relationships (propositions that support), support by contrary statement: concessive, 401; situation-response, 401–2

arcing, and subordinate relationships (propositions that support), support by distinct statement: action-purpose (main clause–purpose clause), 399–400; action-result (main clause–result clause), 399; bilateral, 400–401; conditional (main clause–conditional clause), 400; ground (main clause–causal clause), 399; inference (main clause–inferential clause), 399; locative (main clause–locative clause), 400; temporal (main clause–temporal clause), 400

arcing, and subordinate relationships (propositions that support), support by restatement: action-manner, 397; comparison, 397–98; idea-explanation, 398; negative-positive, 398; question-answer, 398

Augustine, 110, 158, 246; transformation of, 159–60

"Awake, My Soul, and with the Sun" (Ken), 270

Basic Guide to Interpreting the Bible, A: Playing by the Rules (Stein), 227n1

Battling Unbelief: Defeating Sin with Superior Pleasure (Piper), 157n2

sees, scribes, and Sadducees' inability to read the Bible, Jesus's critique of Pharisees, scribes, and Sadducees' inability to read the Bible, Jesus's critique of: and Jesus's question "Have you not read . . ."? 197, 198, 199, 201, 202, 203, 204, 205, 206; their misreading of the Bible, 198–200, 202–3, 205–6; their misreading of him, 201–2, 203–5

Piper, John, 364; *Acting the Miracle: God's Work and Ours in the Mystery of Sanctification* (with Mathis), 43n1, 232n1; *Battling Unbelief: Defeating Sin with Superior Pleasure,* 157n2; *Biblical Exegesis: Discovering the Meaning of Scriptural Texts,* 368, 368n3; *A Camaraderie of Confidence: The Fruit of Unfailing Faith in the Lives of Charles Spurgeon, George Müller, and Hudson Taylor,* 100n3; *Desiring God: Meditations of a Christian Hedonist,* 100n1, 109n12; "Did Christ Die for Us or for God?," 49; *Future Grace: The Purifying Power of the Promises of God,* 100n2, 157n2; *The Legacy of Sovereign Joy: God's Triumphant Grace in the Lives of Augustine, Luther, and Calvin,* 380n2; *A Peculiar Glory: How the Christian Scriptures Reveal Their Complete Truthfulness,* 19, 22, 25–26, 31, 31–32, 32, 314n1; "The Peculiar Marks of Majesty, Part 1," 204n1; "The Peculiar Marks of Majesty, Part 2," 204n1; personal testimony on how he learned to read, 298–99, 326–28, 332, 365–66, 371; *Spectacular Sins: And Their Global Purpose in the Glory of Christ,* 265n1; *What Jesus Demands from the World,* 31n3; "Who Is This Divided Man?," 270n4. *See also* reading the Bible supernaturally, Piper's proposal for the ultimate goal of

"Power of Patience, The: Teaching Students the Value of Deceleration and Immersive Attention" (Roberts), 333–36

prayer, 274; humility as the root of, 249; Jesus died so that our prayer for desire would be answered, 256–58; as the path of perception, 251–53; pray about all because God governs all, 265; the prayer for desire, 254–56; prayer for help to pay attention to what is actually written in the Bible, 266–69; prayer and interpretation, 266; prayer and thinking/study, 253; prayer about the way we read the Bible,

273–74; praying for God's help in grasping the basic meaning of the words of the Bible, 263–65; praying without ceasing, 260–61; and surrendering our identity to God, 258–59. *See also* I.O.U.S.

predestination, 46–47; and worship, 57

propitiation, 48–50; Christ's death as death for God's glory, 49–50; sinning as a discounting of the value of the glory of God, 50; and worship, 57

Protagoras, 307

Proverbs, book of, thirty sayings in, 384–85

Psalms, book of: main summons of (come, see, and savor), 128–29; as modeling how we are to savor God, 127–33

Purity of Heart Is to Will One Thing (Kierkegaard), 269

Qur'an: comparison of the Islamic view of the Qur'an with the Christian view of the Bible, 315–16; Islamic view of, 315, 317

reading, and the basic habits/strategies of good reading, 227; active reading, 327, 339–40, 342, 344; aggressive attentiveness, 327, 342, 344, 348, 361, 362; and genres, 295, 297, 298; and humble skepticism, 297–98; the ordinary aim of reading (*see* meaning, Piper's definition of [what the author intended to communicate]); Piper's testimony on his learning to read, 298–99, 326–28, 332, 365–66, 371; reading to know what we are reading, 295, 297; and unique word combinations, 295–96, 297; we read before we know what we are reading, 296–97

reading the Bible supernaturally, 179–80, 188–89, 221–22, 226; compared to Bible reading that Satan leaves alone, 185; God intends that we read his word supernaturally, 180–81; how reading the Bible is supernatural, 183–84; the necessity of reading the Bible supernaturally, 211; and Satan as the blinding enemy outside, 22, 143, 183, 184–85, 211; there is no opening of the eyes without divine power, 184–85. *See also* Bible, the, as the word of God; new birth, and the spiritual act of reading the Bible; Paul, on receiving the word supernaturally; reading the Bible supernaturally, and God's supernatural act; reading the Bible supernaturally, the natural act of; reading the Bible supernaturally, Piper's proposal for the

Scripture Index

The Glory of God Is Shining
through Scripture

✹ desiringGod

Everyone wants to be happy. Our website was born and built for happiness. We want people everywhere to understand and embrace the truth that *God is most glorified in us when we are most satisfied in him.* We've collected more than thirty years of John Piper's speaking and writing, including translations into more than forty languages. We also provide a daily stream of new written, audio, and video resources to help you find truth, purpose, and satisfaction that never end. And it's all available free of charge, thanks to the generosity of people who've been blessed by the ministry.

If you want more resources for true happiness, or if you want to learn more about our work at Desiring God, we invite you to visit us at www.desiringGod.org.

www.desiringGod.org